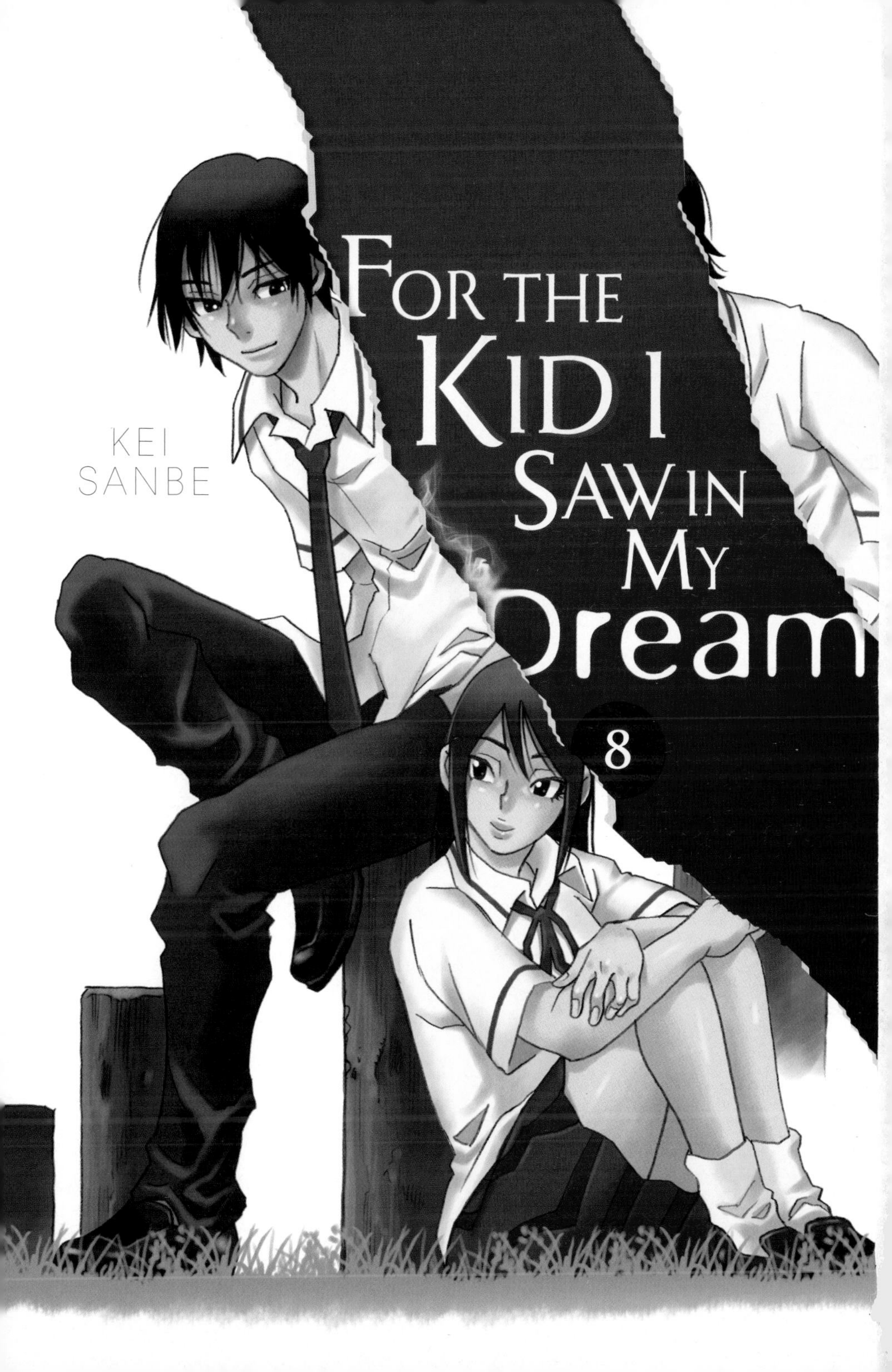
For the Kid I Saw in My Dream
Kei Sanbe
8

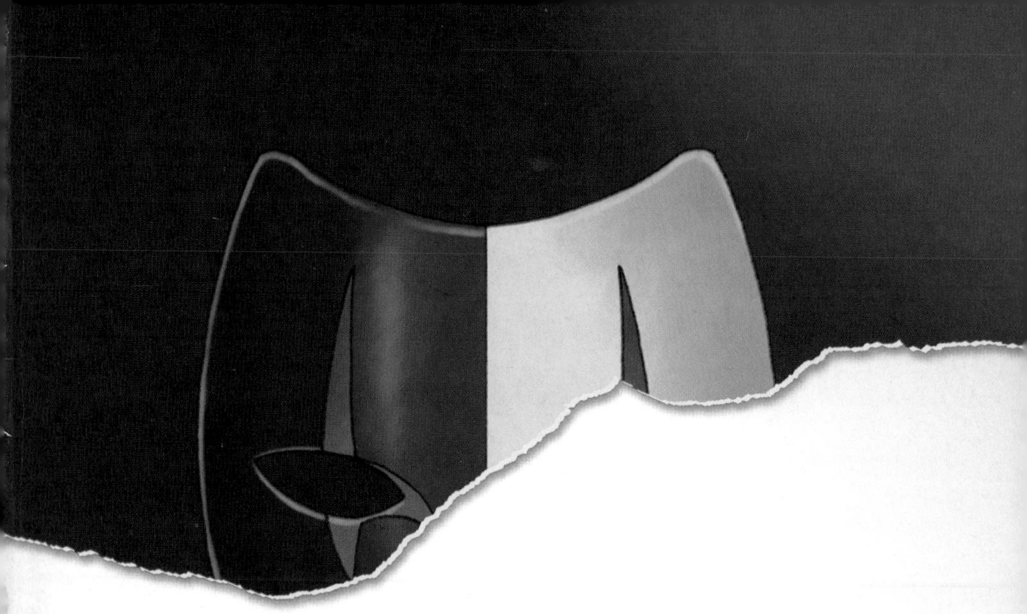

CONTENTS

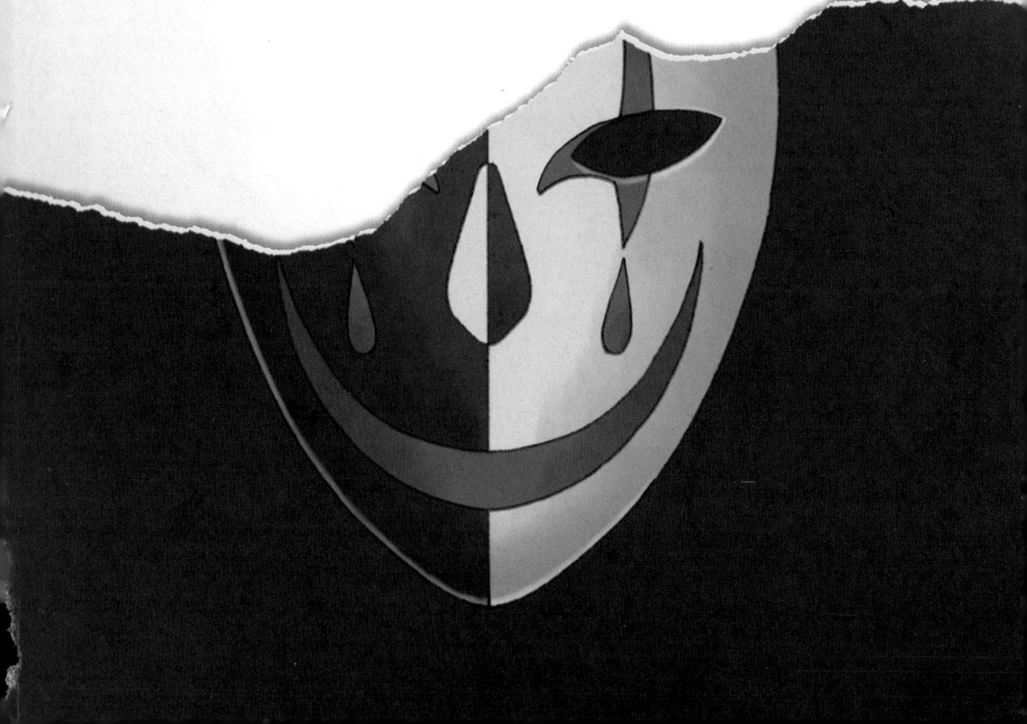

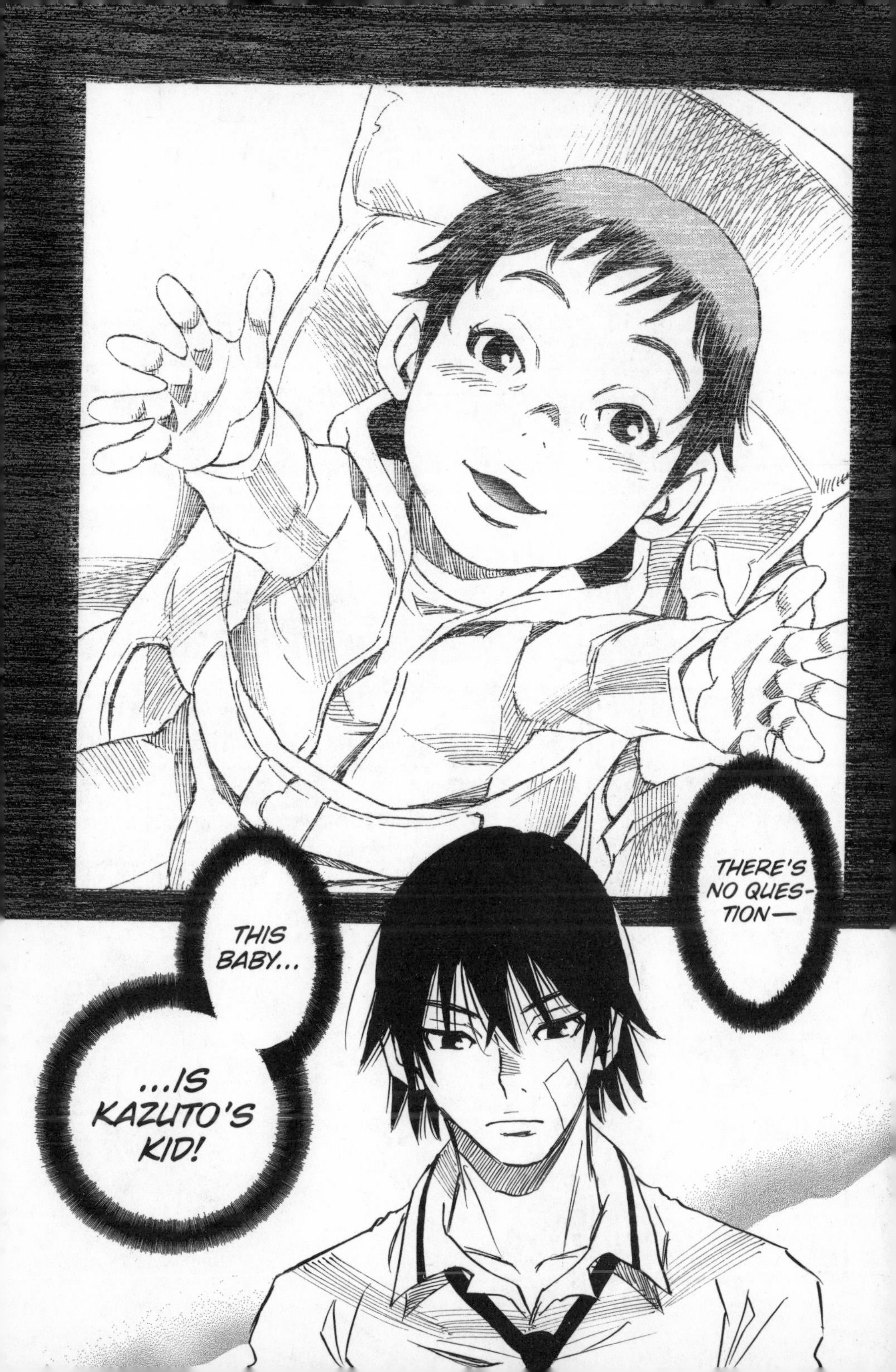
THERE'S NO QUES-TION—
THIS BABY...
...IS KAZUTO'S KID!

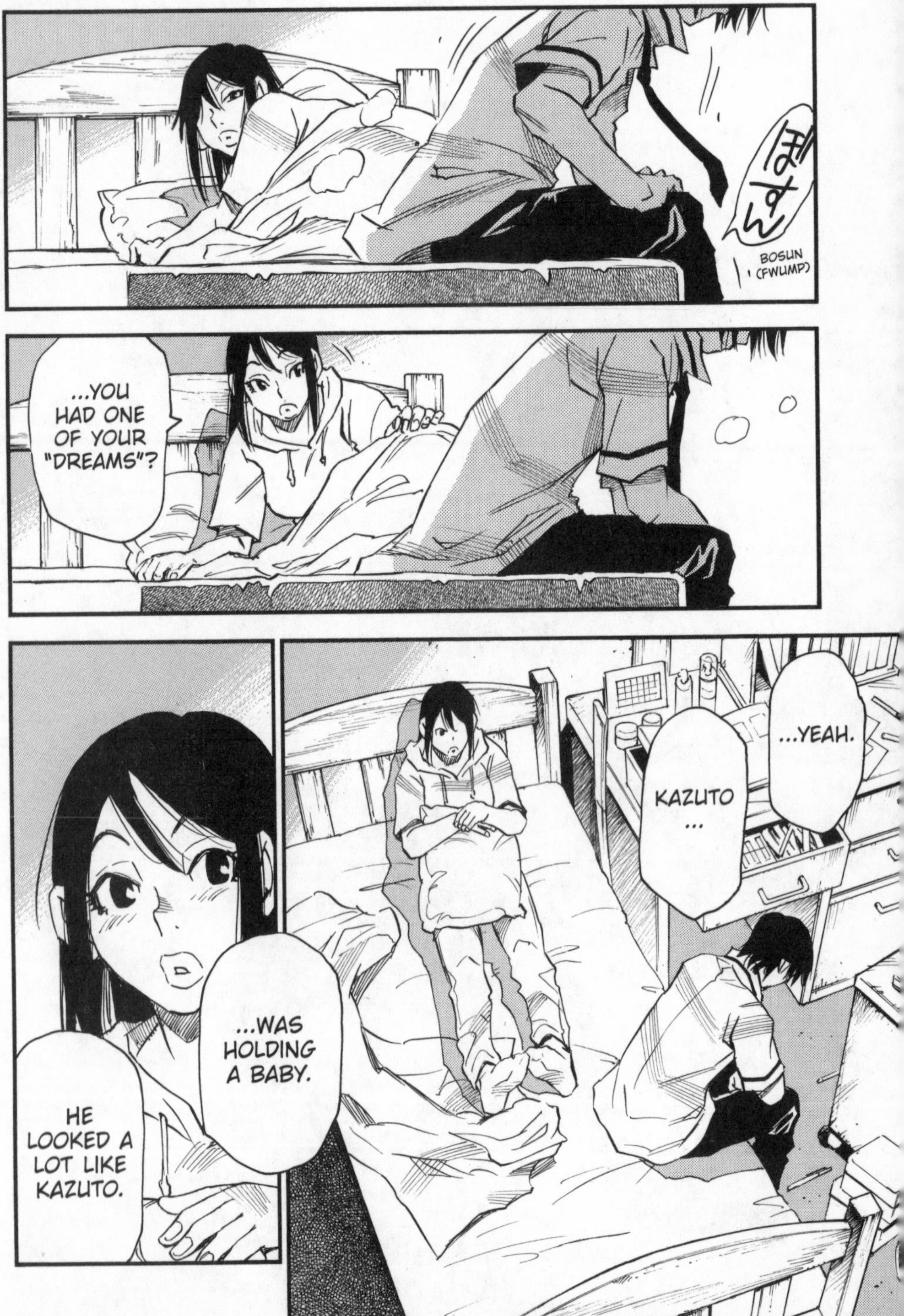
ぼすん
BOSUN (FWUMP)
...YOU HAD ONE OF YOUR "DREAMS"?
...YEAH.
KAZUTO ...
...WAS HOLDING A BABY.
HE LOOKED A LOT LIKE KAZUTO.

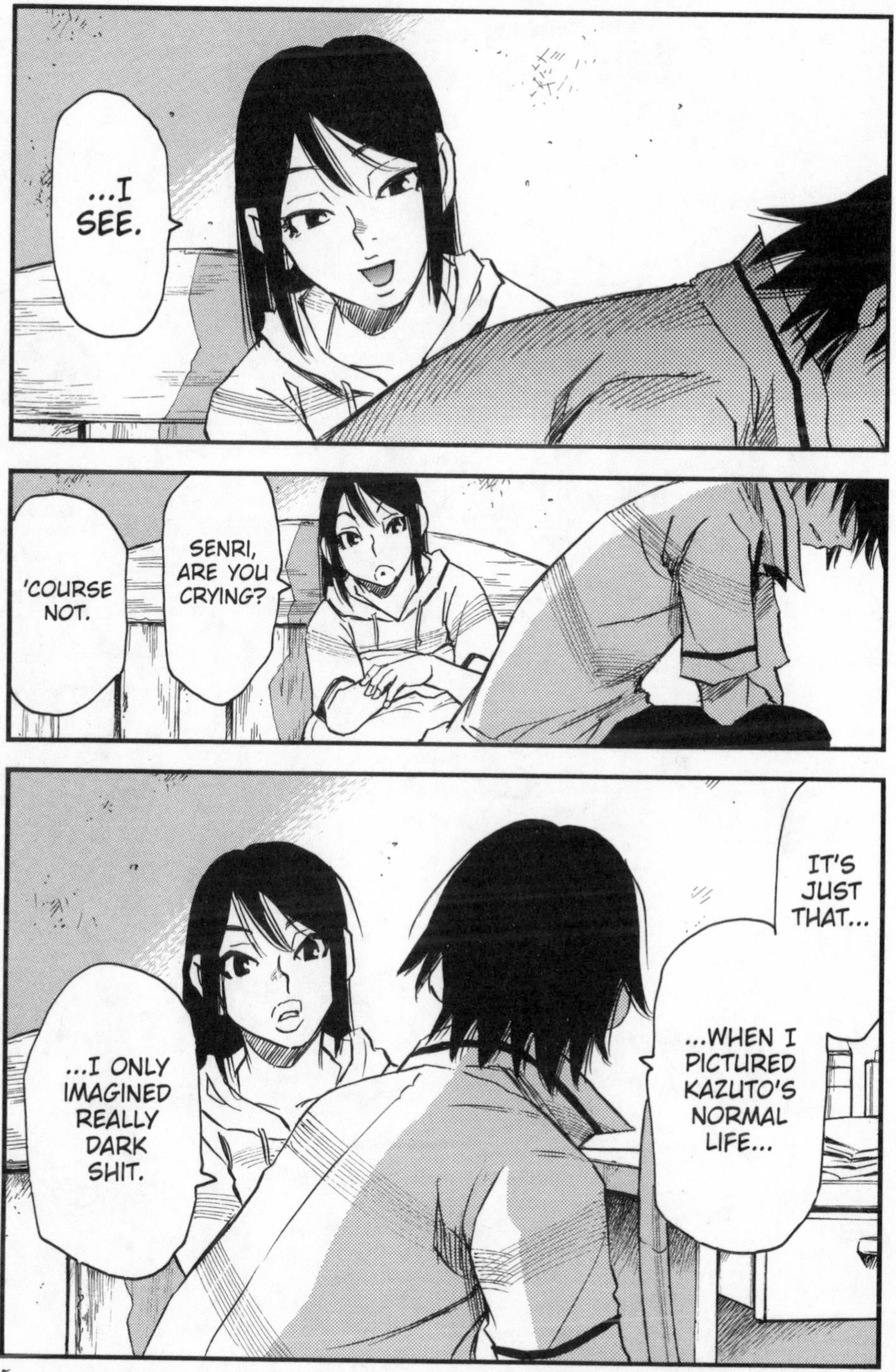
...I SEE.
SENRI, ARE YOU CRYING?
'COURSE NOT.
IT'S JUST THAT...
...WHEN I PICTURED KAZUTO'S NORMAL LIFE...
...I ONLY IMAGINED REALLY DARK SHIT.

#38 I Sensed the Future

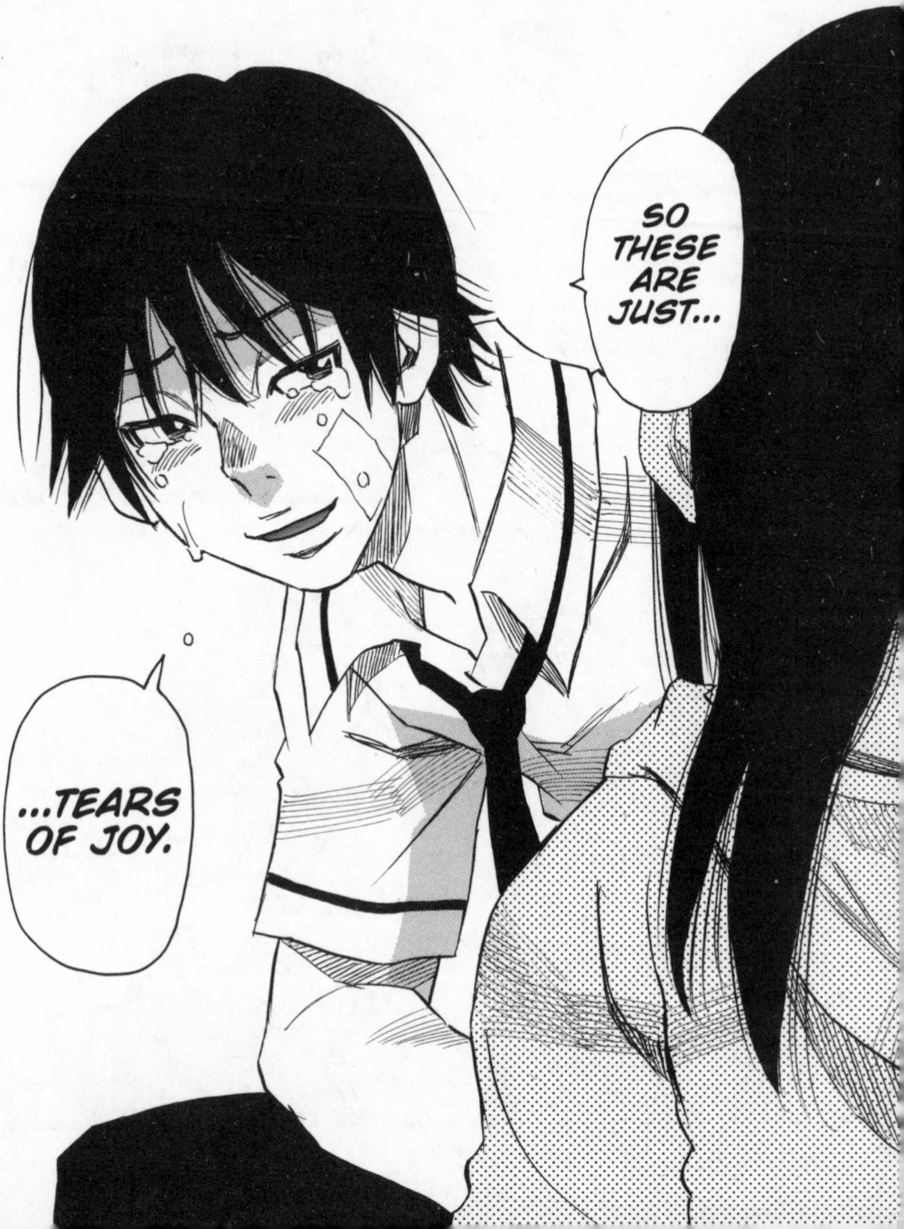

SO THESE ARE JUST...
...TEARS OF JOY.

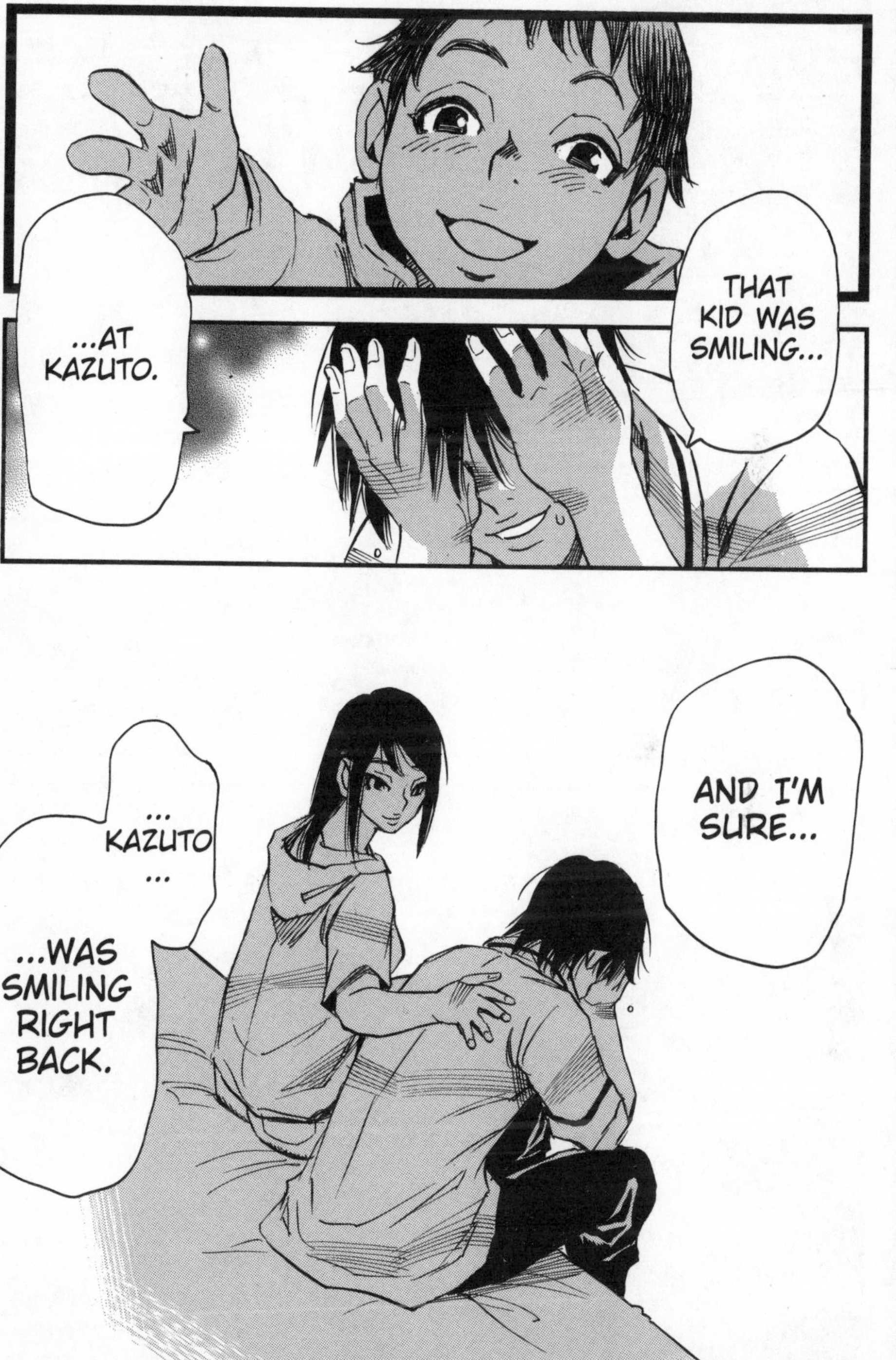
THAT KID WAS SMILING...
...AT KAZUTO.
AND I'M SURE...
... KAZUTO ...
...WAS SMILING RIGHT BACK.

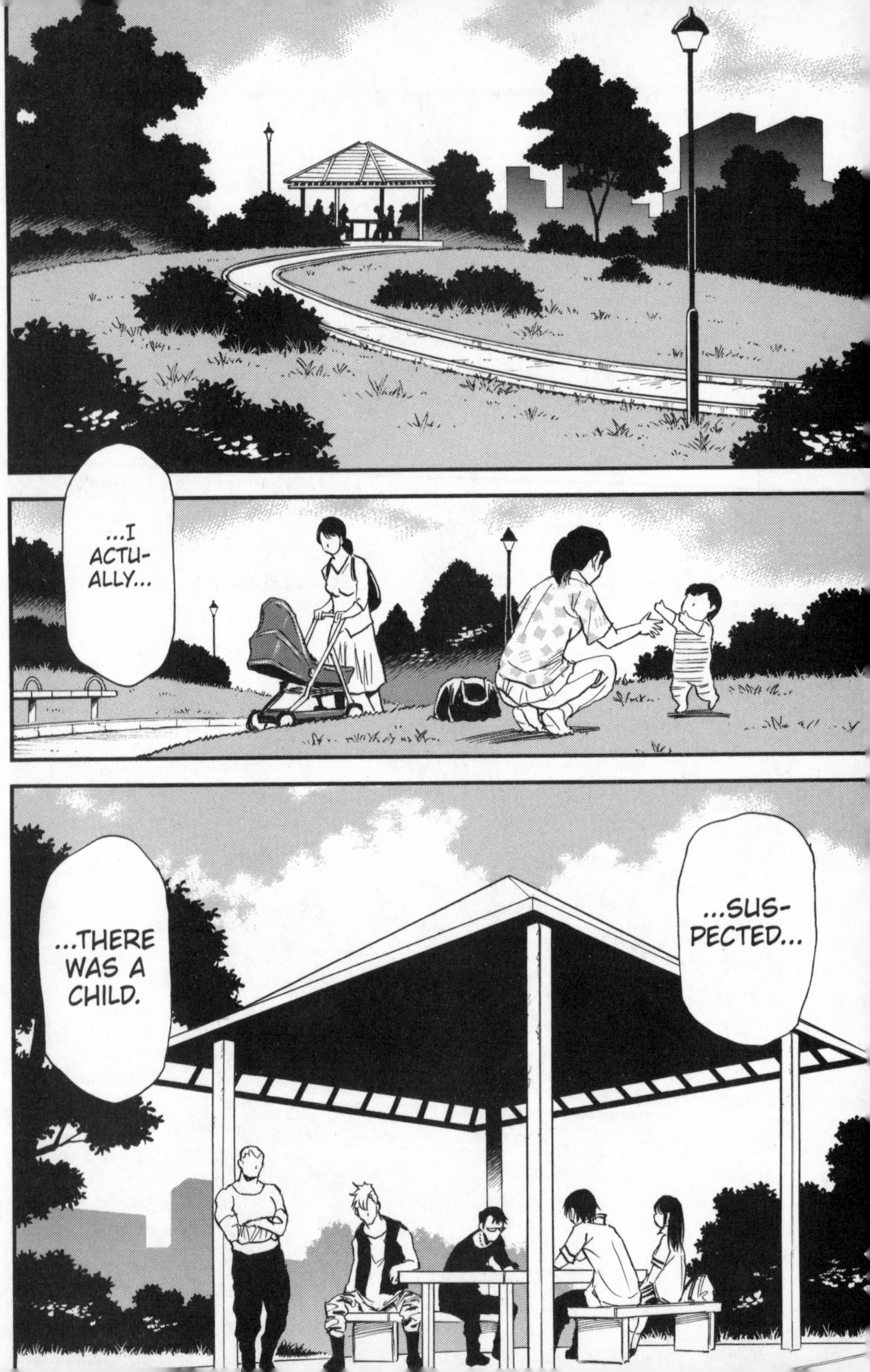
...I ACTU-ALLY...
...SUS-PECTED...
...THERE WAS A CHILD.

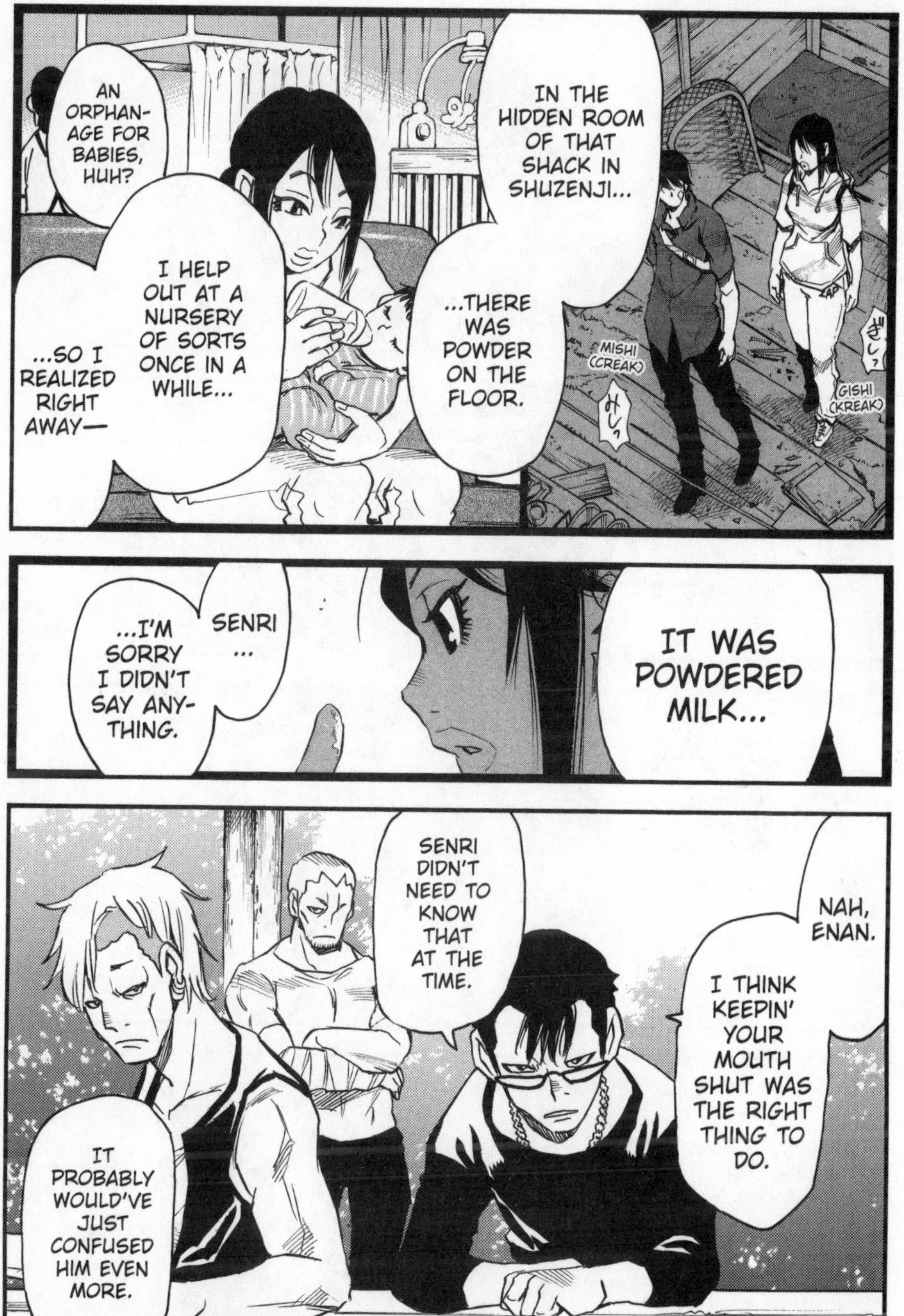
IN THE HIDDEN ROOM OF THAT SHACK IN SHUZENJI...
...THERE WAS POWDER ON THE FLOOR.
ぎしっ
GISHI (KREAK)
みしっ
MISHI (CREAK)
AN ORPHAN-AGE FOR BABIES, HUH?
I HELP OUT AT A NURSERY OF SORTS ONCE IN A WHILE...
...SO I REALIZED RIGHT AWAY—
IT WAS POWDERED MILK...
SENRI ...
...I'M SORRY I DIDN'T SAY ANY-THING.
NAH, ENAN.
I THINK KEEPIN' YOUR MOUTH SHUT WAS THE RIGHT THING TO DO.
SENRI DIDN'T NEED TO KNOW THAT AT THE TIME.
IT PROBABLY WOULD'VE JUST CONFUSED HIM EVEN MORE.

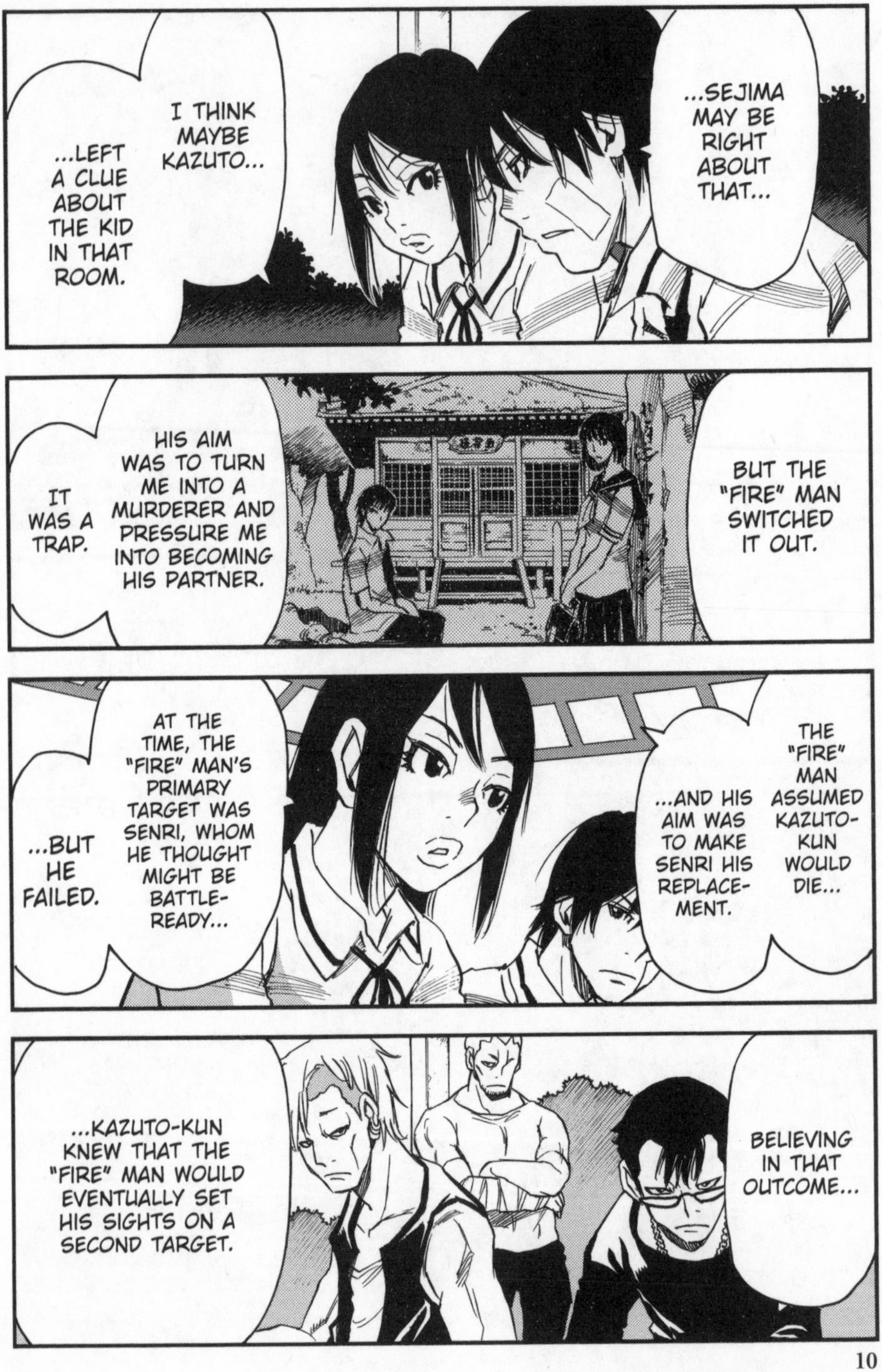
...SEJIMA MAY BE RIGHT ABOUT THAT...
I THINK MAYBE KAZUTO...
...LEFT A CLUE ABOUT THE KID IN THAT ROOM.
BUT THE "FIRE" MAN SWITCHED IT OUT.
HIS AIM WAS TO TURN ME INTO A MURDERER AND PRESSURE ME INTO BECOMING HIS PARTNER.
IT WAS A TRAP.
THE "FIRE" MAN ASSUMED KAZUTO-KUN WOULD DIE...
...AND HIS AIM WAS TO MAKE SENRI HIS REPLACE-MENT.
AT THE TIME, THE "FIRE" MAN'S PRIMARY TARGET WAS SENRI, WHOM HE THOUGHT MIGHT BE BATTLE-READY...
...BUT HE FAILED.
BELIEVING IN THAT OUTCOME...
...KAZUTO-KUN KNEW THAT THE "FIRE" MAN WOULD EVENTUALLY SET HIS SIGHTS ON A SECOND TARGET.

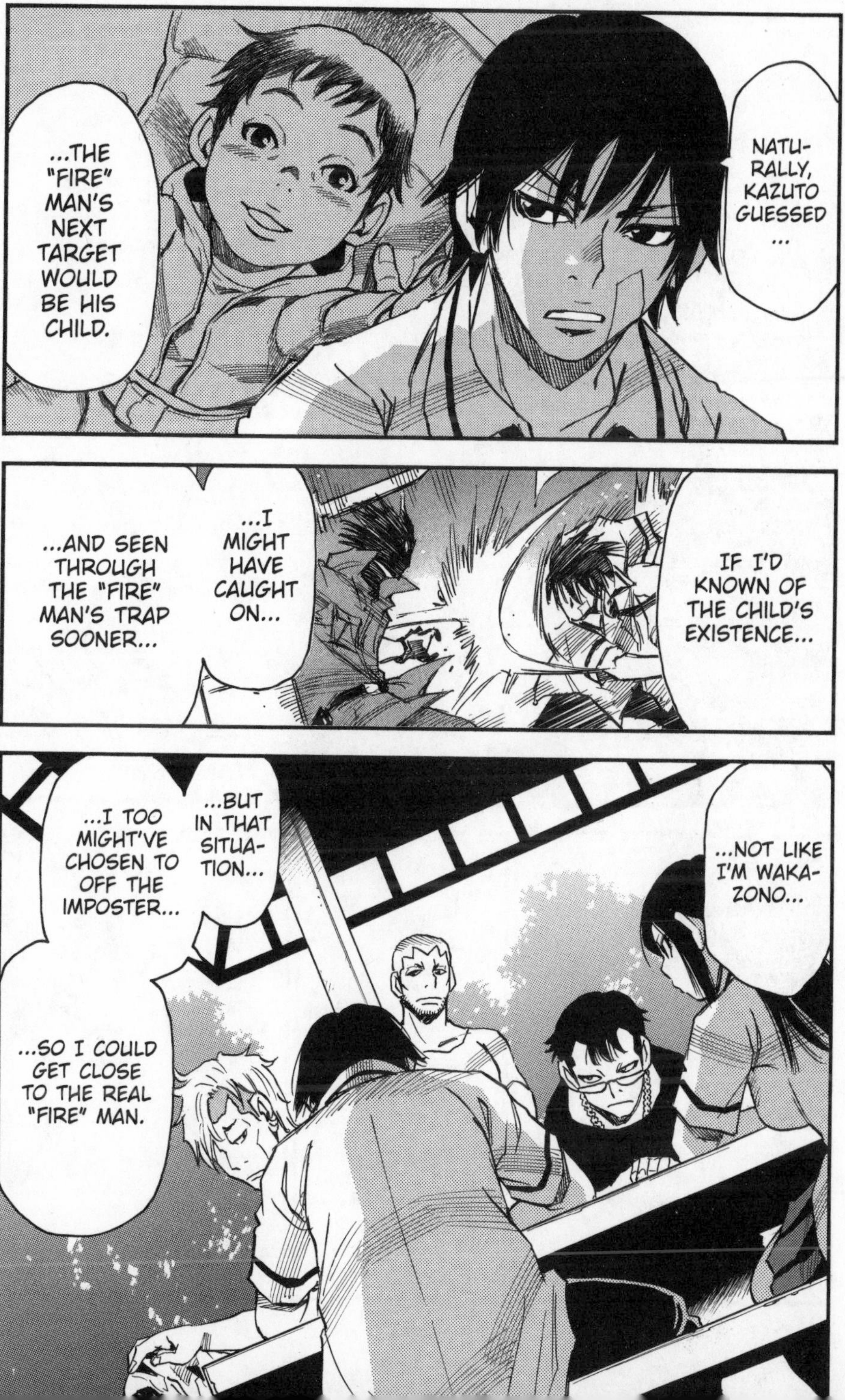
NATURALLY, KAZUTO GUESSED...
...THE "FIRE" MAN'S NEXT TARGET WOULD BE HIS CHILD.
IF I'D KNOWN OF THE CHILD'S EXISTENCE...
...I MIGHT HAVE CAUGHT ON...
...AND SEEN THROUGH THE "FIRE" MAN'S TRAP SOONER...
...NOT LIKE I'M WAKAZONO...
...BUT IN THAT SITUATION...
...I TOO MIGHT'VE CHOSEN TO OFF THE IMPOSTER...
...SO I COULD GET CLOSE TO THE REAL "FIRE" MAN.

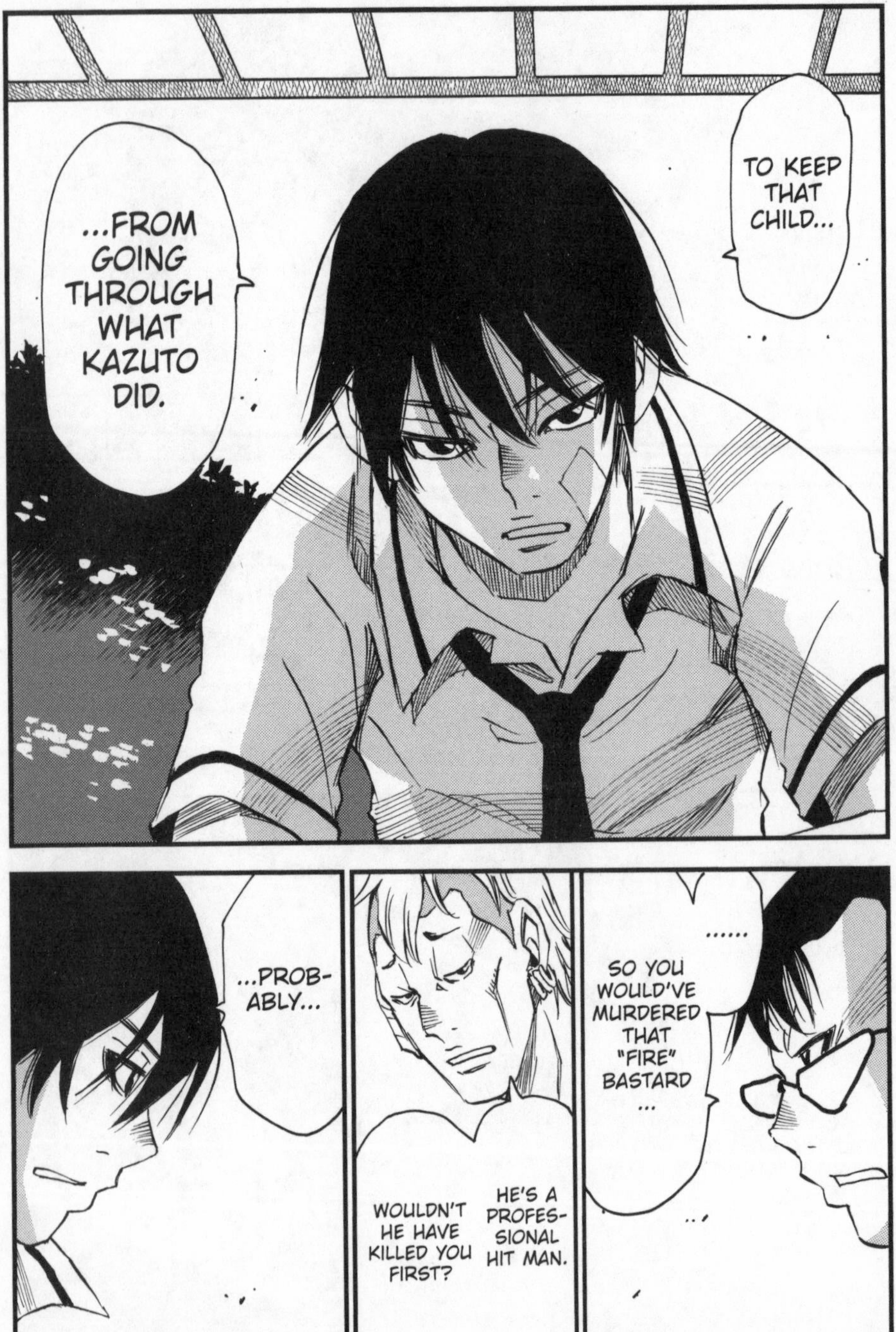
TO KEEP THAT CHILD...
...FROM GOING THROUGH WHAT KAZUTO DID.
......
SO YOU WOULD'VE MURDERED THAT "FIRE" BASTARD ...
HE'S A PROFES- SIONAL HIT MAN.
WOULDN'T HE HAVE KILLED YOU FIRST?
...PROB- ABLY...

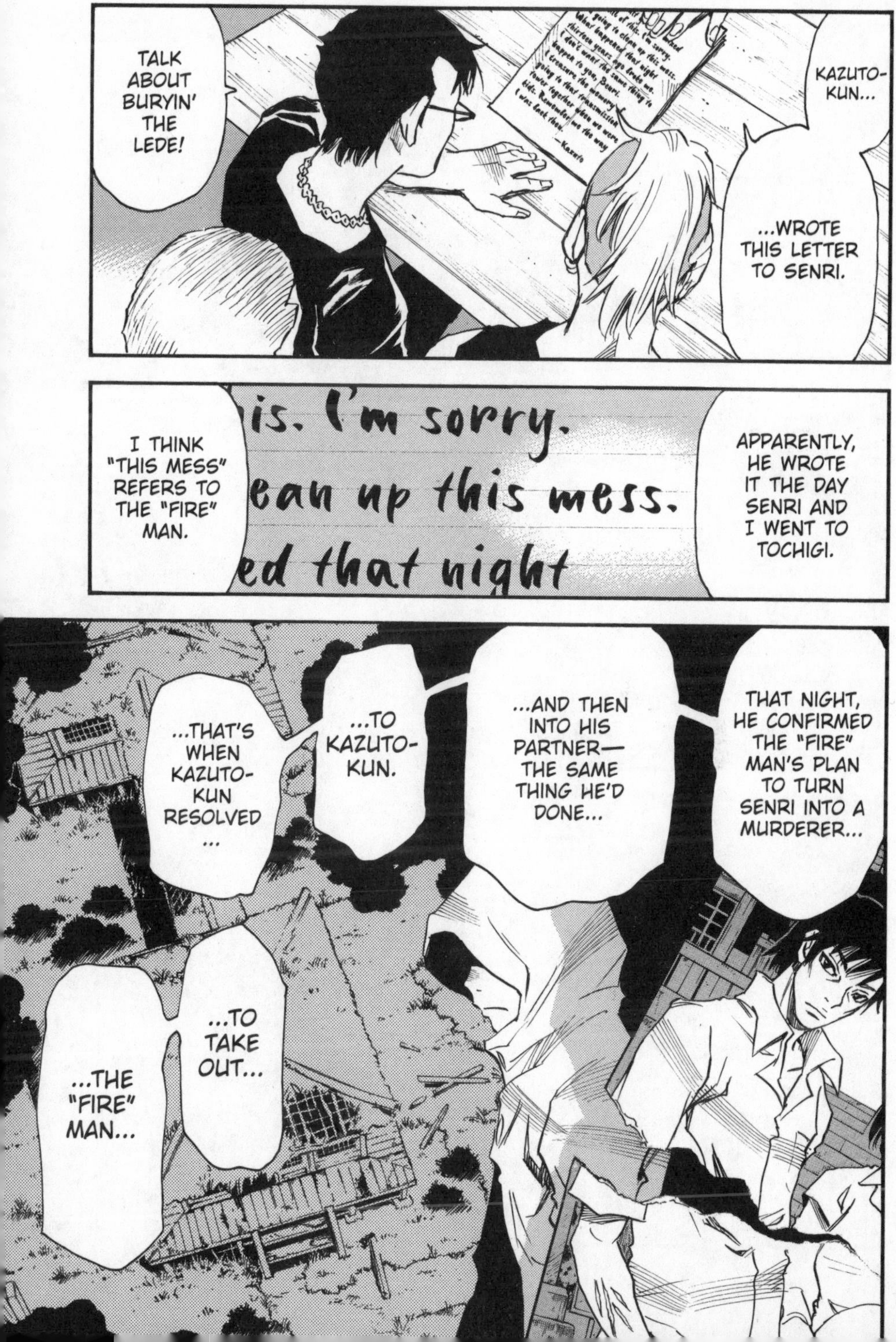
KAZUTO-KUN...
...WROTE THIS LETTER TO SENRI.
of this. I'm sorry.
going to clean up this mess.
What happened that night
thirteen years ago broke me.
I don't want the same thing to
happen to you, Senri.
I treasure the memory of
going to that transmission
tower together when we were
kids. Remember me the way
I was back then.
—Kazuto
TALK ABOUT BURYIN' THE LEDE!
APPARENTLY, HE WROTE IT THE DAY SENRI AND I WENT TO TOCHIGI.
is. I'm sorry.
ean up this mess.
ed that night
I THINK "THIS MESS" REFERS TO THE "FIRE" MAN.
THAT NIGHT, HE CONFIRMED THE "FIRE" MAN'S PLAN TO TURN SENRI INTO A MURDERER...
...AND THEN INTO HIS PARTNER—THE SAME THING HE'D DONE...
...TO KAZUTO-KUN.
...THAT'S WHEN KAZUTO-KUN RESOLVED...
...TO TAKE OUT...
...THE "FIRE" MAN...

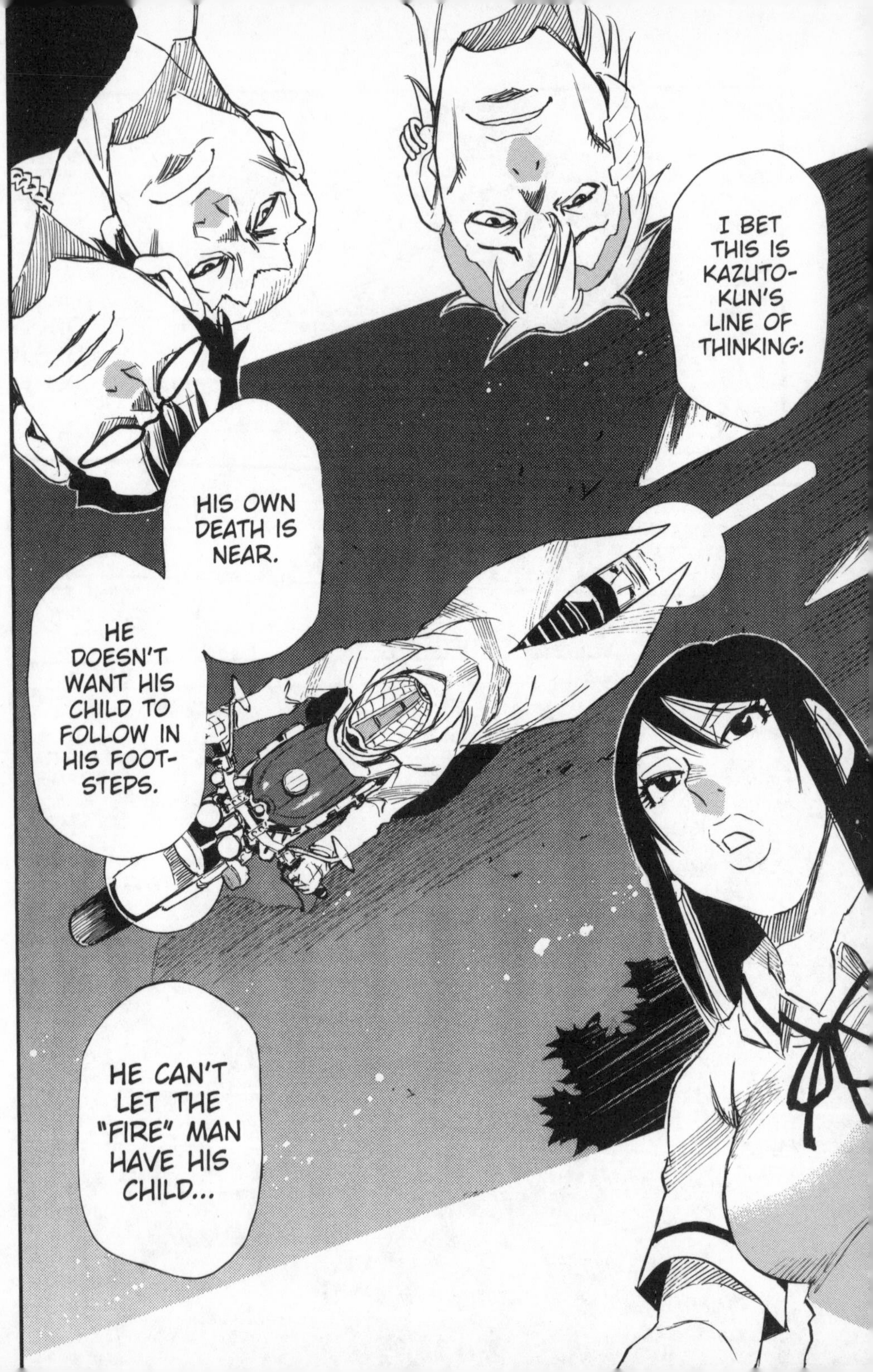
I BET THIS IS KAZUTO-KUN'S LINE OF THINKING:
HIS OWN DEATH IS NEAR.
HE DOESN'T WANT HIS CHILD TO FOLLOW IN HIS FOOT-STEPS.
HE CAN'T LET THE "FIRE" MAN HAVE HIS CHILD...

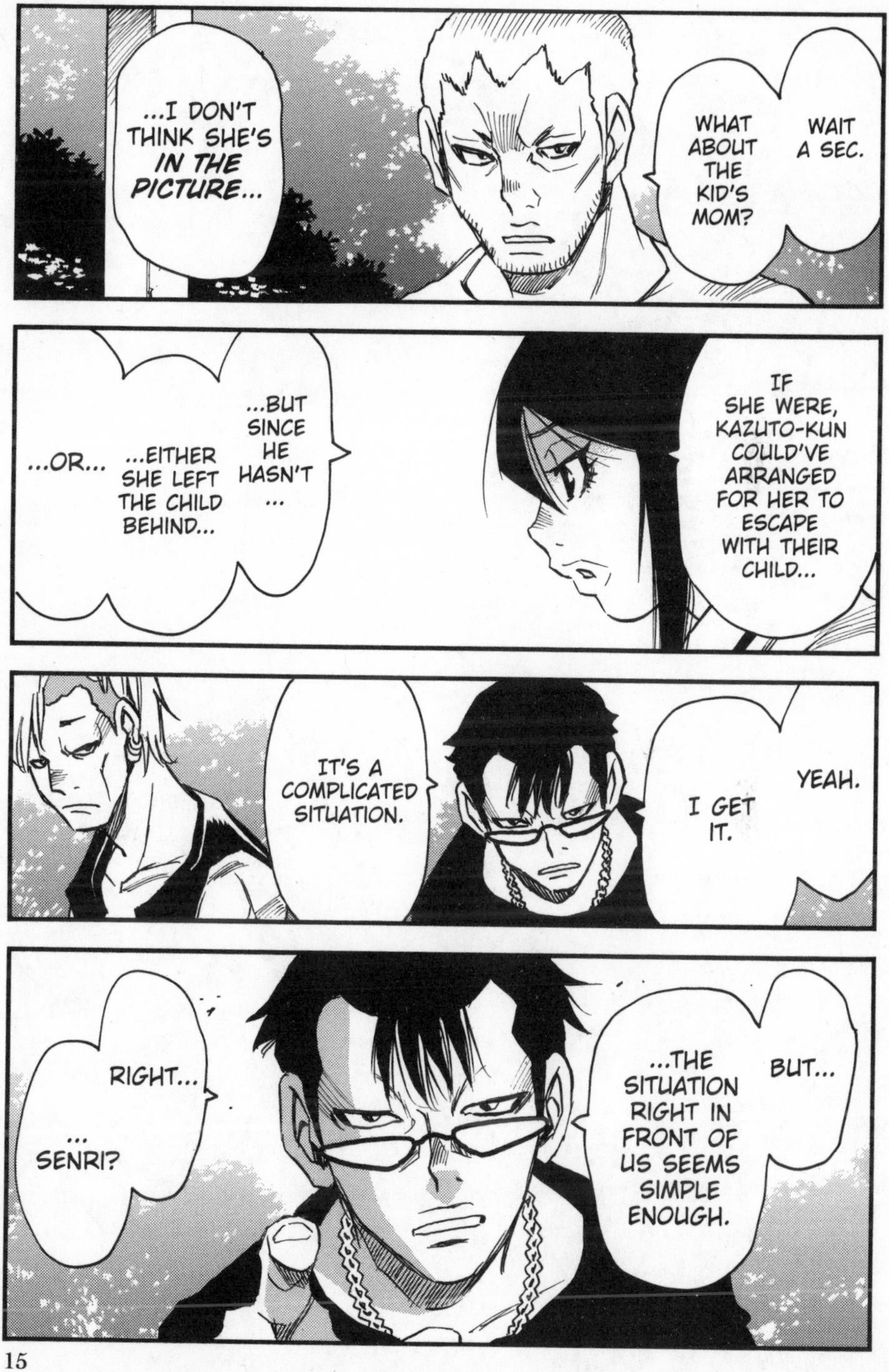
WAIT A SEC.
WHAT ABOUT THE KID'S MOM?
...I DON'T THINK SHE'S *IN THE PICTURE...*
IF SHE WERE, KAZUTO-KUN COULD'VE ARRANGED FOR HER TO ESCAPE WITH THEIR CHILD...
...BUT SINCE HE HASN'T ...
...EITHER SHE LEFT THE CHILD BEHIND...
...OR...
YEAH.
I GET IT.
IT'S A COMPLICATED SITUATION.
BUT...
...THE SITUATION RIGHT IN FRONT OF US SEEMS SIMPLE ENOUGH.
RIGHT...
... SENRI?

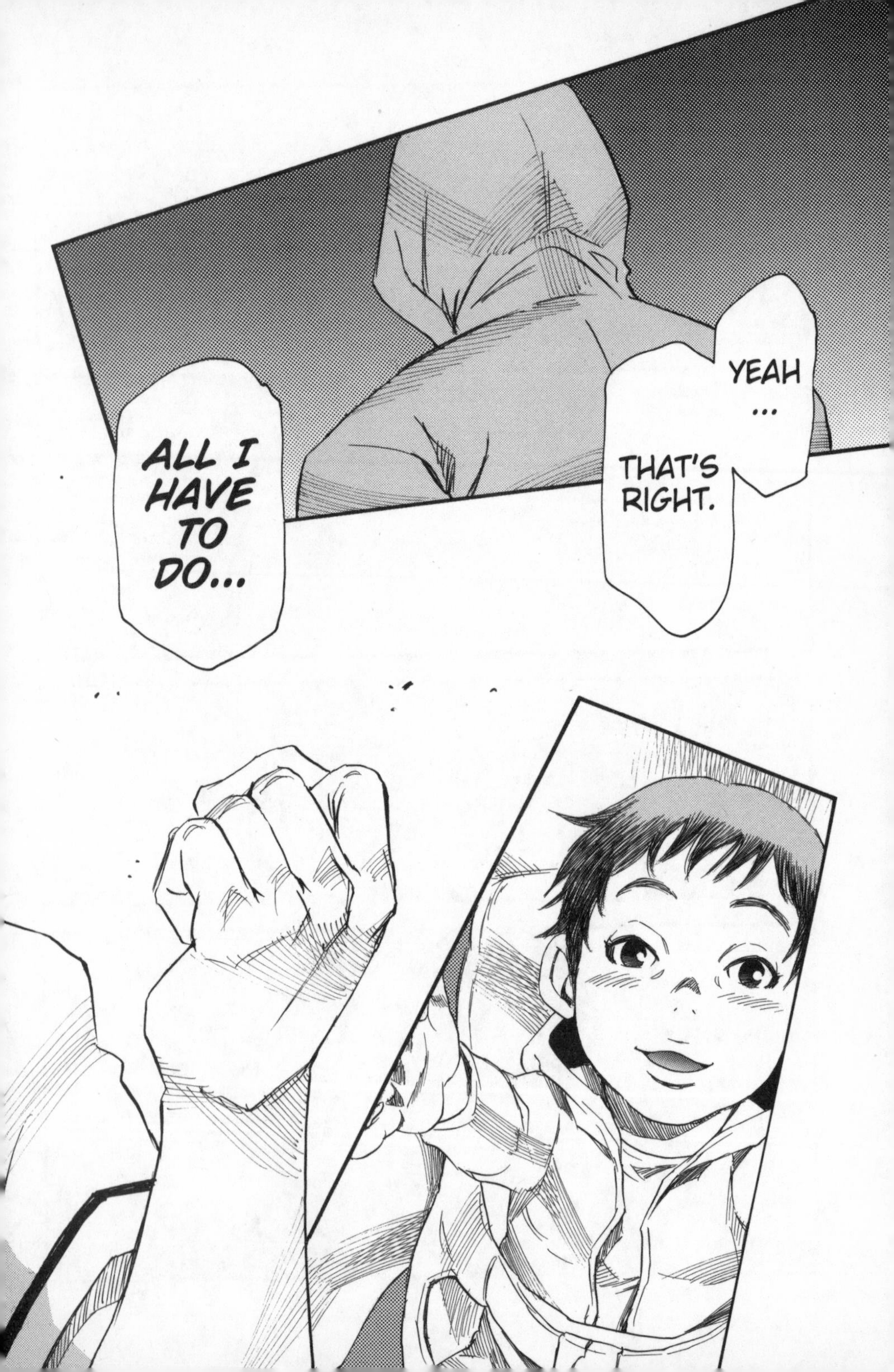
YEAH ... THAT'S RIGHT.
ALL I HAVE TO DO...

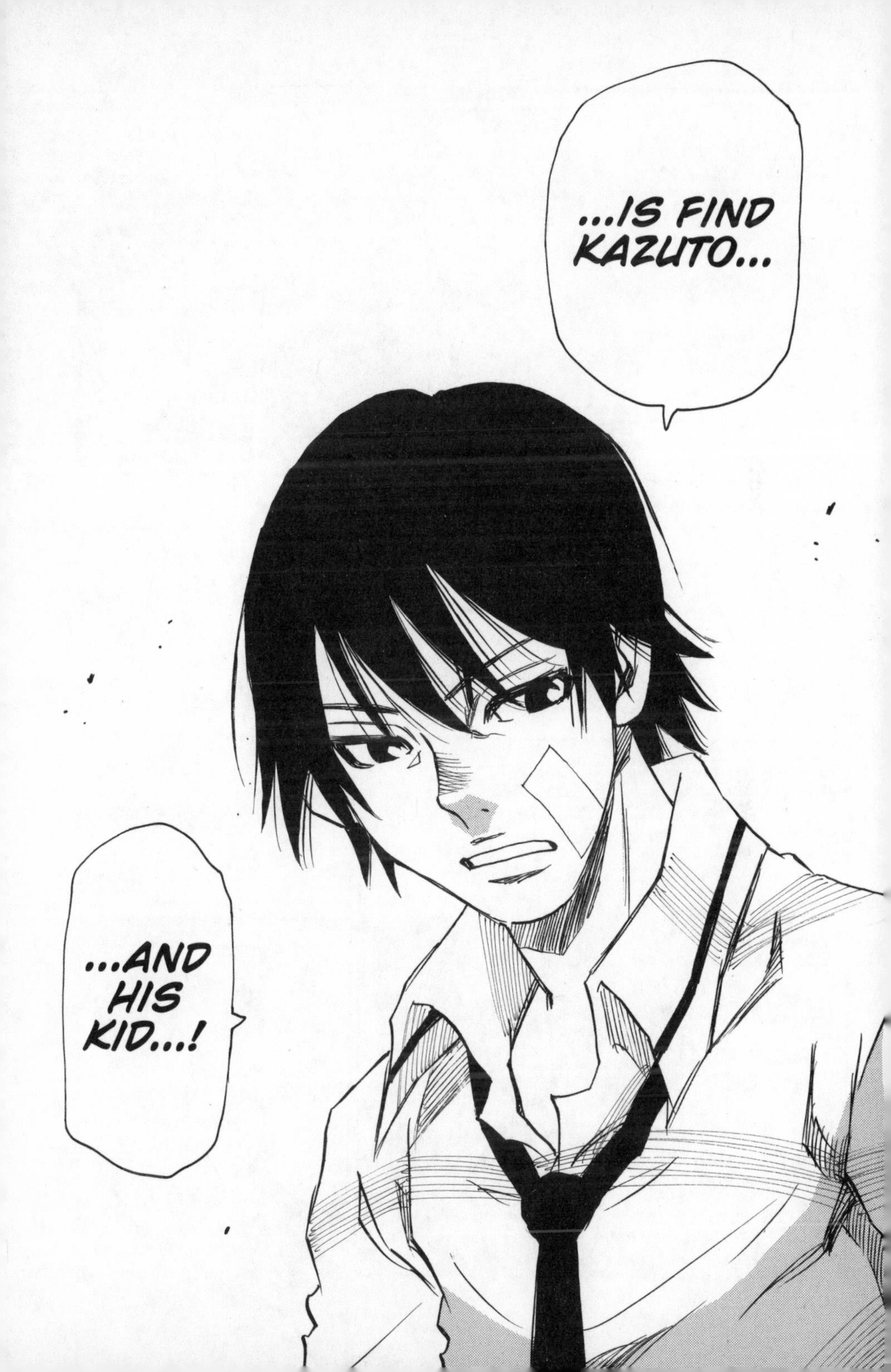
...IS FIND KAZUTO...
...AND HIS KID...!

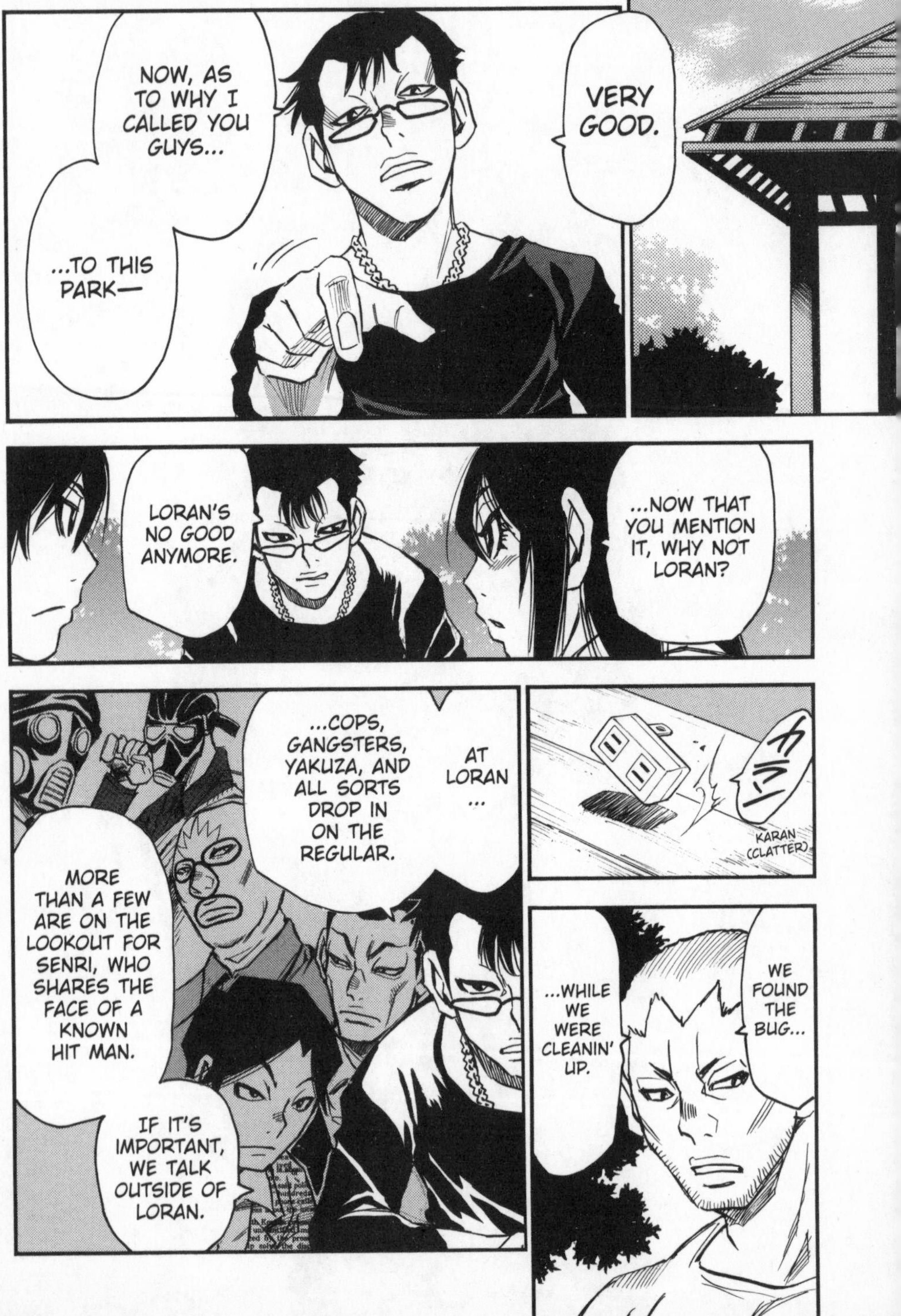
VERY GOOD.
NOW, AS TO WHY I CALLED YOU GUYS...
...TO THIS PARK—
...NOW THAT YOU MENTION IT, WHY NOT LORAN?
LORAN'S NO GOOD ANYMORE.
KARAN (CLATTER)
WE FOUND THE BUG...
...WHILE WE WERE CLEANIN' UP.
AT LORAN ...
...COPS, GANGSTERS, YAKUZA, AND ALL SORTS DROP IN ON THE REGULAR.
MORE THAN A FEW ARE ON THE LOOKOUT FOR SENRI, WHO SHARES THE FACE OF A KNOWN HIT MAN.
IF IT'S IMPORTANT, WE TALK OUTSIDE OF LORAN.

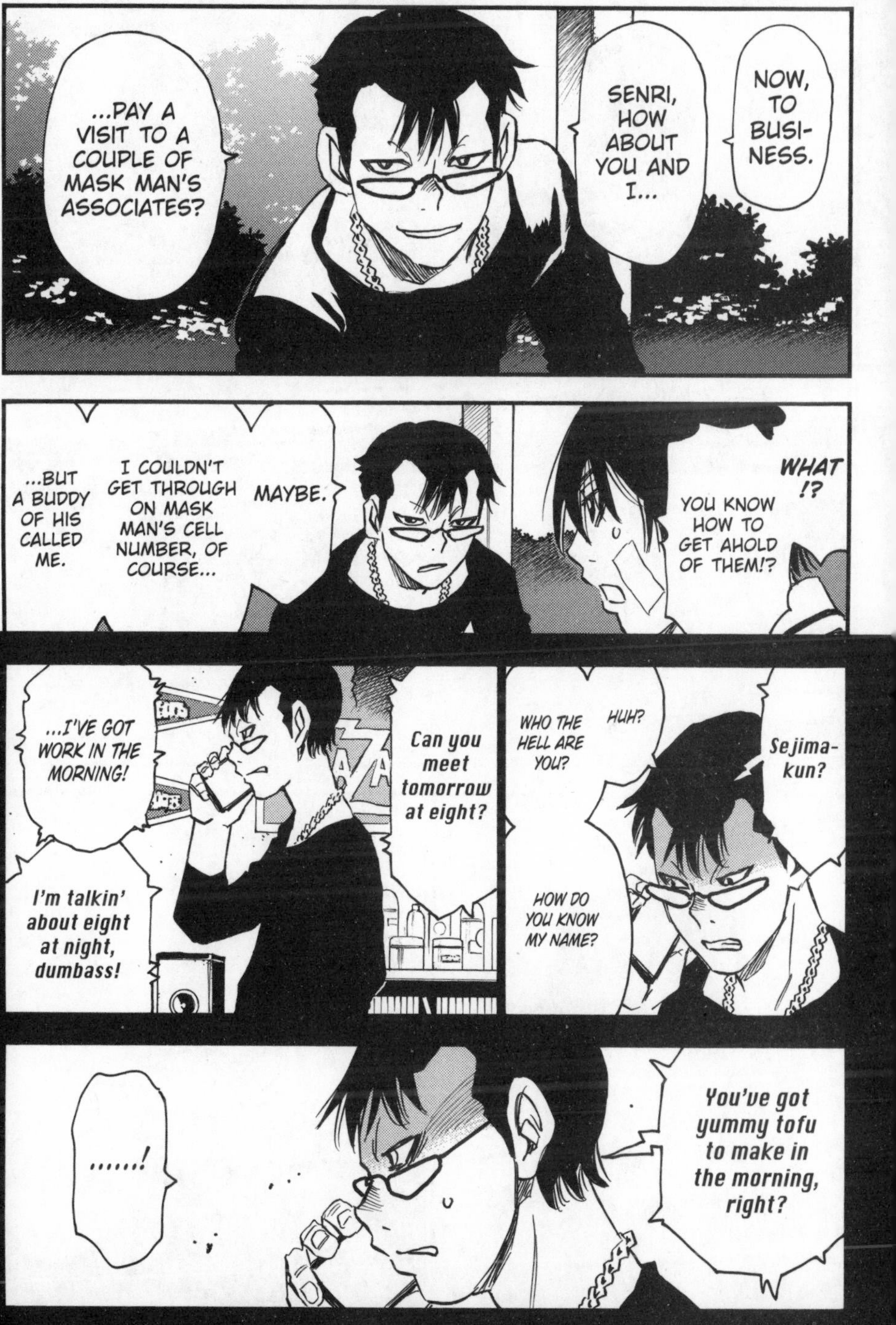
NOW, TO BUSI-NESS.
SENRI, HOW ABOUT YOU AND I...
...PAY A VISIT TO A COUPLE OF MASK MAN'S ASSOCIATES?
WHAT!?
YOU KNOW HOW TO GET AHOLD OF THEM!?
MAYBE.
I COULDN'T GET THROUGH ON MASK MAN'S CELL NUMBER, OF COURSE...
...BUT A BUDDY OF HIS CALLED ME.
Sejima-kun?
HUH?
WHO THE HELL ARE YOU?
HOW DO YOU KNOW MY NAME?
Can you meet tomorrow at eight?
...I'VE GOT WORK IN THE MORNING!
I'm talkin' about eight at night, dumbass!
You've got yummy tofu to make in the morning, right?
......!

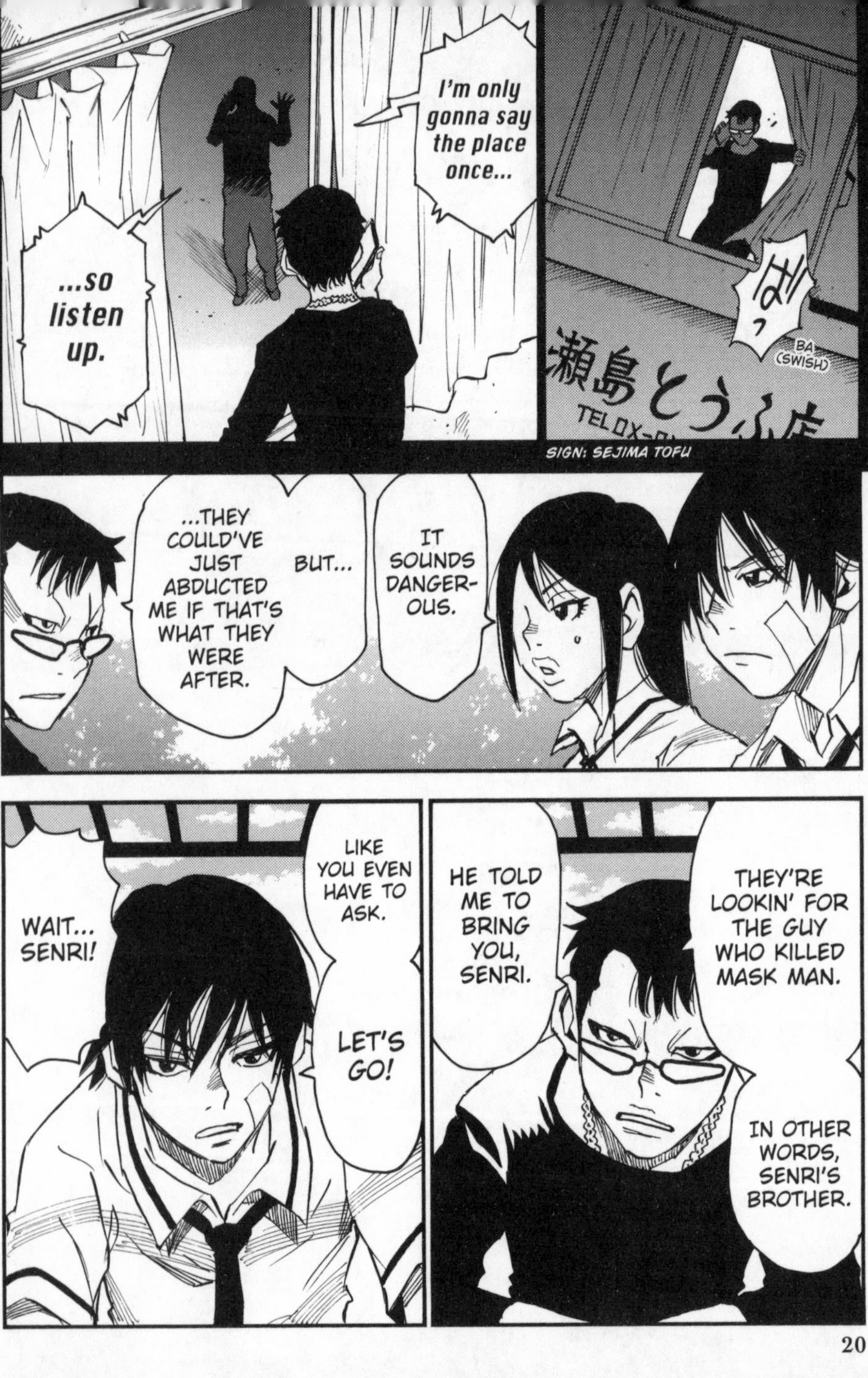

瀬島とうふ
はっ
BA (SWISH)
SIGN: SEJIMA TOFU
I'm only gonna say the place once...
...so listen up.
IT SOUNDS DANGEROUS.
BUT...
...THEY COULD'VE JUST ABDUCTED ME IF THAT'S WHAT THEY WERE AFTER.
THEY'RE LOOKIN' FOR THE GUY WHO KILLED MASK MAN.
IN OTHER WORDS, SENRI'S BROTHER.
HE TOLD ME TO BRING YOU, SENRI.
LIKE YOU EVEN HAVE TO ASK.
LET'S GO!
WAIT... SENRI!

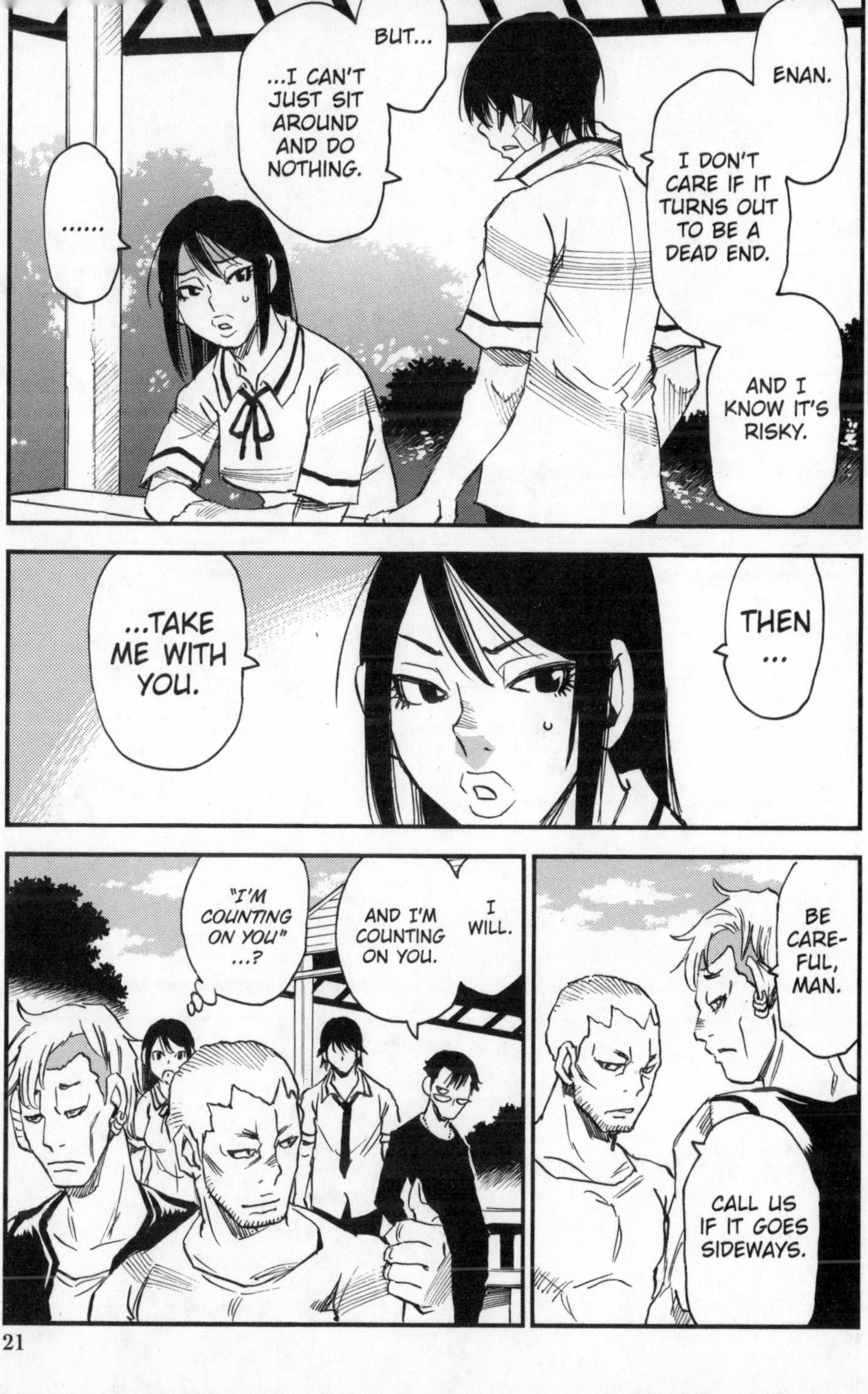
ENAN.
I DON'T CARE IF IT TURNS OUT TO BE A DEAD END.
AND I KNOW IT'S RISKY.
BUT...
...I CAN'T JUST SIT AROUND AND DO NOTHING.
......
THEN...
...TAKE ME WITH YOU.
BE CARE-FUL, MAN.
CALL US IF IT GOES SIDEWAYS.
I WILL.
AND I'M COUNTING ON YOU.
"I'M COUNTING ON YOU" ...?

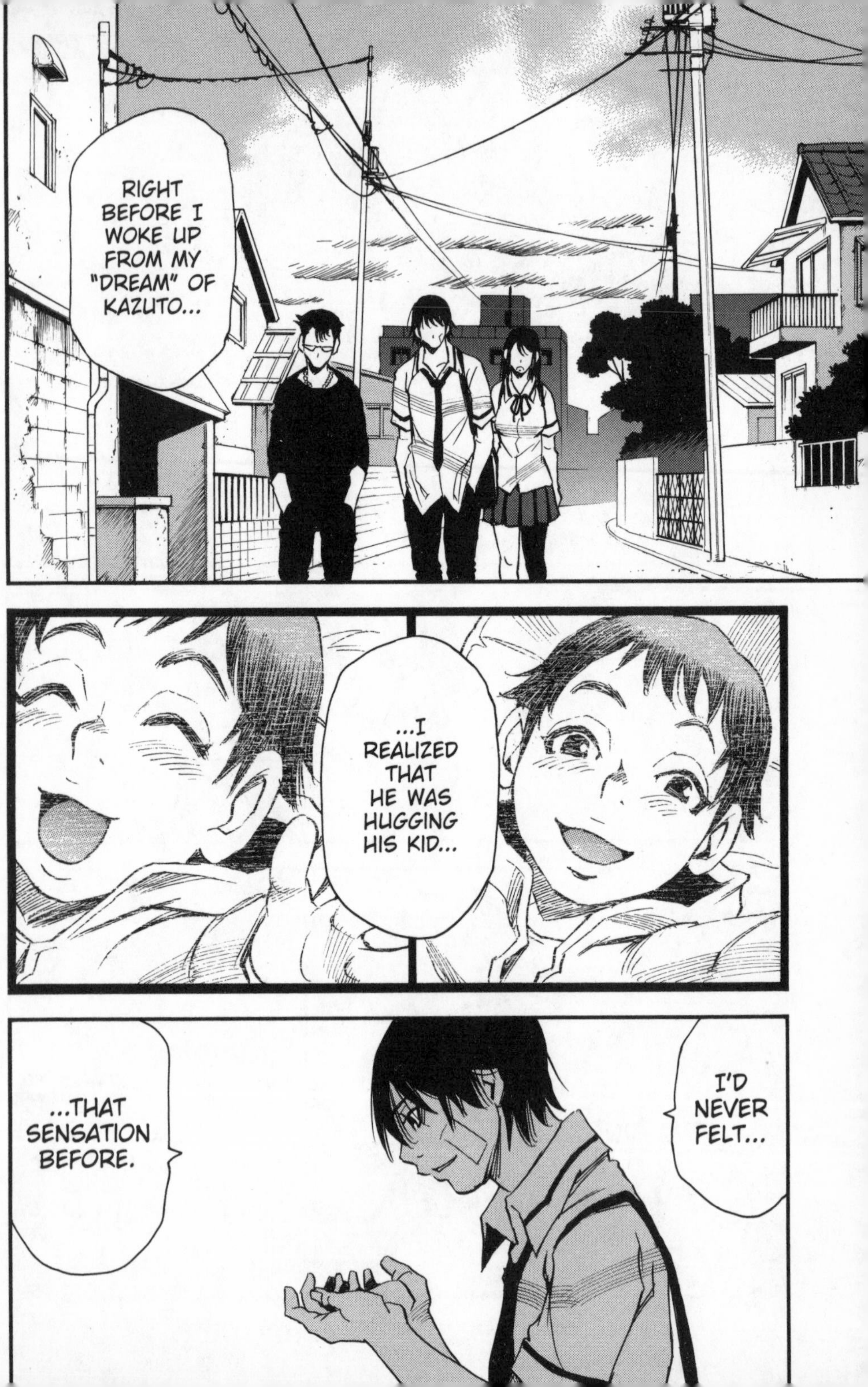
RIGHT BEFORE I WOKE UP FROM MY "DREAM" OF KAZUTO...
...I REALIZED THAT HE WAS HUGGING HIS KID...
I'D NEVER FELT...
...THAT SENSATION BEFORE.

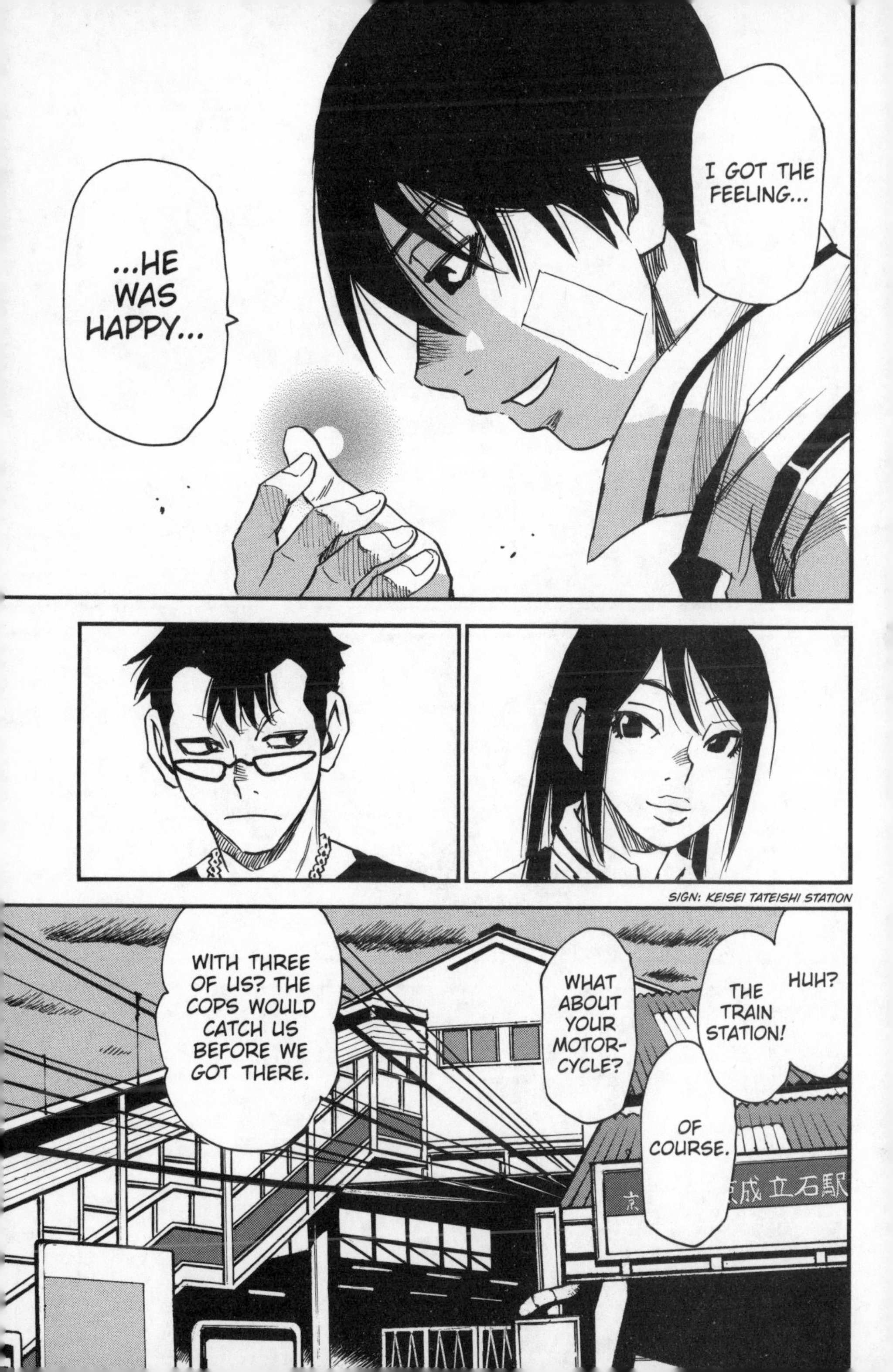
I GOT THE FEELING...
...HE WAS HAPPY...
SIGN: KEISEI TATEISHI STATION
HUH?
THE TRAIN STATION!
OF COURSE.
WHAT ABOUT YOUR MOTOR-CYCLE?
WITH THREE OF US? THE COPS WOULD CATCH US BEFORE WE GOT THERE.
京成立石駅

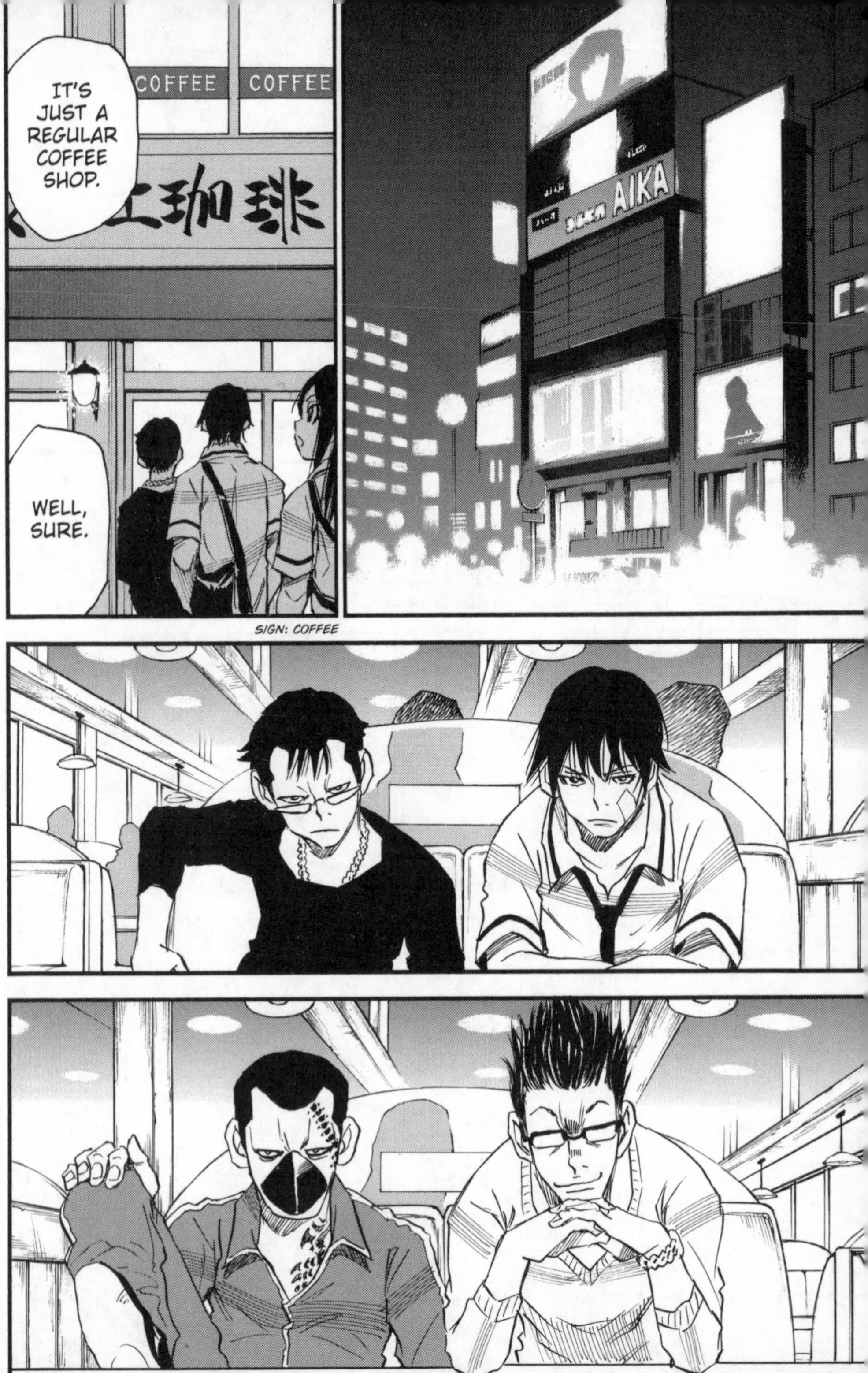
AIKA
COFFEE COFFEE
IT'S JUST A REGULAR COFFEE SHOP.
WELL, SURE.
SIGN: COFFEE

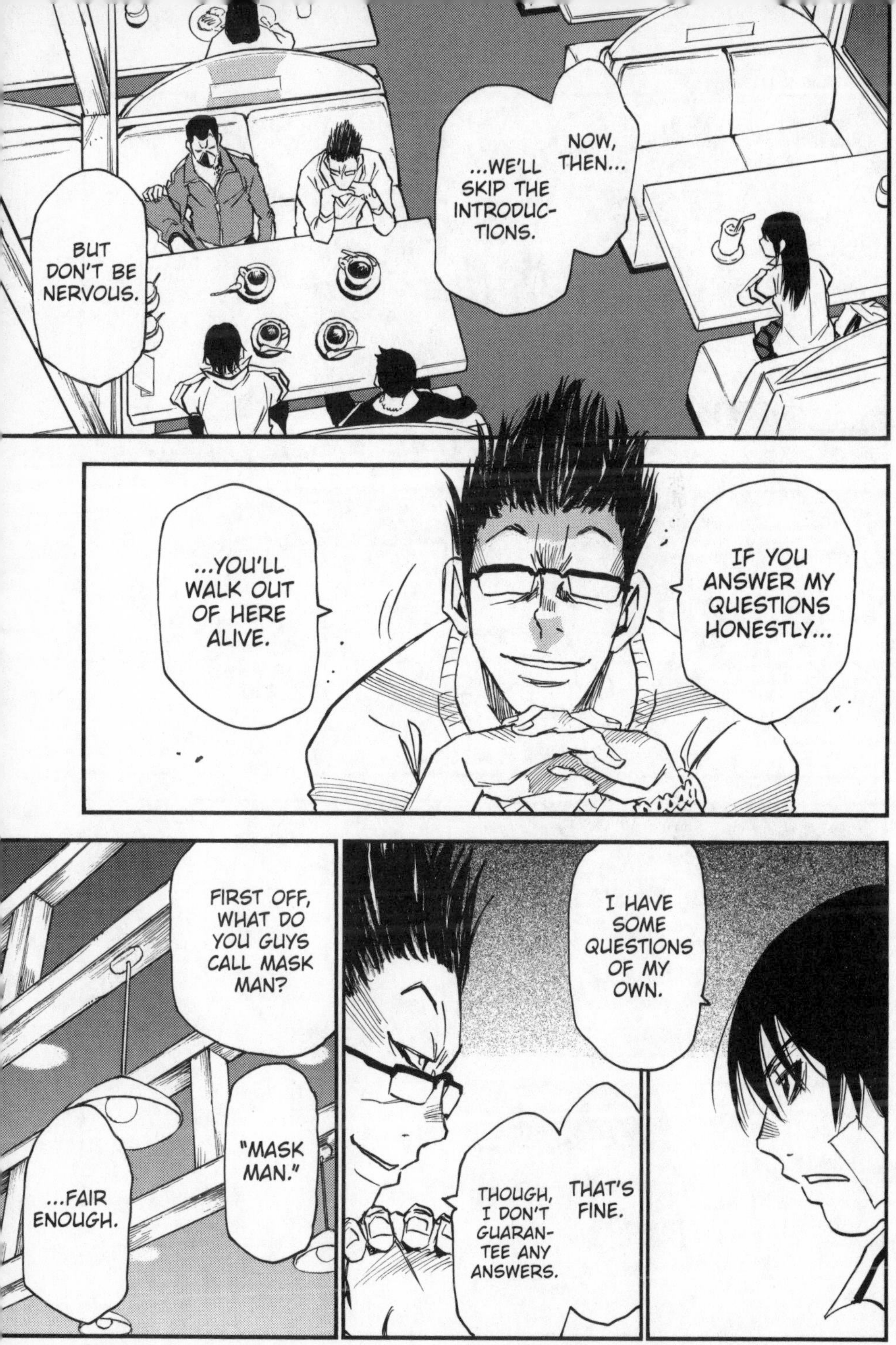
NOW, THEN... ...WE'LL SKIP THE INTRODUCTIONS.
BUT DON'T BE NERVOUS.
IF YOU ANSWER MY QUESTIONS HONESTLY...
...YOU'LL WALK OUT OF HERE ALIVE.
I HAVE SOME QUESTIONS OF MY OWN.
THAT'S FINE.
THOUGH, I DON'T GUARANTEE ANY ANSWERS.
FIRST OFF, WHAT DO YOU GUYS CALL MASK MAN?
"MASK MAN."
...FAIR ENOUGH.

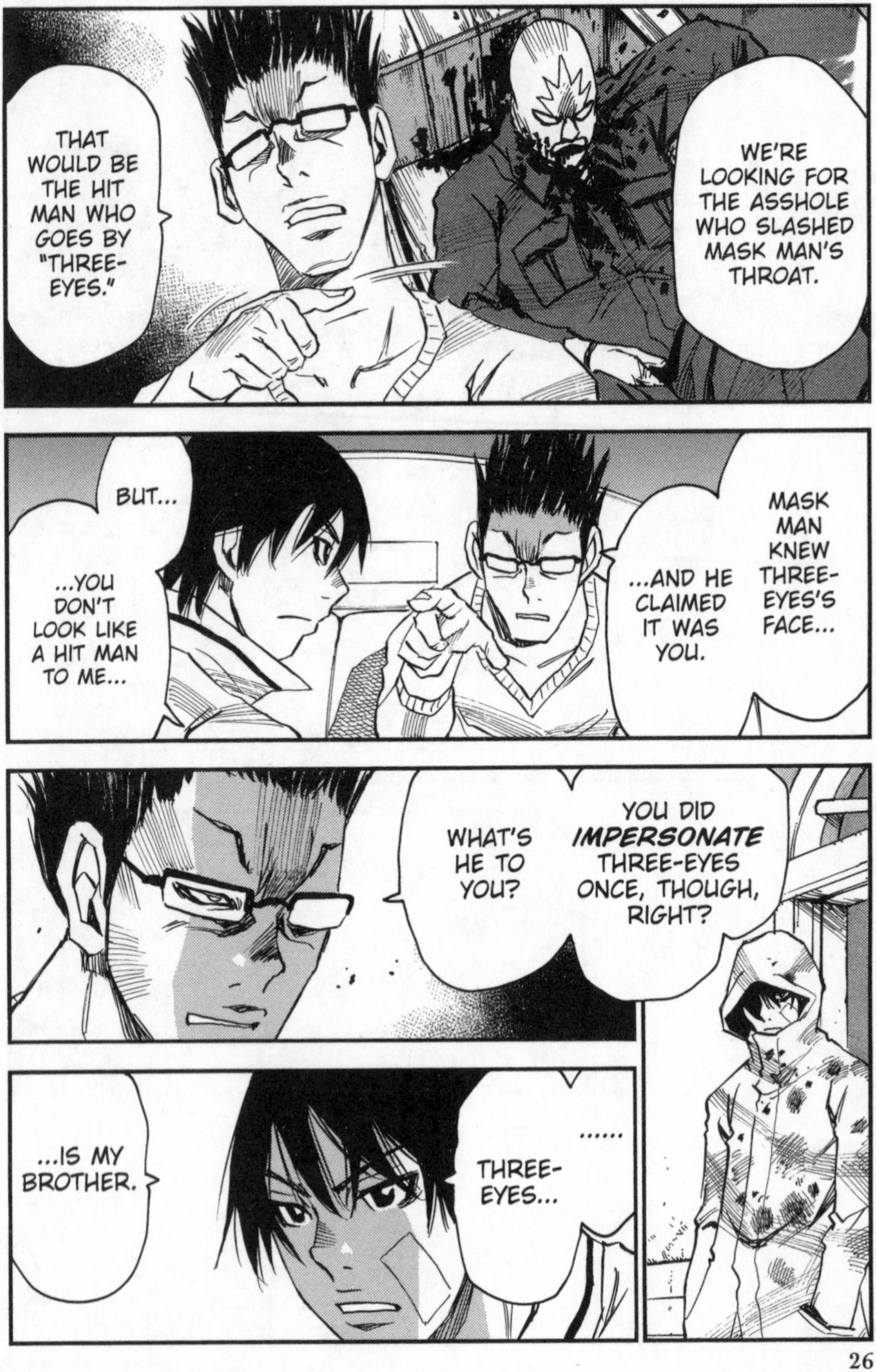
WE'RE LOOKING FOR THE ASSHOLE WHO SLASHED MASK MAN'S THROAT.
THAT WOULD BE THE HIT MAN WHO GOES BY "THREE-EYES."
MASK MAN KNEW THREE-EYES'S FACE...
...AND HE CLAIMED IT WAS YOU.
BUT...
...YOU DON'T LOOK LIKE A HIT MAN TO ME...
YOU DID *IMPERSONATE* THREE-EYES ONCE, THOUGH, RIGHT?
WHAT'S HE TO YOU?
......
THREE-EYES...
...IS MY BROTHER.

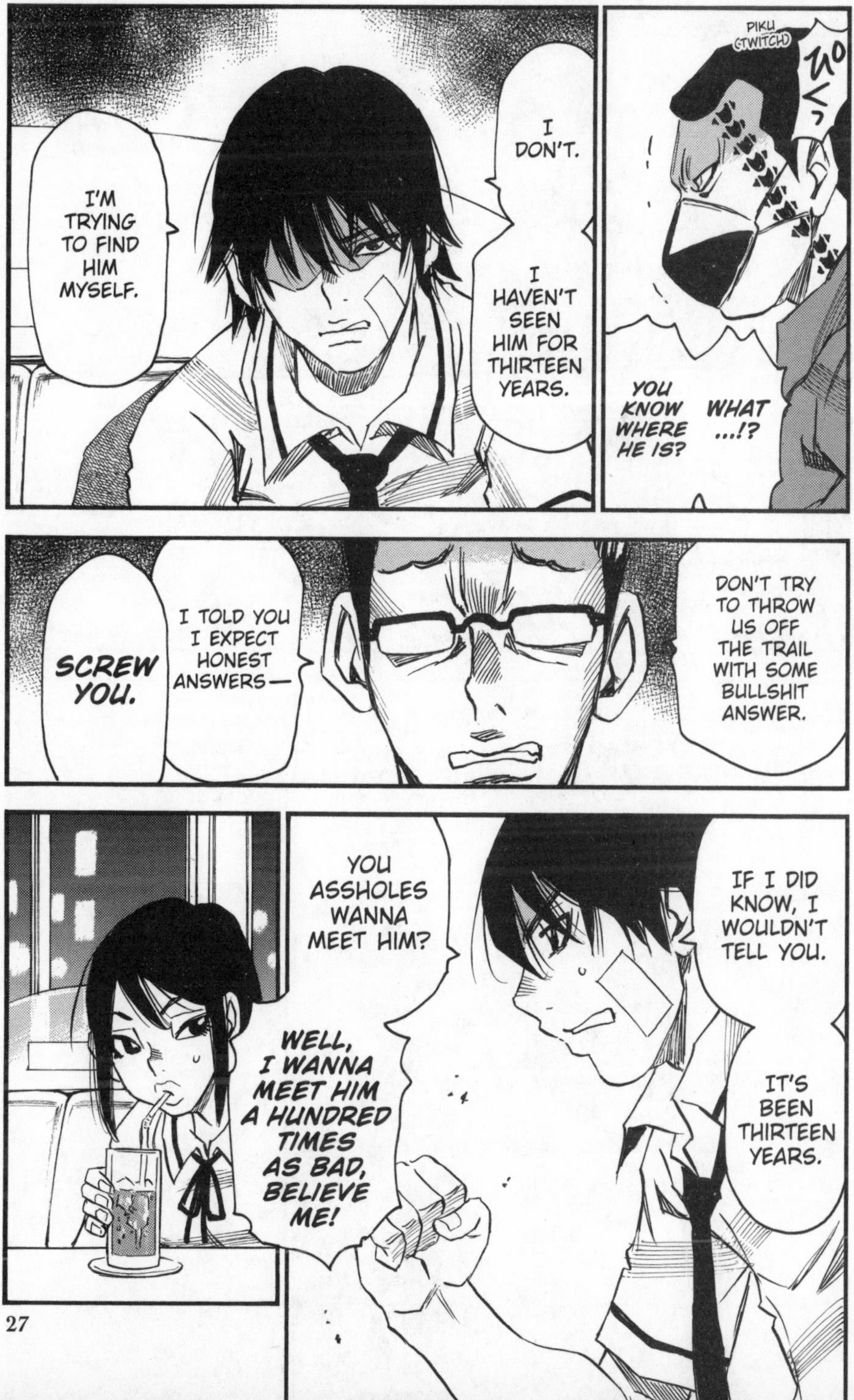
PIKU (TWITCH)
ぴくっ
WHAT ...!?
YOU KNOW WHERE HE IS?
I DON'T.
I HAVEN'T SEEN HIM FOR THIRTEEN YEARS.
I'M TRYING TO FIND HIM MYSELF.
DON'T TRY TO THROW US OFF THE TRAIL WITH SOME BULLSHIT ANSWER.
I TOLD YOU I EXPECT HONEST ANSWERS—
SCREW YOU.
IF I DID KNOW, I WOULDN'T TELL YOU.
IT'S BEEN THIRTEEN YEARS.
YOU ASSHOLES WANNA MEET HIM?
WELL, I WANNA MEET HIM A HUNDRED TIMES AS BAD, BELIEVE ME!

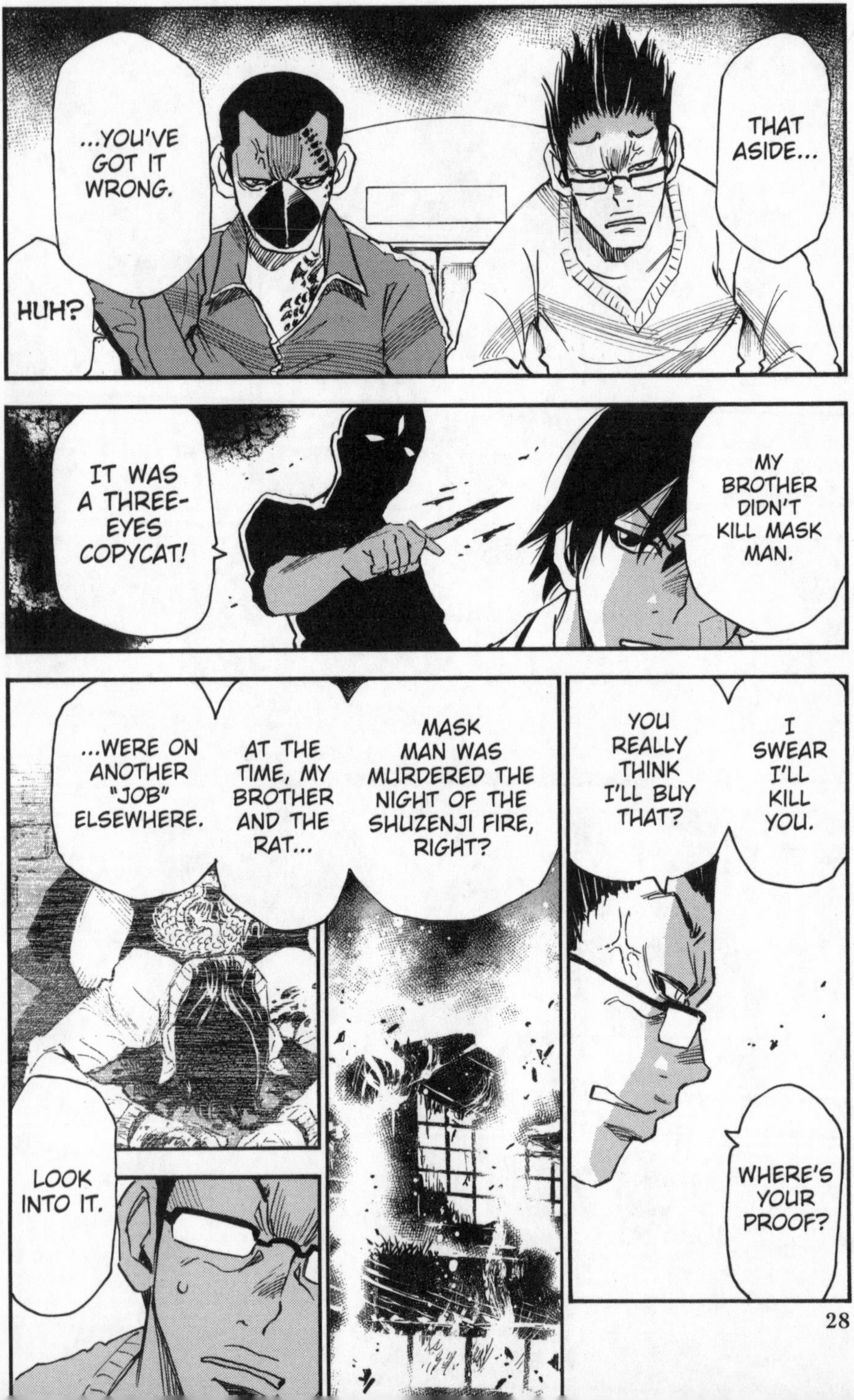
THAT ASIDE...
...YOU'VE GOT IT WRONG.
HUH?
MY BROTHER DIDN'T KILL MASK MAN.
IT WAS A THREE-EYES COPYCAT!
I SWEAR I'LL KILL YOU.
YOU REALLY THINK I'LL BUY THAT?
WHERE'S YOUR PROOF?
MASK MAN WAS MURDERED THE NIGHT OF THE SHUZENJI FIRE, RIGHT?
AT THE TIME, MY BROTHER AND THE RAT...
...WERE ON ANOTHER "JOB" ELSEWHERE.
LOOK INTO IT.

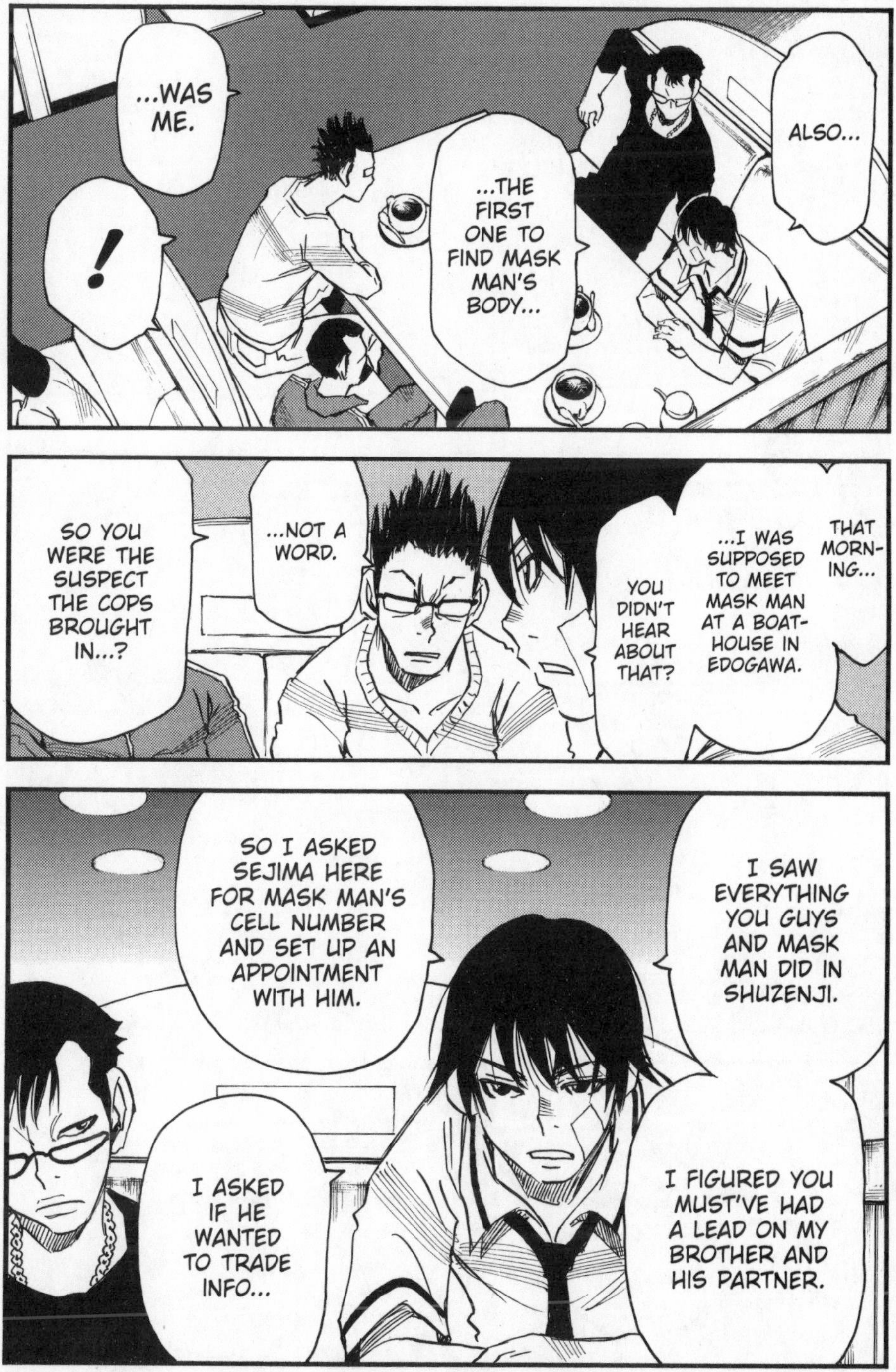
ALSO...
...THE FIRST ONE TO FIND MASK MAN'S BODY...
...WAS ME.
!
THAT MORNING...
...I WAS SUPPOSED TO MEET MASK MAN AT A BOATHOUSE IN EDOGAWA.
YOU DIDN'T HEAR ABOUT THAT?
...NOT A WORD.
SO YOU WERE THE SUSPECT THE COPS BROUGHT IN...?
I SAW EVERYTHING YOU GUYS AND MASK MAN DID IN SHUZENJI.
SO I ASKED SEJIMA HERE FOR MASK MAN'S CELL NUMBER AND SET UP AN APPOINTMENT WITH HIM.
I FIGURED YOU MUST'VE HAD A LEAD ON MY BROTHER AND HIS PARTNER.
I ASKED IF HE WANTED TO TRADE INFO...

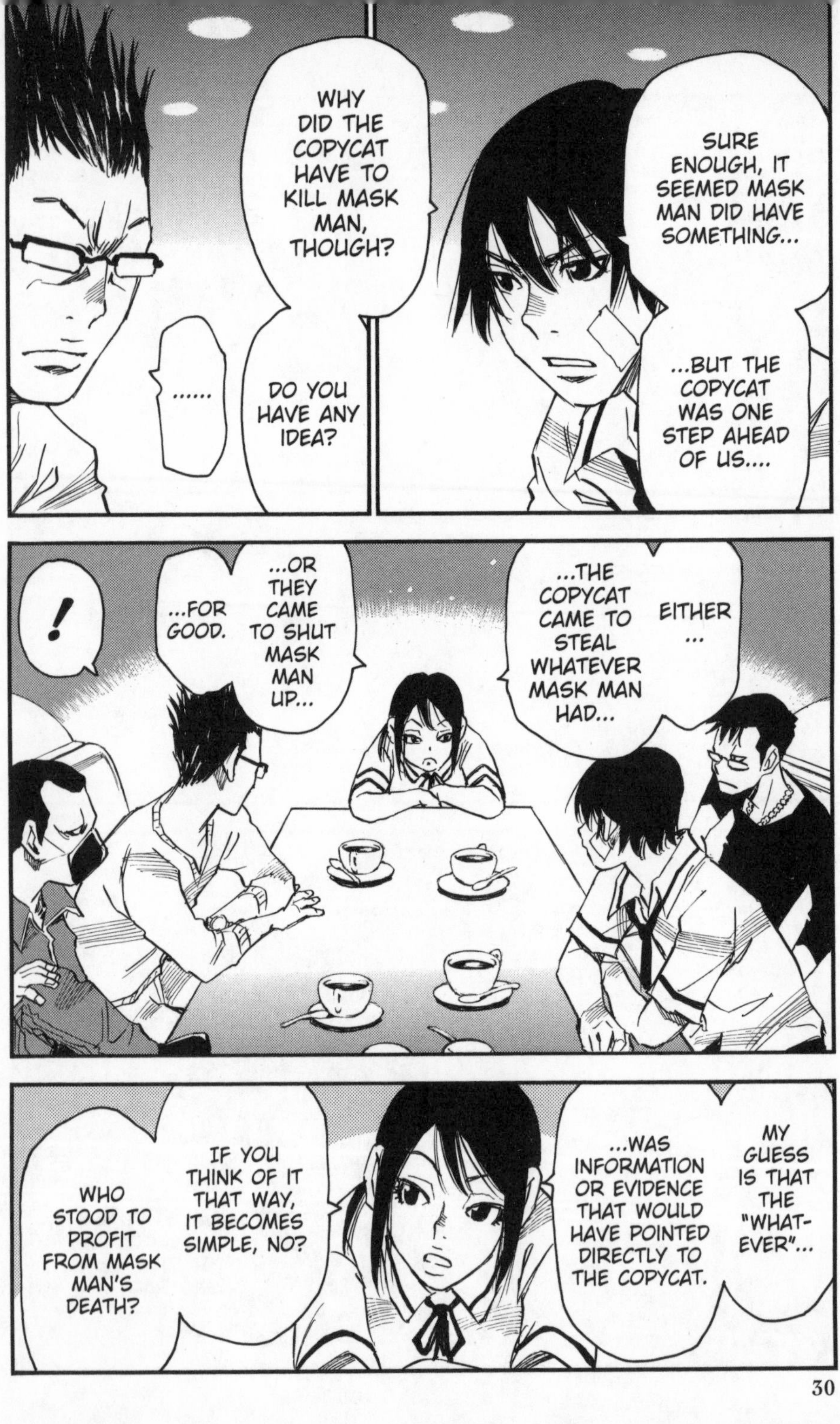

SURE ENOUGH, IT SEEMED MASK MAN DID HAVE SOMETHING...
...BUT THE COPYCAT WAS ONE STEP AHEAD OF US....
WHY DID THE COPYCAT HAVE TO KILL MASK MAN, THOUGH?
DO YOU HAVE ANY IDEA?
......
EITHER...
...THE COPYCAT CAME TO STEAL WHATEVER MASK MAN HAD...
...OR THEY CAME TO SHUT MASK MAN UP...
...FOR GOOD.
!
MY GUESS IS THAT THE "WHAT-EVER"...
...WAS INFORMATION OR EVIDENCE THAT WOULD HAVE POINTED DIRECTLY TO THE COPYCAT.
IF YOU THINK OF IT THAT WAY, IT BECOMES SIMPLE, NO?
WHO STOOD TO PROFIT FROM MASK MAN'S DEATH?

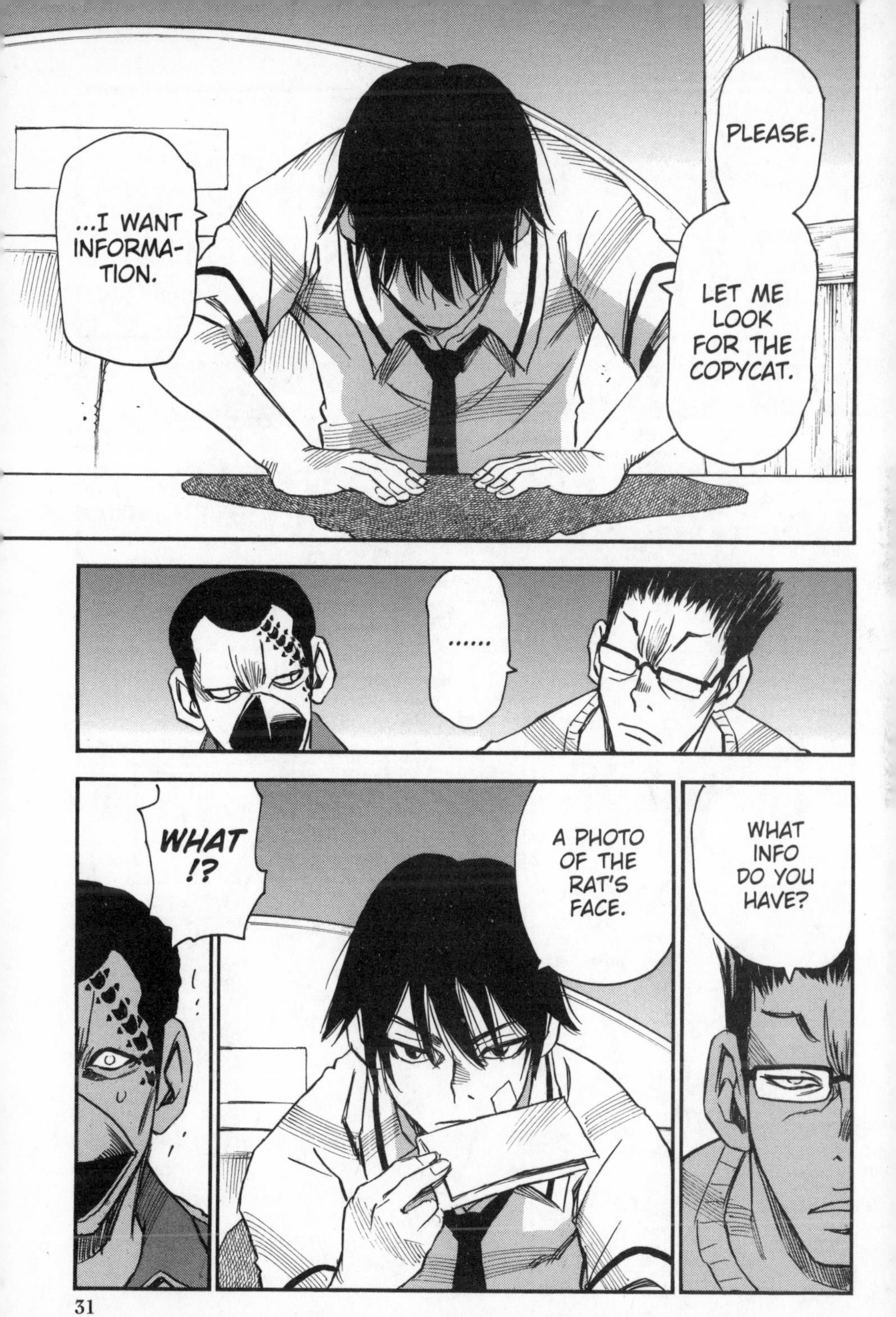
PLEASE.
LET ME LOOK FOR THE COPYCAT.
...I WANT INFORMATION.
......
WHAT INFO DO YOU HAVE?
A PHOTO OF THE RAT'S FACE.
WHAT!?

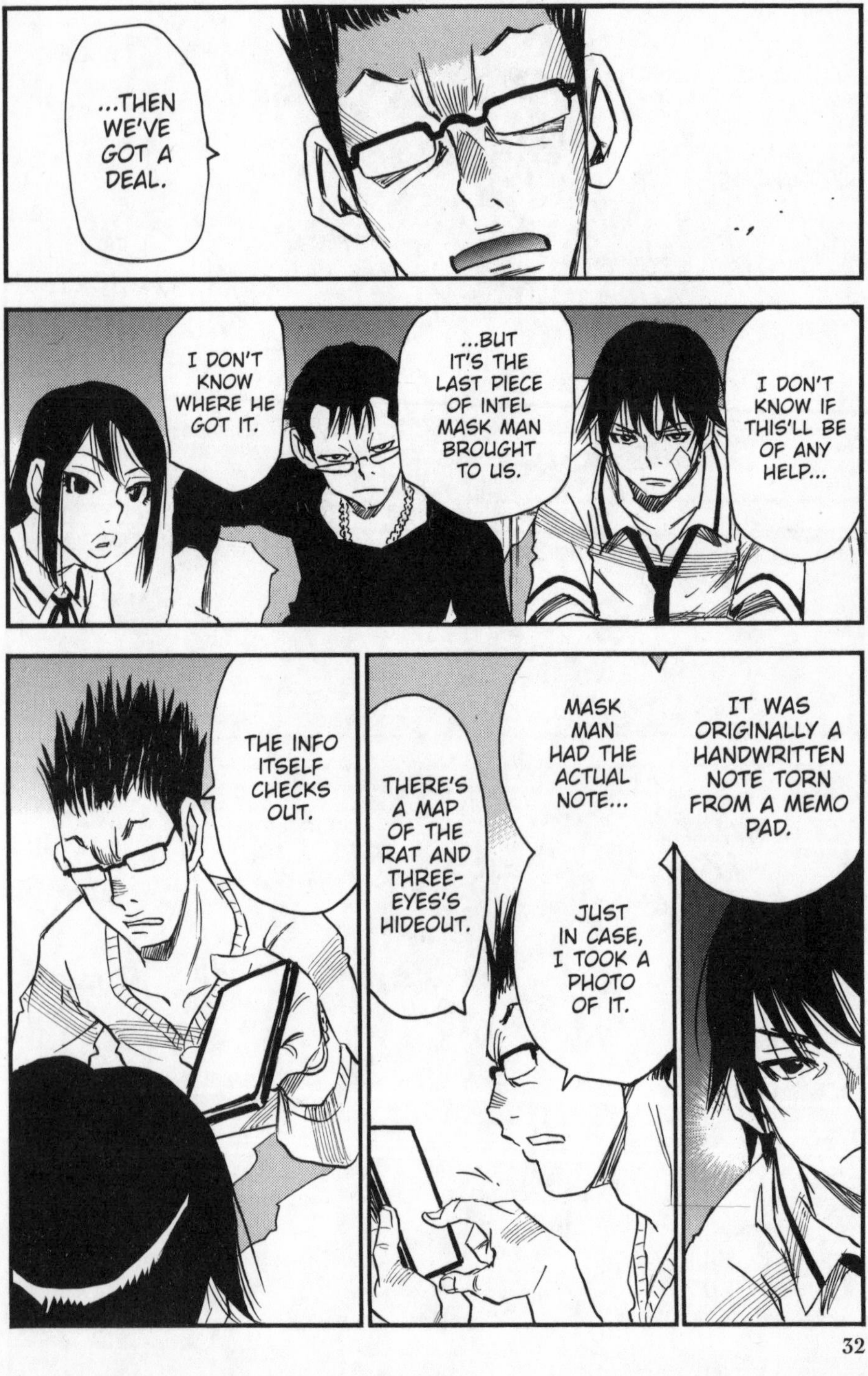
...THEN WE'VE GOT A DEAL.
I DON'T KNOW IF THIS'LL BE OF ANY HELP...
...BUT IT'S THE LAST PIECE OF INTEL MASK MAN BROUGHT TO US.
I DON'T KNOW WHERE HE GOT IT.
IT WAS ORIGINALLY A HANDWRITTEN NOTE TORN FROM A MEMO PAD.
MASK MAN HAD THE ACTUAL NOTE...
JUST IN CASE, I TOOK A PHOTO OF IT.
THERE'S A MAP OF THE RAT AND THREE-EYES'S HIDEOUT.
THE INFO ITSELF CHECKS OUT.

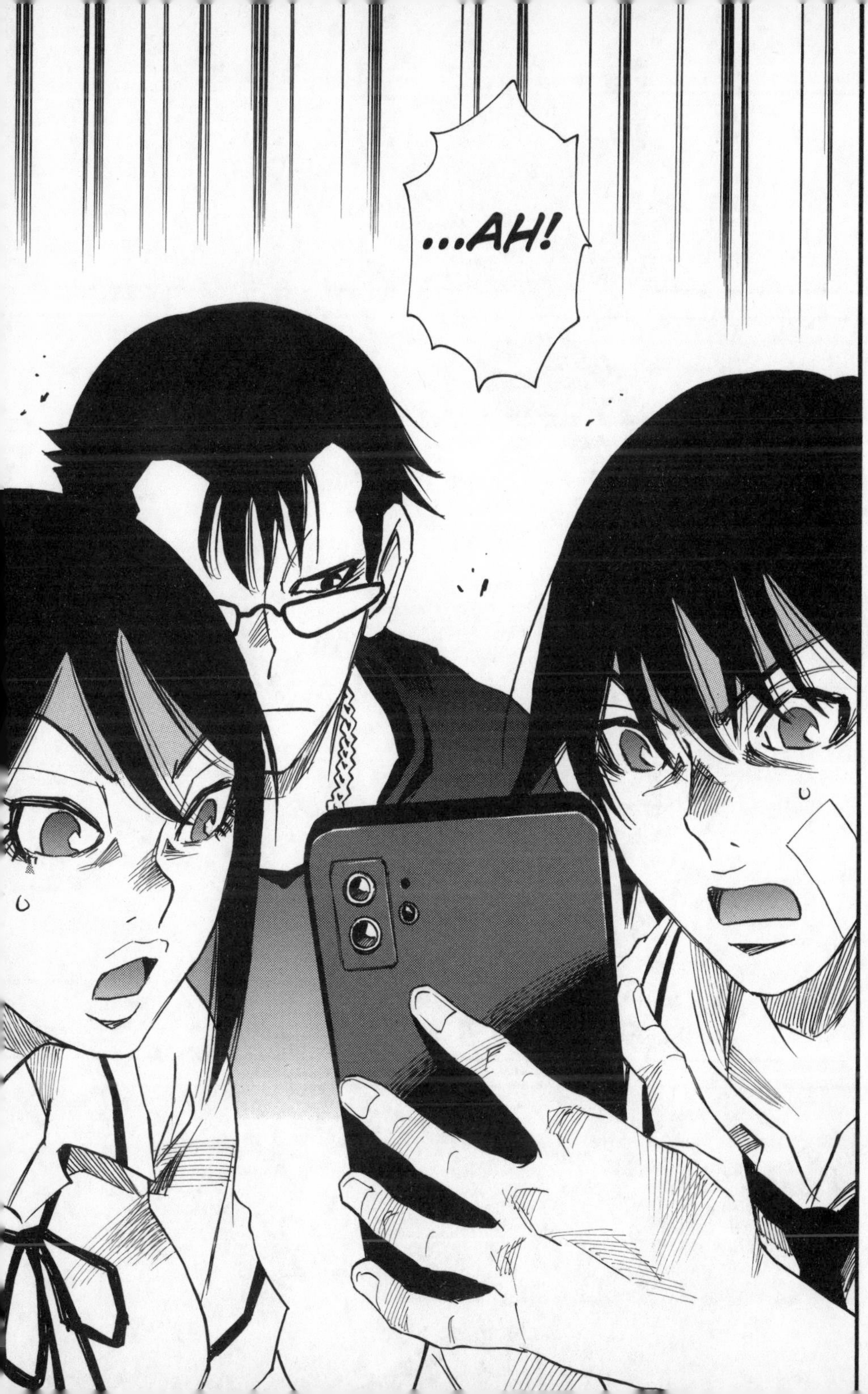
...AH!

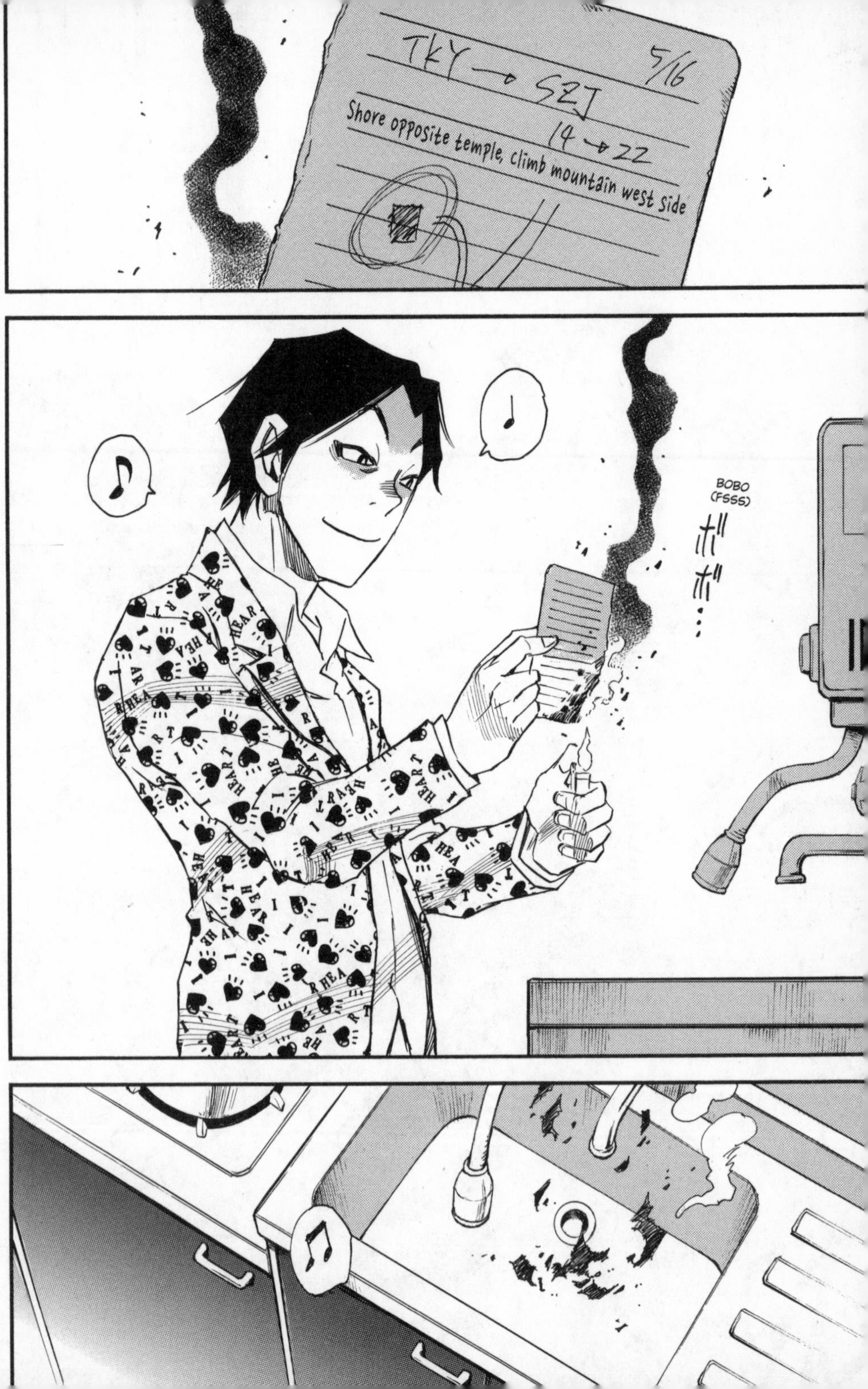

TKY → SZJ 5/16
14 → 22
Shore opposite temple, climb mountain west side
♪
♪
BOBO (FSSS)
ボ ボ…
♪

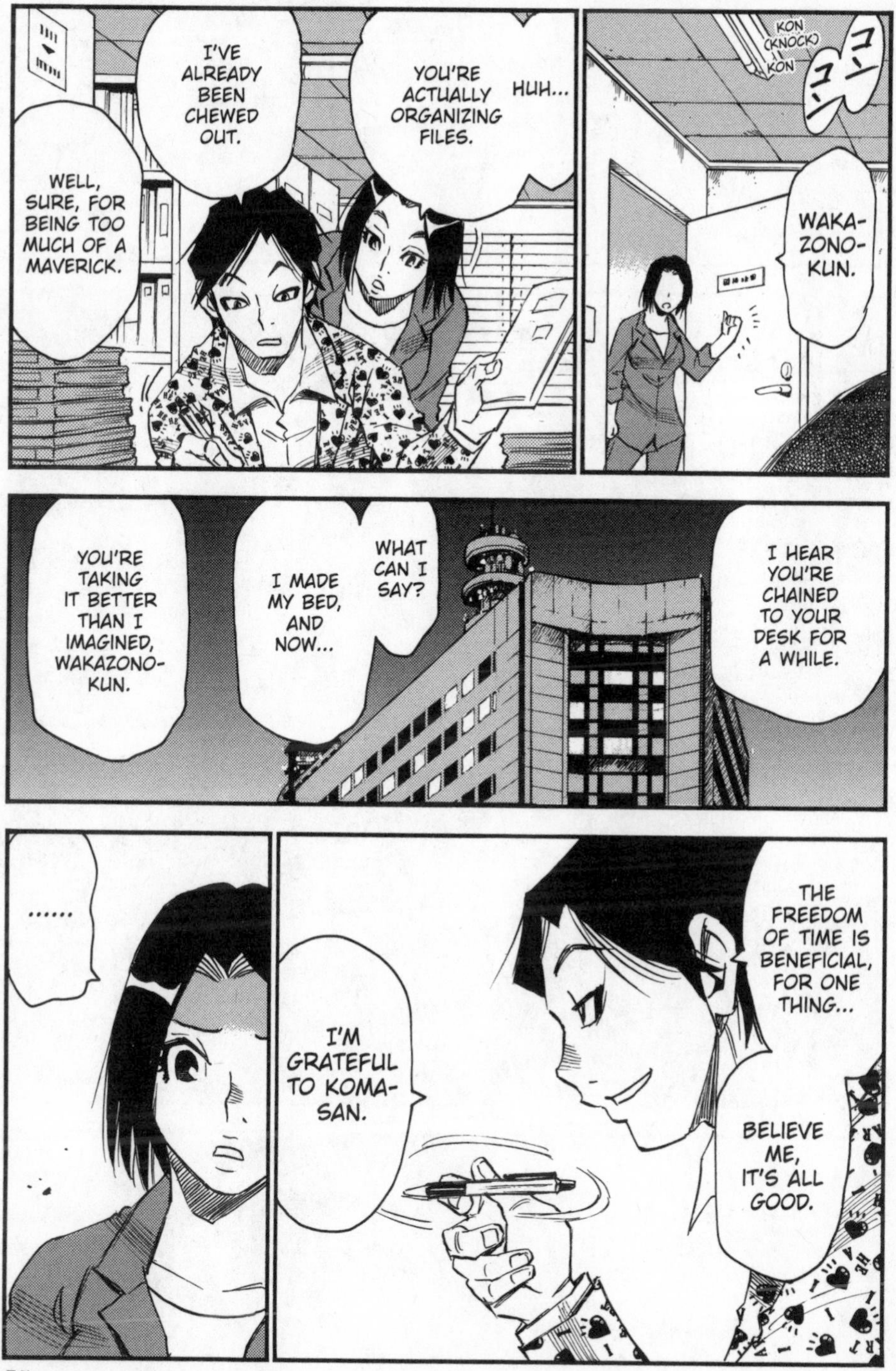
KON (KNOCK) KON
WAKAZONO-KUN.
HUH...
YOU'RE ACTUALLY ORGANIZING FILES.
I'VE ALREADY BEEN CHEWED OUT.
WELL, SURE, FOR BEING TOO MUCH OF A MAVERICK.
I HEAR YOU'RE CHAINED TO YOUR DESK FOR A WHILE.
WHAT CAN I SAY?
I MADE MY BED, AND NOW...
YOU'RE TAKING IT BETTER THAN I IMAGINED, WAKAZONO-KUN.
THE FREEDOM OF TIME IS BENEFICIAL, FOR ONE THING...
BELIEVE ME, IT'S ALL GOOD.
I'M GRATEFUL TO KOMA-SAN.
......

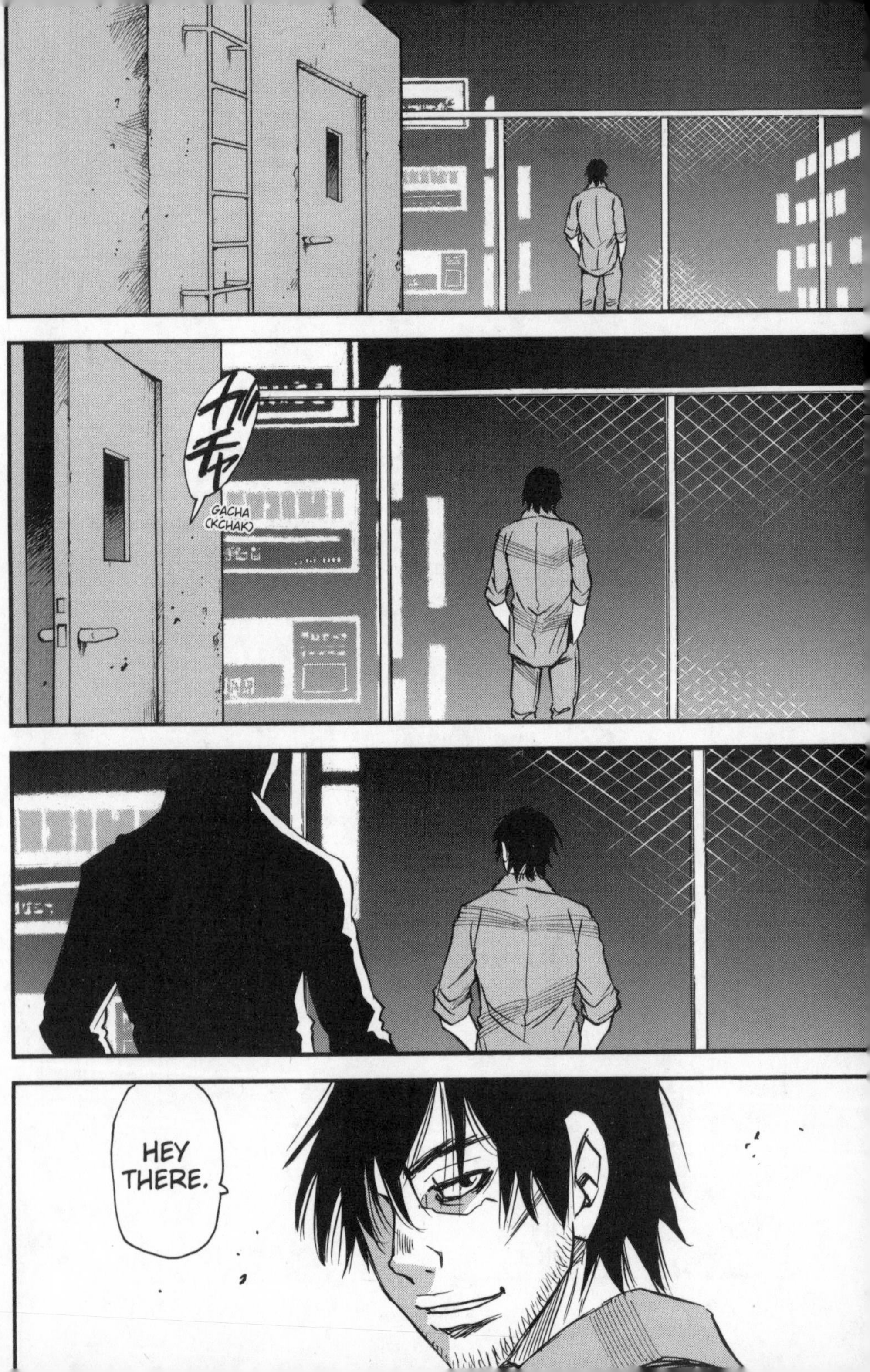
ガチャ
GACHA (KCHAK)
HEY THERE.

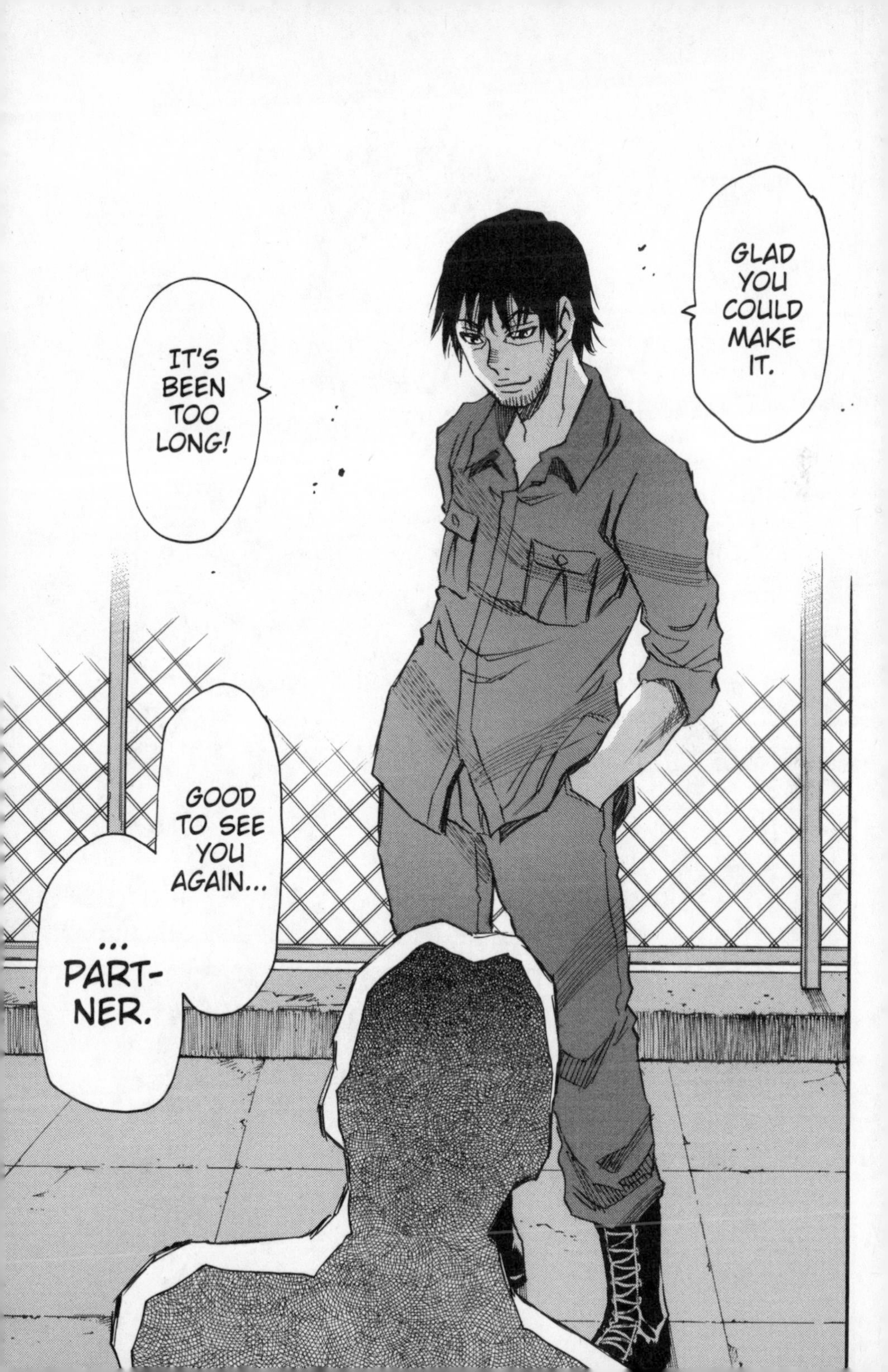
GLAD YOU COULD MAKE IT.
IT'S BEEN TOO LONG!
GOOD TO SEE YOU AGAIN...
...PART-NER.

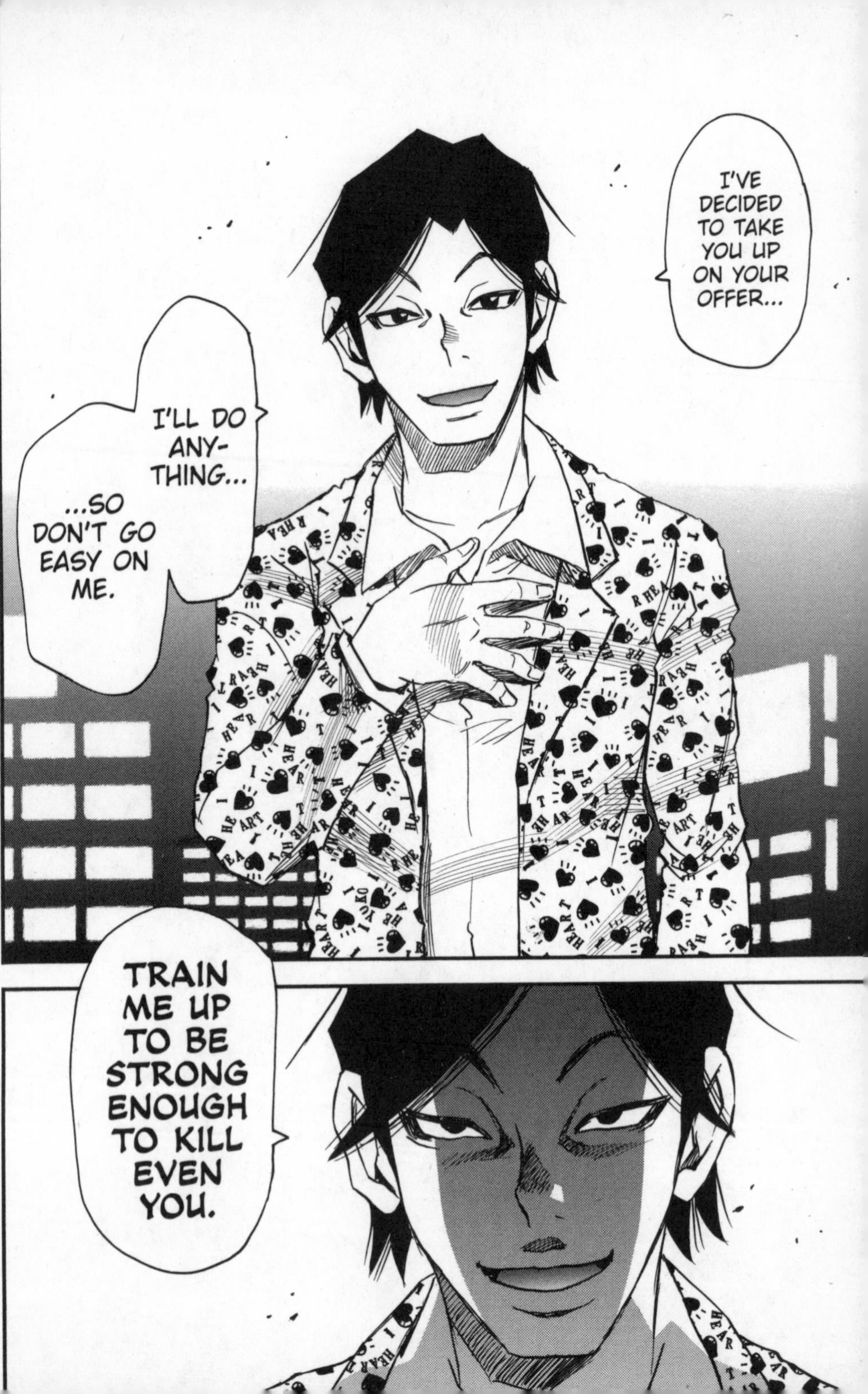
I'VE DECIDED TO TAKE YOU UP ON YOUR OFFER...
I'LL DO ANYTHING...
...SO DON'T GO EASY ON ME.
TRAIN ME UP TO BE STRONG ENOUGH TO KILL EVEN YOU.

#38 END

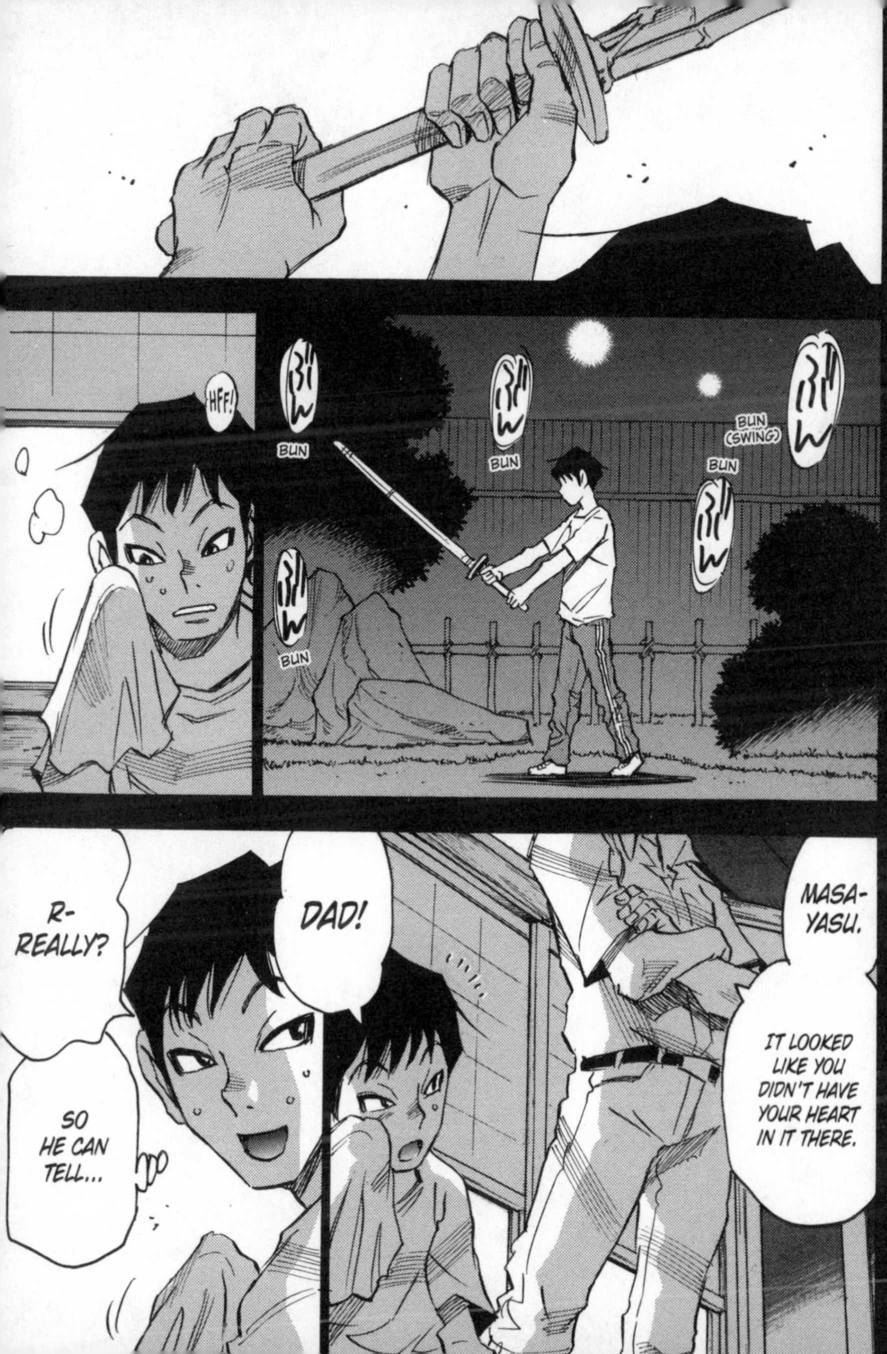
BUN (SWING)
BUN
BUN
BUN
BUN
HFF!
MASA-YASU.
IT LOOKED LIKE YOU DIDN'T HAVE YOUR HEART IN IT THERE.
DAD!
R-REALLY?
SO HE CAN TELL...

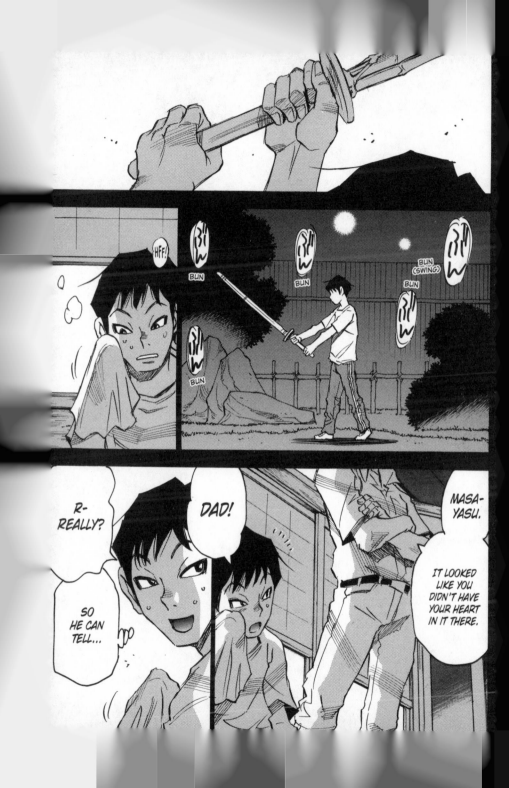

#39 The Man Who Was Bound by His Past

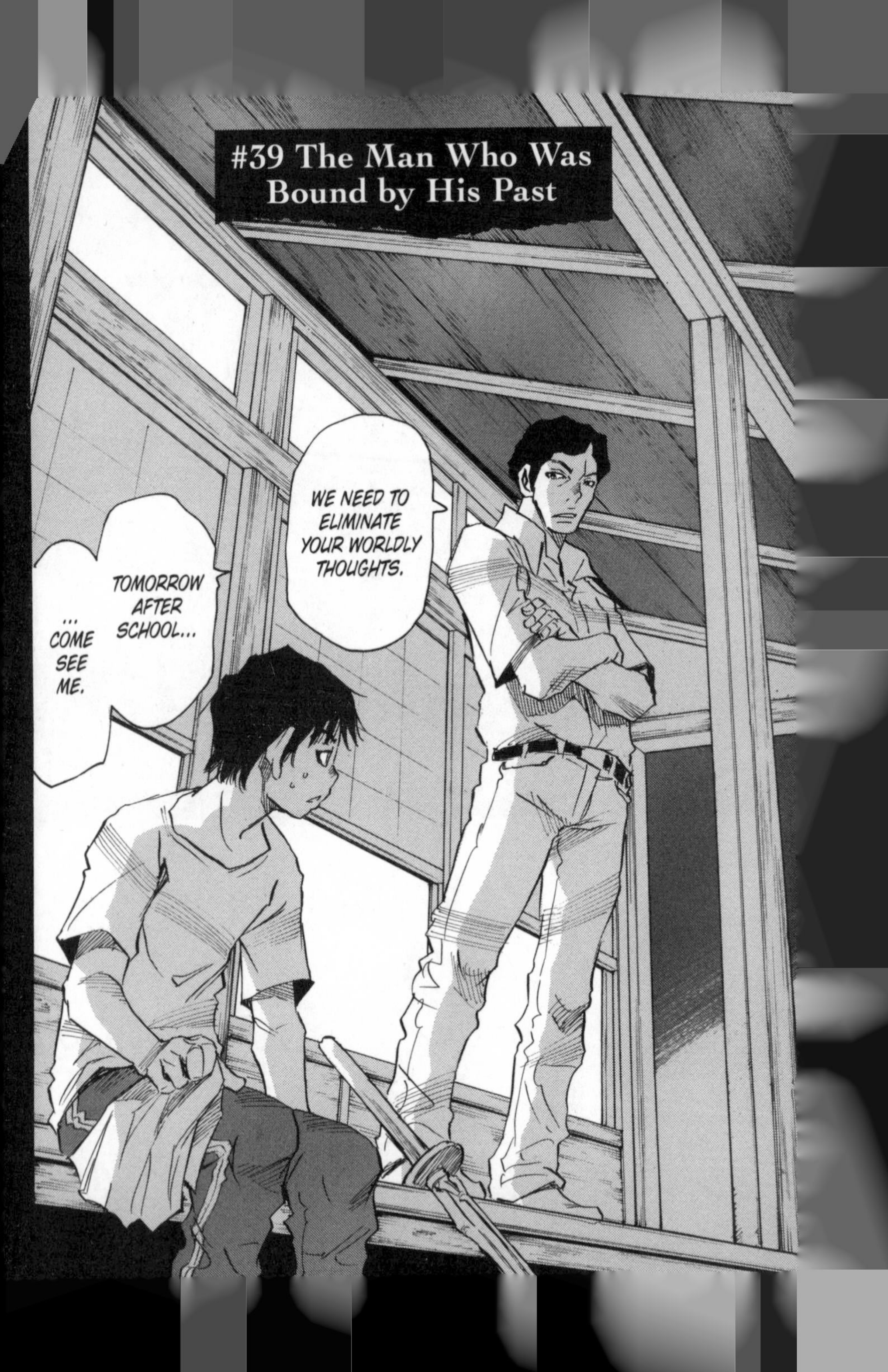
WE NEED TO ELIMINATE YOUR WORLDLY THOUGHTS.
TOMORROW AFTER SCHOOL...
...COME SEE ME.

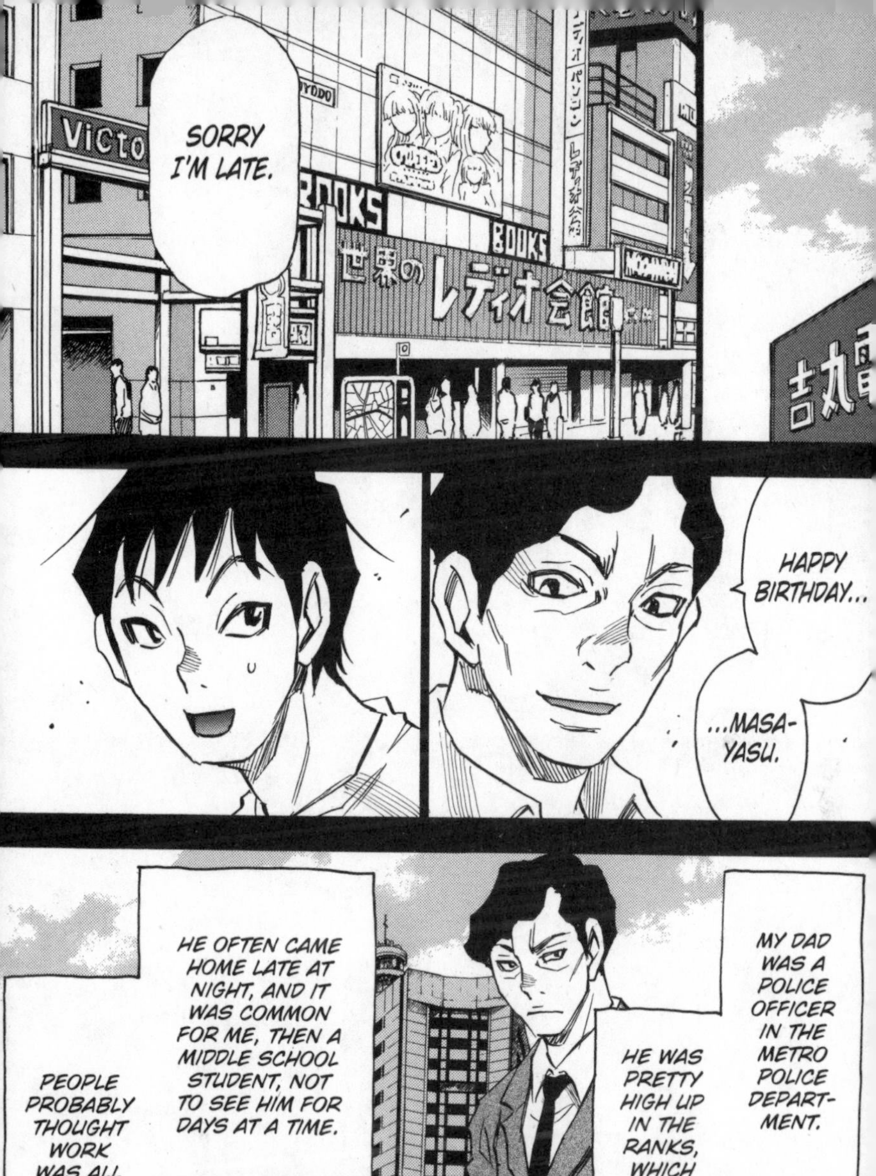
SORRY I'M LATE.
Victo
BOOKS
世界のレディオ会館
HAPPY BIRTHDAY...
...MASA-YASU.
MY DAD WAS A POLICE OFFICER IN THE METRO POLICE DEPARTMENT.
HE WAS PRETTY HIGH UP IN THE RANKS, WHICH MEANT HE HAD A LOT OF WORK TO DO.
HE OFTEN CAME HOME LATE AT NIGHT, AND IT WAS COMMON FOR ME, THEN A MIDDLE SCHOOL STUDENT, NOT TO SEE HIM FOR DAYS AT A TIME.
PEOPLE PROBABLY THOUGHT WORK WAS ALL HE CARED ABOUT.

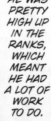

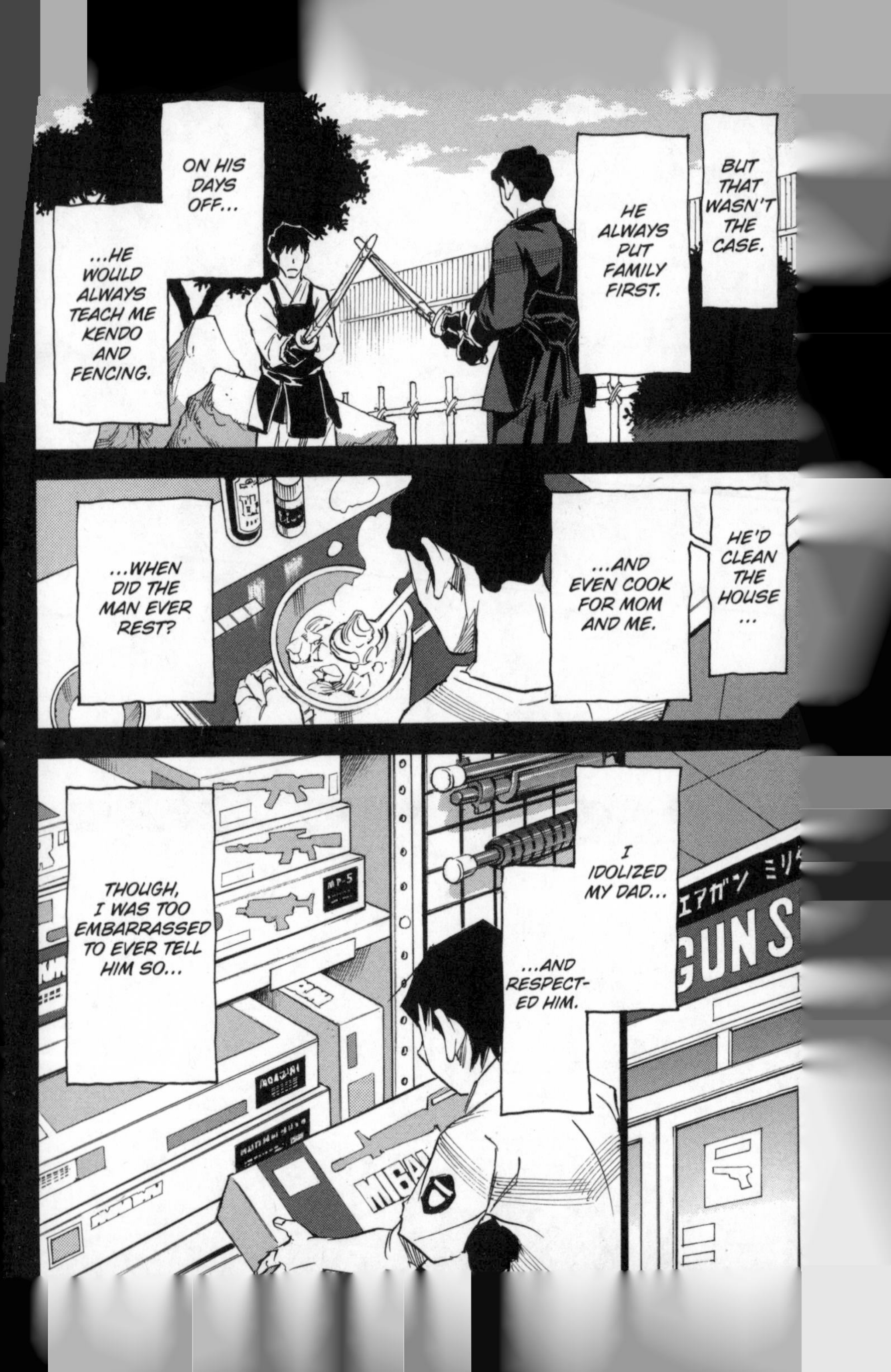
BUT THAT WASN'T THE CASE.
HE ALWAYS PUT FAMILY FIRST.
ON HIS DAYS OFF...
...HE WOULD ALWAYS TEACH ME KENDO AND FENCING.
HE'D CLEAN THE HOUSE ...
...AND EVEN COOK FOR MOM AND ME.
...WHEN DID THE MAN EVER REST?
I IDOLIZED MY DAD...
...AND RESPECTED HIM.
THOUGH, I WAS TOO EMBARRASSED TO EVER TELL HIM SO...

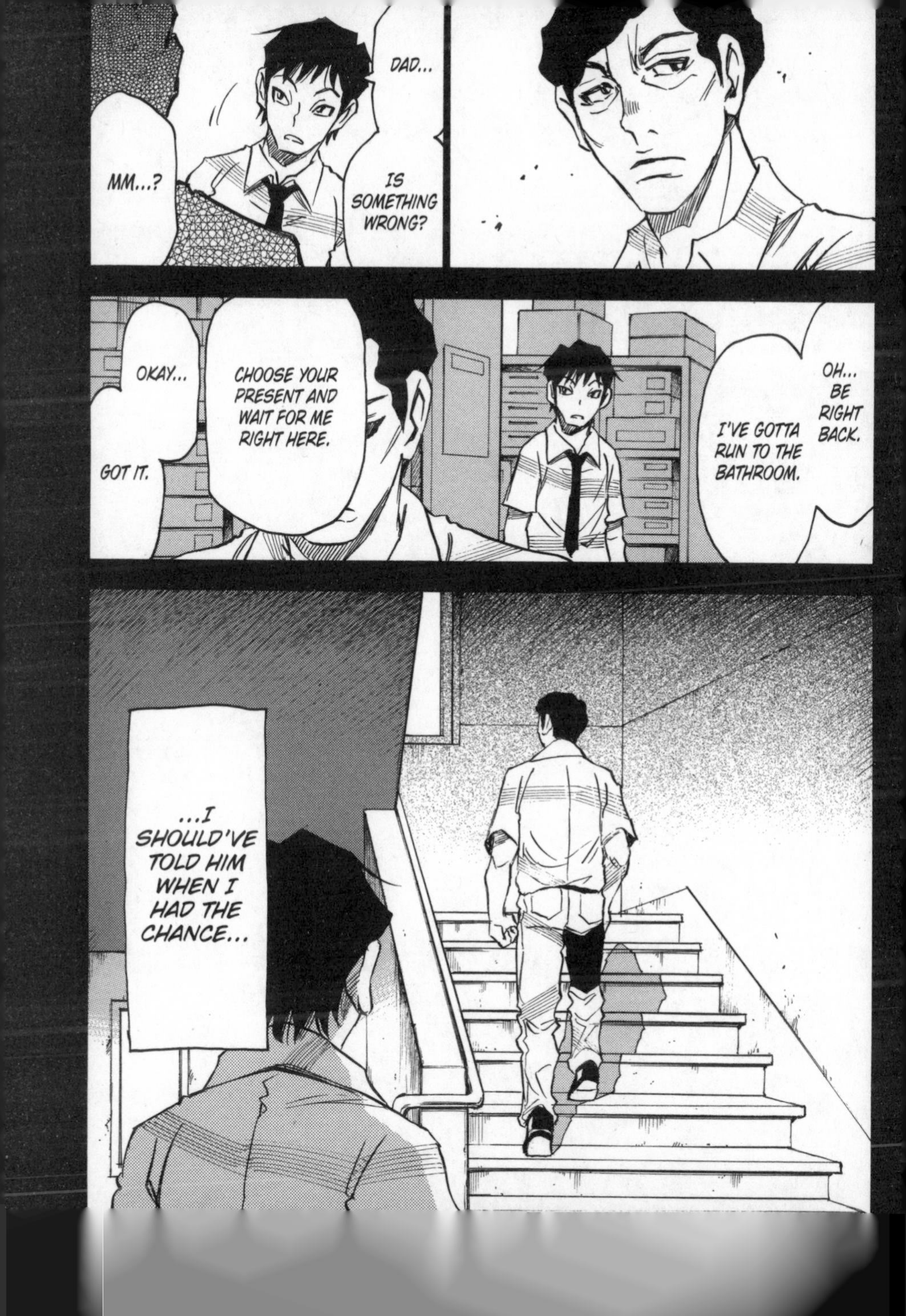
DAD...
IS SOMETHING WRONG?
MM...?
OH... BE RIGHT BACK.
I'VE GOTTA RUN TO THE BATHROOM.
CHOOSE YOUR PRESENT AND WAIT FOR ME RIGHT HERE.
OKAY...
GOT IT.
...I SHOULD'VE TOLD HIM WHEN I HAD THE CHANCE...

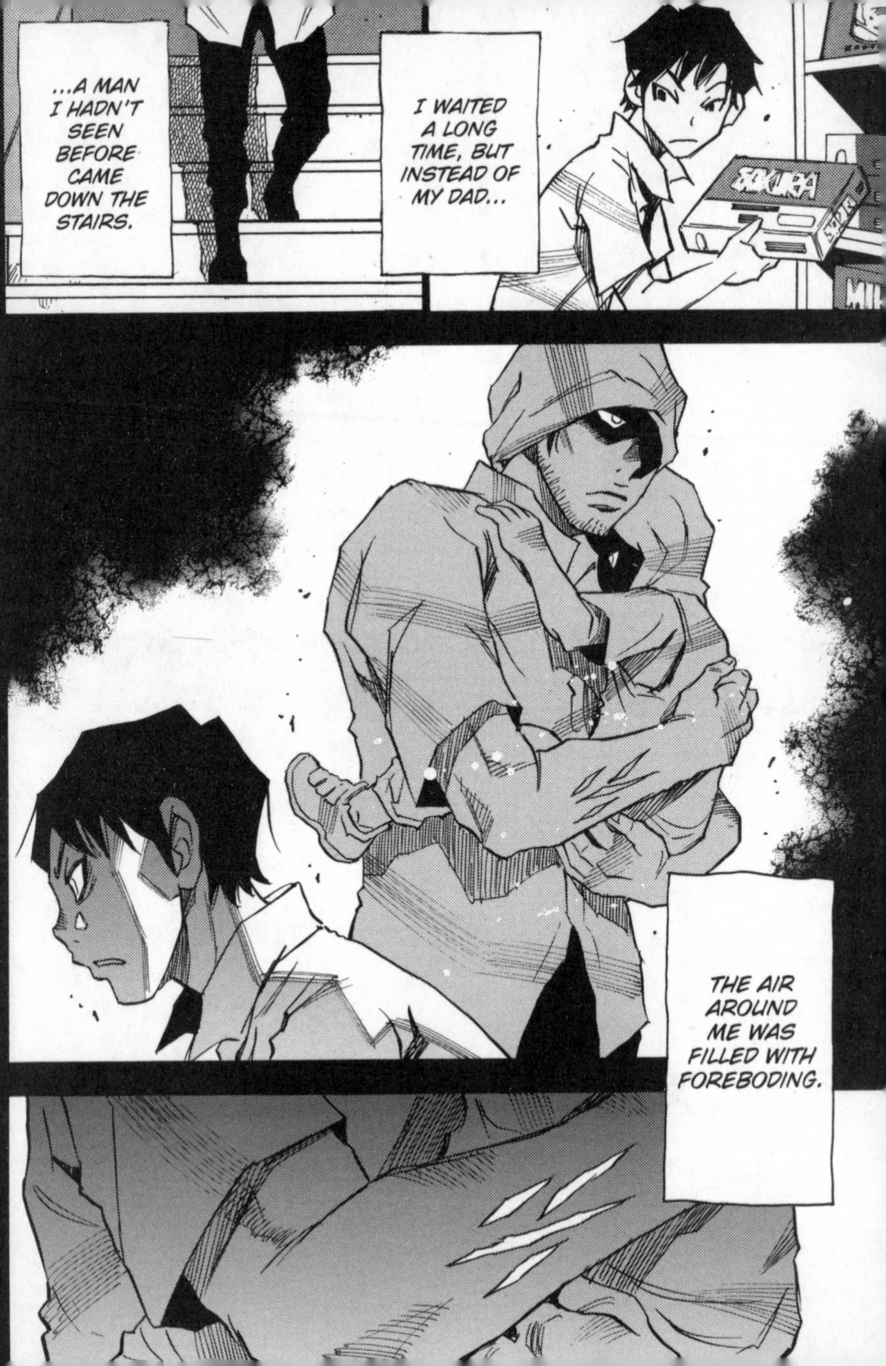
I WAITED A LONG TIME, BUT INSTEAD OF MY DAD...
...A MAN I HADN'T SEEN BEFORE CAME DOWN THE STAIRS.
THE AIR AROUND ME WAS FILLED WITH FOREBODING.

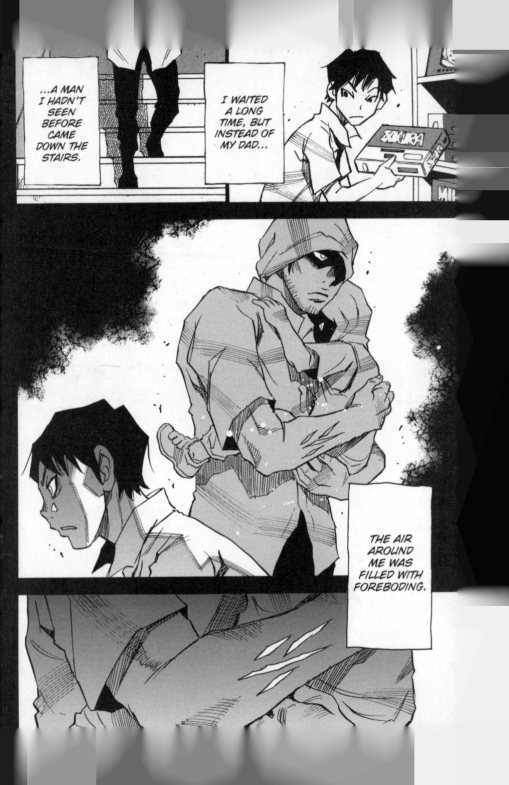

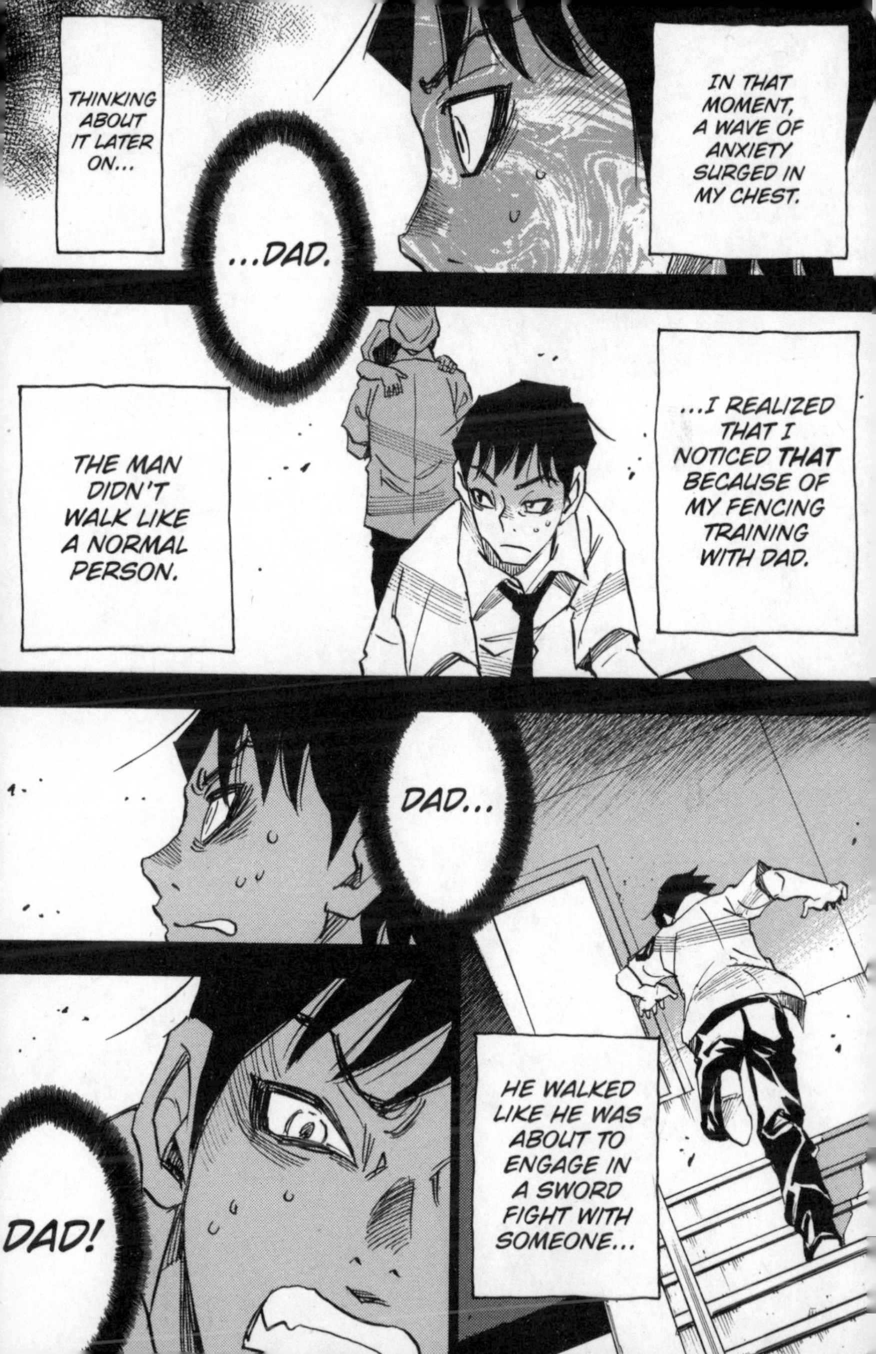
IN THAT MOMENT, A WAVE OF ANXIETY SURGED IN MY CHEST.
...DAD.
THINKING ABOUT IT LATER ON...
...I REALIZED THAT I NOTICED **THAT** BECAUSE OF MY FENCING TRAINING WITH DAD.
THE MAN DIDN'T WALK LIKE A NORMAL PERSON.
HE WALKED LIKE HE WAS ABOUT TO ENGAGE IN A SWORD FIGHT WITH SOMEONE...
DAD...
DAD!

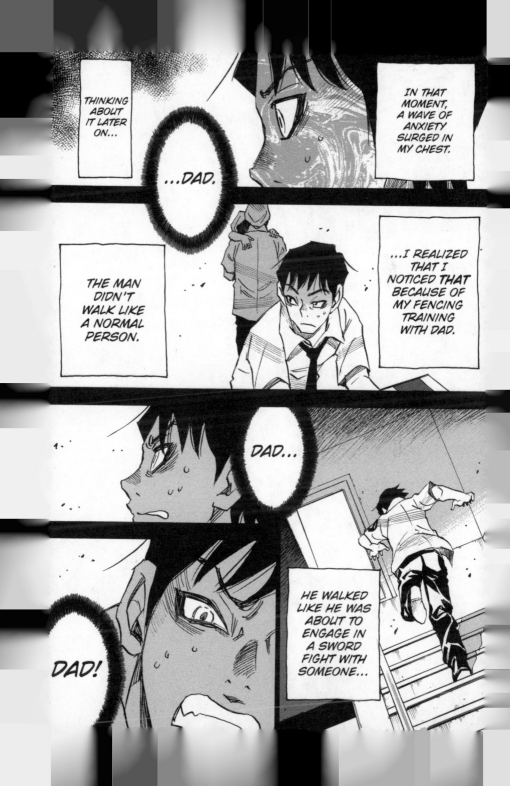

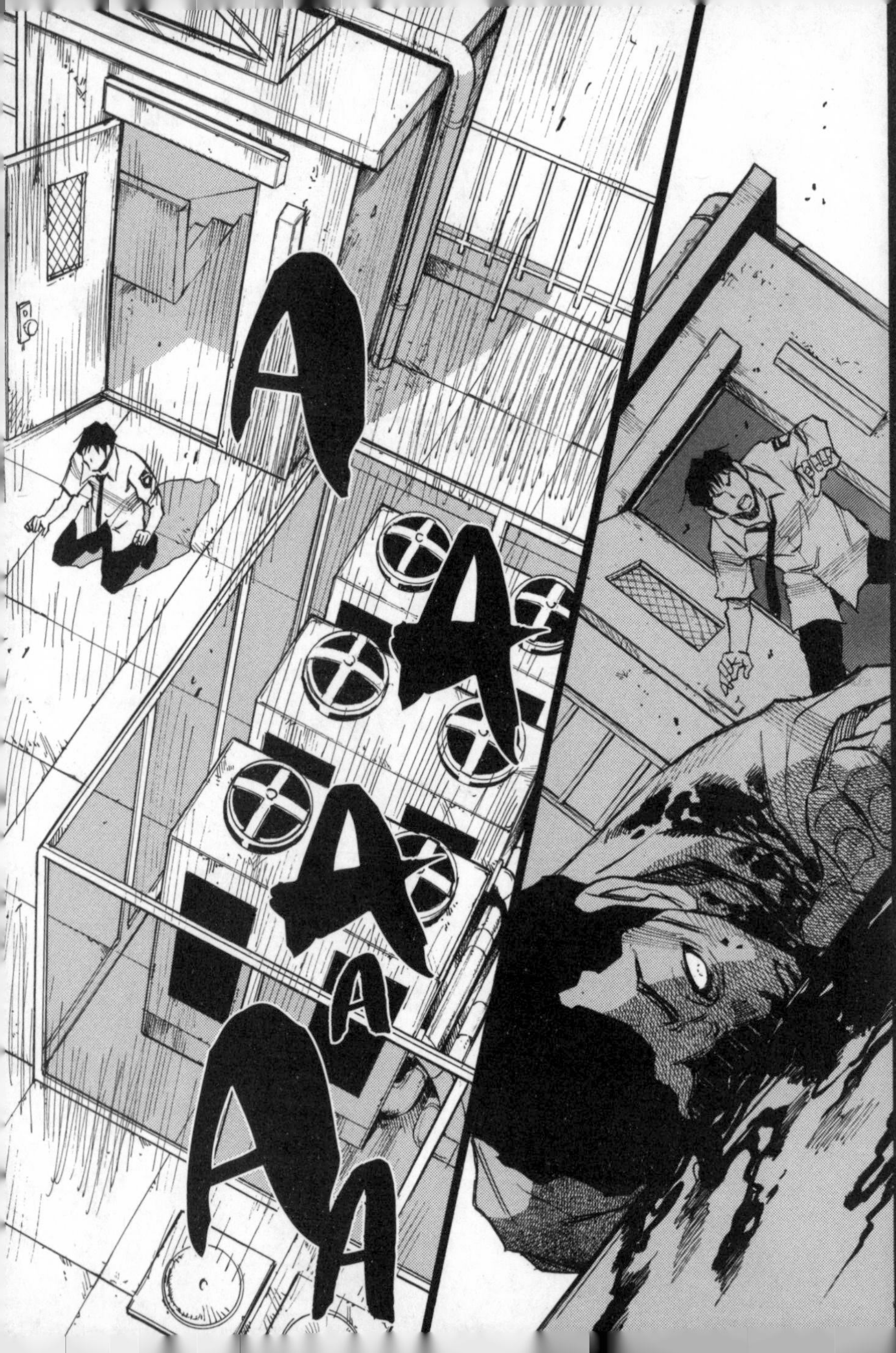
AAAAAAA

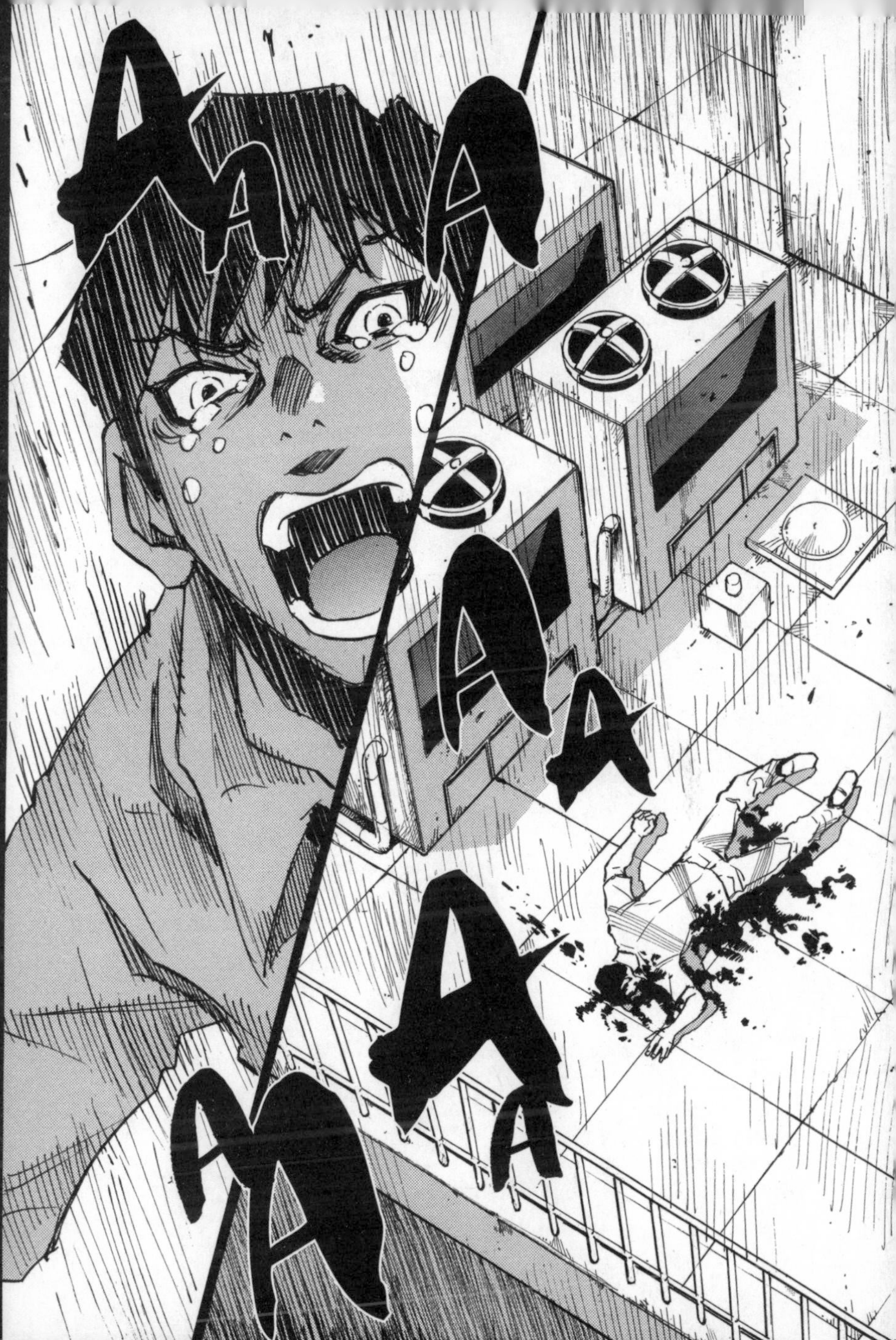
AAAAAAAAAAAA

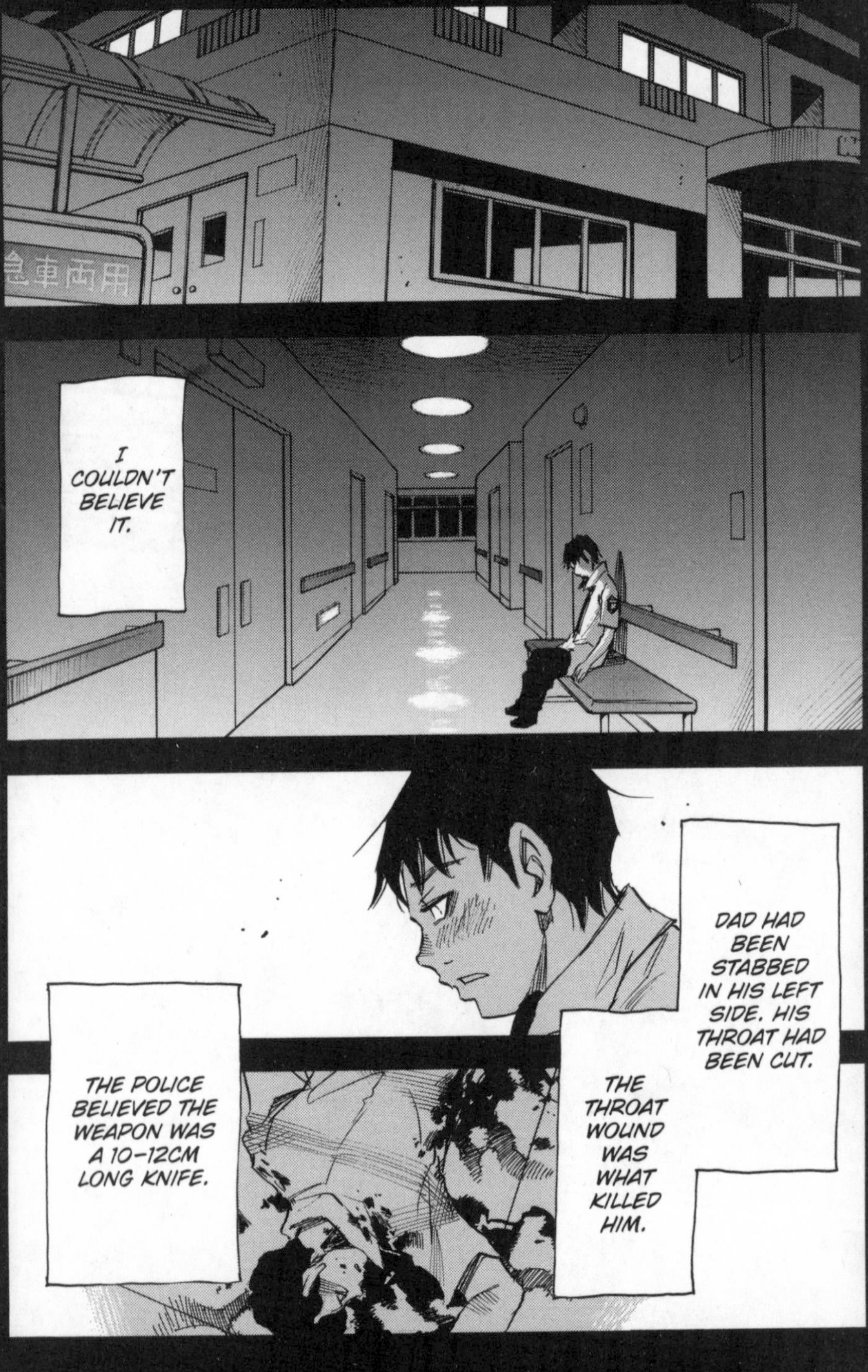
急車両用
I COULDN'T BELIEVE IT.
DAD HAD BEEN STABBED IN HIS LEFT SIDE. HIS THROAT HAD BEEN CUT.
THE THROAT WOUND WAS WHAT KILLED HIM.
THE POLICE BELIEVED THE WEAPON WAS A 10-12CM LONG KNIFE.

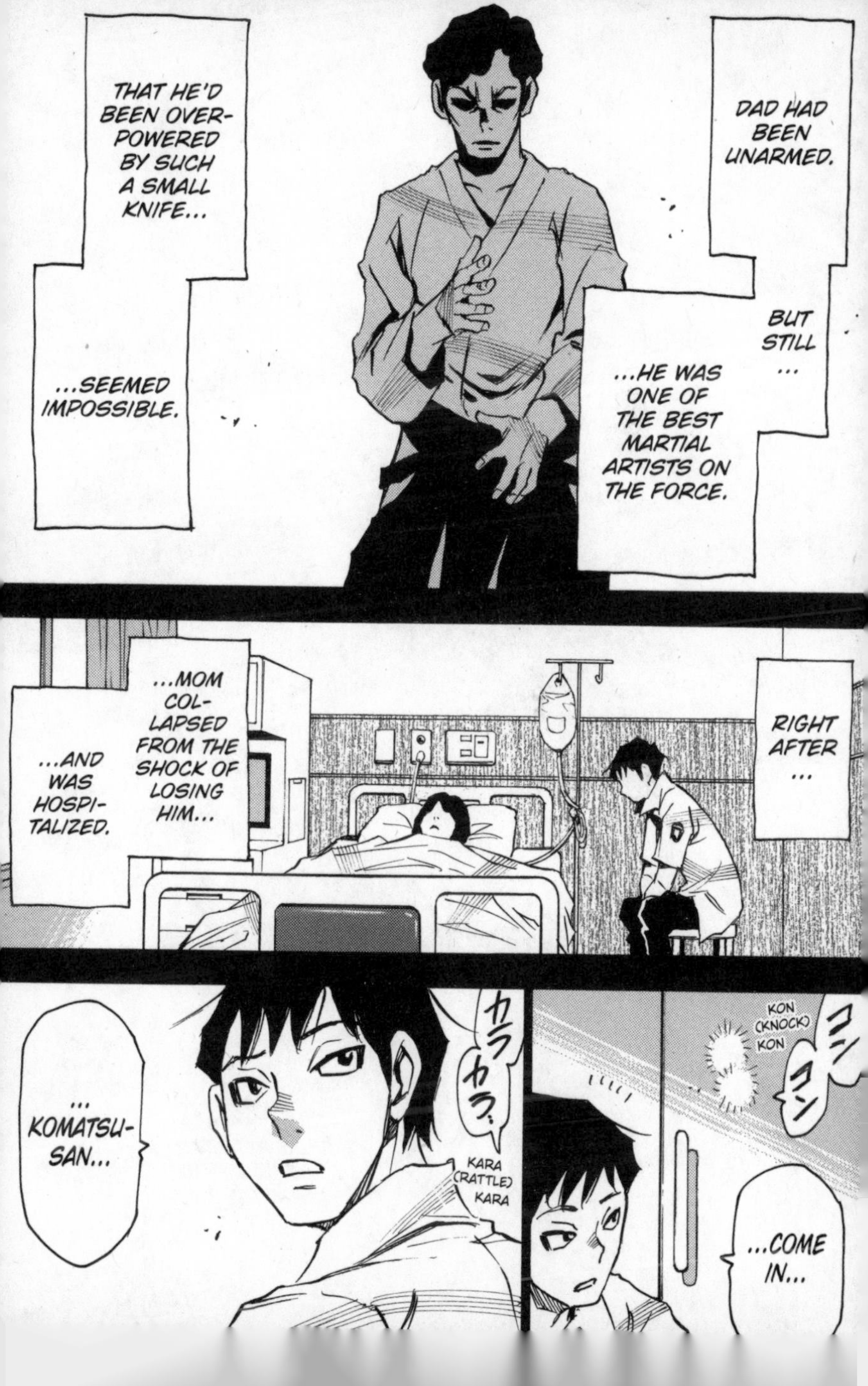
DAD HAD BEEN UNARMED.
BUT STILL...
...HE WAS ONE OF THE BEST MARTIAL ARTISTS ON THE FORCE.
THAT HE'D BEEN OVER-POWERED BY SUCH A SMALL KNIFE...
...SEEMED IMPOSSIBLE.
RIGHT AFTER...
...MOM COL-LAPSED FROM THE SHOCK OF LOSING HIM...
...AND WAS HOSPI-TALIZED.
コンコン
KON (KNOCK) KON
...COME IN...
カラカラ
KARA (RATTLE) KARA
...KOMATSU-SAN...

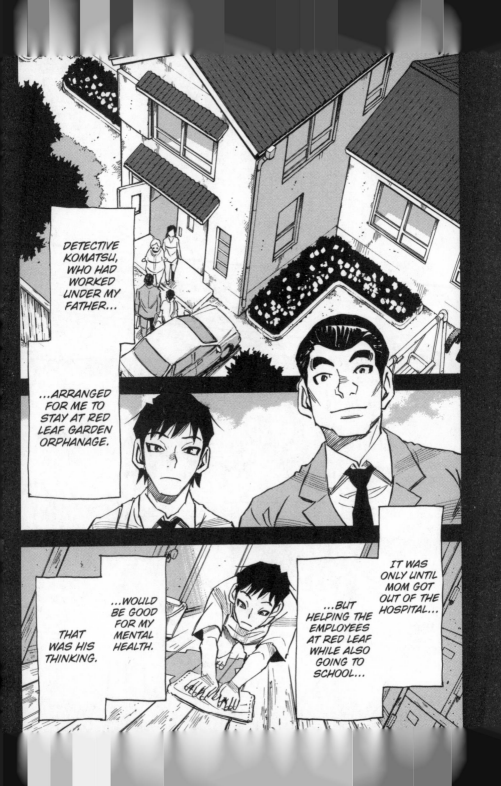

DETECTIVE KOMATSU, WHO HAD WORKED UNDER MY FATHER...
...ARRANGED FOR ME TO STAY AT RED LEAF GARDEN ORPHANAGE.
IT WAS ONLY UNTIL MOM GOT OUT OF THE HOSPITAL...
...BUT HELPING THE EMPLOYEES AT RED LEAF WHILE ALSO GOING TO SCHOOL...
...WOULD BE GOOD FOR MY MENTAL HEALTH.
THAT WAS HIS THINKING.

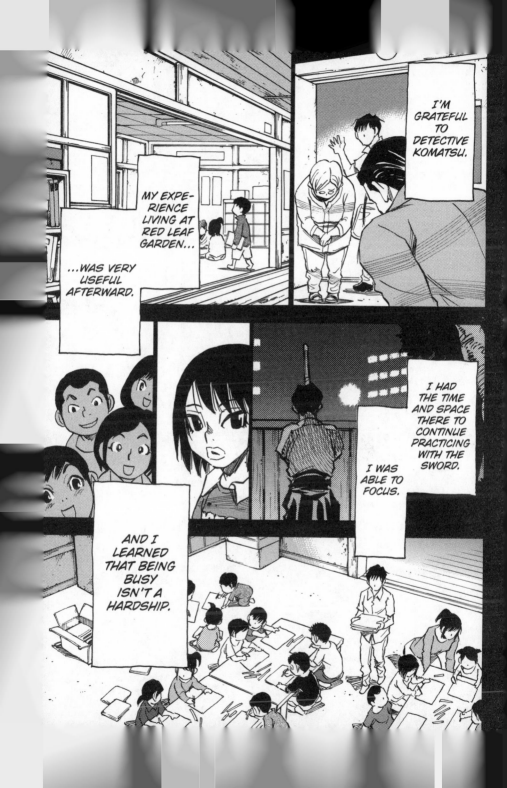

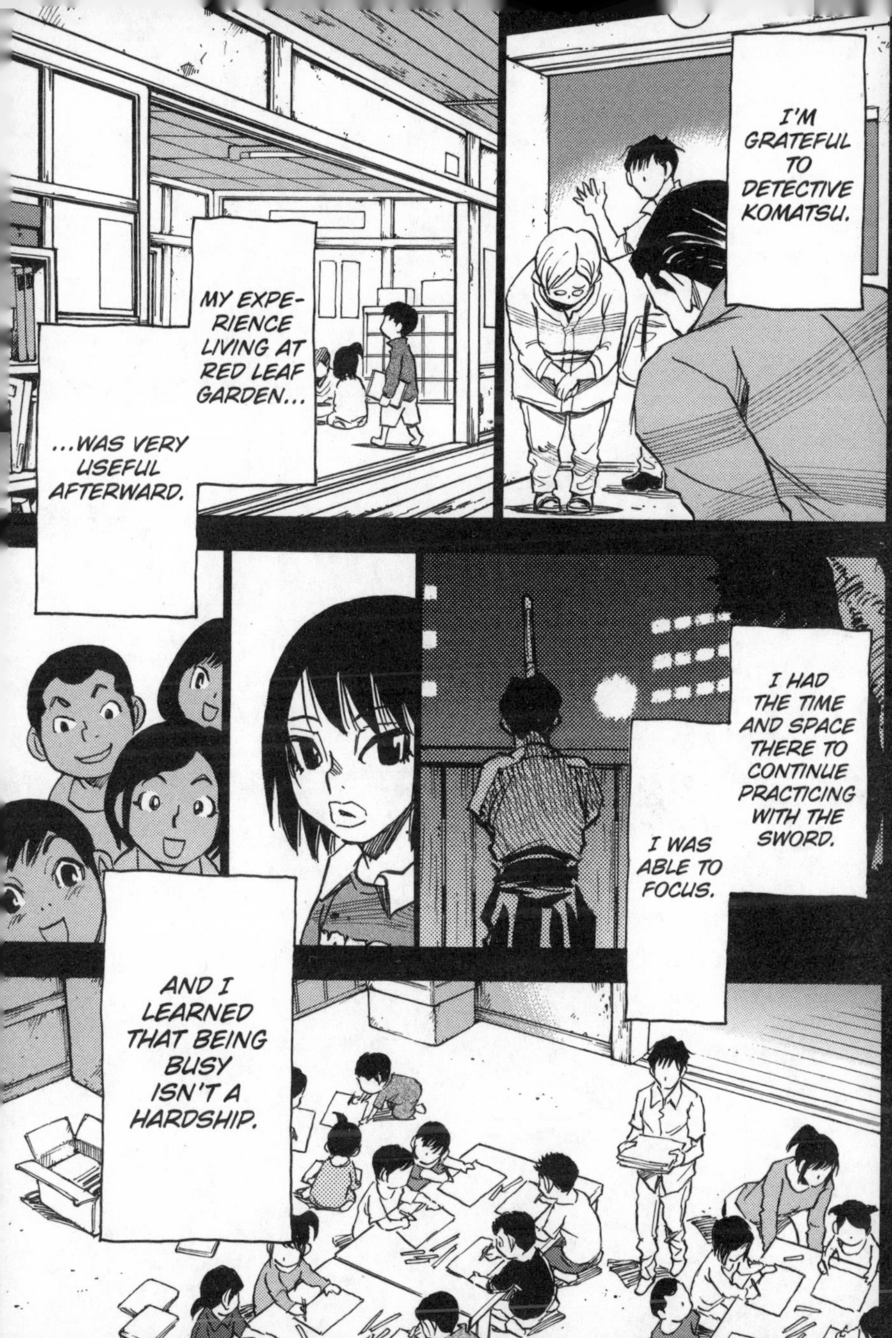
I'M GRATEFUL TO DETECTIVE KOMATSU.
MY EXPE-RIENCE LIVING AT RED LEAF GARDEN...
...WAS VERY USEFUL AFTERWARD.
I HAD THE TIME AND SPACE THERE TO CONTINUE PRACTICING WITH THE SWORD.
I WAS ABLE TO FOCUS.
AND I LEARNED THAT BEING BUSY ISN'T A HARDSHIP.

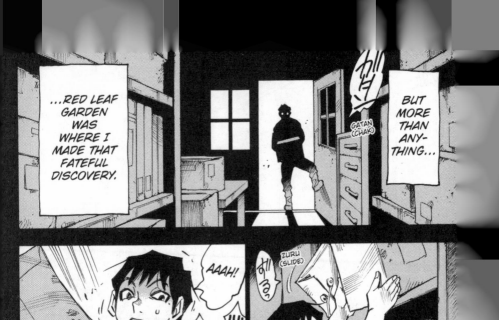

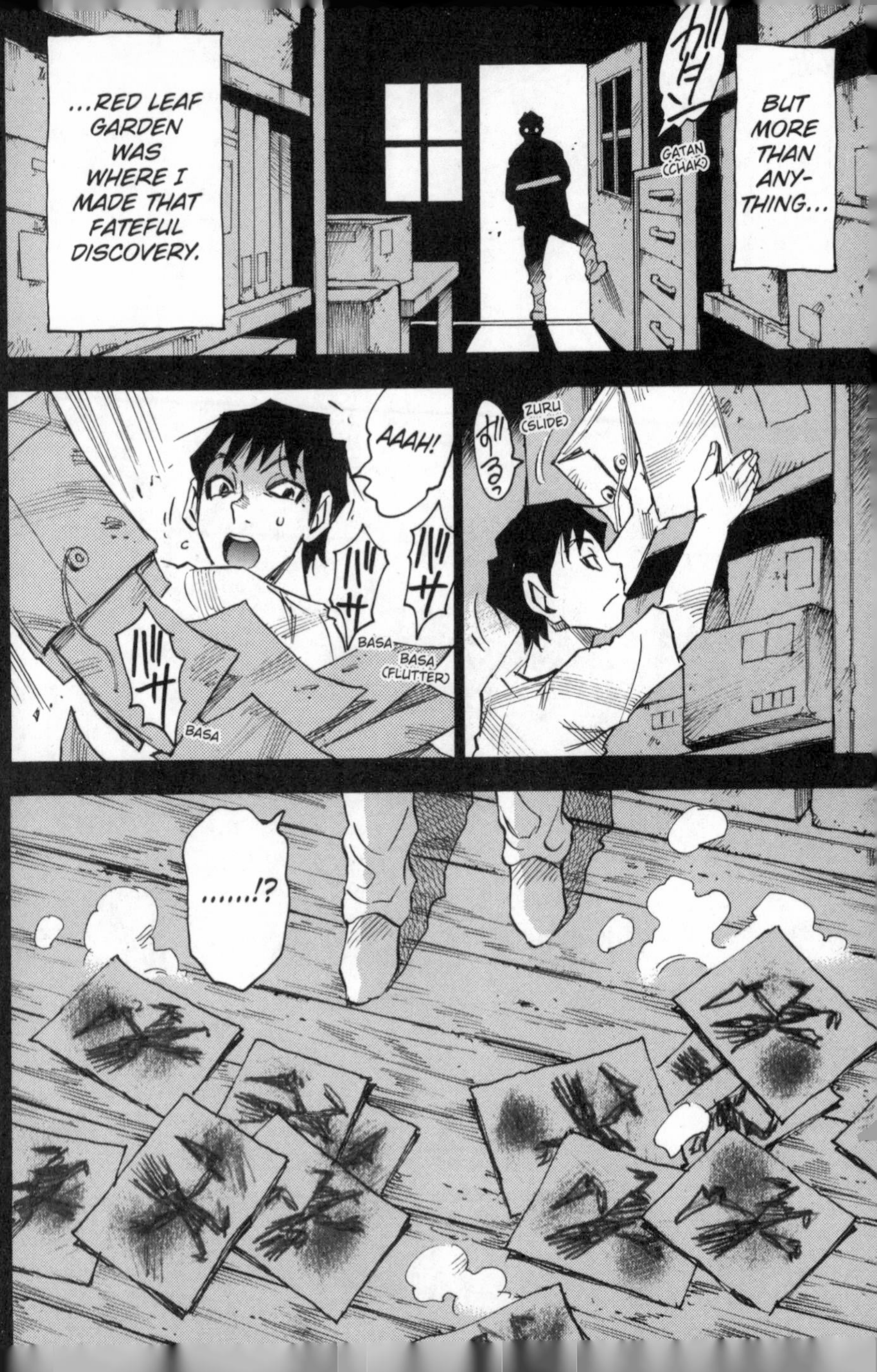
BUT MORE THAN ANY-THING...
GATAN (CHAK)
...RED LEAF GARDEN WAS WHERE I MADE THAT FATEFUL DISCOVERY.
ZURU (SLIDE)
AAAH!
BASA
BASA (FLUTTER)
BASA
......!?

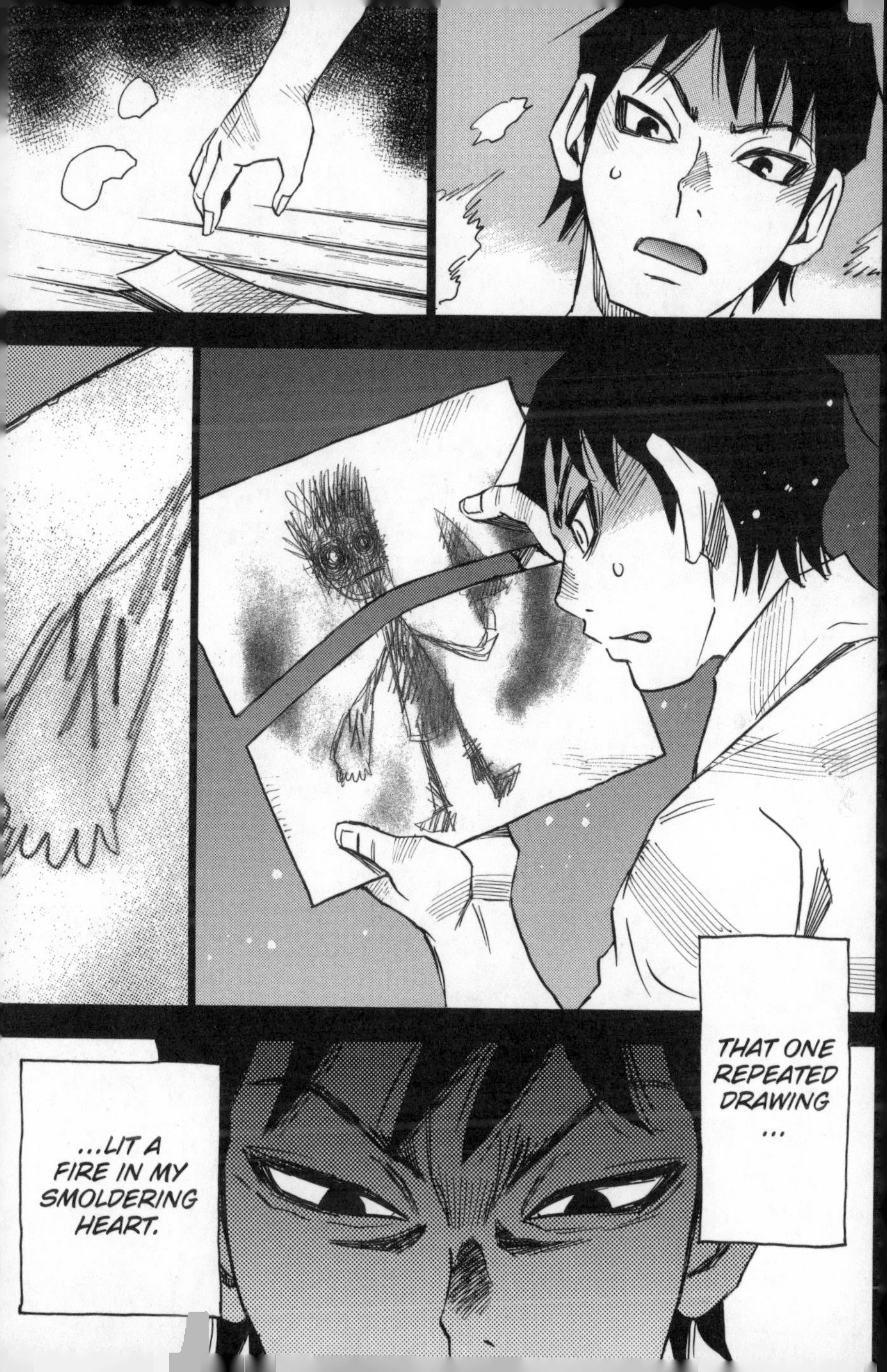
THAT ONE REPEATED DRAWING ...
...LIT A FIRE IN MY SMOLDERING HEART.

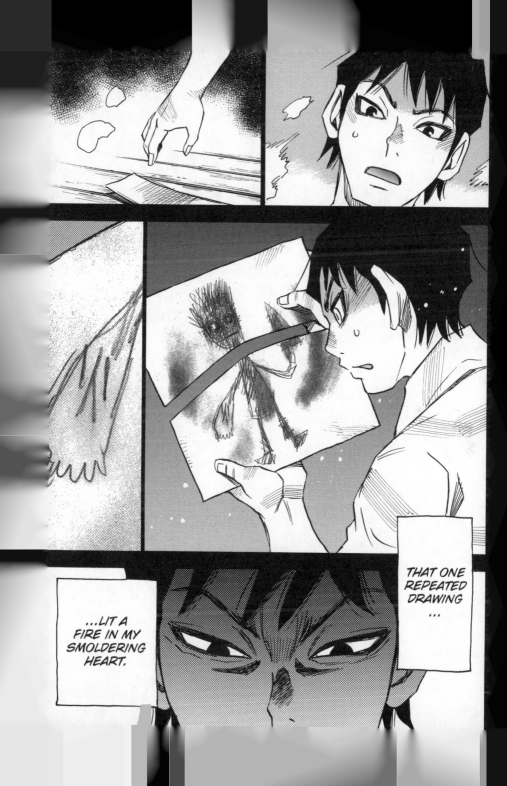

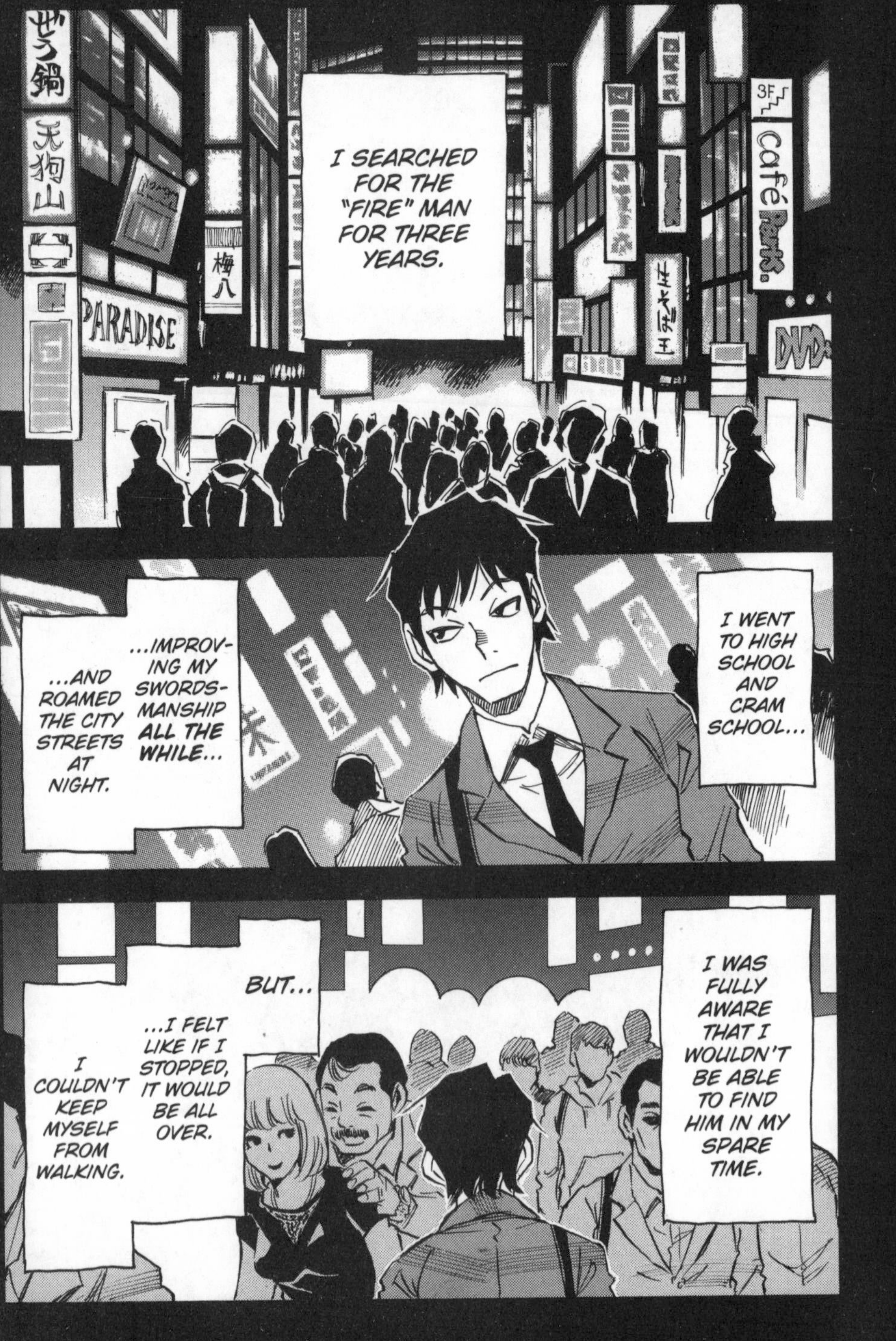
I SEARCHED FOR THE "FIRE" MAN FOR THREE YEARS.
梅八
天狗山
PARADISE
3F
Café
I WENT TO HIGH SCHOOL AND CRAM SCHOOL...
...IMPROVING MY SWORDSMANSHIP **ALL THE WHILE...**
...AND ROAMED THE CITY STREETS AT NIGHT.
I WAS FULLY AWARE THAT I WOULDN'T BE ABLE TO FIND HIM IN MY SPARE TIME.
BUT...
...I FELT LIKE IF I STOPPED, IT WOULD BE ALL OVER.
I COULDN'T KEEP MYSELF FROM WALKING.

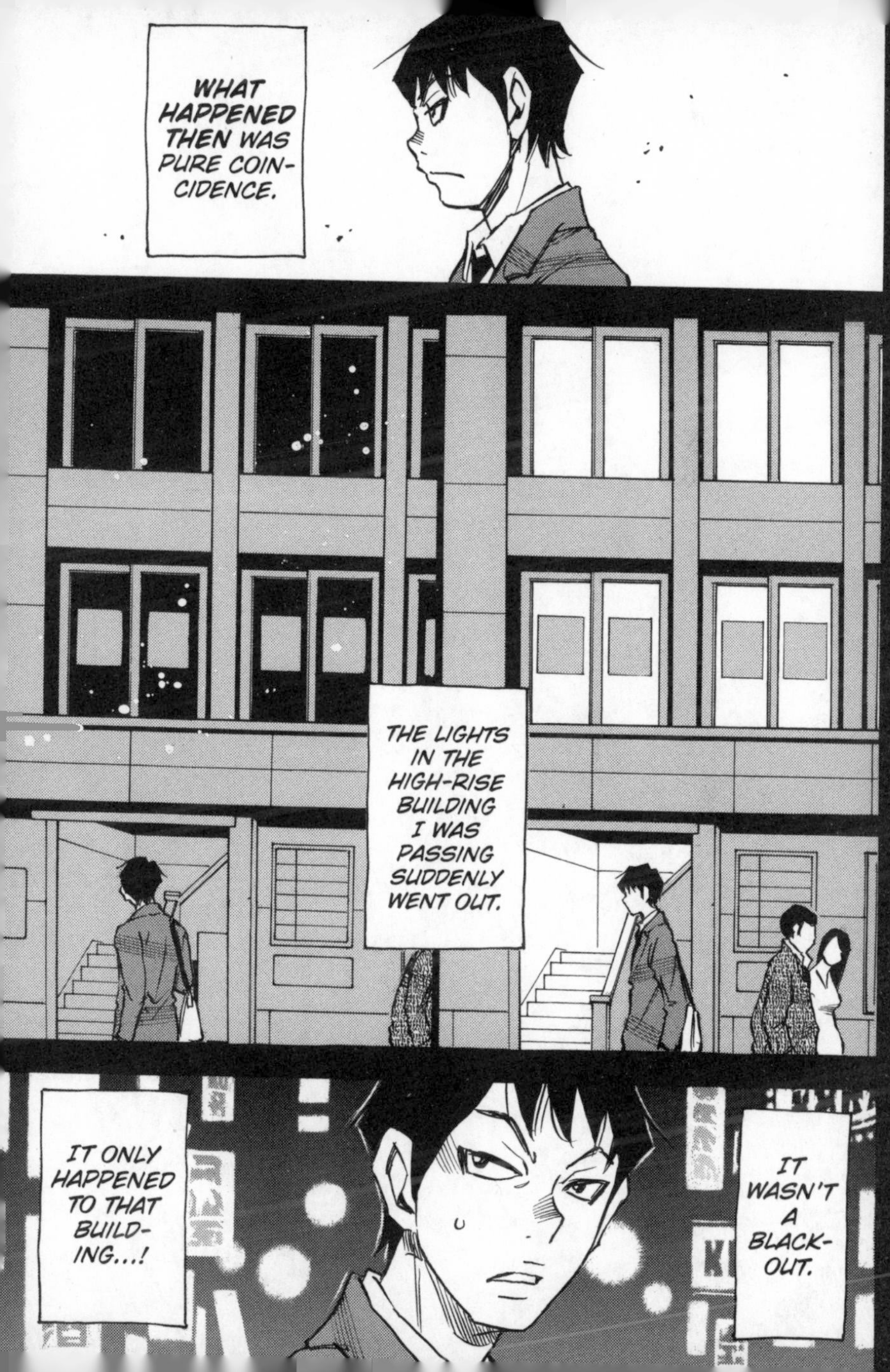
WHAT HAPPENED THEN WAS PURE COIN-CIDENCE.
THE LIGHTS IN THE HIGH-RISE BUILDING I WAS PASSING SUDDENLY WENT OUT.
IT WASN'T A BLACK-OUT.
IT ONLY HAPPENED TO THAT BUILD-ING...!

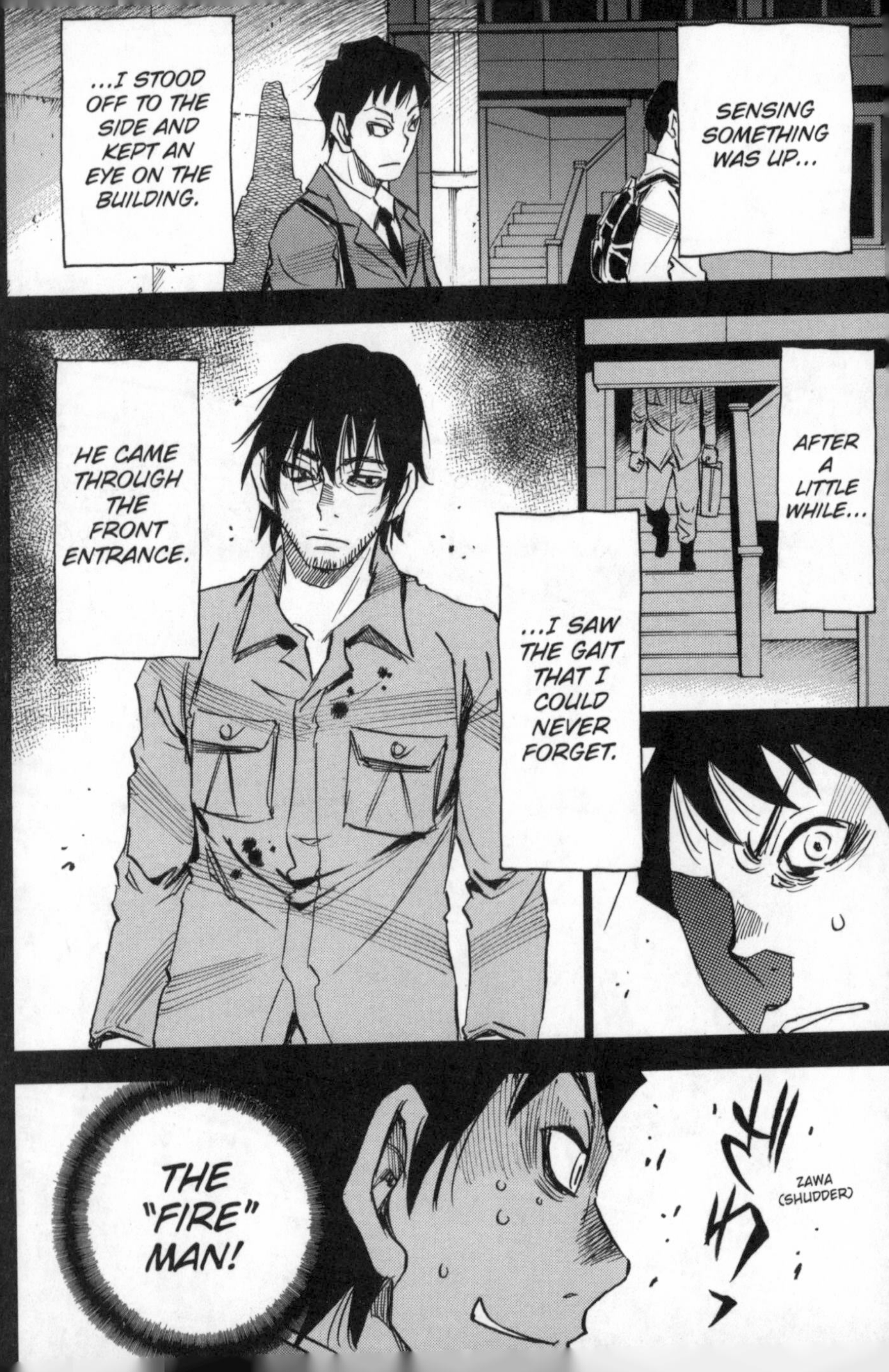
SENSING SOMETHING WAS UP...
...I STOOD OFF TO THE SIDE AND KEPT AN EYE ON THE BUILDING.
AFTER A LITTLE WHILE...
HE CAME THROUGH THE FRONT ENTRANCE.
...I SAW THE GAIT THAT I COULD NEVER FORGET.
ZAWA (SHUDDER)
THE "FIRE" MAN!

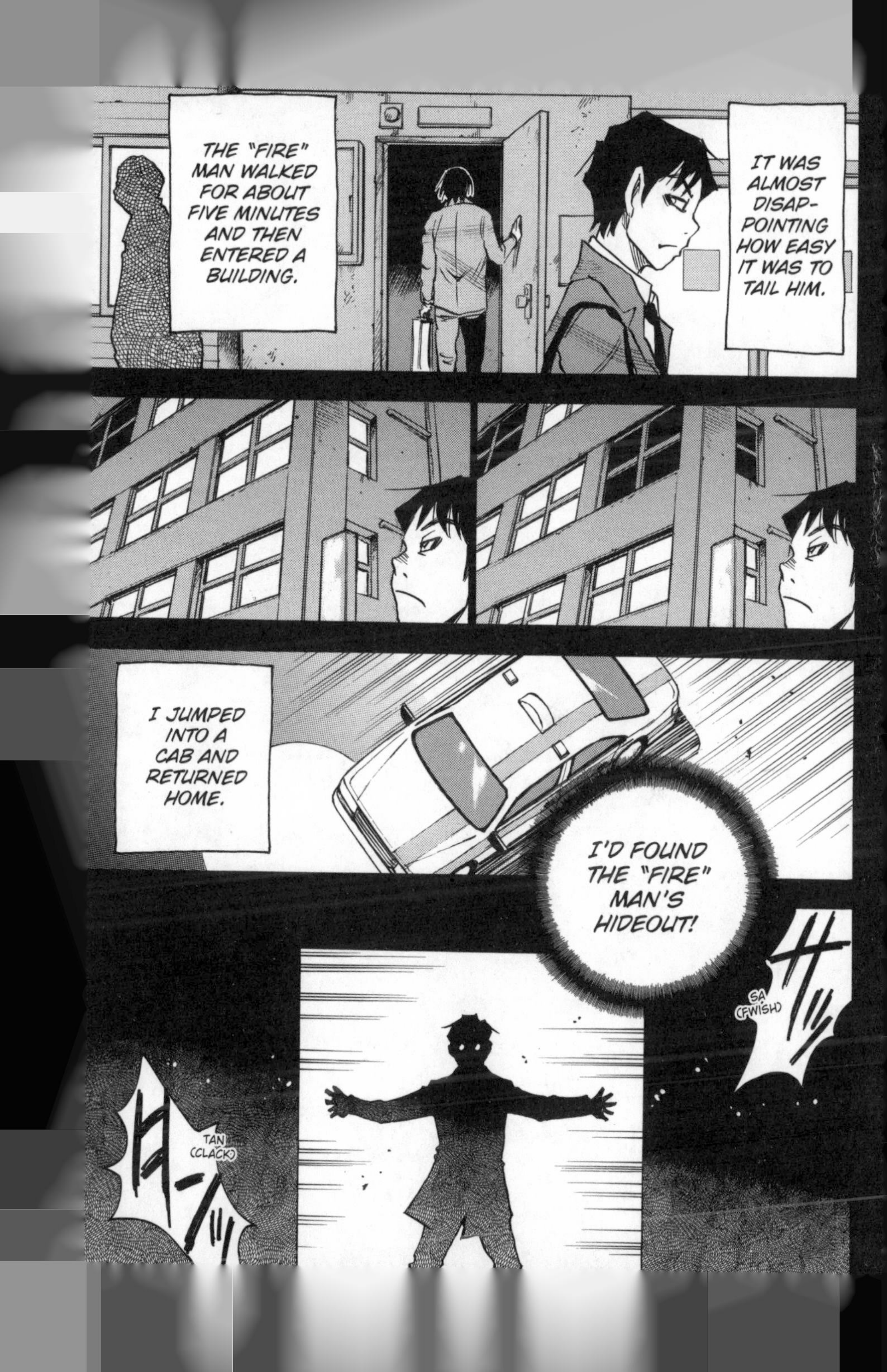
IT WAS ALMOST DISAP-POINTING HOW EASY IT WAS TO TAIL HIM.
THE "FIRE" MAN WALKED FOR ABOUT FIVE MINUTES AND THEN ENTERED A BUILDING.
I JUMPED INTO A CAB AND RETURNED HOME.
I'D FOUND THE "FIRE" MAN'S HIDEOUT!
SA (FWISH)
TAN (CLACK)

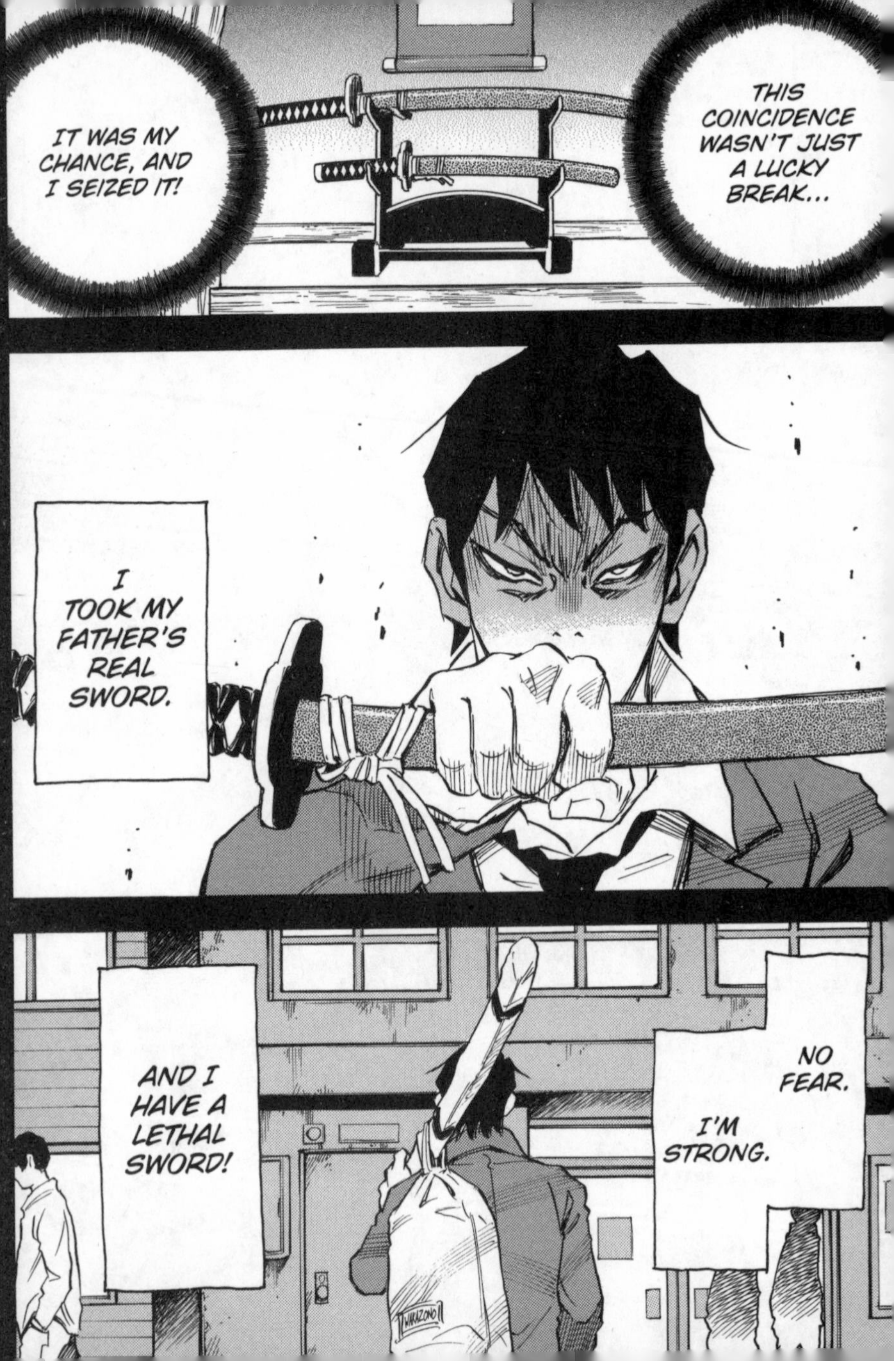
THIS COINCIDENCE WASN'T JUST A LUCKY BREAK...
IT WAS MY CHANCE, AND I SEIZED IT!
I TOOK MY FATHER'S REAL SWORD.
NO FEAR.
I'M STRONG.
AND I HAVE A LETHAL SWORD!

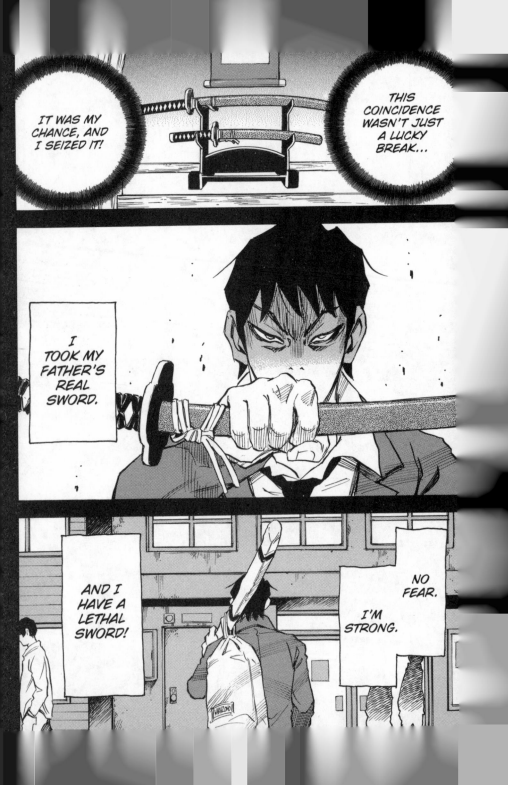

THIS'LL ALL BE OVER IN A MATTER OF MINUTES...!

KATSU

KATSU

JUST YOU WAIT...

KATSU (CLACK)

GACHA (CLICK)

OKAY...

NOW, HOW DO I GET IN...?

...IT'S OPEN ...!?

!

I DON'T KNOW IF HE'S MAKING LIGHT OF ME...

DOSUN (FWUMP)

...BUT IT'S CERTAINLY CONVENIENT.

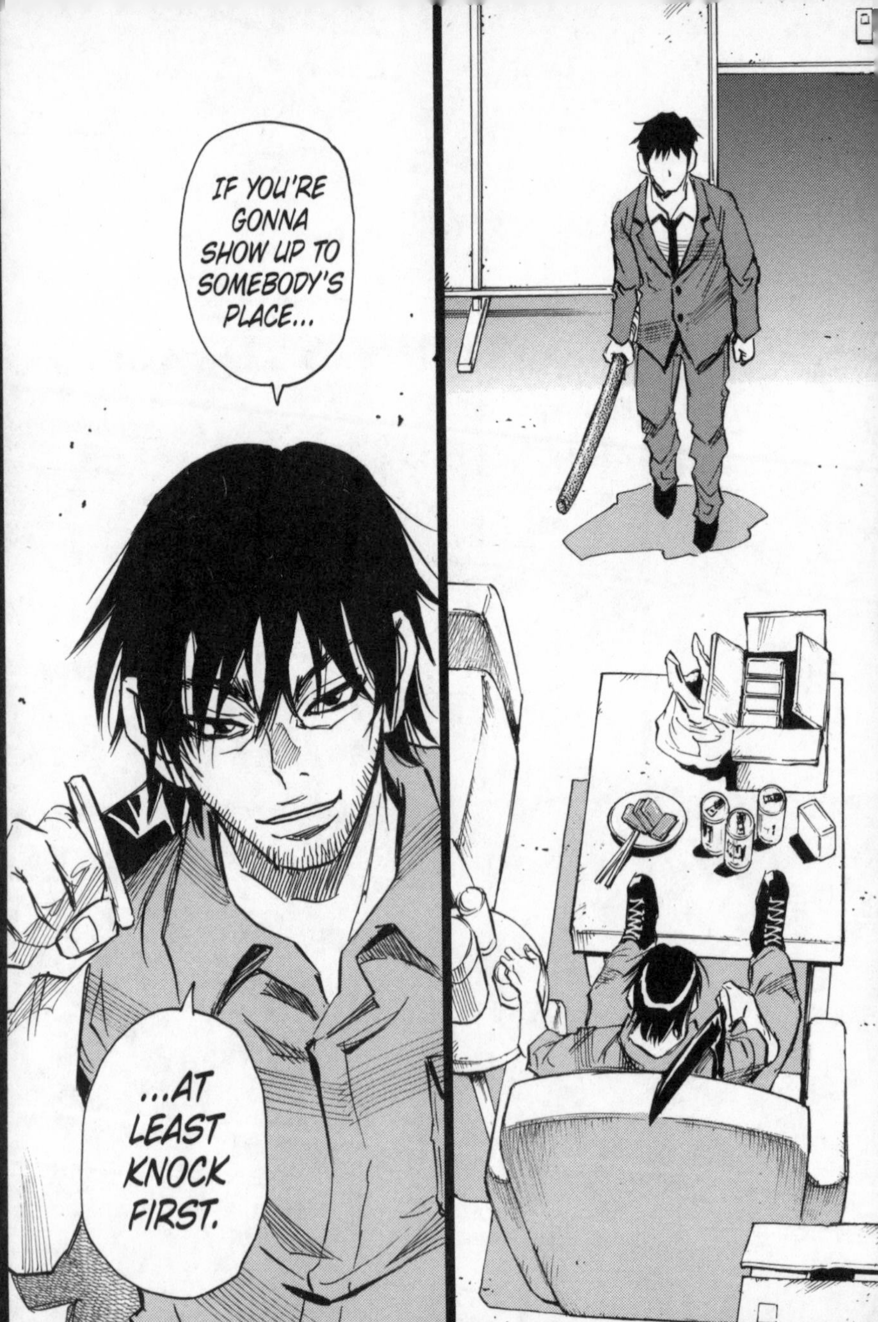
IF YOU'RE GONNA SHOW UP TO SOMEBODY'S PLACE...
...AT LEAST KNOCK FIRST.

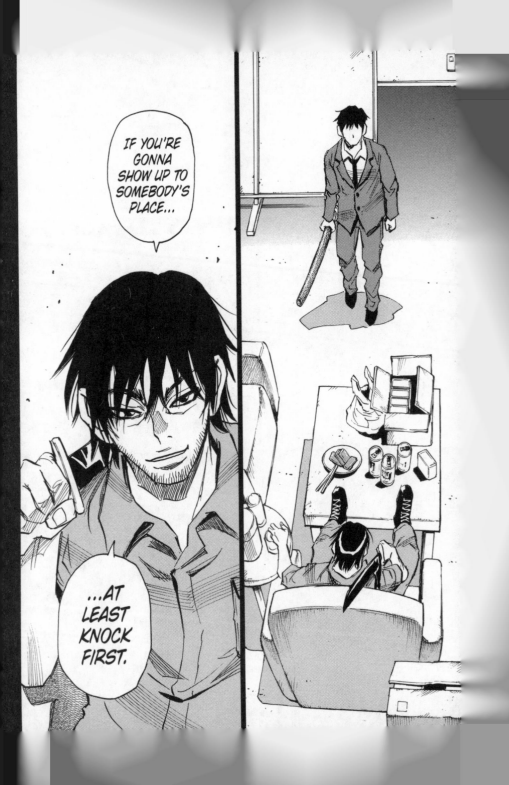

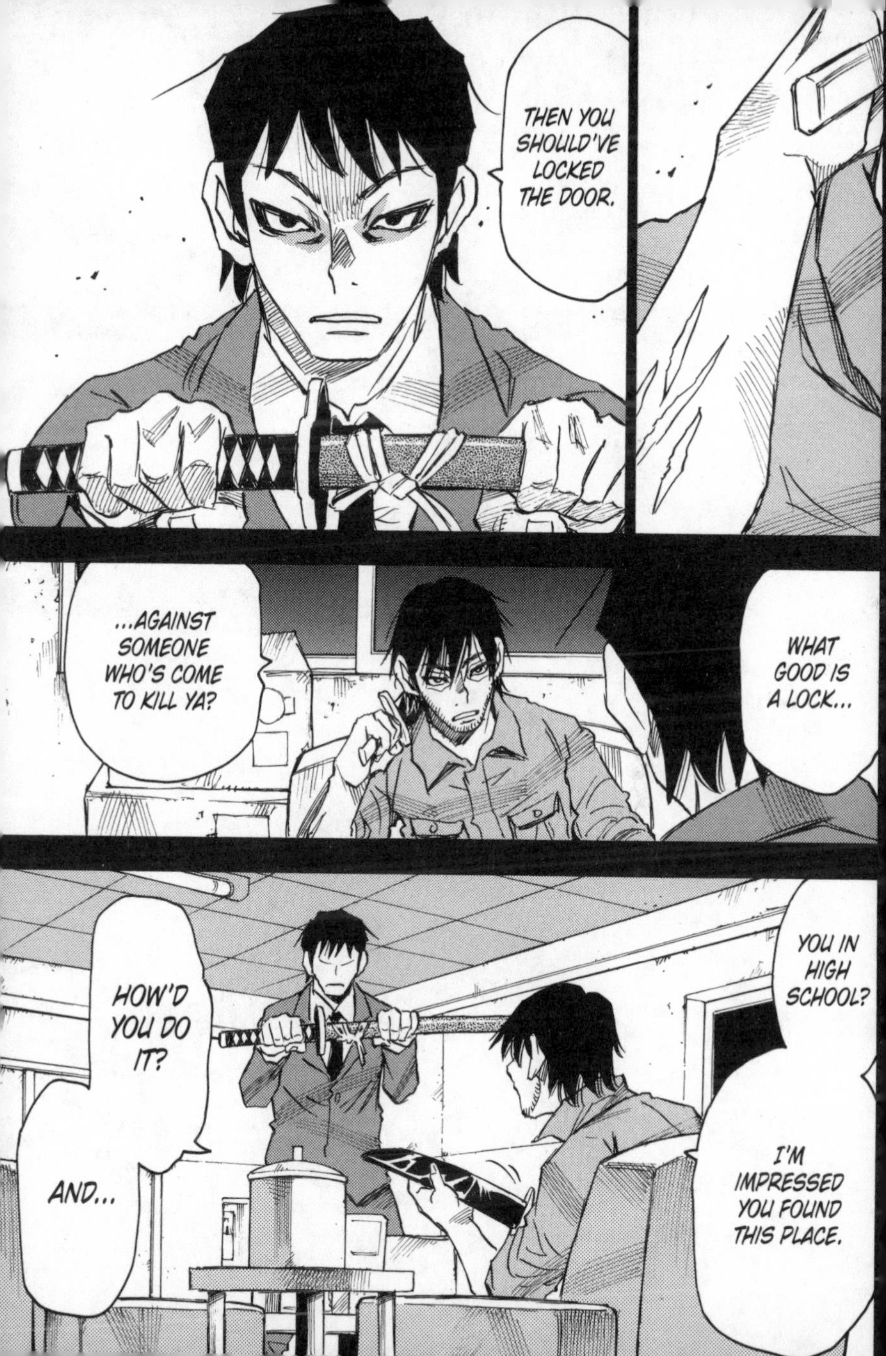
THEN YOU SHOULD'VE LOCKED THE DOOR.
WHAT GOOD IS A LOCK...
...AGAINST SOMEONE WHO'S COME TO KILL YA?
YOU IN HIGH SCHOOL?
I'M IMPRESSED YOU FOUND THIS PLACE.
HOW'D YOU DO IT?
AND...

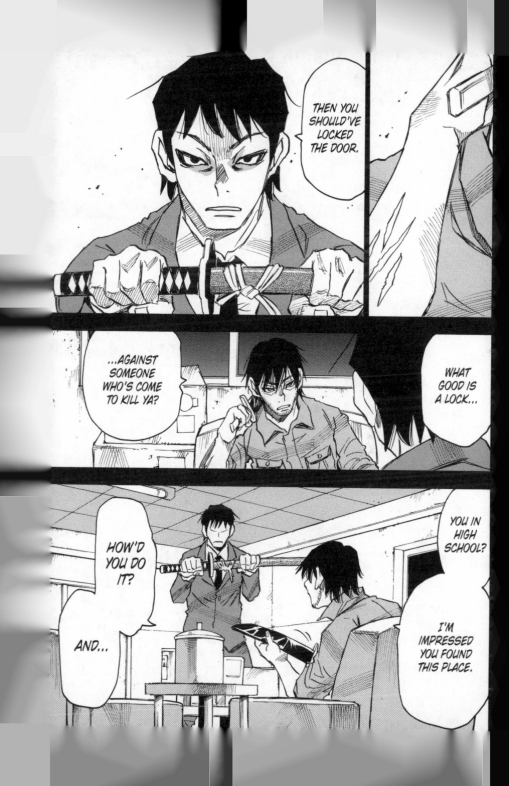

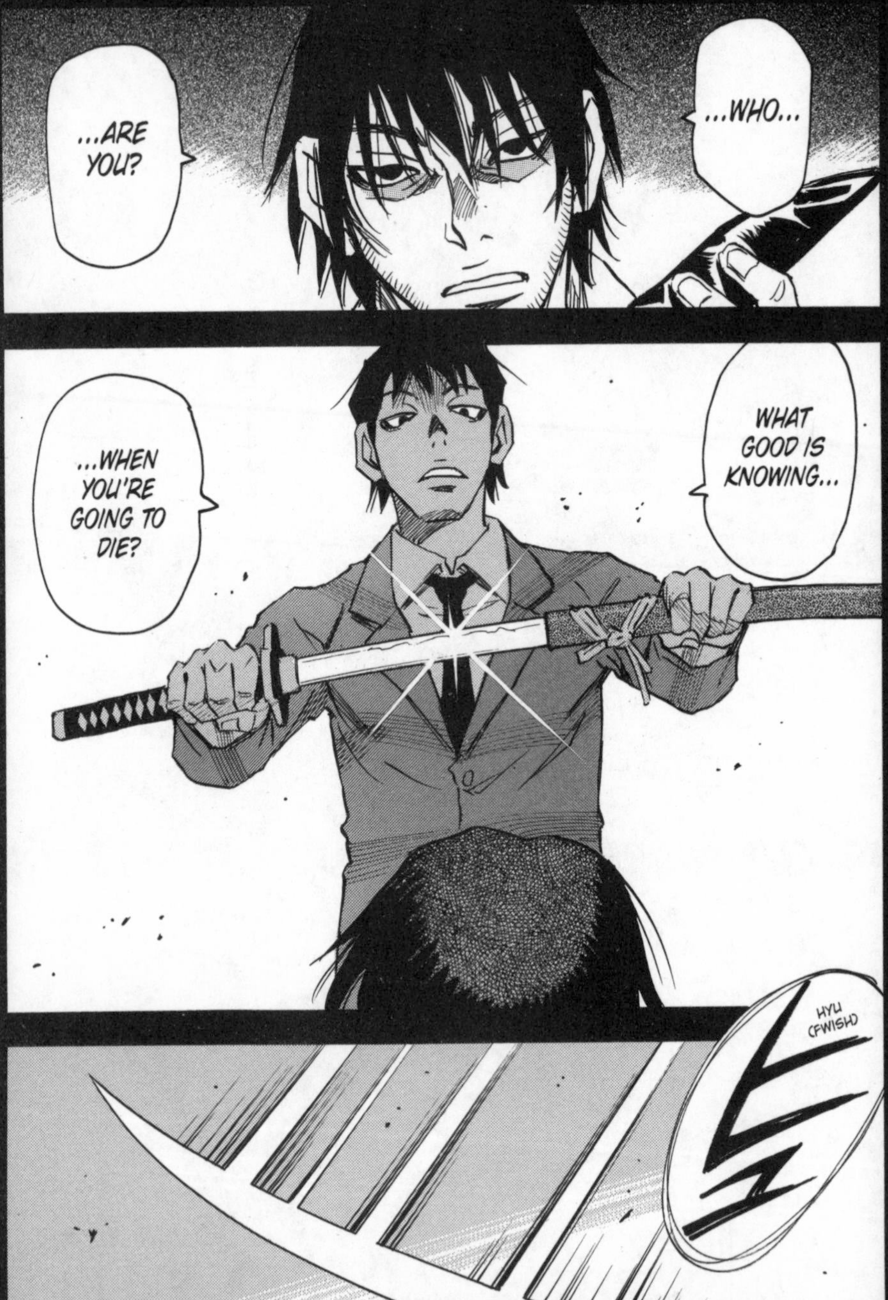
...WHO...
...ARE YOU?
WHAT GOOD IS KNOWING...
...WHEN YOU'RE GOING TO DIE?
HYU (FWISH)

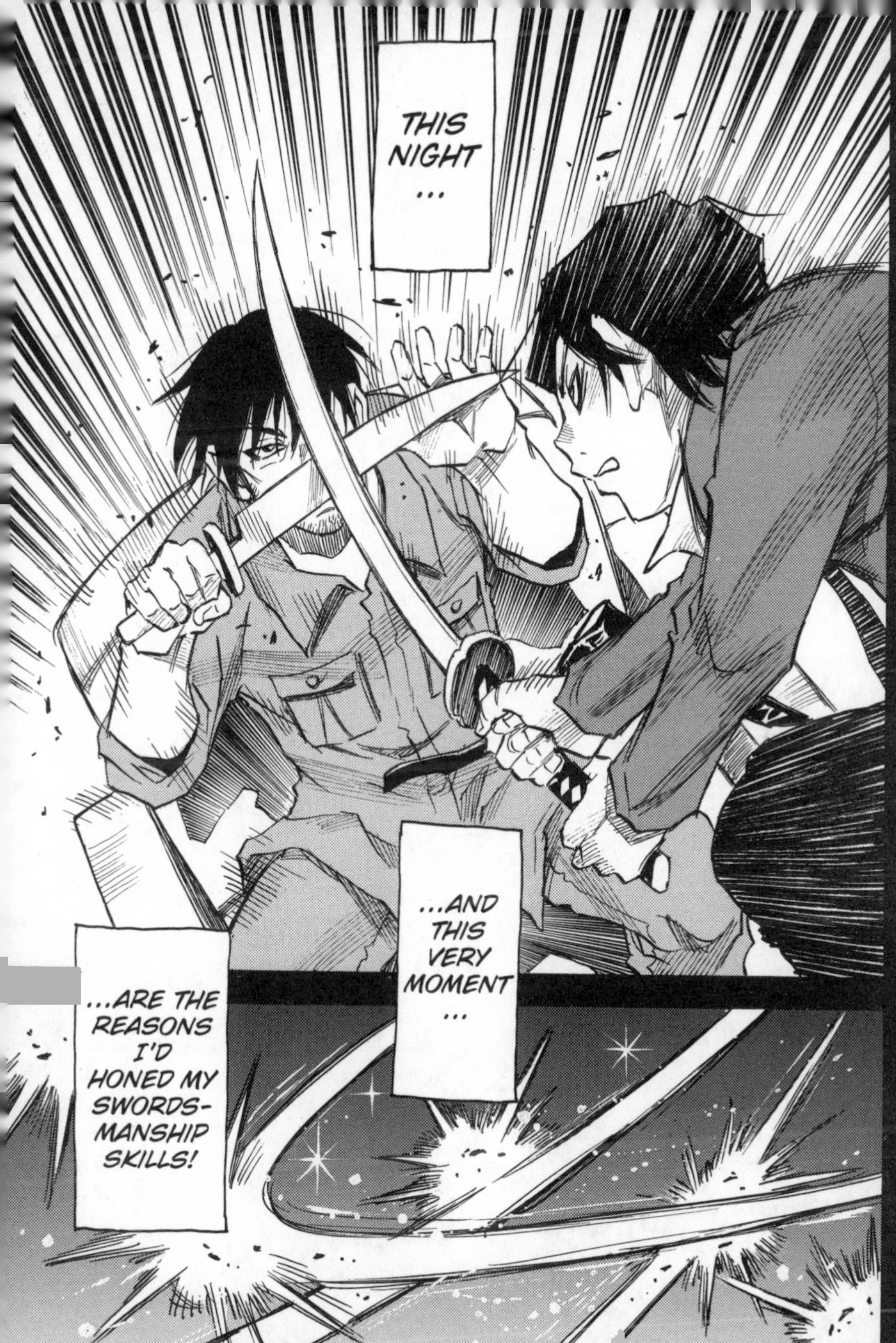
THIS NIGHT ...
...AND THIS VERY MOMENT ...
...ARE THE REASONS I'D HONED MY SWORDS-MANSHIP SKILLS!

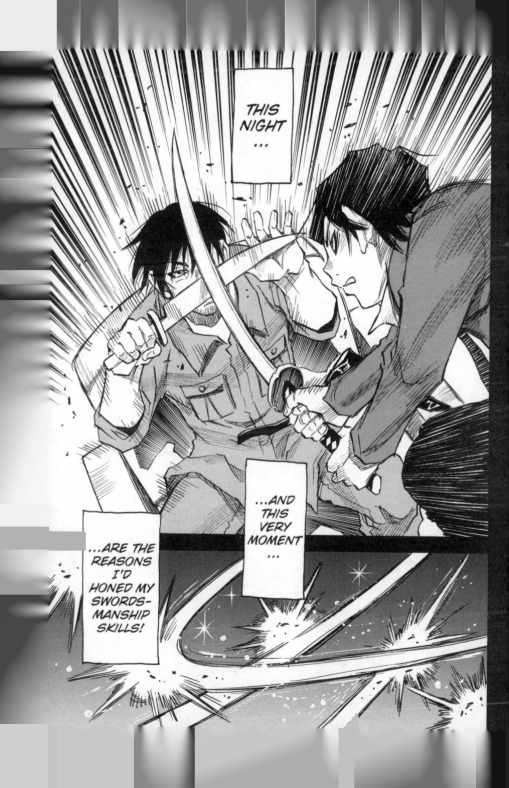

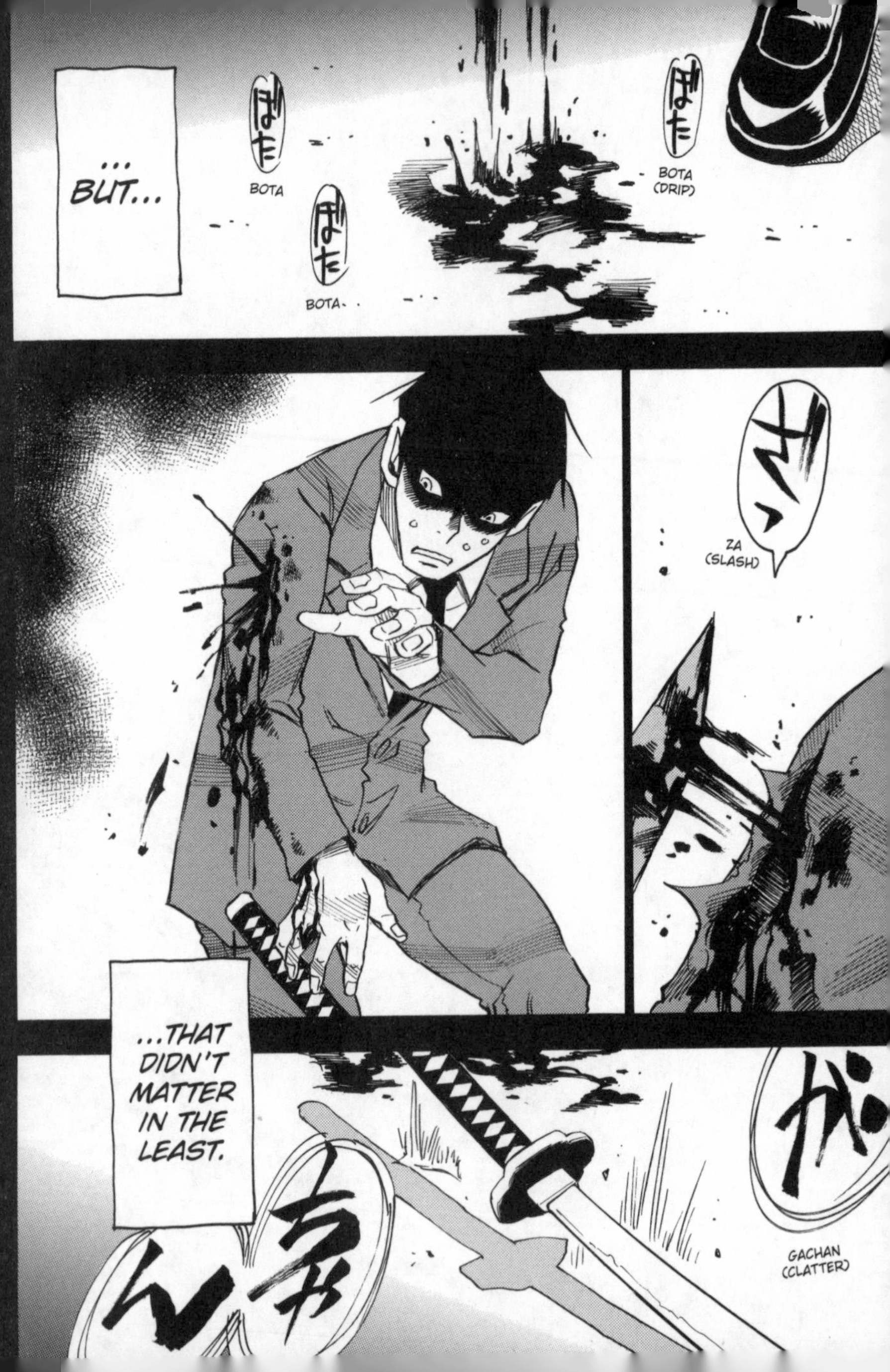
ぼた
BOTA (DRIP)
ぼた
BOTA
...BUT...
ぼた
BOTA
ざっ
ZA (SLASH)
が
GACHAN (CLATTER)
...THAT DIDN'T MATTER IN THE LEAST.
ちゃん

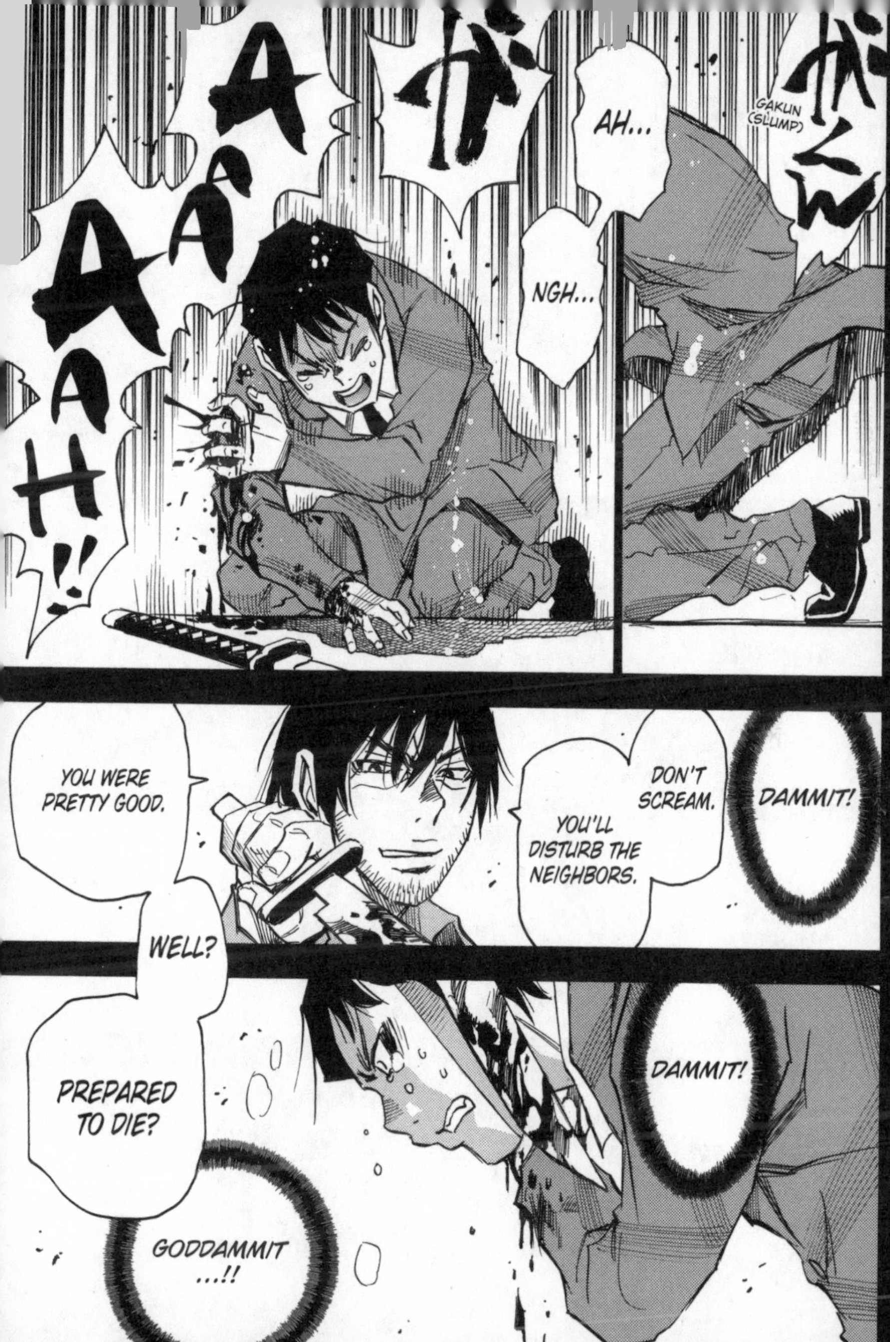
がくん
GAKUN (SLUMP)
AH...
NGH...
が
AAAAAH!!
DAMMIT!
DON'T SCREAM.
YOU'LL DISTURB THE NEIGHBORS.
YOU WERE PRETTY GOOD.
WELL?
DAMMIT!
PREPARED TO DIE?
GODDAMMIT ...!!

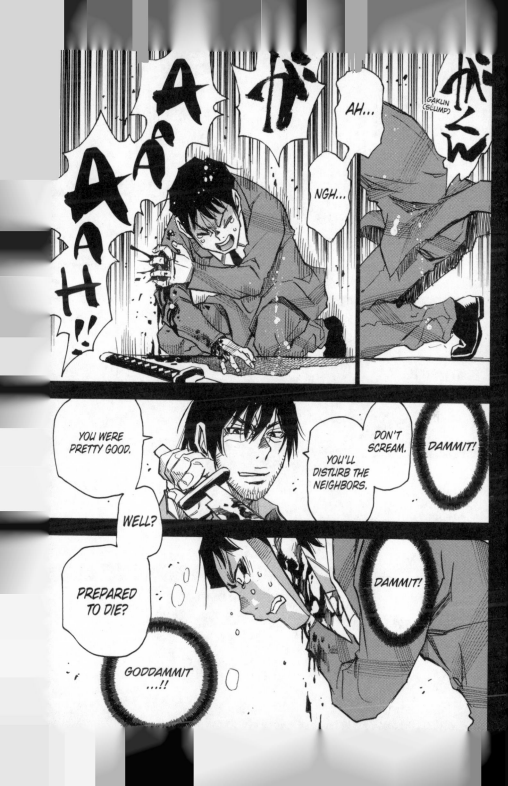

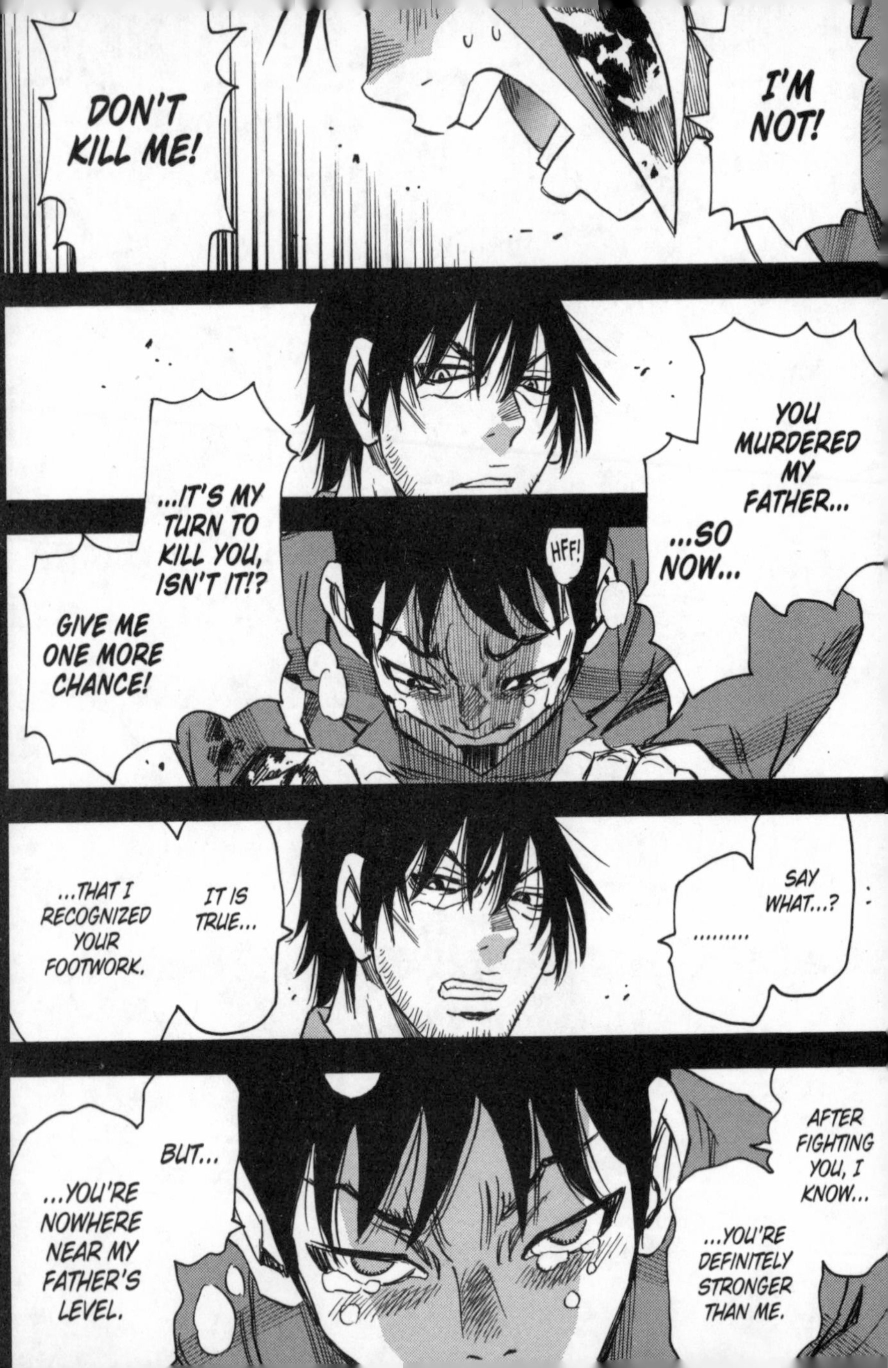
I'M NOT!
DON'T KILL ME!
YOU MURDERED MY FATHER...
...SO NOW...
...IT'S MY TURN TO KILL YOU, ISN'T IT!?
HFF!
GIVE ME ONE MORE CHANCE!
SAY WHAT...?
....
IT IS TRUE...
...THAT I RECOGNIZED YOUR FOOTWORK.
AFTER FIGHTING YOU, I KNOW...
...YOU'RE DEFINITELY STRONGER THAN ME.
BUT...
...YOU'RE NOWHERE NEAR MY FATHER'S LEVEL.

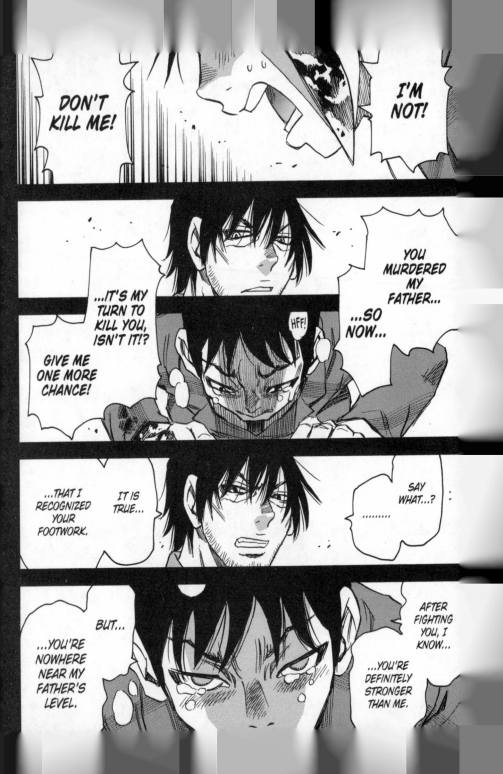

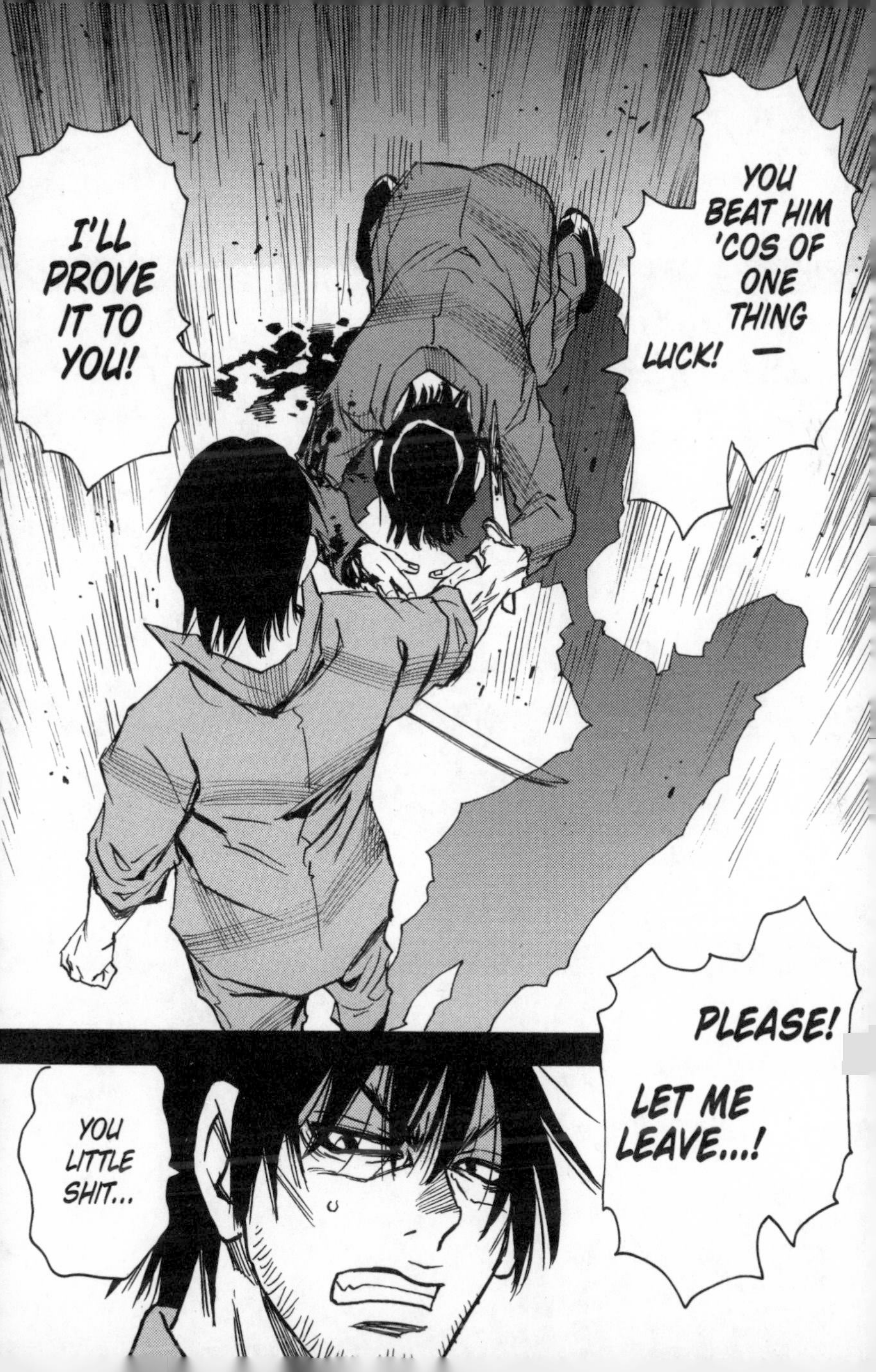
YOU BEAT HIM 'COS OF ONE THING — LUCK!
I'LL PROVE IT TO YOU!
PLEASE!
LET ME LEAVE...!
YOU LITTLE SHIT...

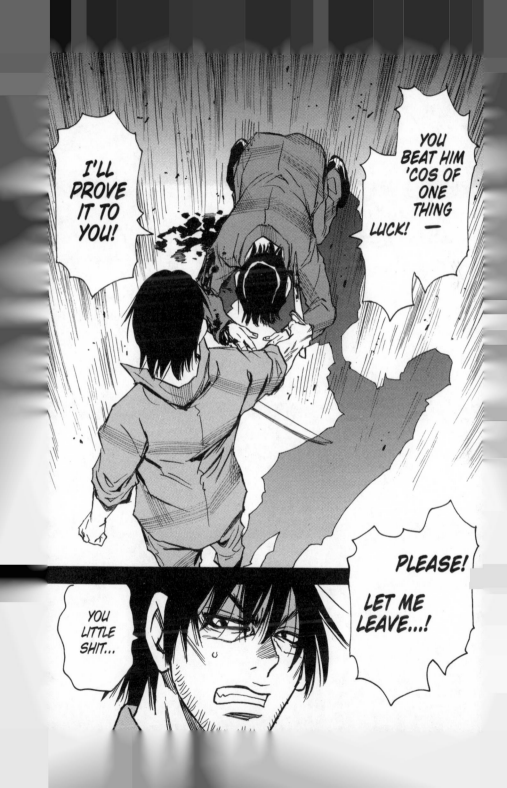

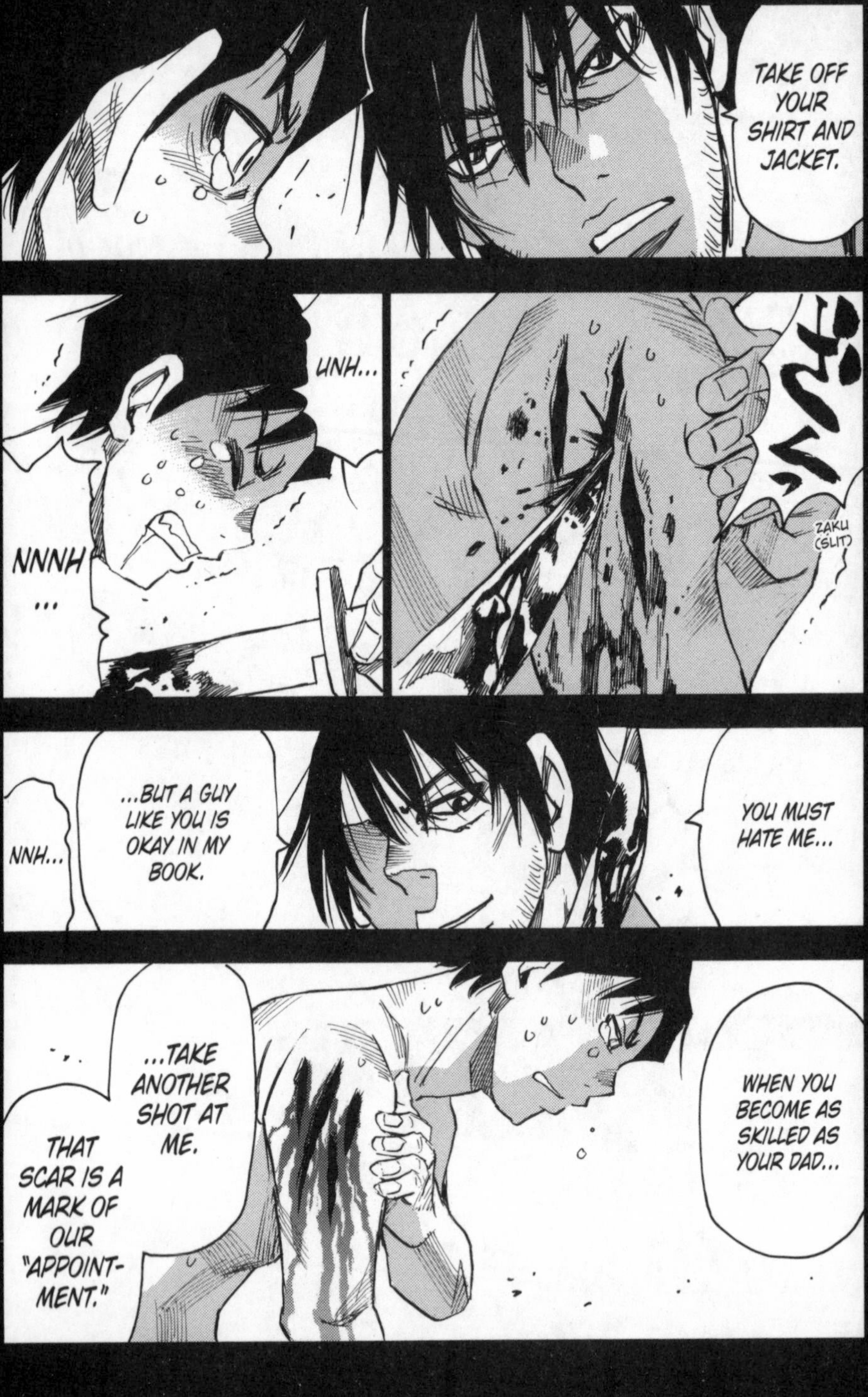
TAKE OFF YOUR SHIRT AND JACKET.
ZAKU (SLIT)
UNH...
NNNH ...
YOU MUST HATE ME...
...BUT A GUY LIKE YOU IS OKAY IN MY BOOK.
NNH...
WHEN YOU BECOME AS SKILLED AS YOUR DAD...
...TAKE ANOTHER SHOT AT ME.
THAT SCAR IS A MARK OF OUR "APPOINTMENT."

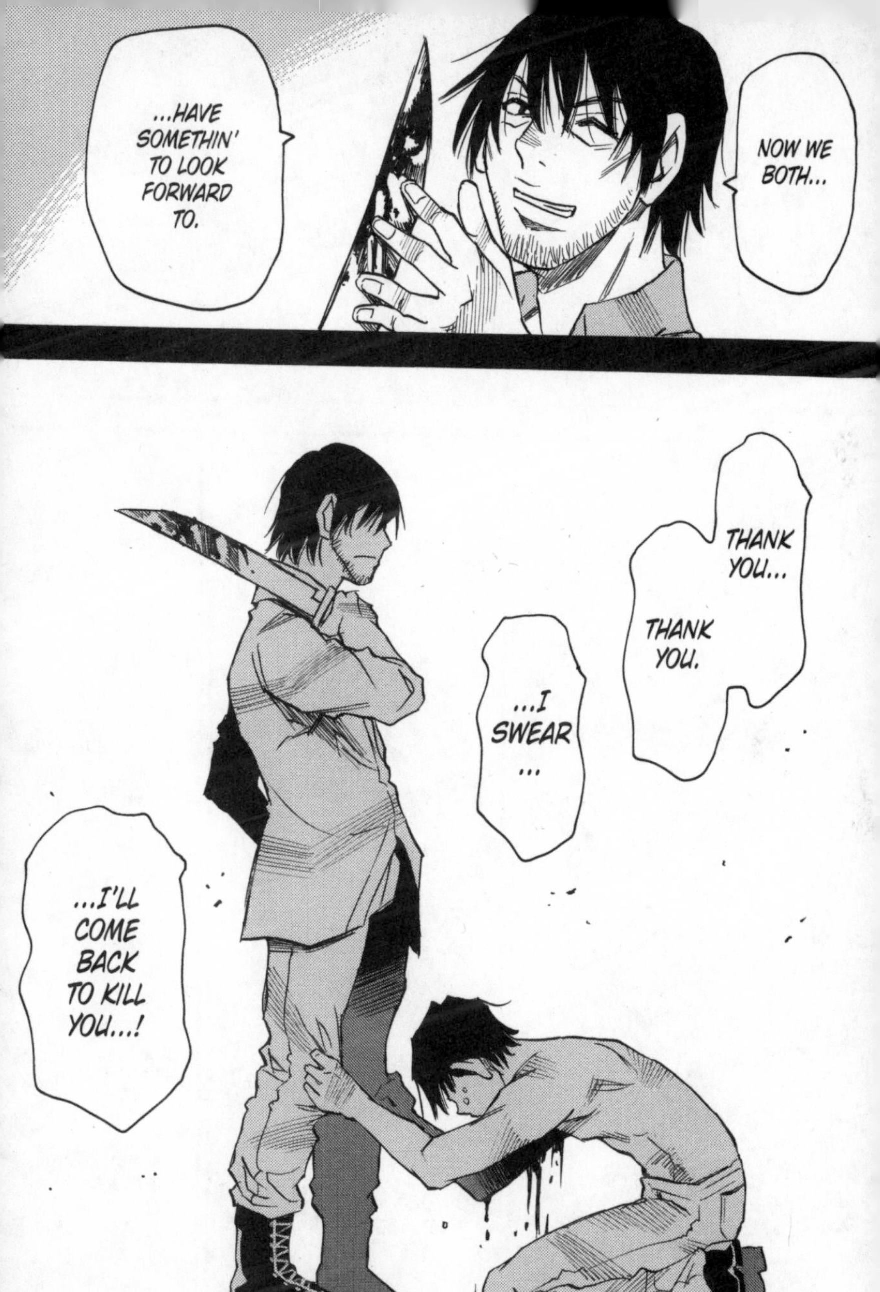
NOW WE BOTH...
...HAVE SOMETHIN' TO LOOK FORWARD TO.
THANK YOU... THANK YOU.
...I SWEAR ...
...I'LL COME BACK TO KILL YOU...!

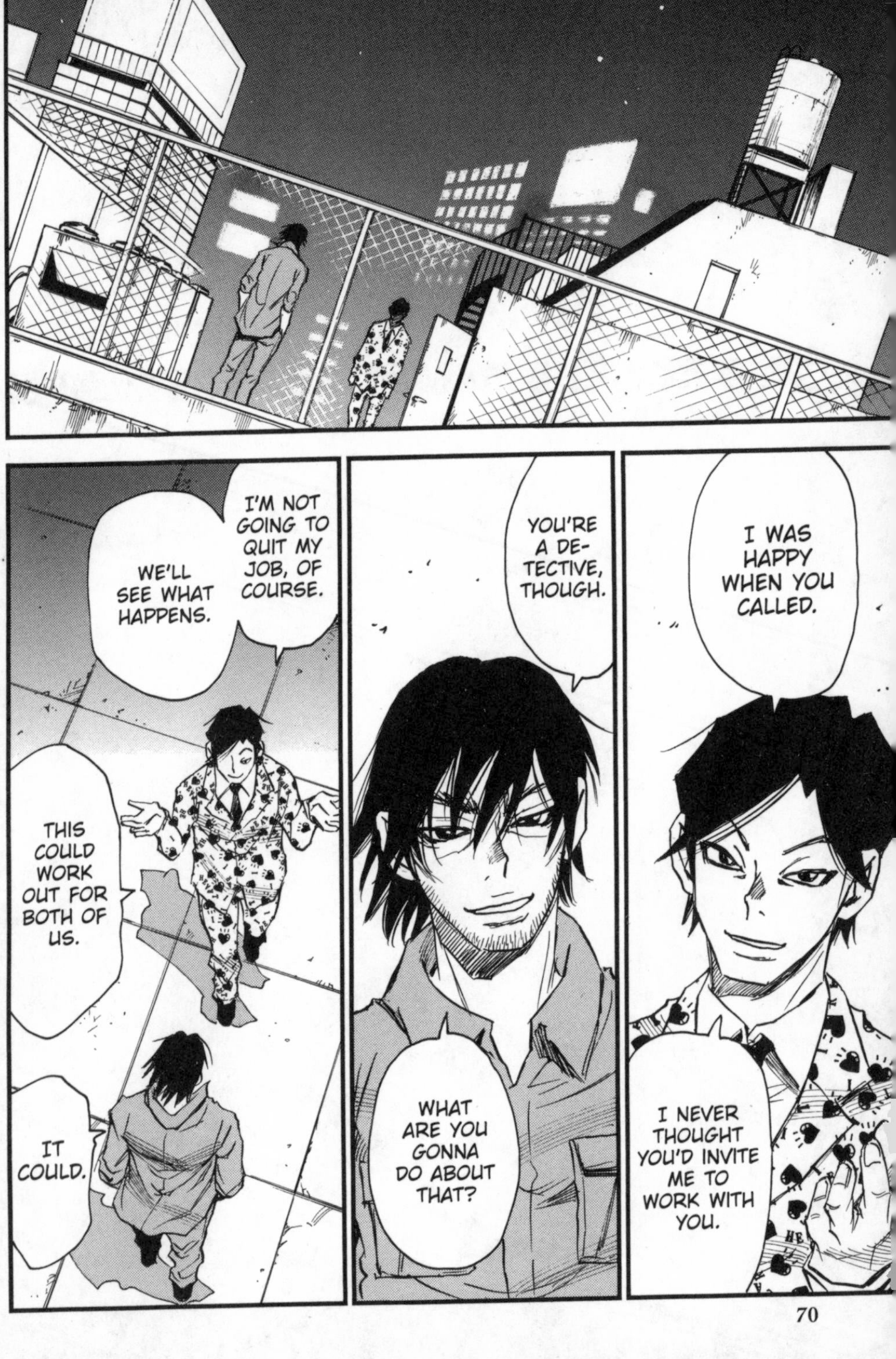
I WAS HAPPY WHEN YOU CALLED.
I NEVER THOUGHT YOU'D INVITE ME TO WORK WITH YOU.
YOU'RE A DETECTIVE, THOUGH.
WHAT ARE YOU GONNA DO ABOUT THAT?
I'M NOT GOING TO QUIT MY JOB, OF COURSE.
WE'LL SEE WHAT HAPPENS.
THIS COULD WORK OUT FOR BOTH OF US.
IT COULD.

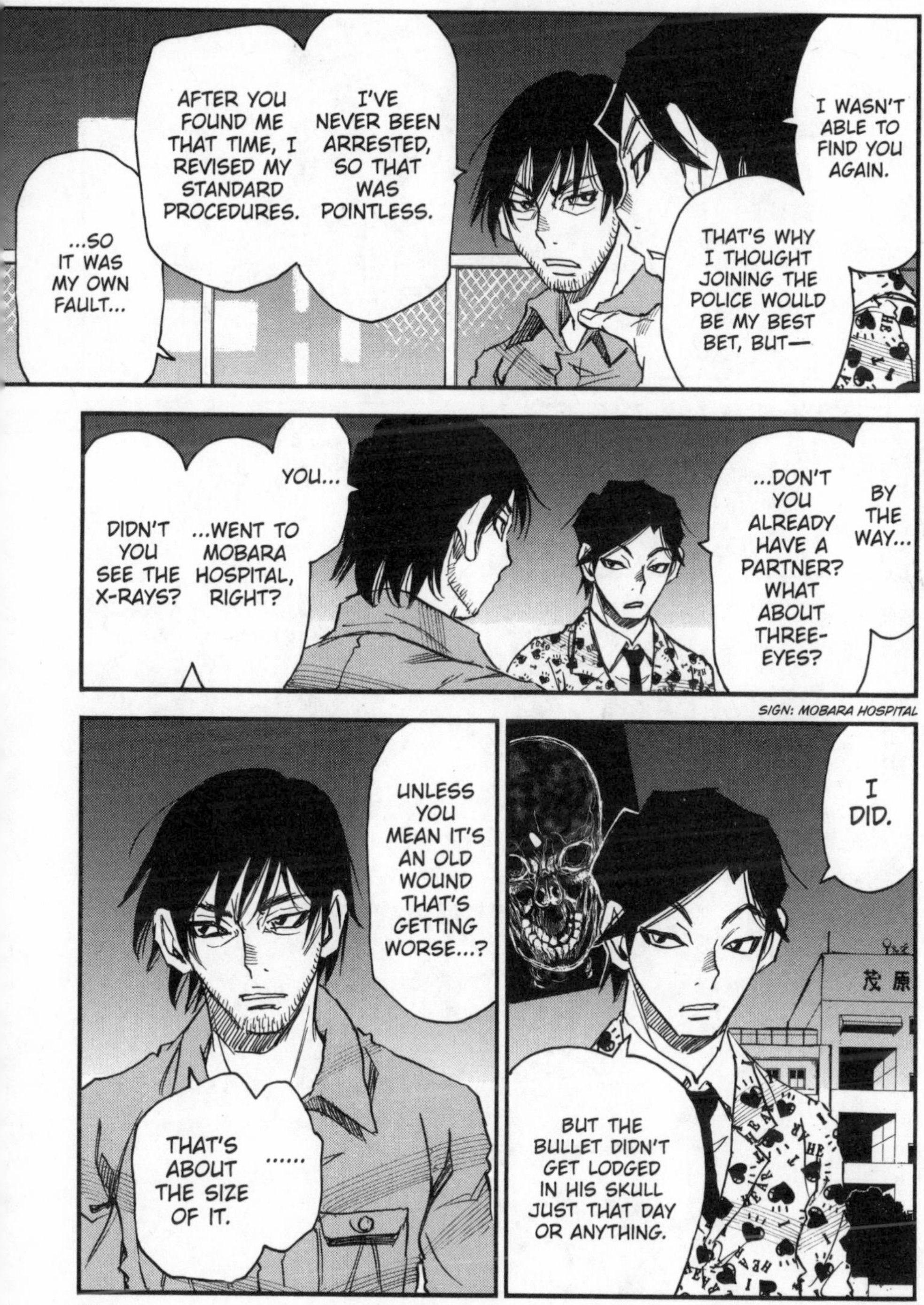
I WASN'T ABLE TO FIND YOU AGAIN.
THAT'S WHY I THOUGHT JOINING THE POLICE WOULD BE MY BEST BET, BUT—
I'VE NEVER BEEN ARRESTED, SO THAT WAS POINTLESS.
AFTER YOU FOUND ME THAT TIME, I REVISED MY STANDARD PROCEDURES.
...SO IT WAS MY OWN FAULT...
BY THE WAY...
...DON'T YOU ALREADY HAVE A PARTNER? WHAT ABOUT THREE-EYES?
YOU...
...WENT TO MOBARA HOSPITAL, RIGHT?
DIDN'T YOU SEE THE X-RAYS?
I DID.
BUT THE BULLET DIDN'T GET LODGED IN HIS SKULL JUST THAT DAY OR ANYTHING.
茂原
UNLESS YOU MEAN IT'S AN OLD WOUND THAT'S GETTING WORSE...?
......
THAT'S ABOUT THE SIZE OF IT.
SIGN: MOBARA HOSPITAL

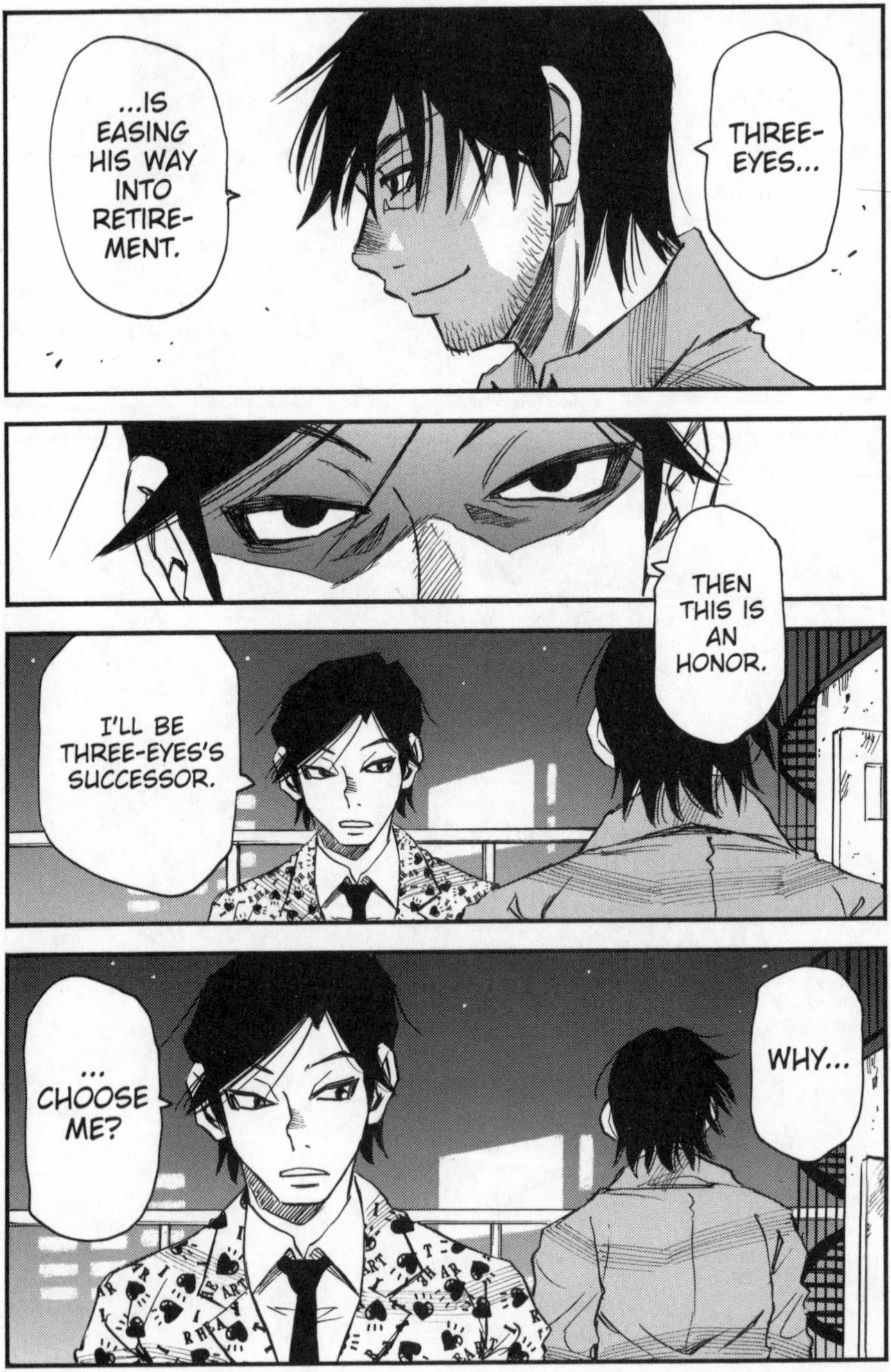
THREE-EYES...
...IS EASING HIS WAY INTO RETIRE-MENT.
THEN THIS IS AN HONOR.
I'LL BE THREE-EYES'S SUCCESSOR.
WHY...
...CHOOSE ME?

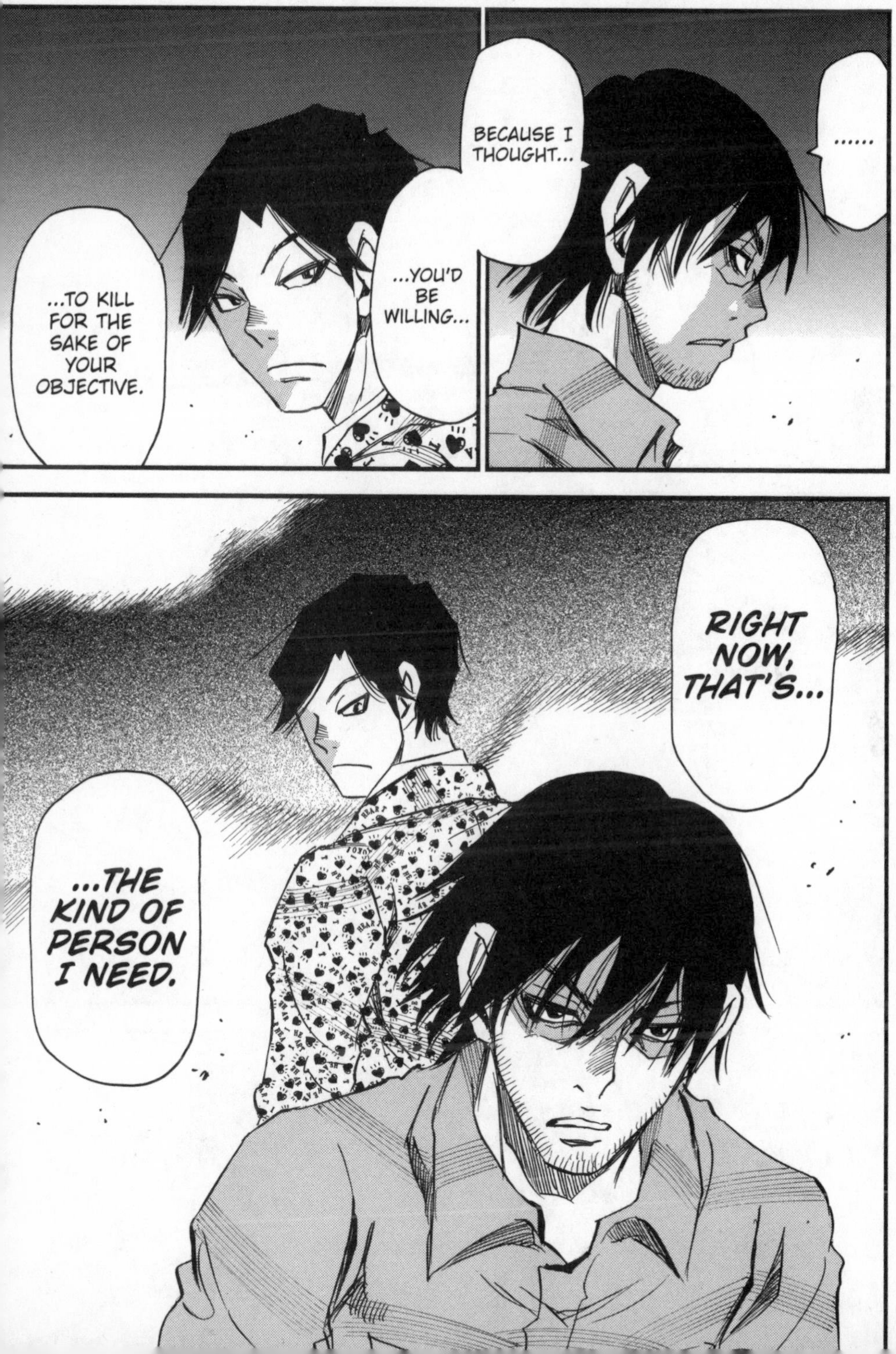
......
BECAUSE I THOUGHT...
...YOU'D BE WILLING...
...TO KILL FOR THE SAKE OF YOUR OBJECTIVE.
RIGHT NOW, THAT'S...
...THE KIND OF PERSON I NEED.

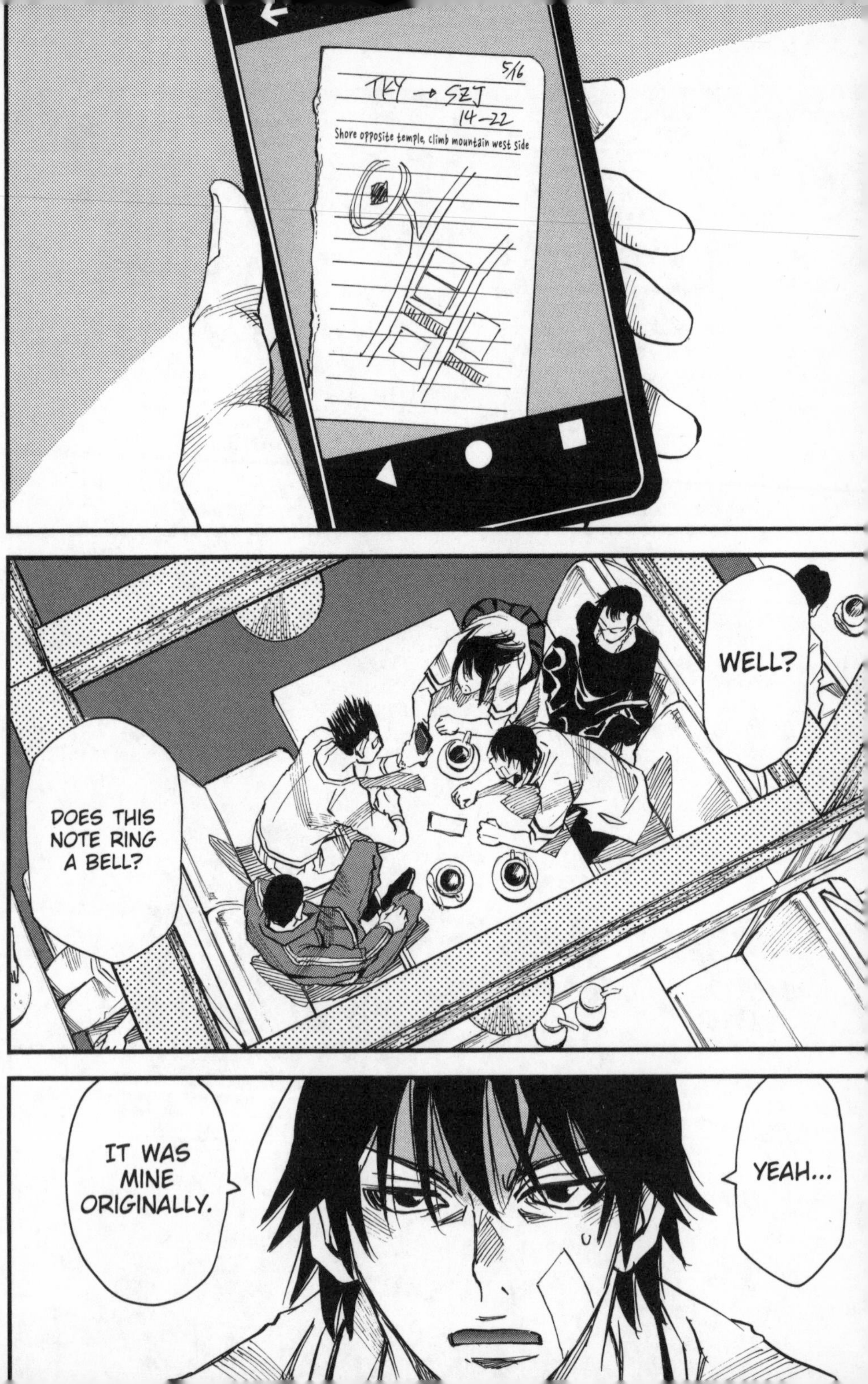
5/16
TKY → SZJ
14–22
Shore opposite temple, climb mountain west side
WELL?
DOES THIS NOTE RING A BELL?
YEAH...
IT WAS MINE ORIGINALLY.

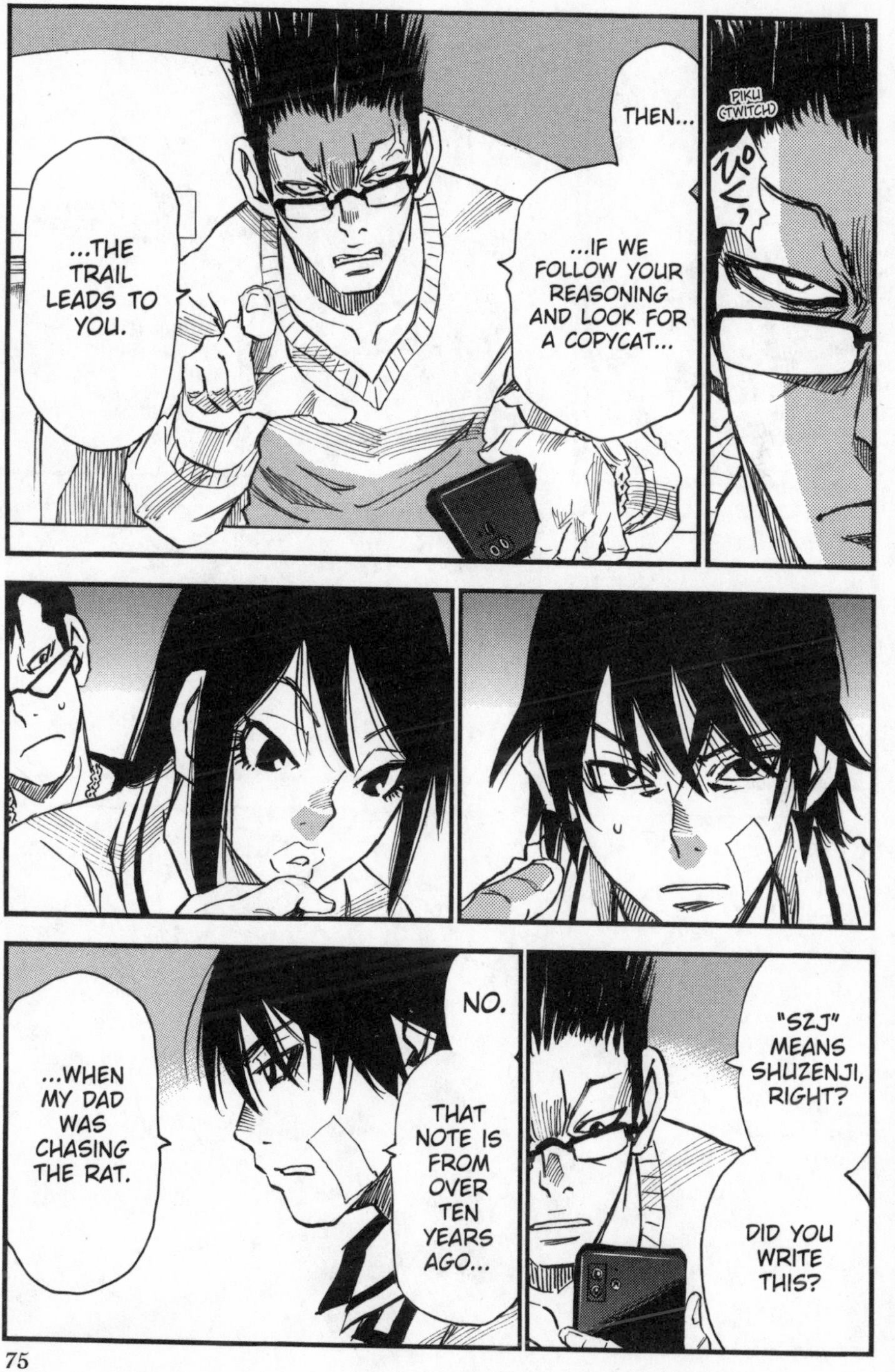
PIKU (TWITCH)
ぴくっ
THEN...
...IF WE FOLLOW YOUR REASONING AND LOOK FOR A COPYCAT...
...THE TRAIL LEADS TO YOU.
"SZJ" MEANS SHUZENJI, RIGHT?
DID YOU WRITE THIS?
NO.
THAT NOTE IS FROM OVER TEN YEARS AGO...
...WHEN MY DAD WAS CHASING THE RAT.

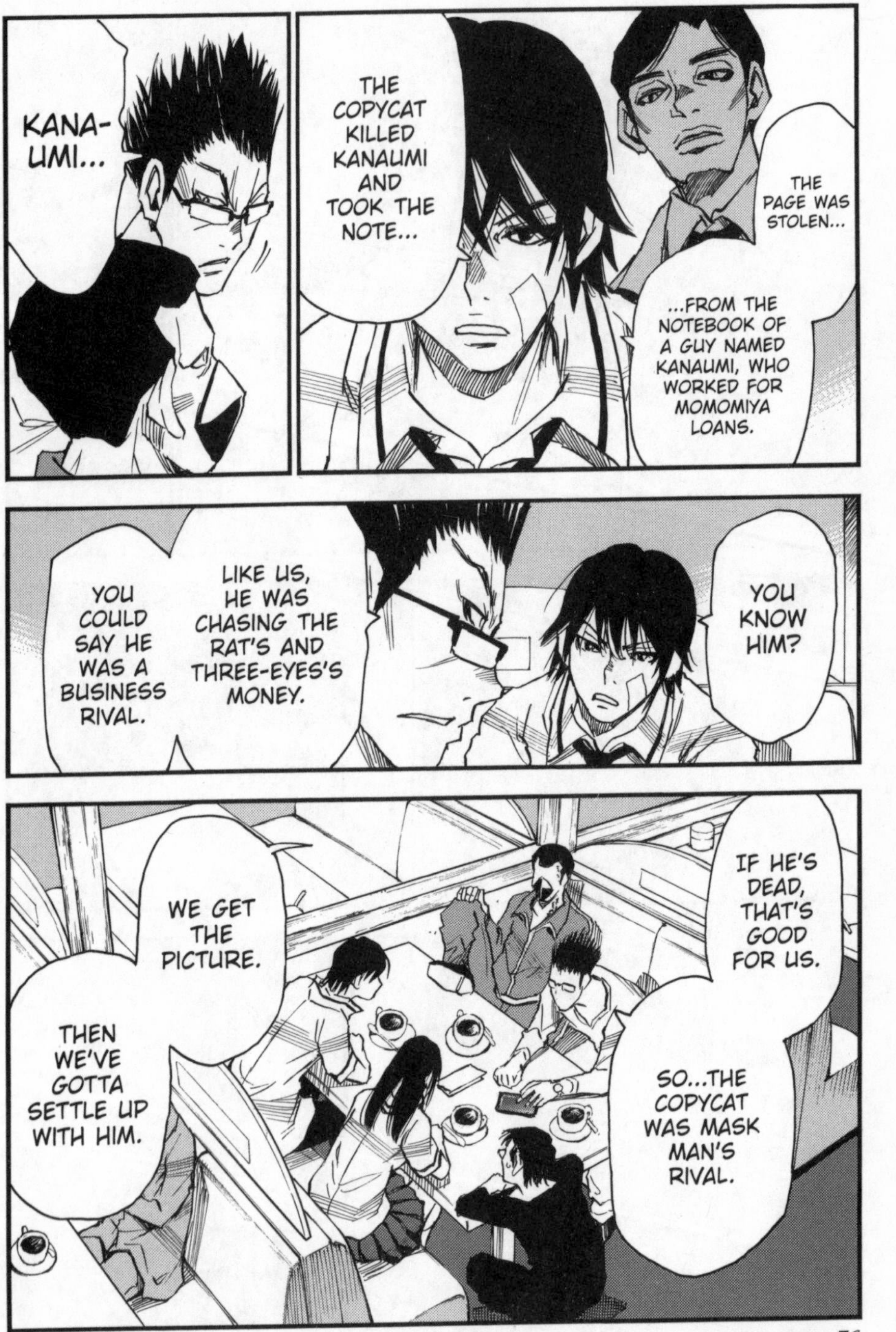
THE PAGE WAS STOLEN...
...FROM THE NOTEBOOK OF A GUY NAMED KANAUMI, WHO WORKED FOR MOMOMIYA LOANS.
THE COPYCAT KILLED KANAUMI AND TOOK THE NOTE...
KANA-UMI...
YOU KNOW HIM?
LIKE US, HE WAS CHASING THE RAT'S AND THREE-EYES'S MONEY.
YOU COULD SAY HE WAS A BUSINESS RIVAL.
IF HE'S DEAD, THAT'S GOOD FOR US.
SO...THE COPYCAT WAS MASK MAN'S RIVAL.
WE GET THE PICTURE.
THEN WE'VE GOTTA SETTLE UP WITH HIM.

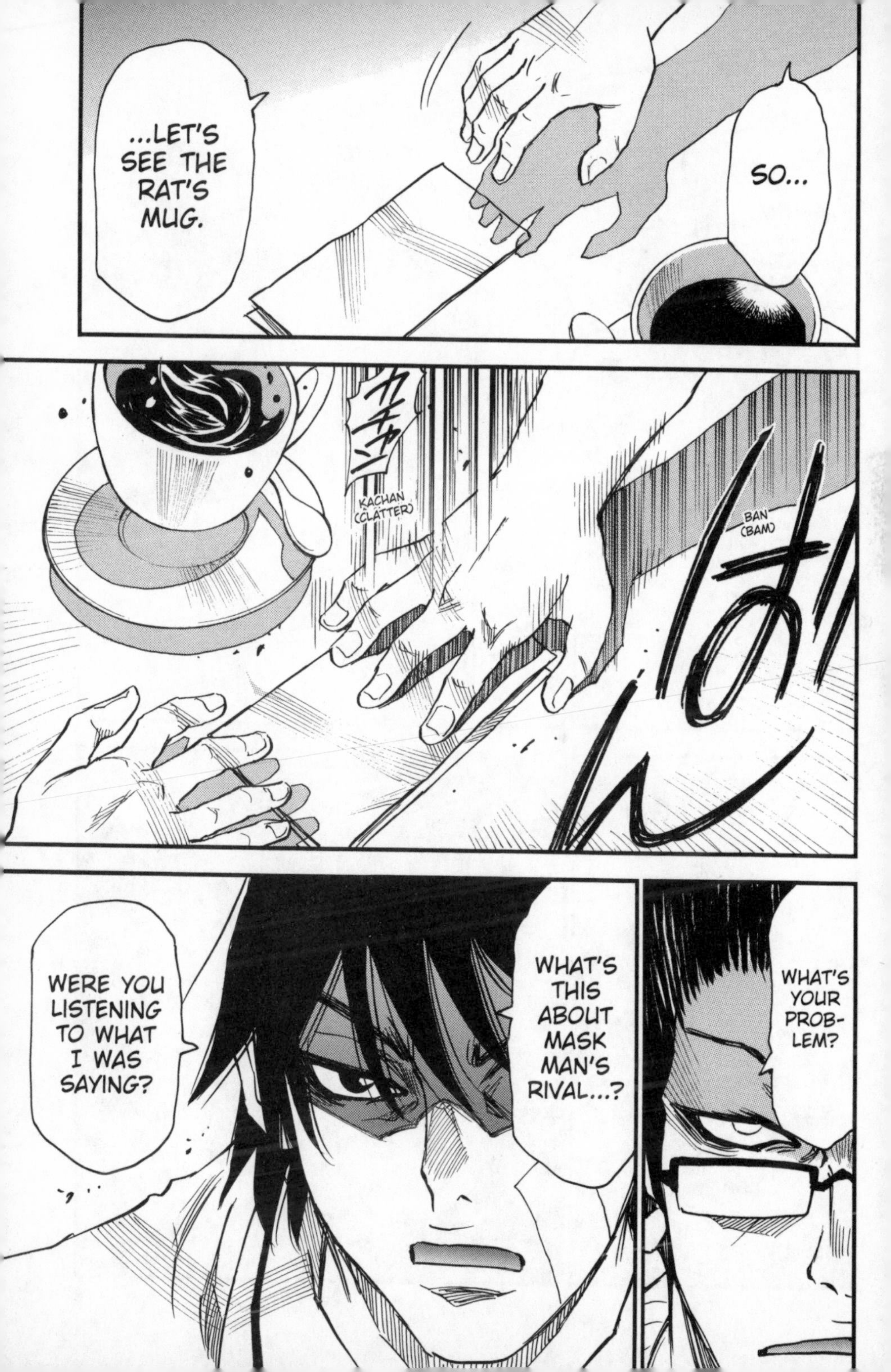
SO...
...LET'S SEE THE RAT'S MUG.
BAN (BAM)
KACHAN (CLATTER)
WHAT'S YOUR PROB-LEM?
WHAT'S THIS ABOUT MASK MAN'S RIVAL...?
WERE YOU LISTENING TO WHAT I WAS SAYING?

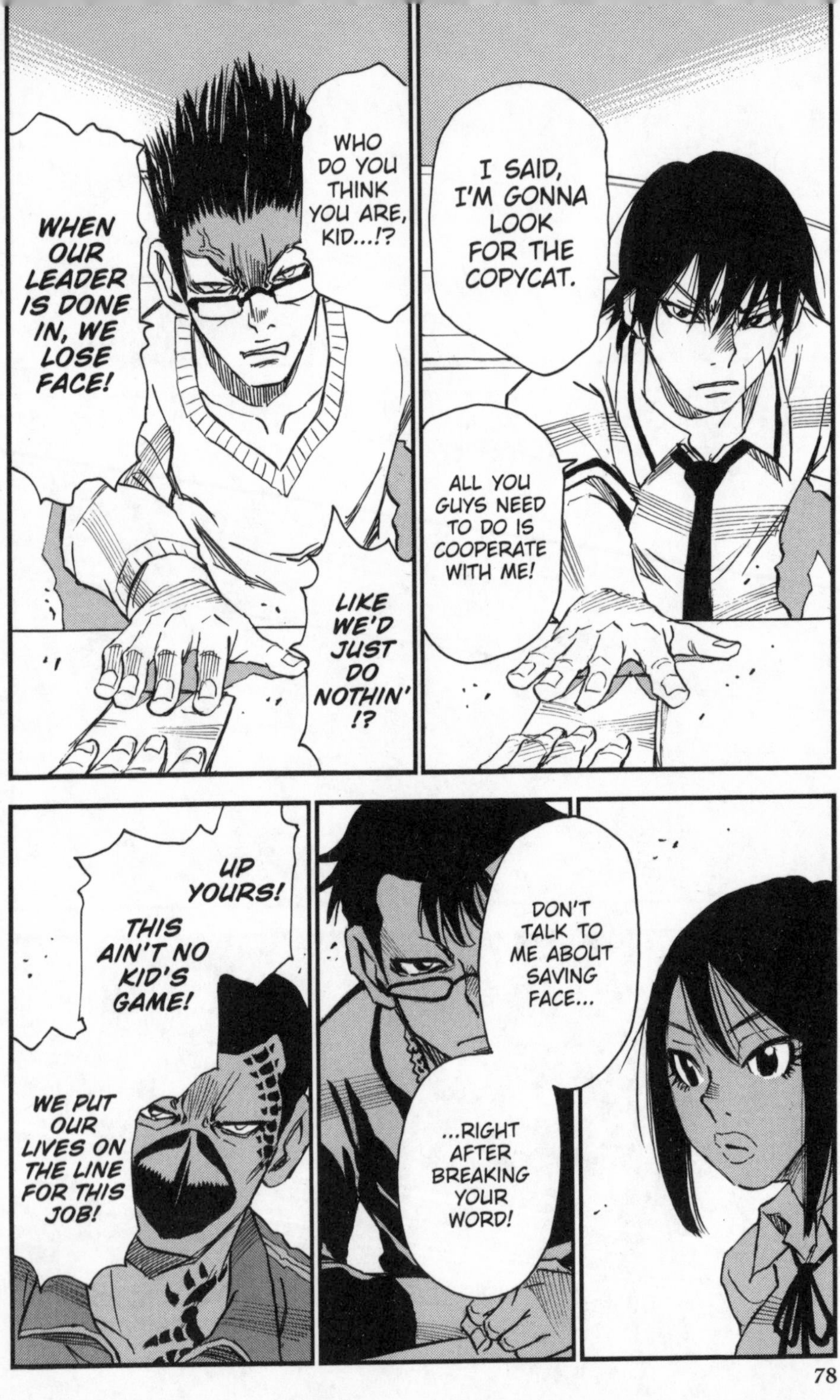
I SAID, I'M GONNA LOOK FOR THE COPYCAT.
ALL YOU GUYS NEED TO DO IS COOPERATE WITH ME!
WHO DO YOU THINK YOU ARE, KID...!?
WHEN OUR LEADER IS DONE IN, WE LOSE FACE!
LIKE WE'D JUST DO NOTHIN' !?
DON'T TALK TO ME ABOUT SAVING FACE...
...RIGHT AFTER BREAKING YOUR WORD!
UP YOURS!
THIS AIN'T NO KID'S GAME!
WE PUT OUR LIVES ON THE LINE FOR THIS JOB!

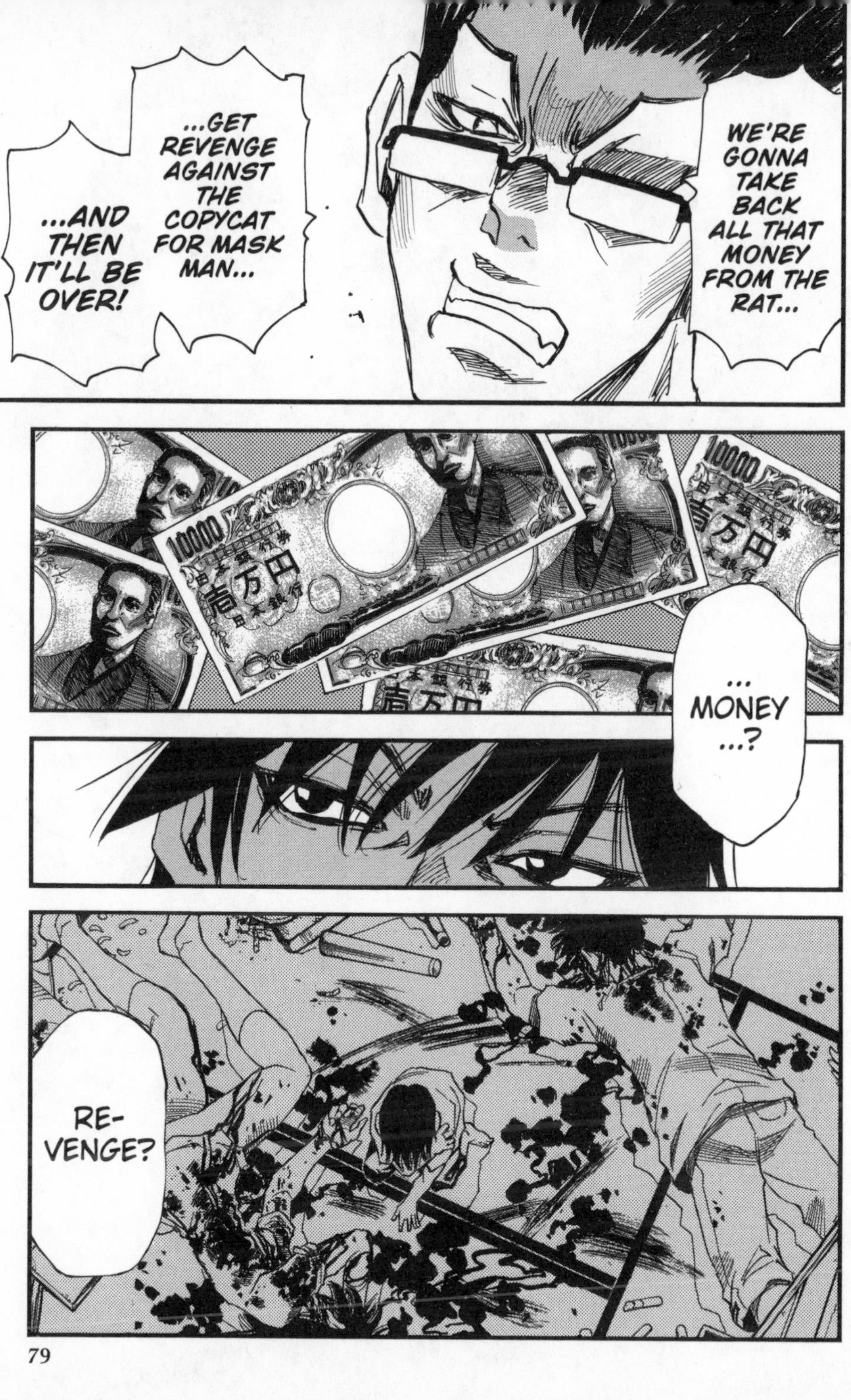
WE'RE GONNA TAKE BACK ALL THAT MONEY FROM THE RAT...
...GET REVENGE AGAINST THE COPYCAT FOR MASK MAN...
...AND THEN IT'LL BE OVER!
...MONEY...?
RE-VENGE?

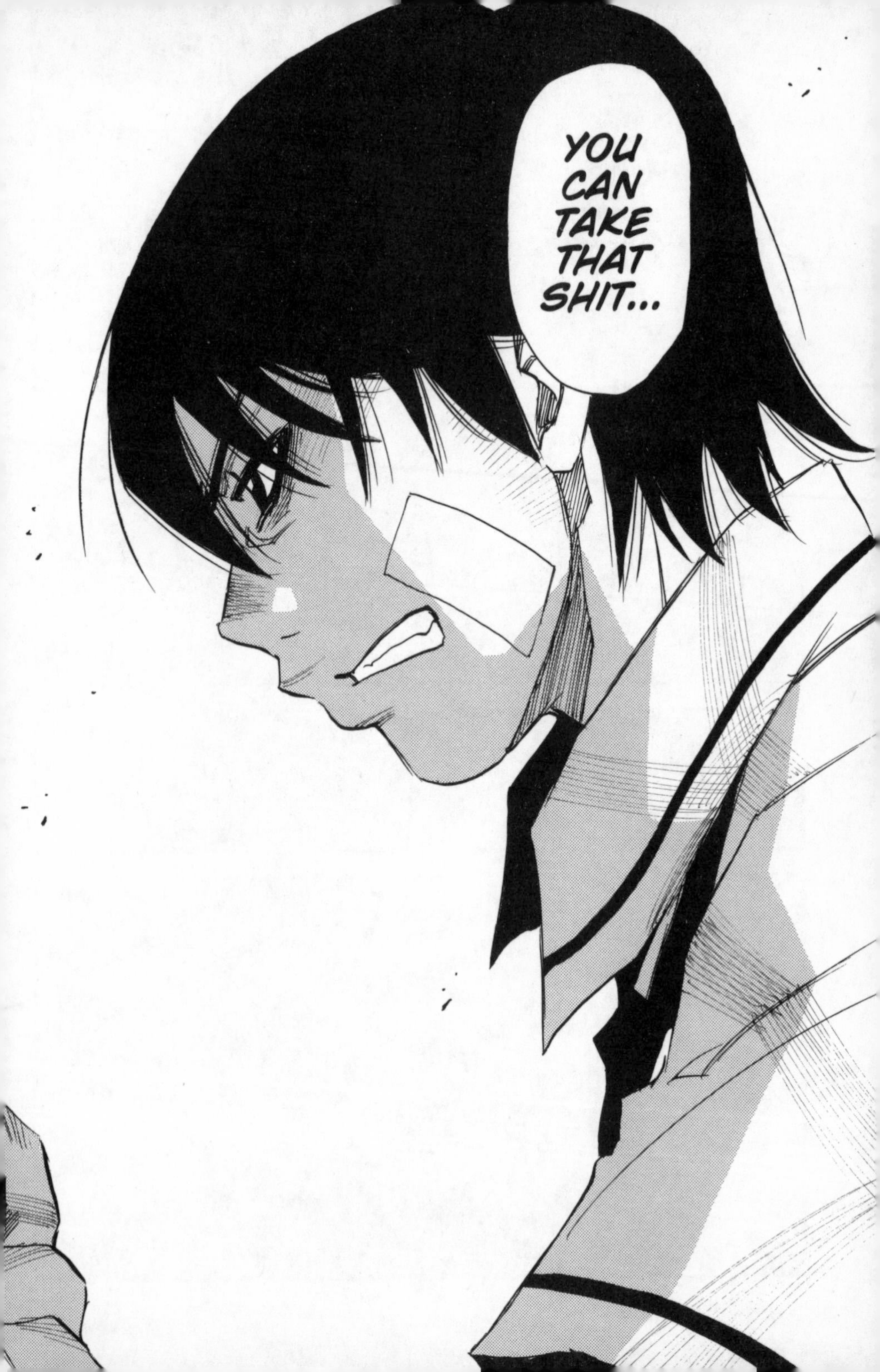
YOU CAN TAKE THAT SHIT...

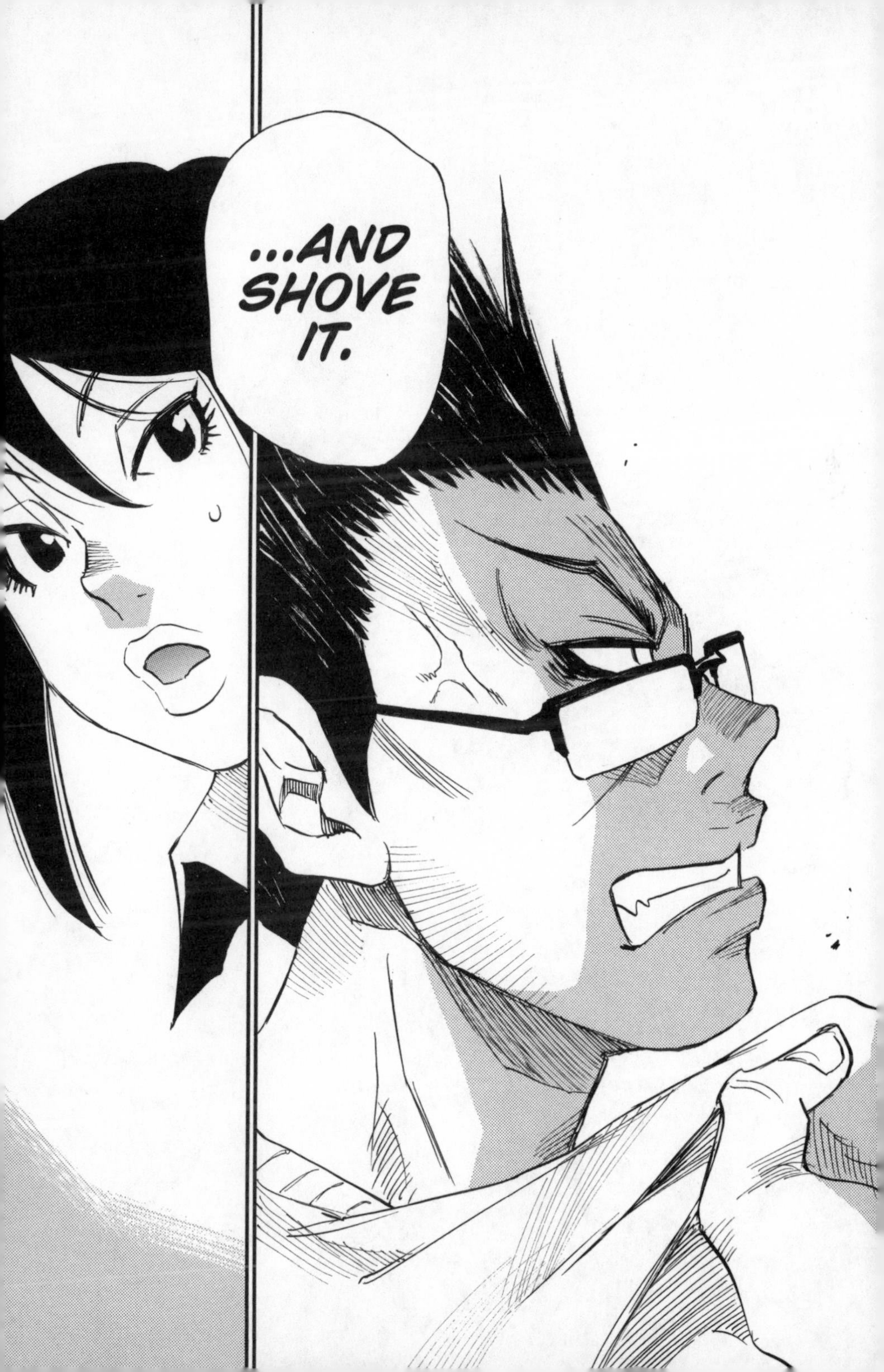
...AND SHOVE IT.

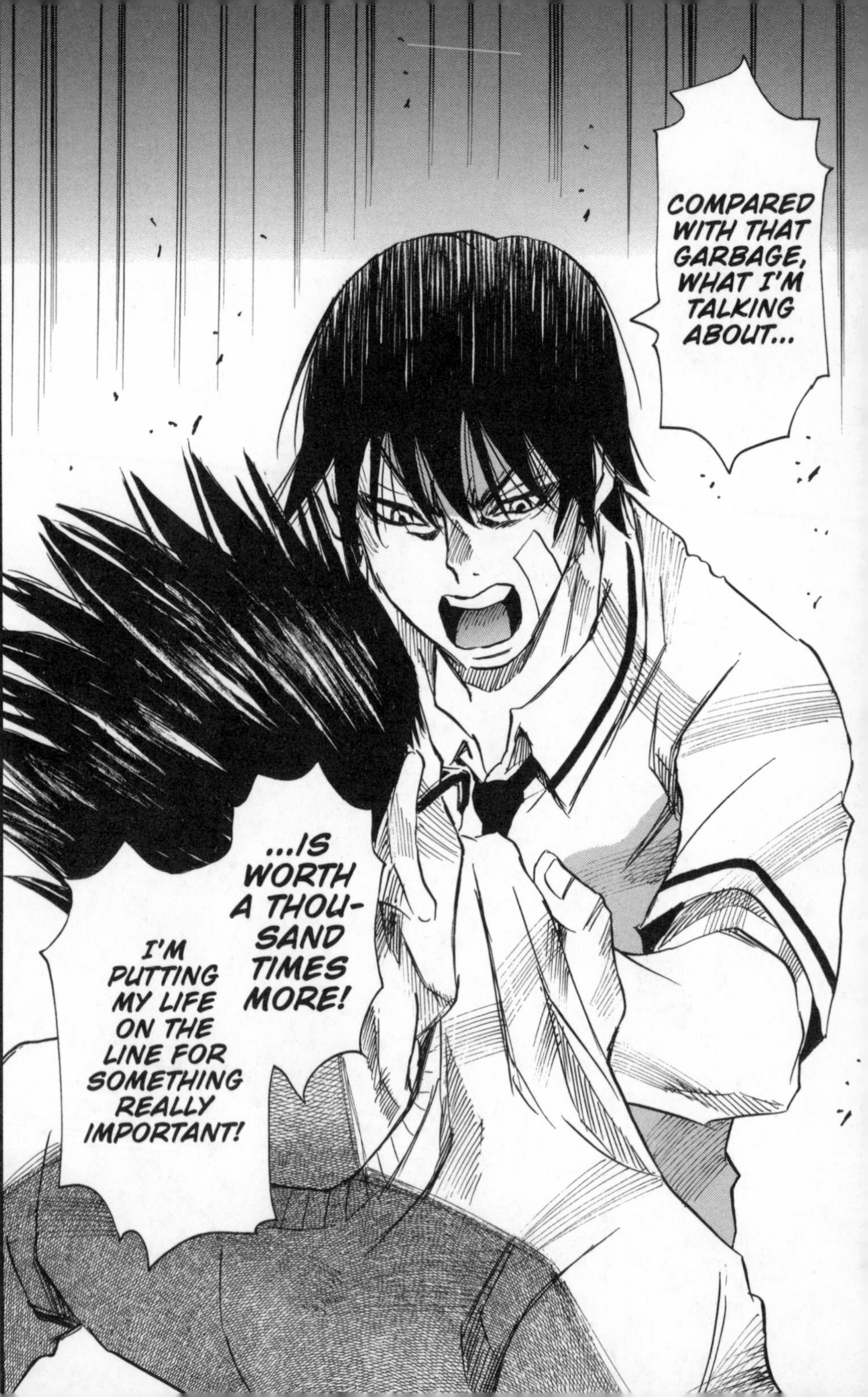
COMPARED WITH THAT GARBAGE, WHAT I'M TALKING ABOUT...
...IS WORTH A THOU-SAND TIMES MORE!
I'M PUTTING MY LIFE ON THE LINE FOR SOMETHING REALLY IMPORTANT!

#39 END

#40 The Identity of the Copycat

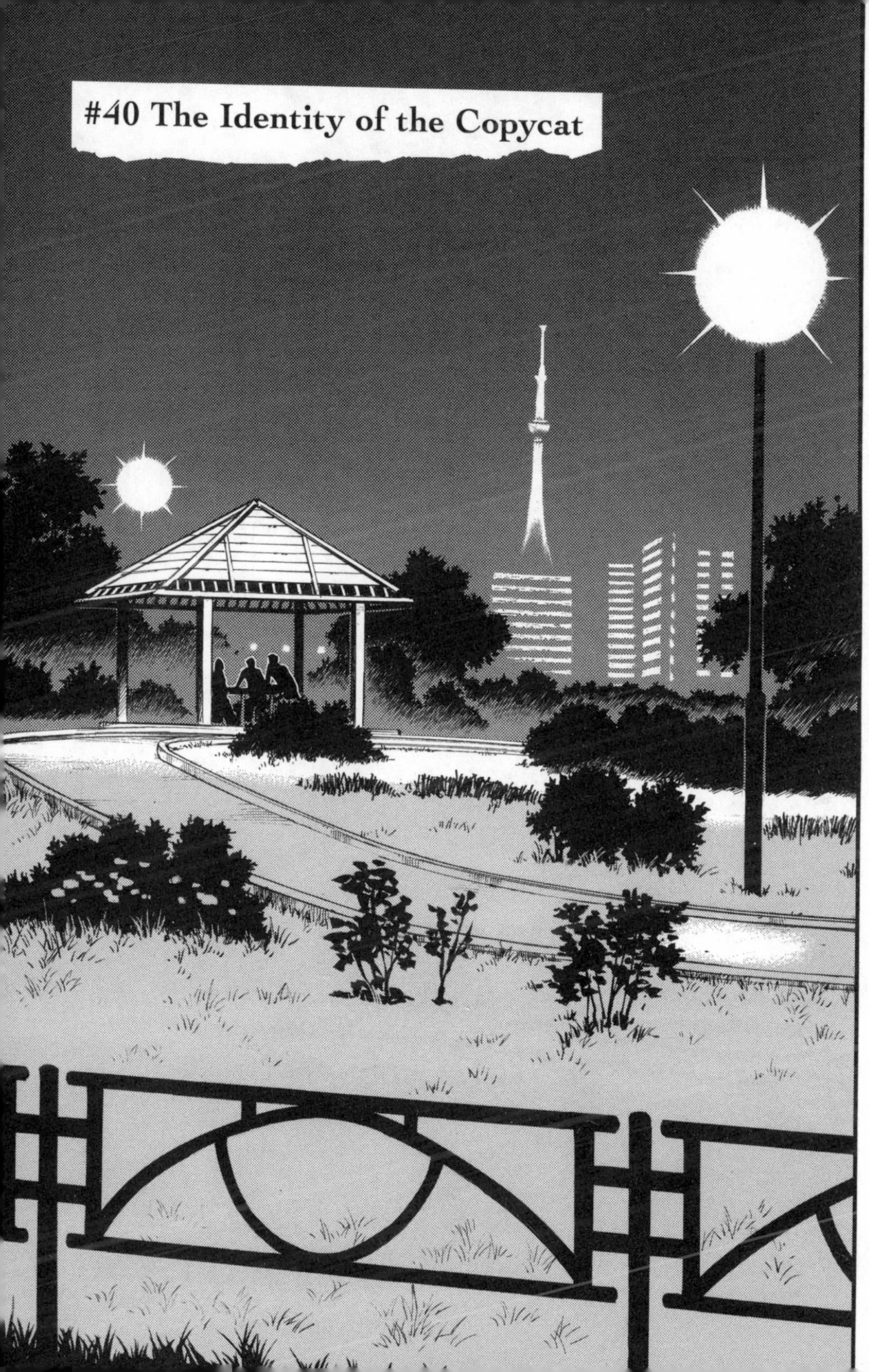

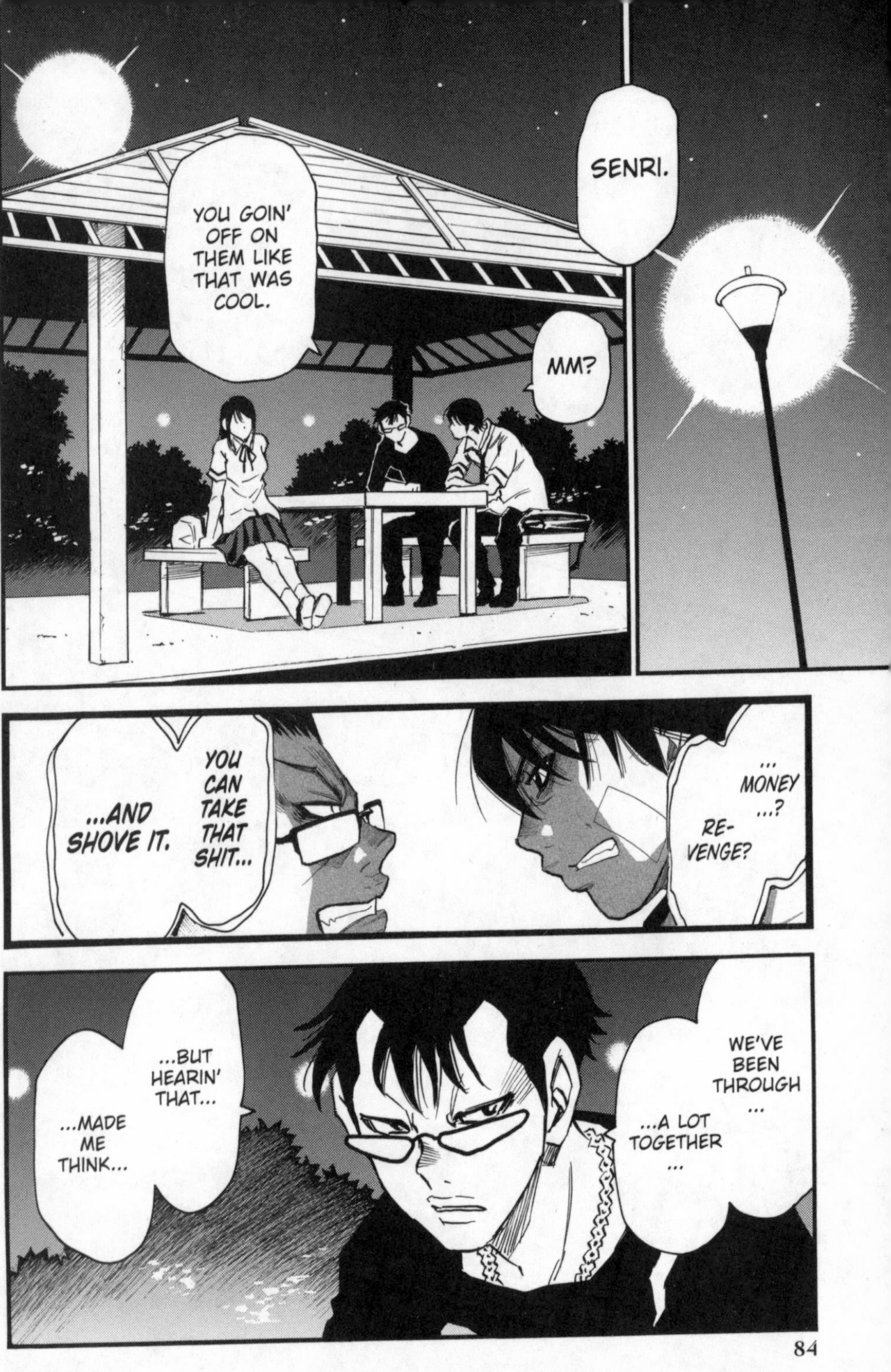
SENRI.
MM?
YOU GOIN' OFF ON THEM LIKE THAT WAS COOL.
... MONEY ...?
RE-VENGE?
YOU CAN TAKE THAT SHIT...
...AND SHOVE IT.
WE'VE BEEN THROUGH ...
...A LOT TOGETHER ...
...BUT HEARIN' THAT...
...MADE ME THINK...

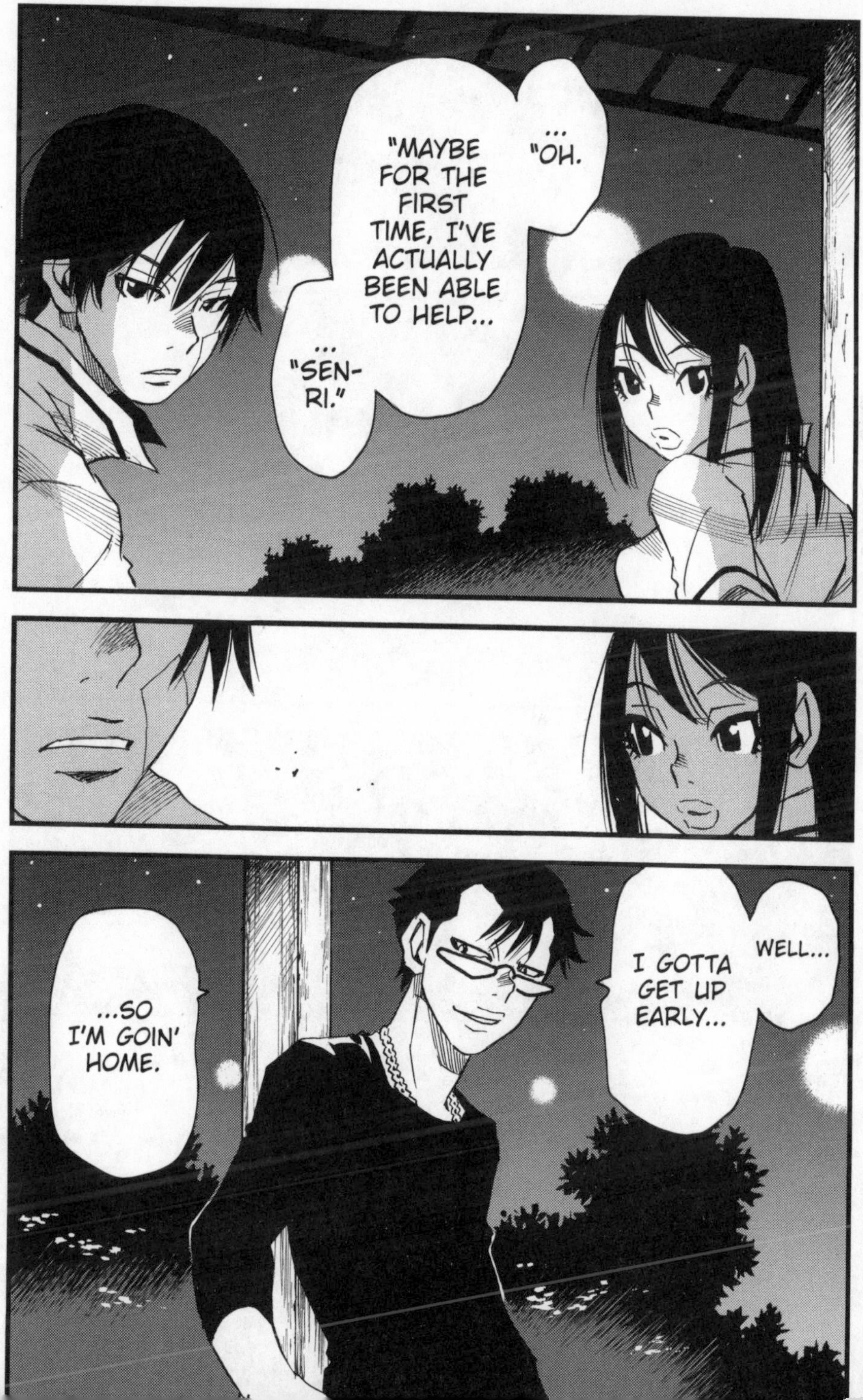
..."OH.
"MAYBE FOR THE FIRST TIME, I'VE ACTUALLY BEEN ABLE TO HELP...
..."SEN-RI."
WELL...
I GOTTA GET UP EARLY...
...SO I'M GOIN' HOME.

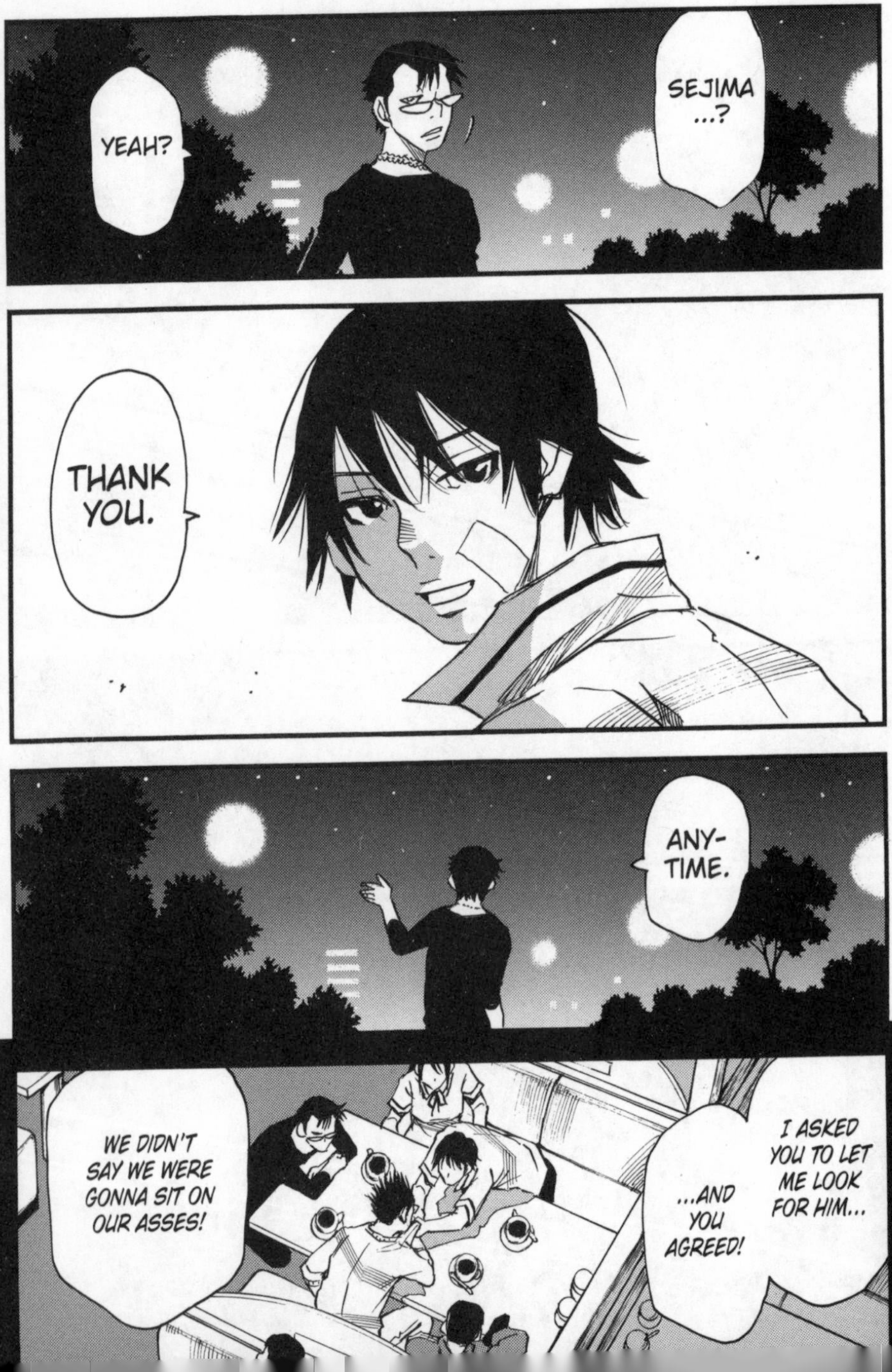
SEJIMA ...?
YEAH?
THANK YOU.
ANY-TIME.
I ASKED YOU TO LET ME LOOK FOR HIM...
...AND YOU AGREED!
WE DIDN'T SAY WE WERE GONNA SIT ON OUR ASSES!

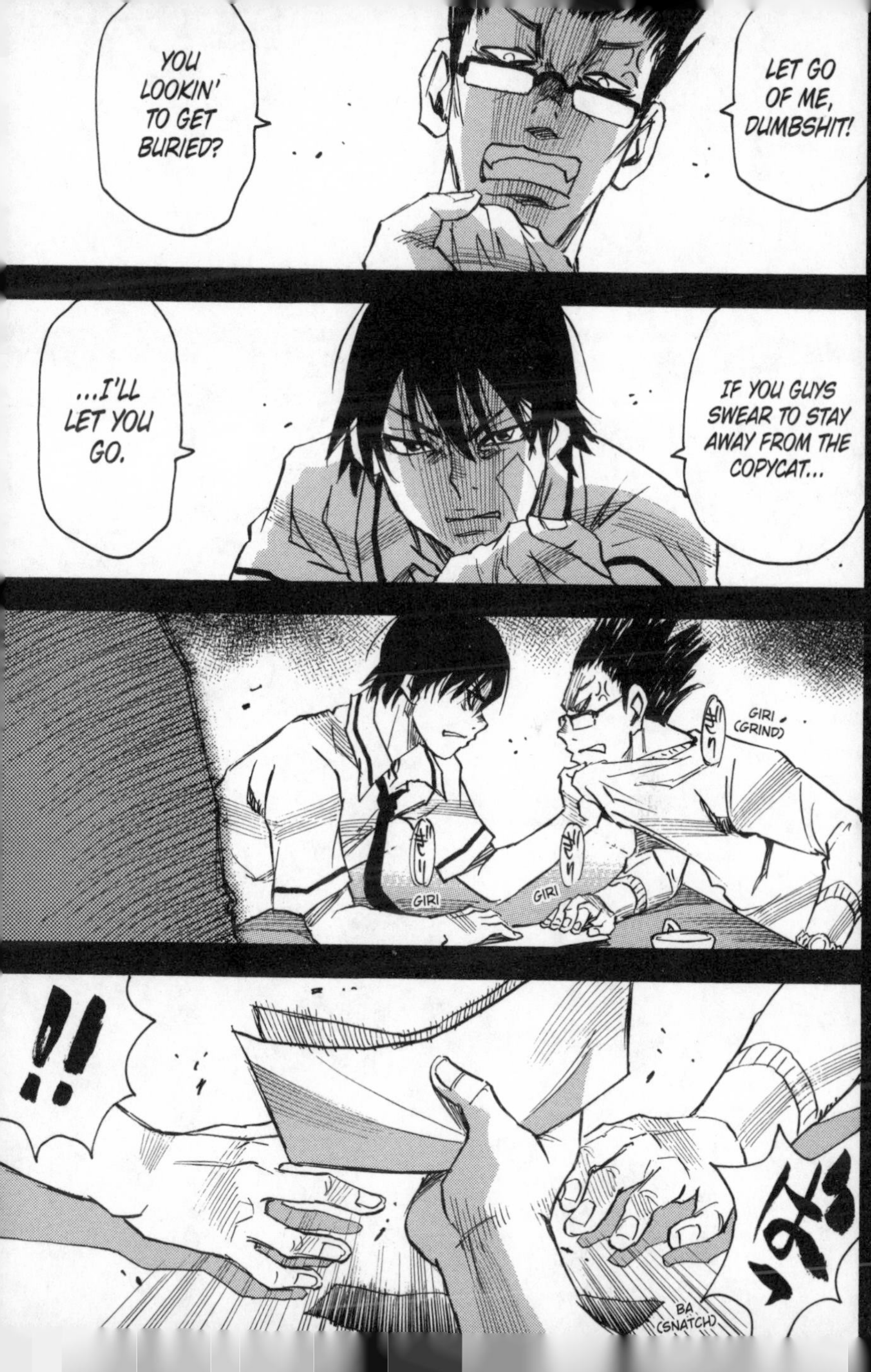
LET GO OF ME, DUMBSHIT!
YOU LOOKIN' TO GET BURIED?
IF YOU GUYS SWEAR TO STAY AWAY FROM THE COPYCAT...
...I'LL LET YOU GO.
GIRI (GRIND)
GIRI
GIRI
BA (SNATCH)
!!

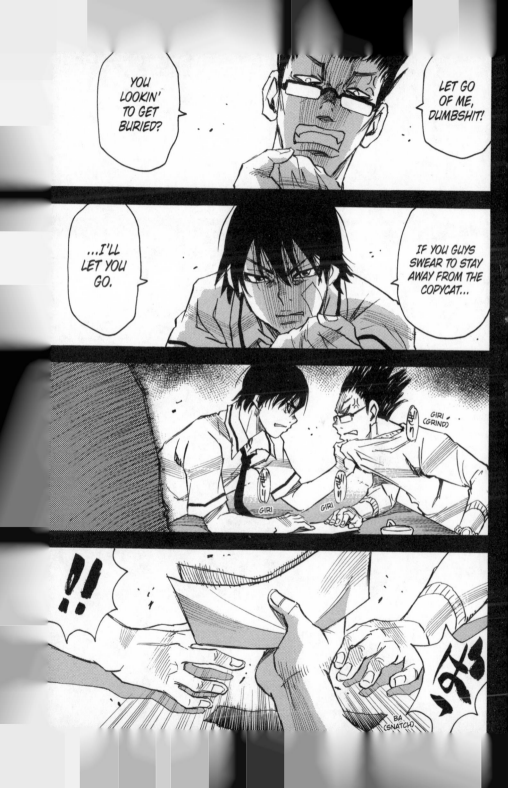

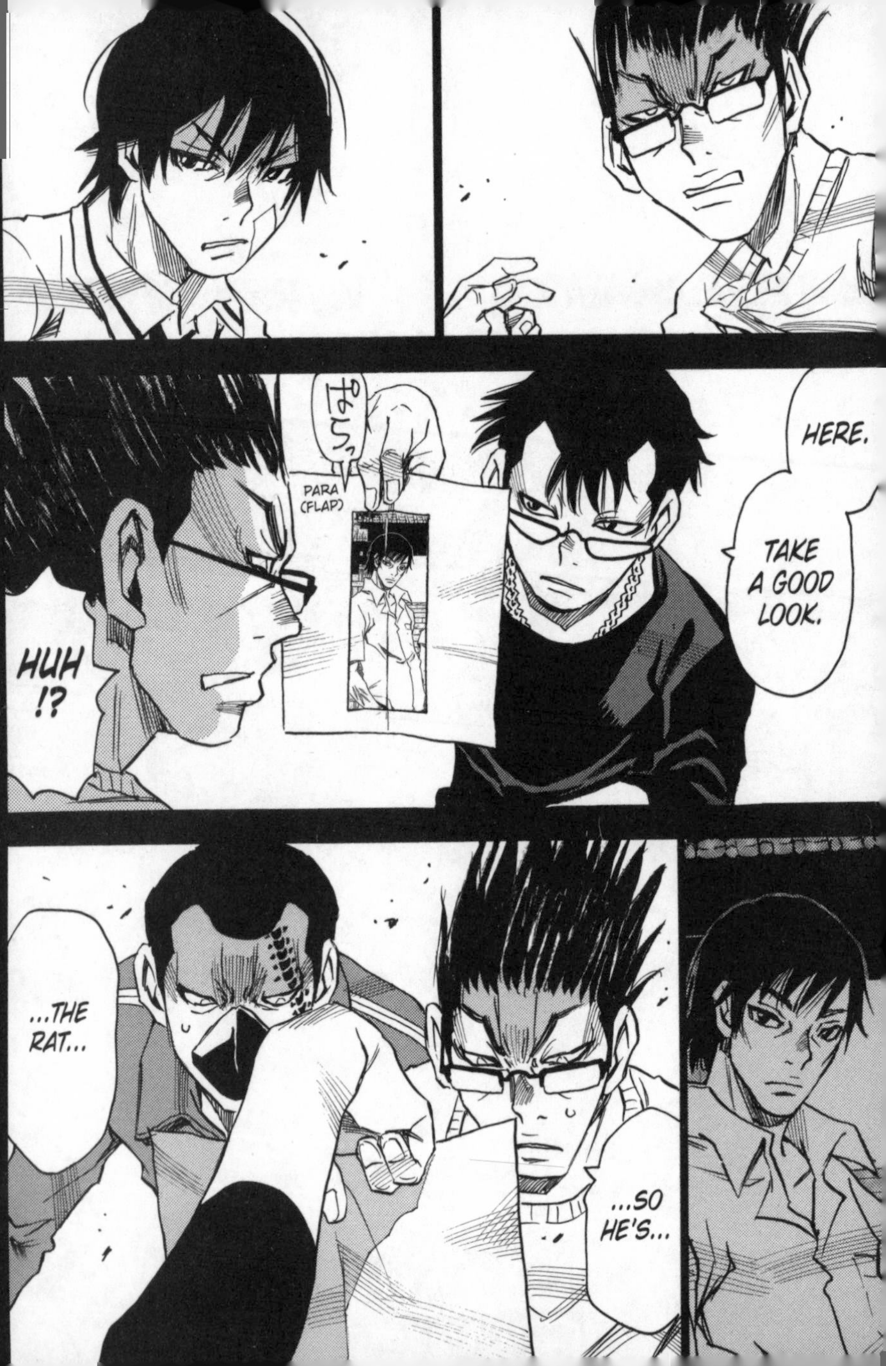
HERE.
TAKE A GOOD LOOK.
ぱらっ
PARA (FLAP)
HUH!?
...SO HE'S...
...THE RAT...

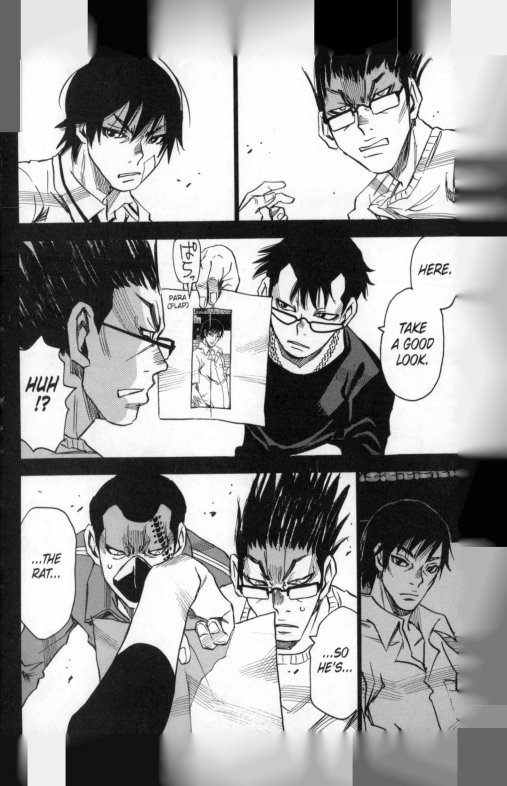

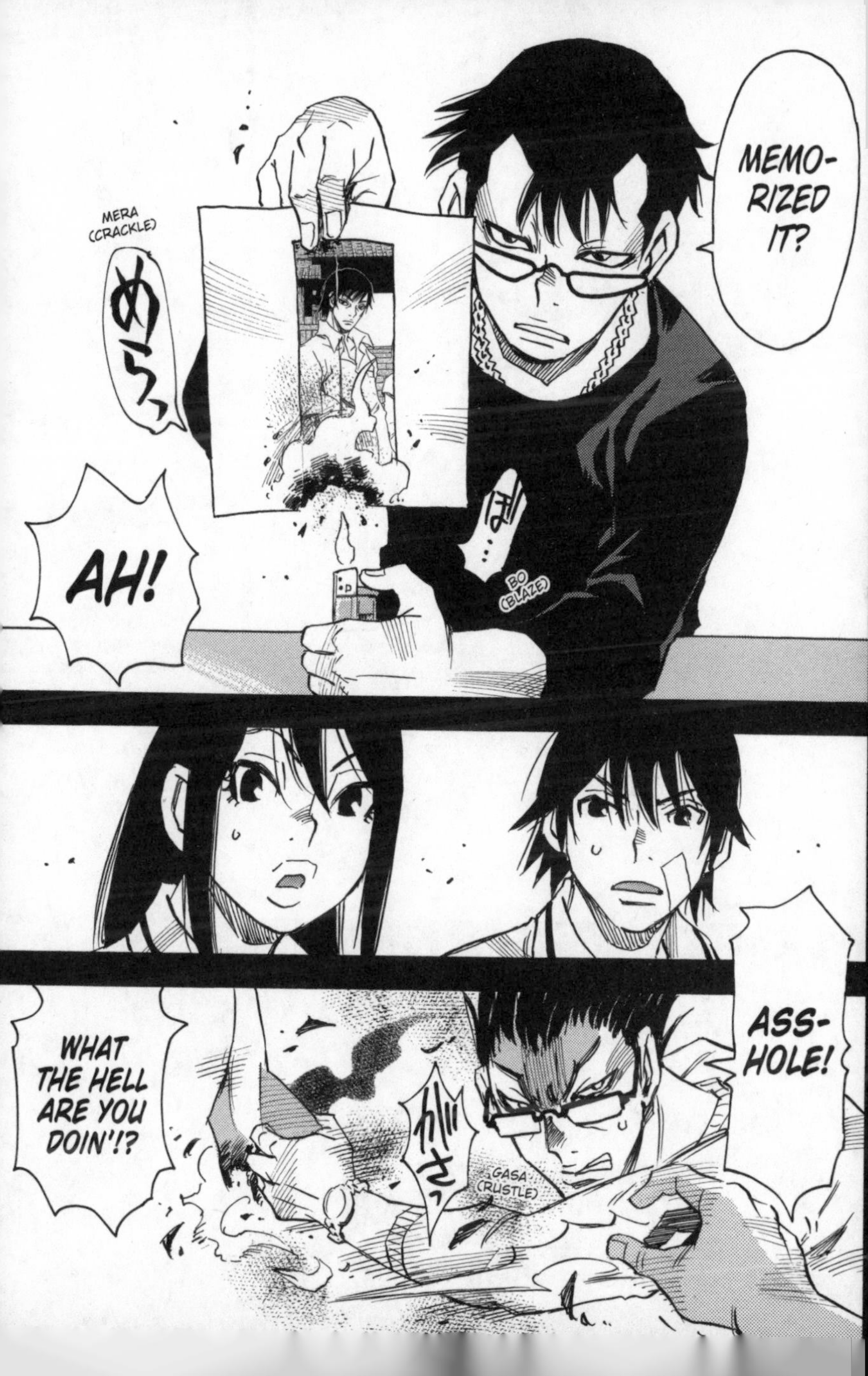
MEMO-RIZED IT?
ぼ…
BO (BLAZE)
MERA (CRACKLE)
めらっ
AH!
ASS-HOLE!
がさっ
GASA (RUSTLE)
WHAT THE HELL ARE YOU DOIN'!?

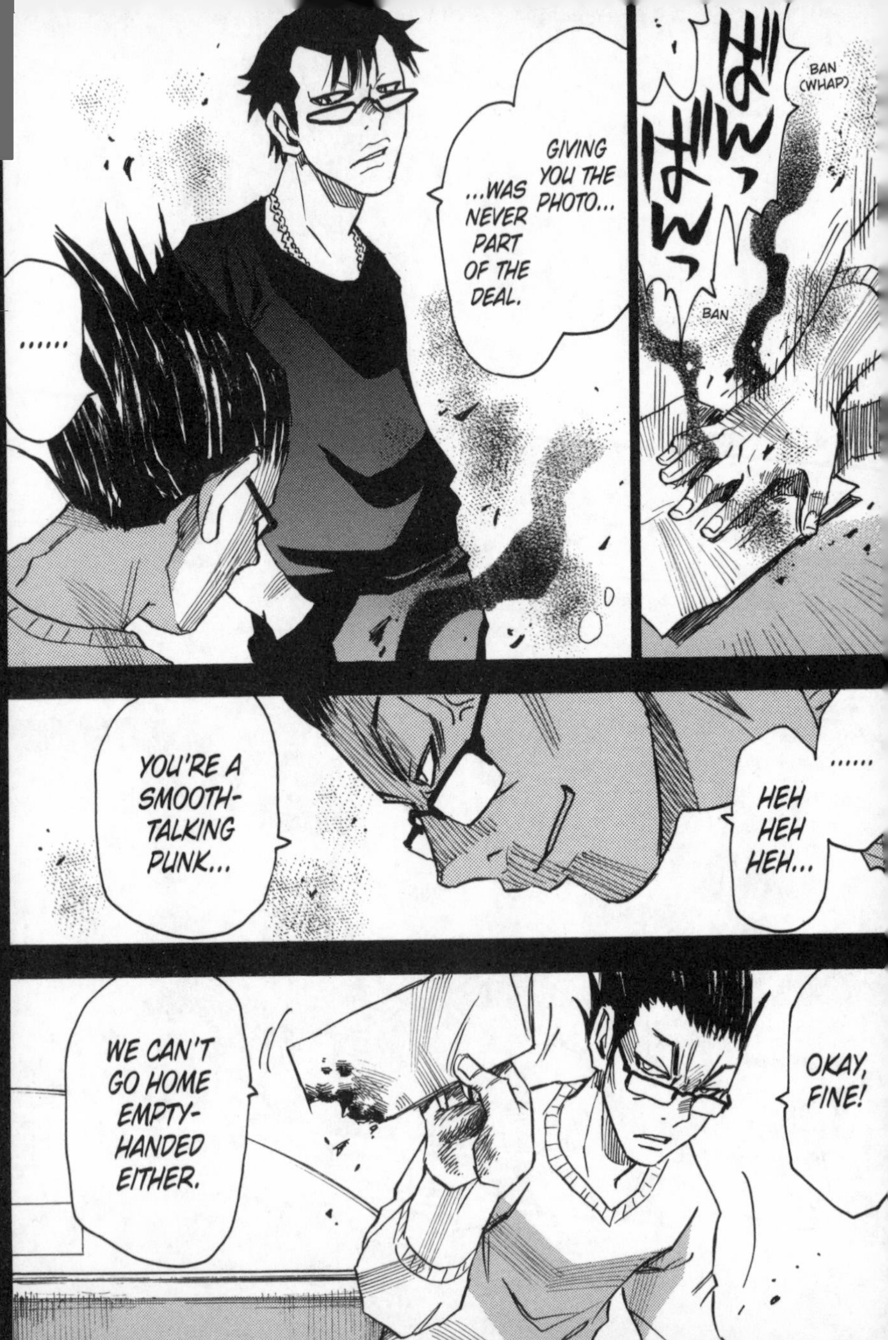
ばんっ
BAN (WHAP)
ばんっ
BAN
GIVING YOU THE PHOTO...
...WAS NEVER PART OF THE DEAL.
......
......
HEH HEH HEH...
YOU'RE A SMOOTH-TALKING PUNK...
OKAY, FINE!
WE CAN'T GO HOME EMPTY-HANDED EITHER.

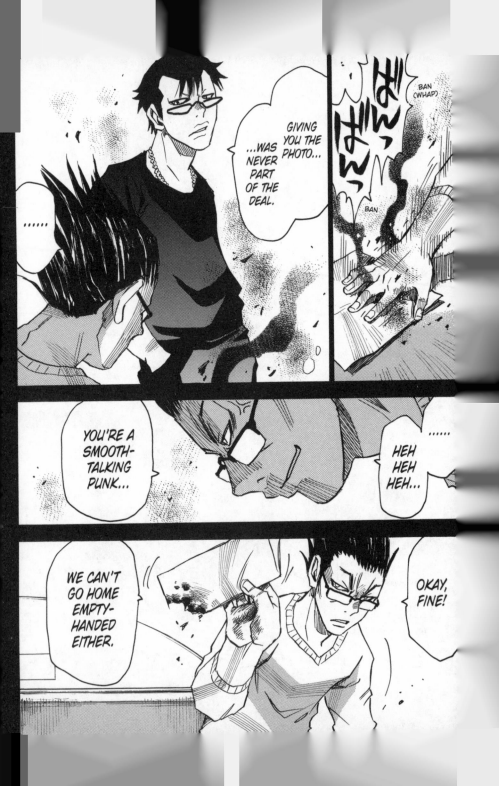

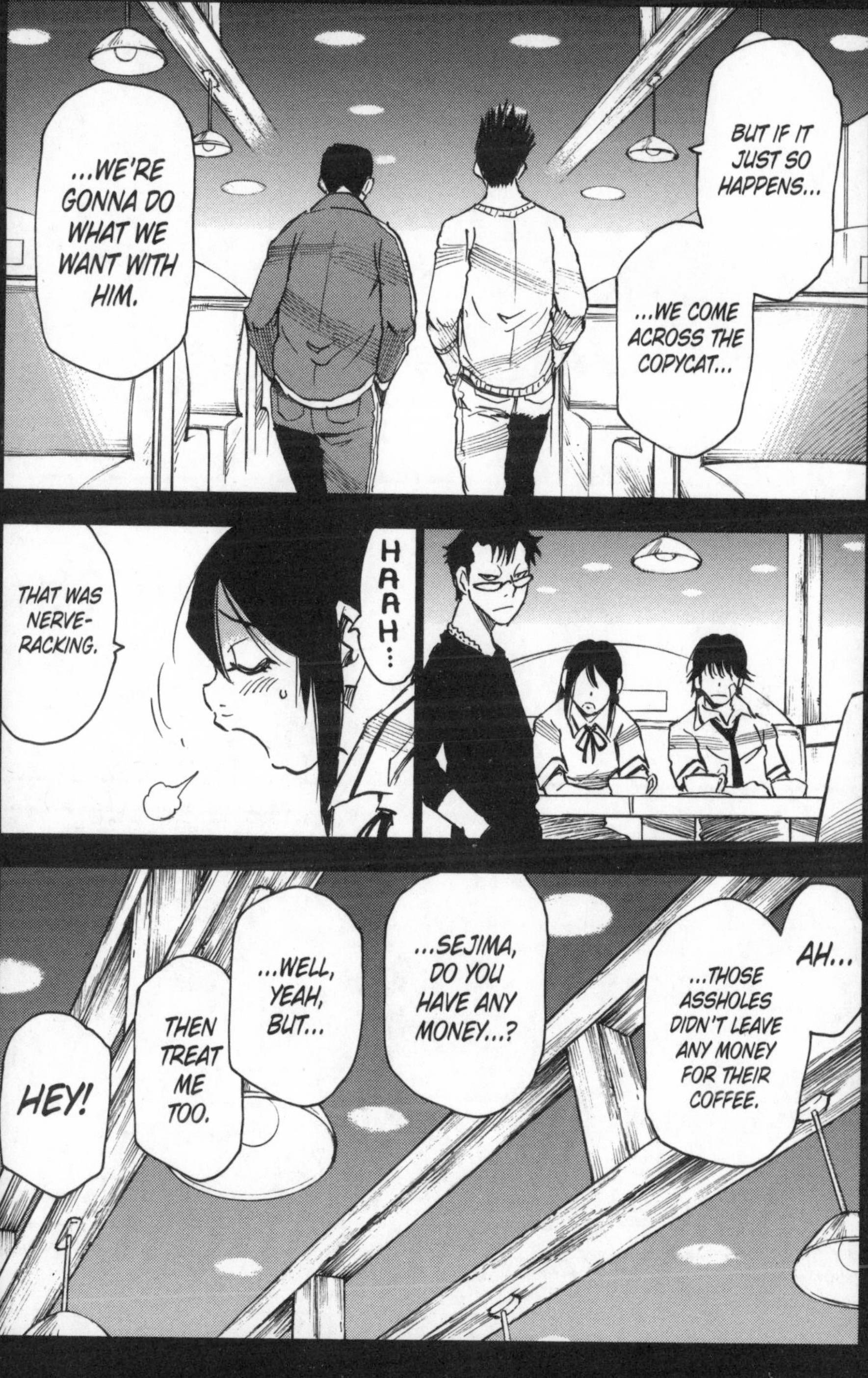
BUT IF IT JUST SO HAPPENS...
...WE COME ACROSS THE COPYCAT...
...WE'RE GONNA DO WHAT WE WANT WITH HIM.
HAAH...
THAT WAS NERVE-RACKING.
AH...
...THOSE ASSHOLES DIDN'T LEAVE ANY MONEY FOR THEIR COFFEE.
...SEJIMA, DO YOU HAVE ANY MONEY...?
...WELL, YEAH, BUT...
THEN TREAT ME TOO.
HEY!

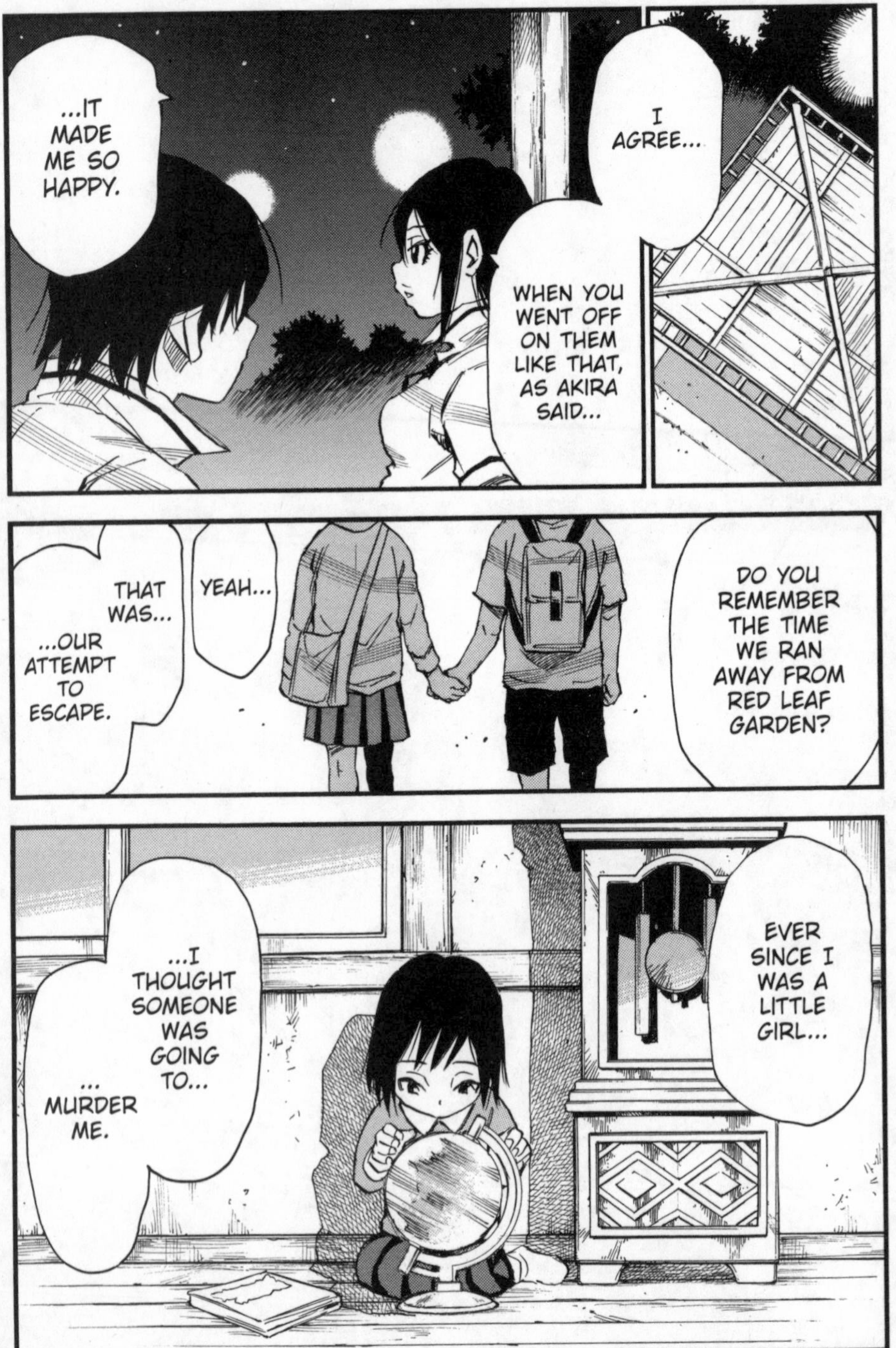
I AGREE...
WHEN YOU WENT OFF ON THEM LIKE THAT, AS AKIRA SAID...
...IT MADE ME SO HAPPY.
DO YOU REMEMBER THE TIME WE RAN AWAY FROM RED LEAF GARDEN?
YEAH...
THAT WAS...
...OUR ATTEMPT TO ESCAPE.
EVER SINCE I WAS A LITTLE GIRL...
...I THOUGHT SOMEONE WAS GOING TO...
... MURDER ME.

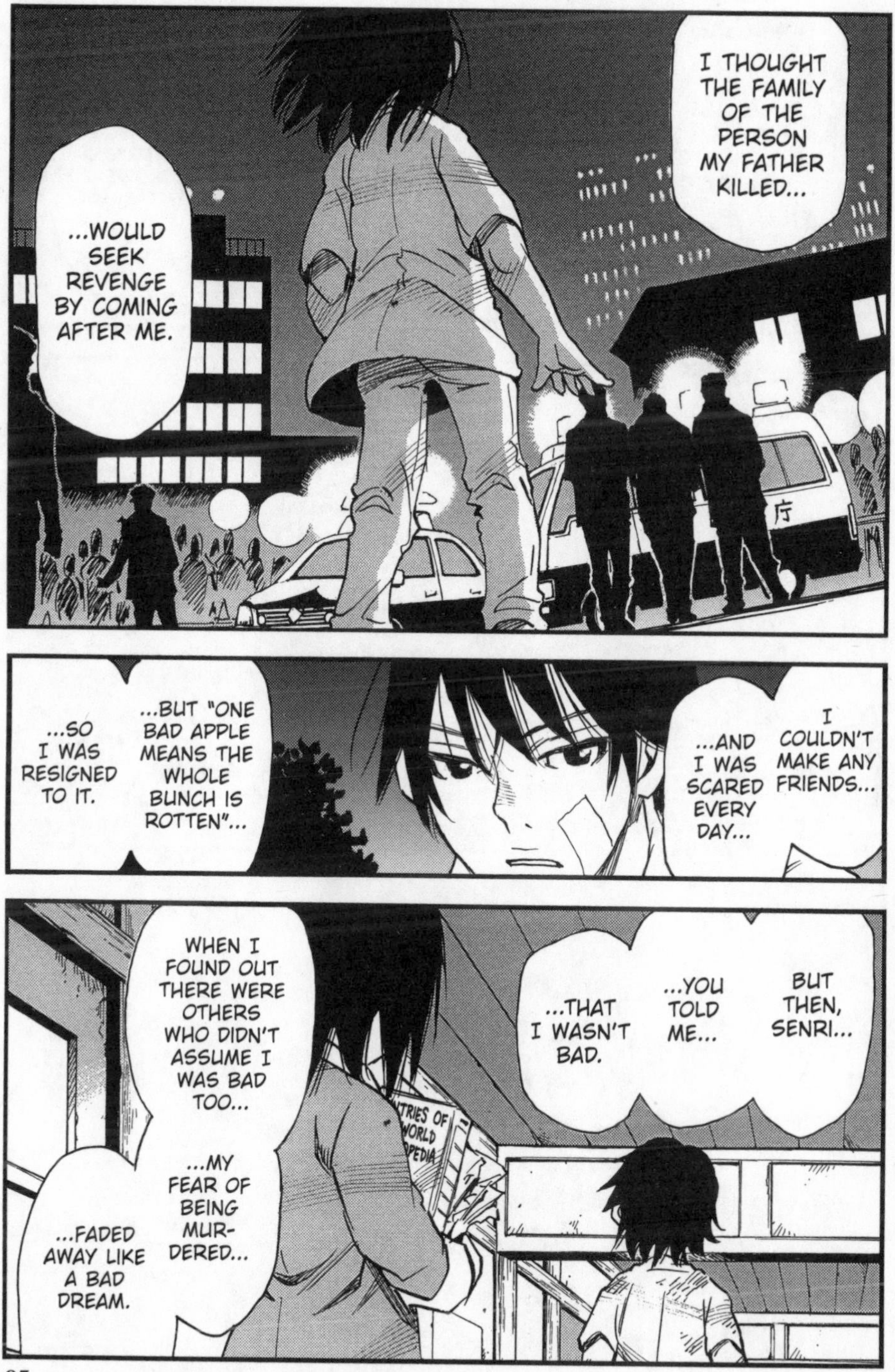
I THOUGHT THE FAMILY OF THE PERSON MY FATHER KILLED...
...WOULD SEEK REVENGE BY COMING AFTER ME.
I COULDN'T MAKE ANY FRIENDS...
...AND I WAS SCARED EVERY DAY...
...BUT "ONE BAD APPLE MEANS THE WHOLE BUNCH IS ROTTEN"...
...SO I WAS RESIGNED TO IT.
BUT THEN, SENRI...
...YOU TOLD ME...
...THAT I WASN'T BAD.
WHEN I FOUND OUT THERE WERE OTHERS WHO DIDN'T ASSUME I WAS BAD TOO...
...MY FEAR OF BEING MUR-DERED...
...FADED AWAY LIKE A BAD DREAM.

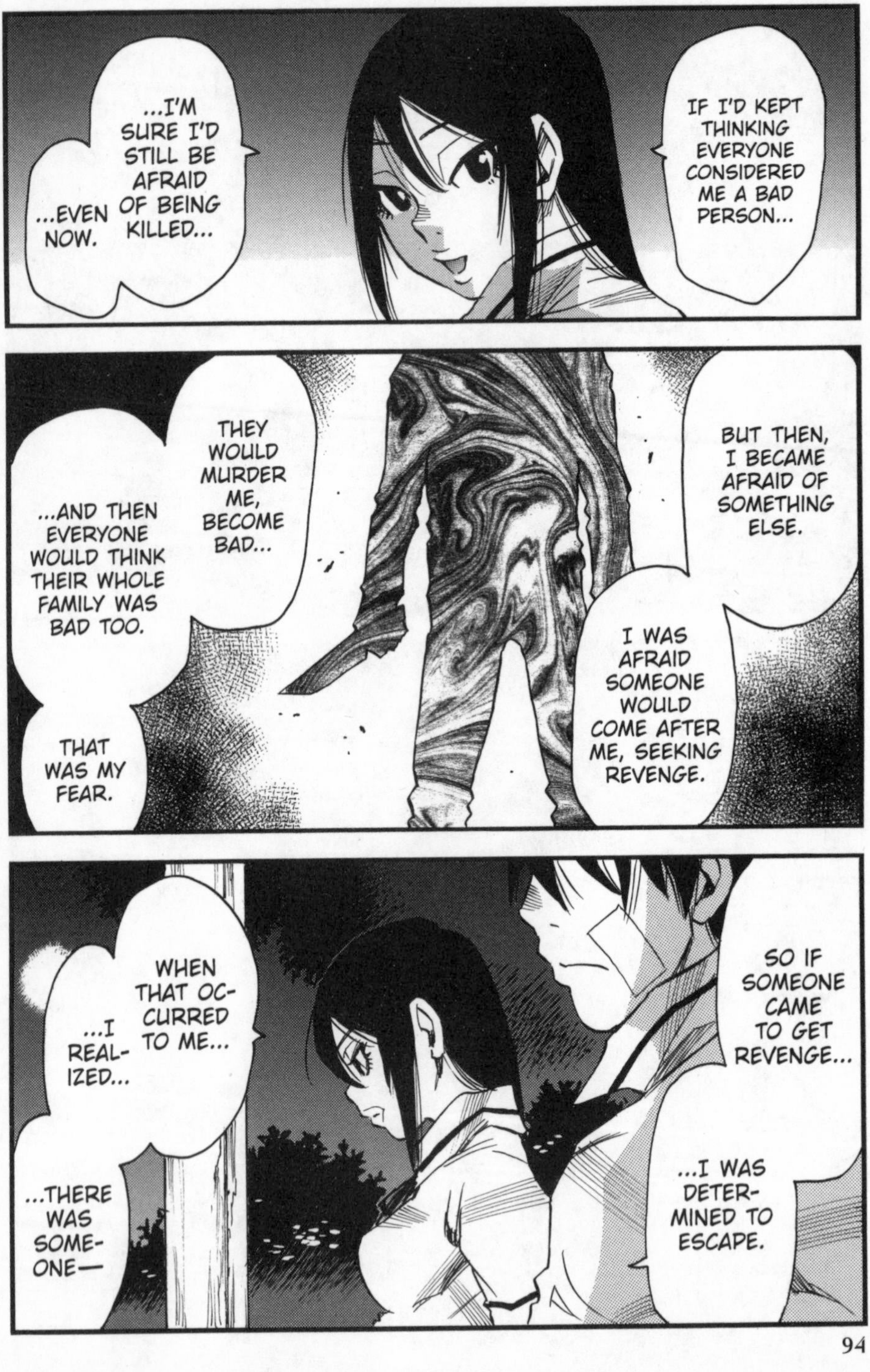
IF I'D KEPT THINKING EVERYONE CONSIDERED ME A BAD PERSON...
...I'M SURE I'D STILL BE AFRAID OF BEING KILLED...
...EVEN NOW.
BUT THEN, I BECAME AFRAID OF SOMETHING ELSE.
I WAS AFRAID SOMEONE WOULD COME AFTER ME, SEEKING REVENGE.
THEY WOULD MURDER ME, BECOME BAD...
...AND THEN EVERYONE WOULD THINK THEIR WHOLE FAMILY WAS BAD TOO.
THAT WAS MY FEAR.
SO IF SOMEONE CAME TO GET REVENGE...
...I WAS DETER-MINED TO ESCAPE.
WHEN THAT OC-CURRED TO ME...
...I REAL-IZED...
...THERE WAS SOME-ONE—

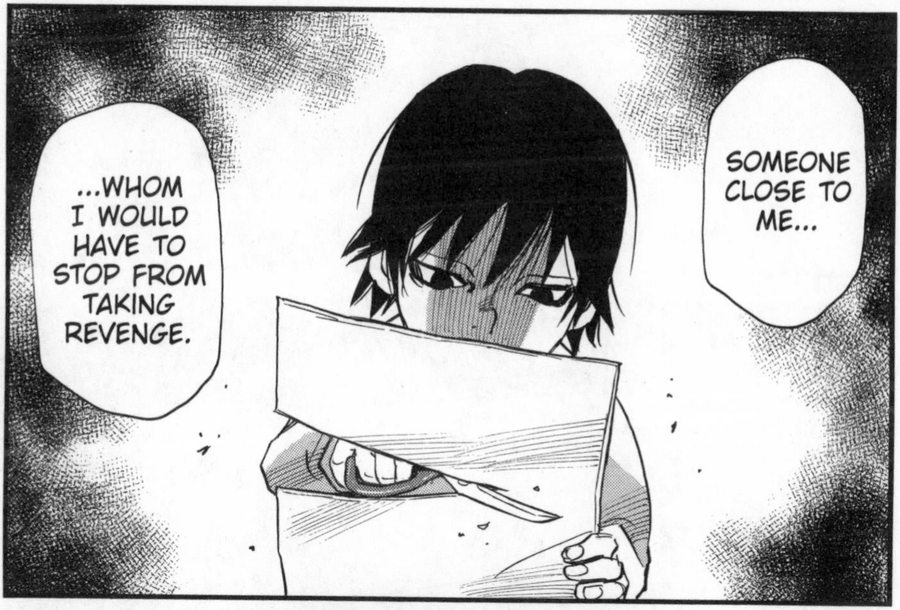
SOMEONE CLOSE TO ME...
...WHOM I WOULD HAVE TO STOP FROM TAKING REVENGE.

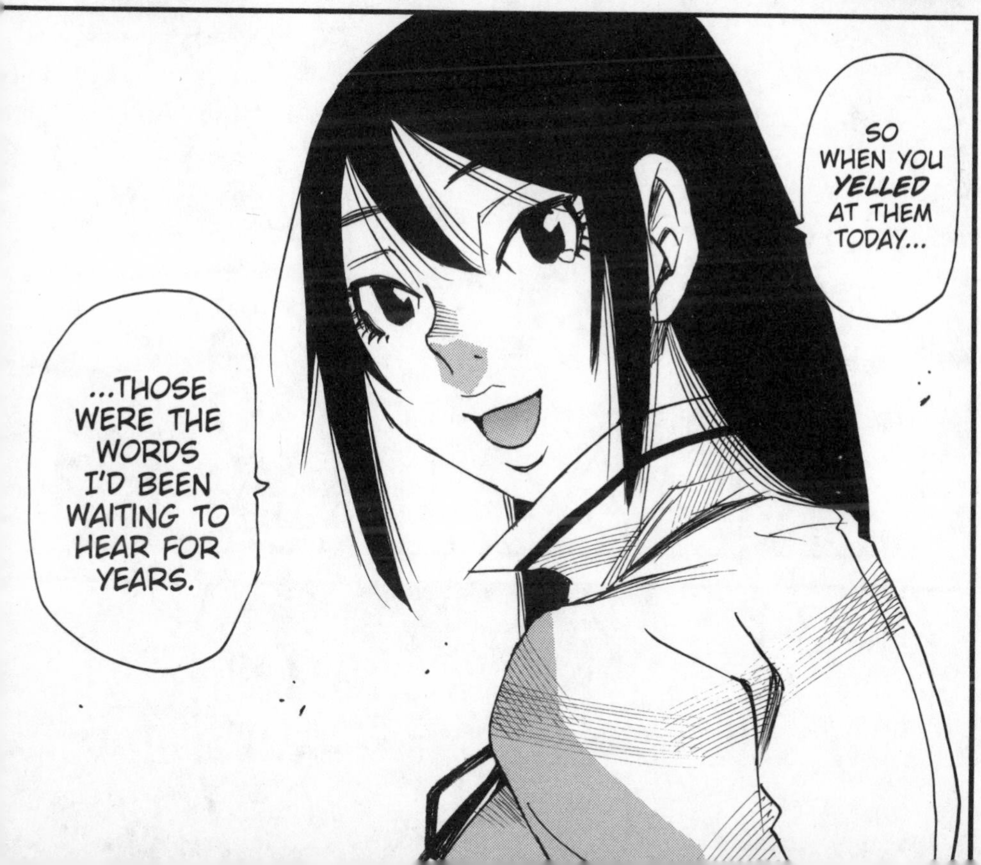
SO WHEN YOU *YELLED* AT THEM TODAY...
...THOSE WERE THE WORDS I'D BEEN WAITING TO HEAR FOR YEARS.

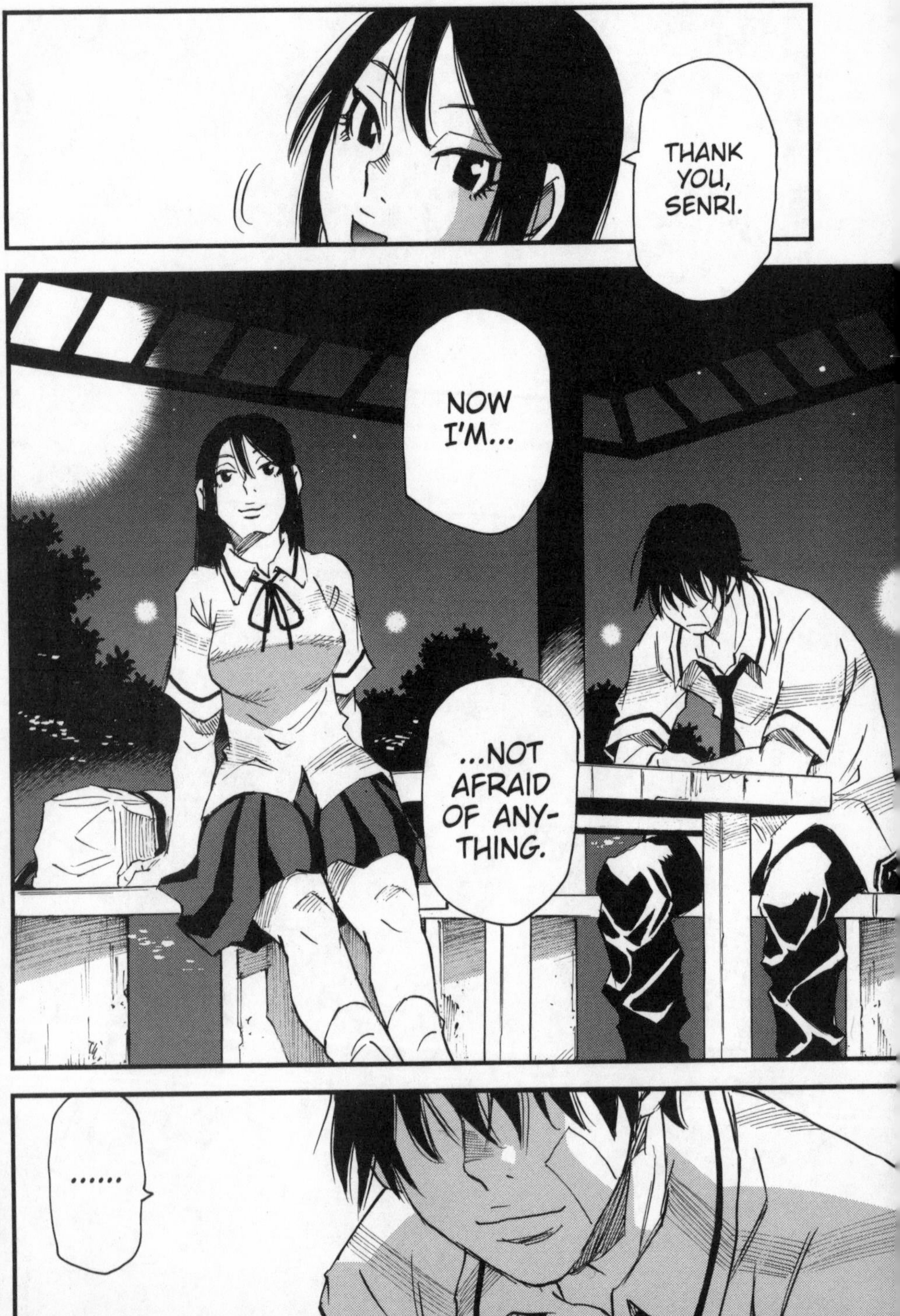
THANK YOU, SENRI.
NOW I'M...
...NOT AFRAID OF ANY-THING.
......

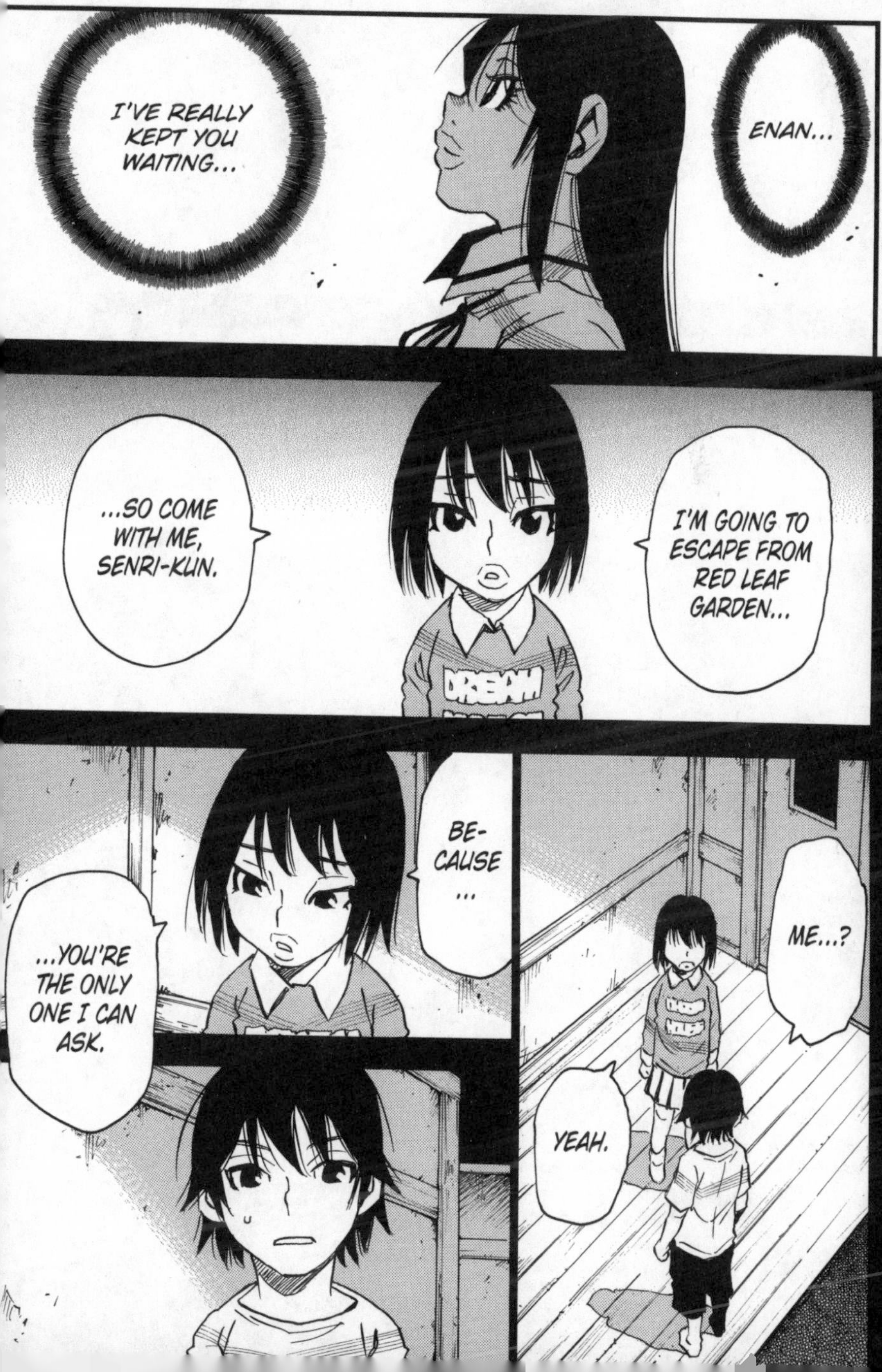
ENAN...
I'VE REALLY KEPT YOU WAITING...
I'M GOING TO ESCAPE FROM RED LEAF GARDEN...
...SO COME WITH ME, SENRI-KUN.
ME...?
YEAH.
BE-CAUSE ...
...YOU'RE THE ONLY ONE I CAN ASK.

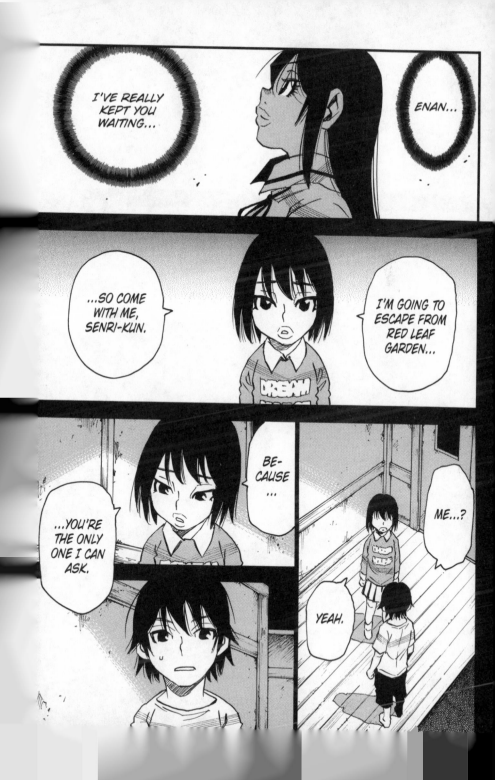

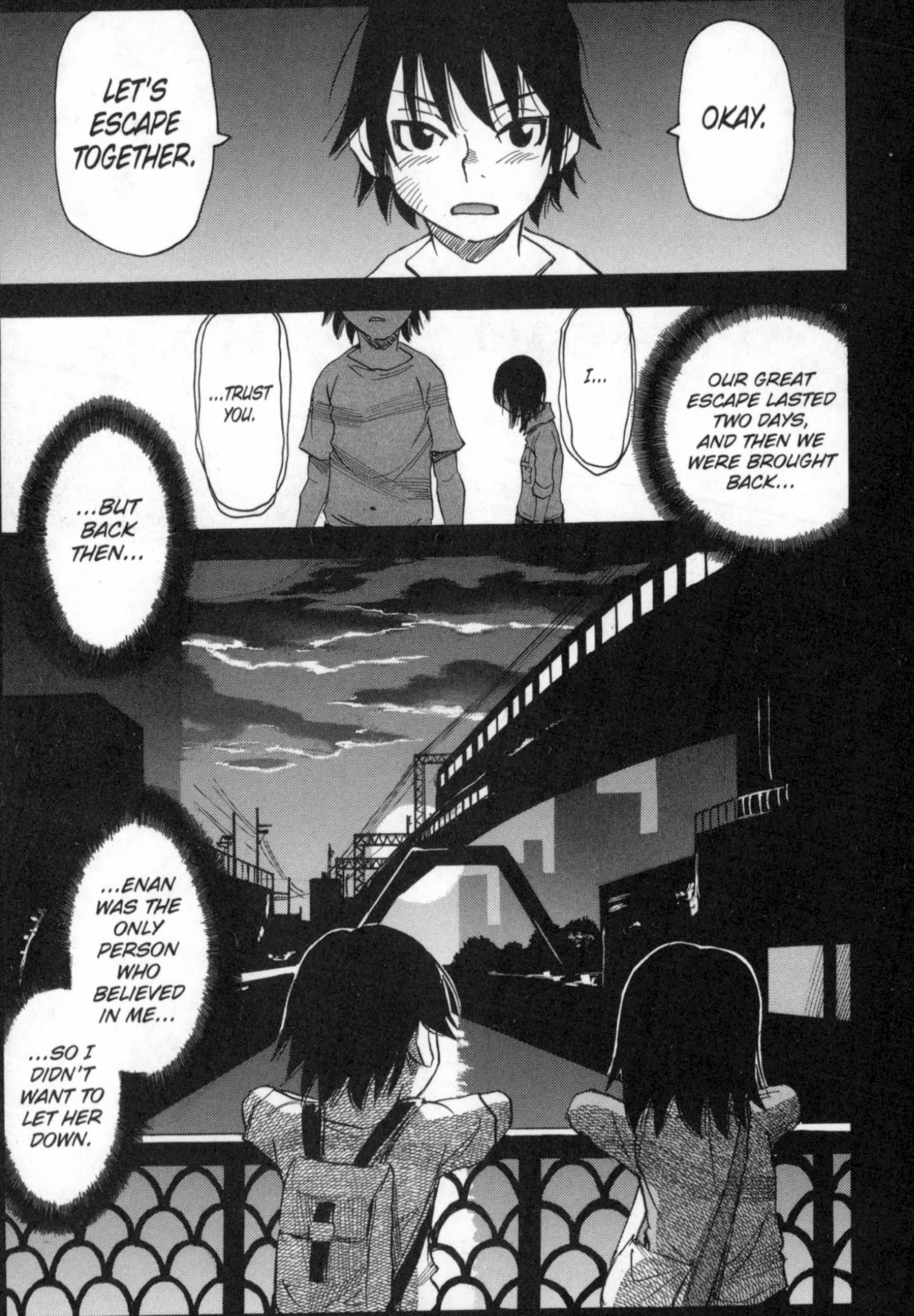
OKAY.
LET'S ESCAPE TOGETHER.
OUR GREAT ESCAPE LASTED TWO DAYS, AND THEN WE WERE BROUGHT BACK...
I...
...TRUST YOU.
...BUT BACK THEN...
...ENAN WAS THE ONLY PERSON WHO BELIEVED IN ME...
...SO I DIDN'T WANT TO LET HER DOWN.

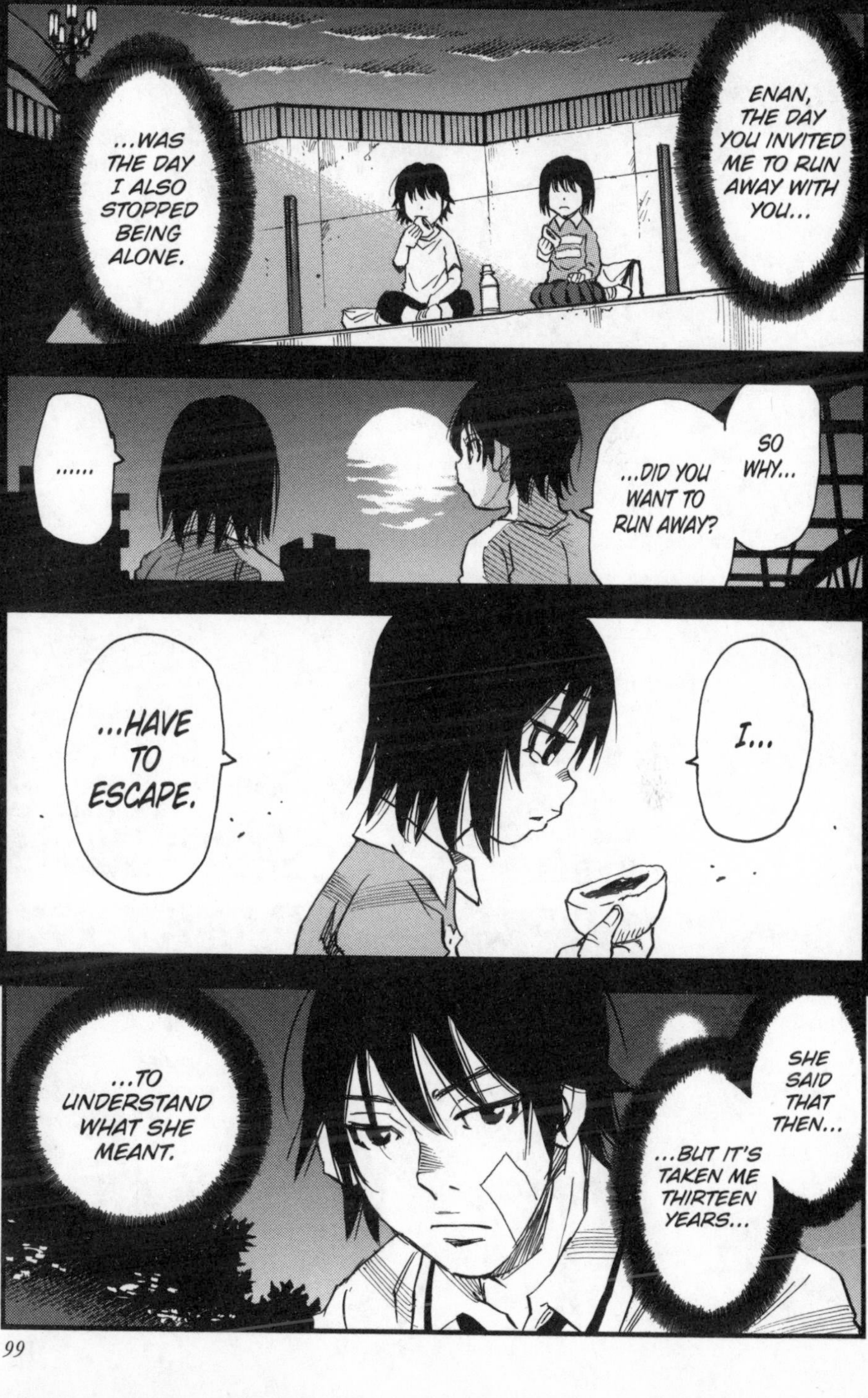
ENAN, THE DAY YOU INVITED ME TO RUN AWAY WITH YOU...
...WAS THE DAY I ALSO STOPPED BEING ALONE.
SO WHY...
...DID YOU WANT TO RUN AWAY?
......
I...
...HAVE TO ESCAPE.
SHE SAID THAT THEN...
...BUT IT'S TAKEN ME THIRTEEN YEARS...
...TO UNDERSTAND WHAT SHE MEANT.

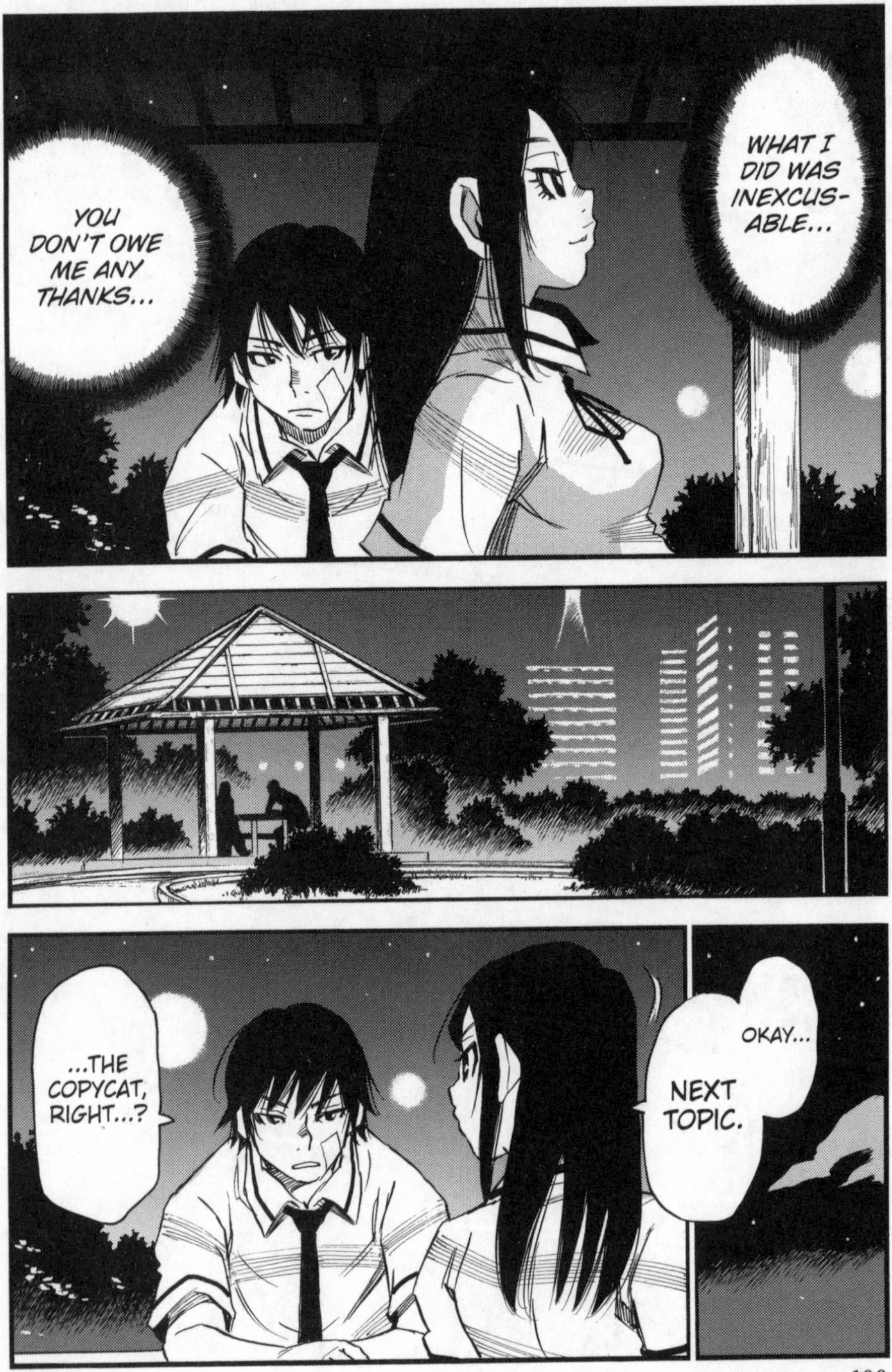
WHAT I DID WAS INEXCUSABLE...
YOU DON'T OWE ME ANY THANKS...
OKAY... NEXT TOPIC.
...THE COPYCAT, RIGHT...?

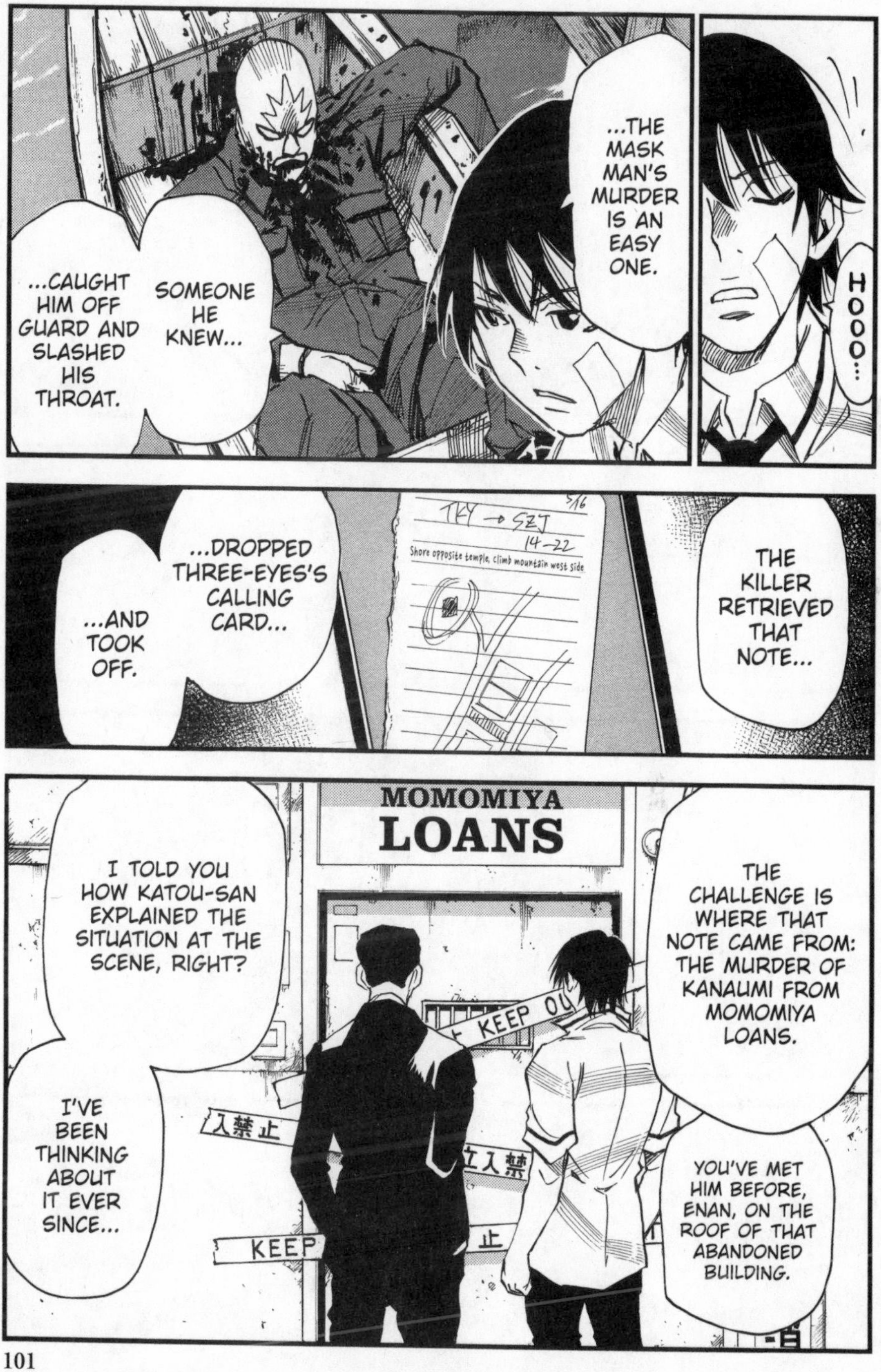
HOOO...
...THE MASK MAN'S MURDER IS AN EASY ONE.
SOMEONE HE KNEW...
...CAUGHT HIM OFF GUARD AND SLASHED HIS THROAT.
THE KILLER RETRIEVED THAT NOTE...
TKY → SZJ 5/16 14-22
Shore opposite temple, climb mountain west side
...DROPPED THREE-EYES'S CALLING CARD...
...AND TOOK OFF.
MOMOMIYA LOANS
THE CHALLENGE IS WHERE THAT NOTE CAME FROM: THE MURDER OF KANAUMI FROM MOMOMIYA LOANS.
YOU'VE MET HIM BEFORE, ENAN, ON THE ROOF OF THAT ABANDONED BUILDING.
I TOLD YOU HOW KATOU-SAN EXPLAINED THE SITUATION AT THE SCENE, RIGHT?
I'VE BEEN THINKING ABOUT IT EVER SINCE...
KEEP OU
入禁止
立入禁
KEEP
止

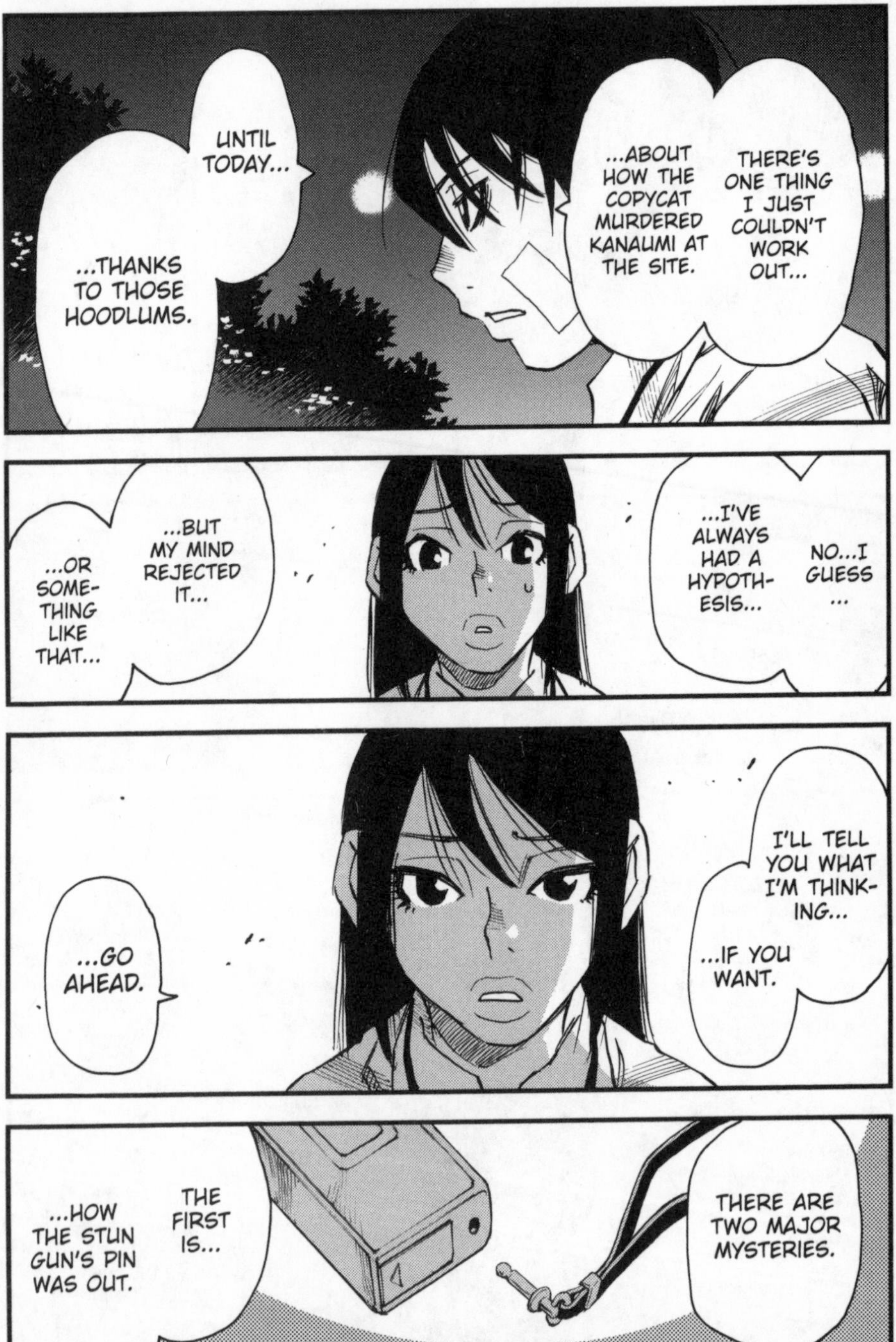
THERE'S ONE THING I JUST COULDN'T WORK OUT...
...ABOUT HOW THE COPYCAT MURDERED KANAUMI AT THE SITE.
UNTIL TODAY...
...THANKS TO THOSE HOODLUMS.
NO...I GUESS ...
...I'VE ALWAYS HAD A HYPOTH-ESIS...
...BUT MY MIND REJECTED IT...
...OR SOME-THING LIKE THAT...
I'LL TELL YOU WHAT I'M THINK-ING...
...IF YOU WANT.
...GO AHEAD.
THERE ARE TWO MAJOR MYSTERIES.
THE FIRST IS...
...HOW THE STUN GUN'S PIN WAS OUT.

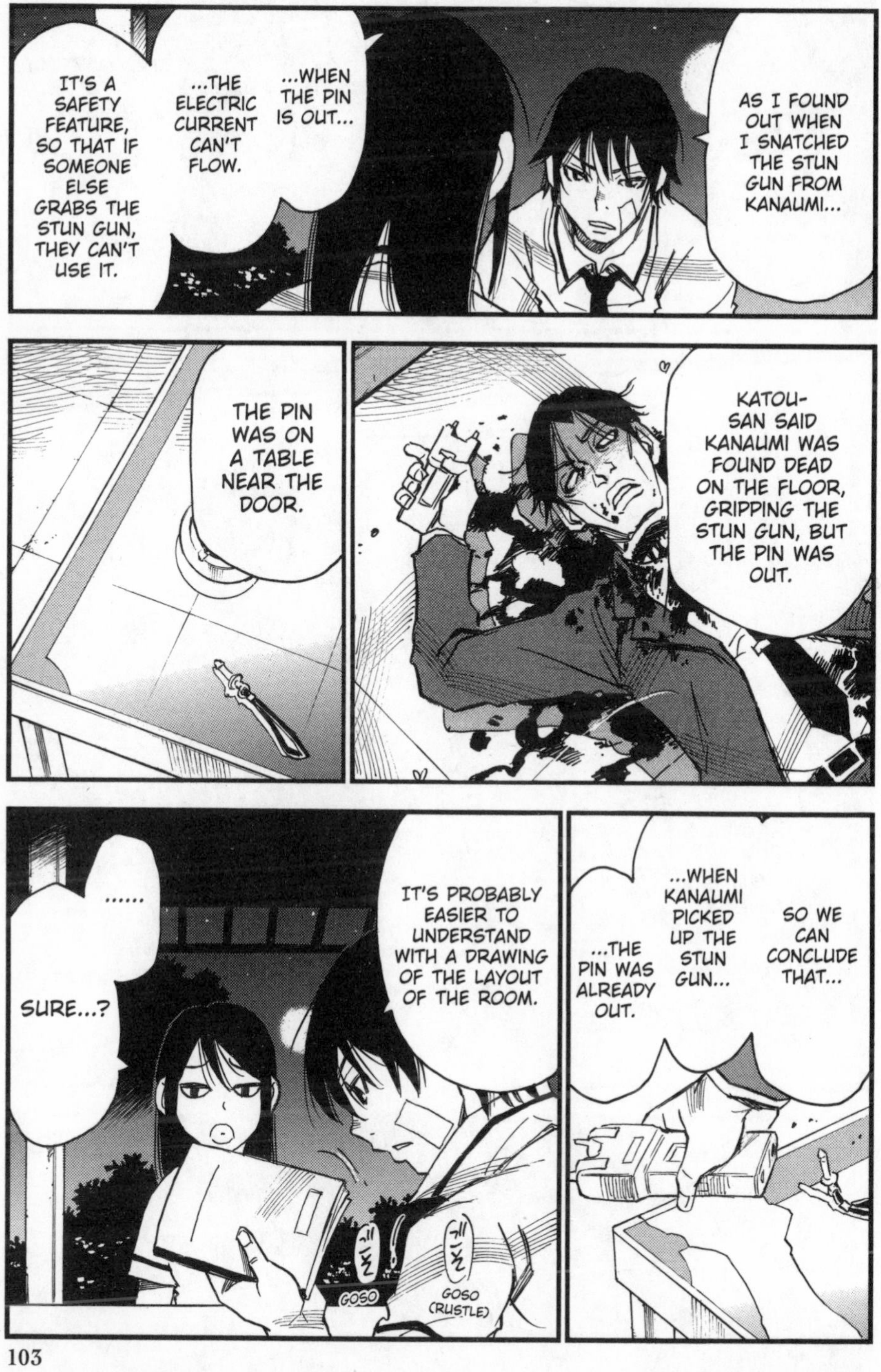
AS I FOUND OUT WHEN I SNATCHED THE STUN GUN FROM KANAUMI...
...WHEN THE PIN IS OUT...
...THE ELECTRIC CURRENT CAN'T FLOW.
IT'S A SAFETY FEATURE, SO THAT IF SOMEONE ELSE GRABS THE STUN GUN, THEY CAN'T USE IT.
KATOU-SAN SAID KANAUMI WAS FOUND DEAD ON THE FLOOR, GRIPPING THE STUN GUN, BUT THE PIN WAS OUT.
THE PIN WAS ON A TABLE NEAR THE DOOR.
SO WE CAN CONCLUDE THAT...
...WHEN KANAUMI PICKED UP THE STUN GUN...
...THE PIN WAS ALREADY OUT.
IT'S PROBABLY EASIER TO UNDERSTAND WITH A DRAWING OF THE LAYOUT OF THE ROOM.
......
SURE...?
GOSO (RUSTLE)
GOSO

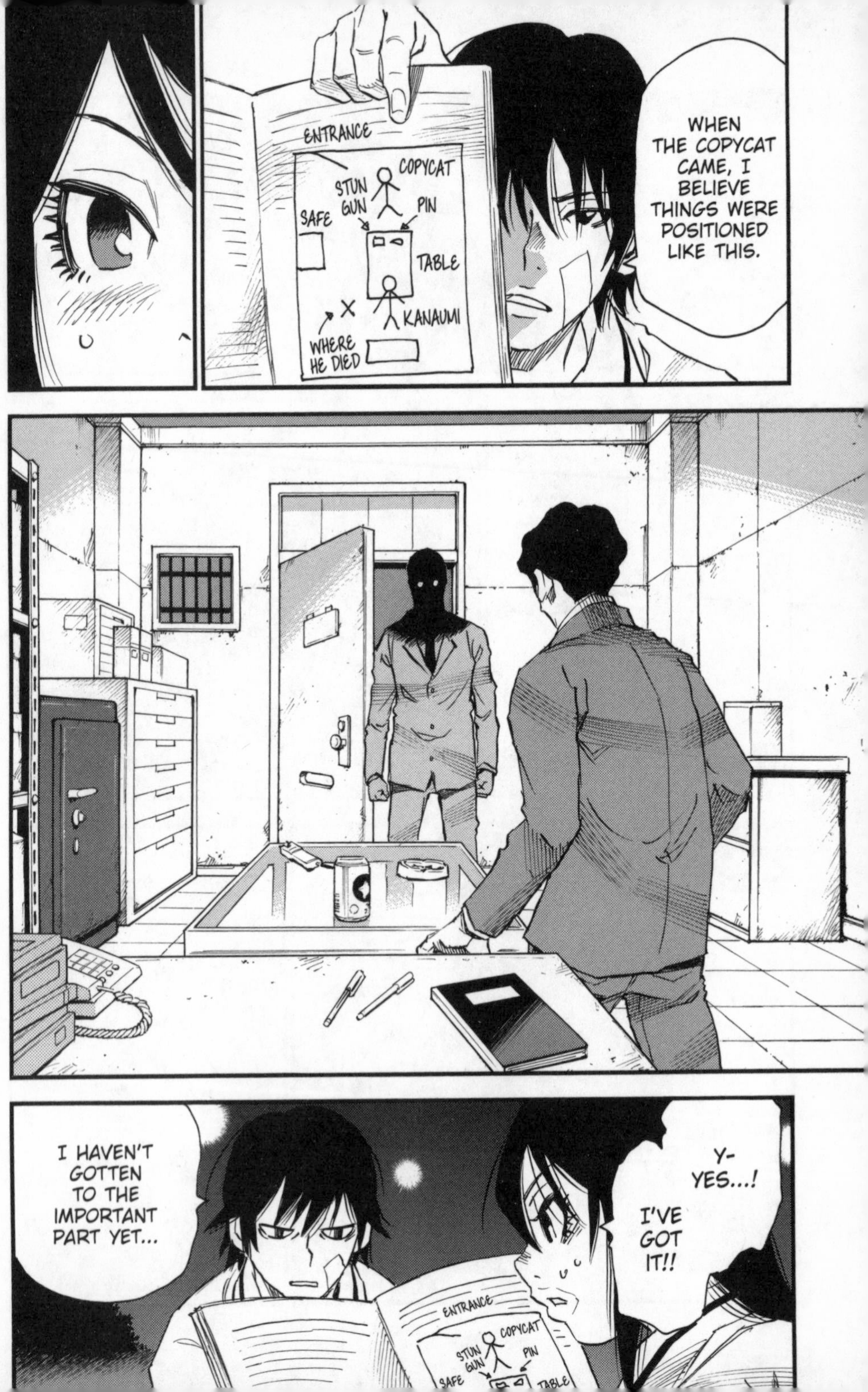
WHEN THE COPYCAT CAME, I BELIEVE THINGS WERE POSITIONED LIKE THIS.
ENTRANCE
COPYCAT
STUN GUN
PIN
SAFE
TABLE
KANAUMI
WHERE HE DIED
Y- YES...!
I'VE GOT IT!!
I HAVEN'T GOTTEN TO THE IMPORTANT PART YET...
ENTRANCE
COPYCAT
STUN GUN
PIN
SAFE
TABLE

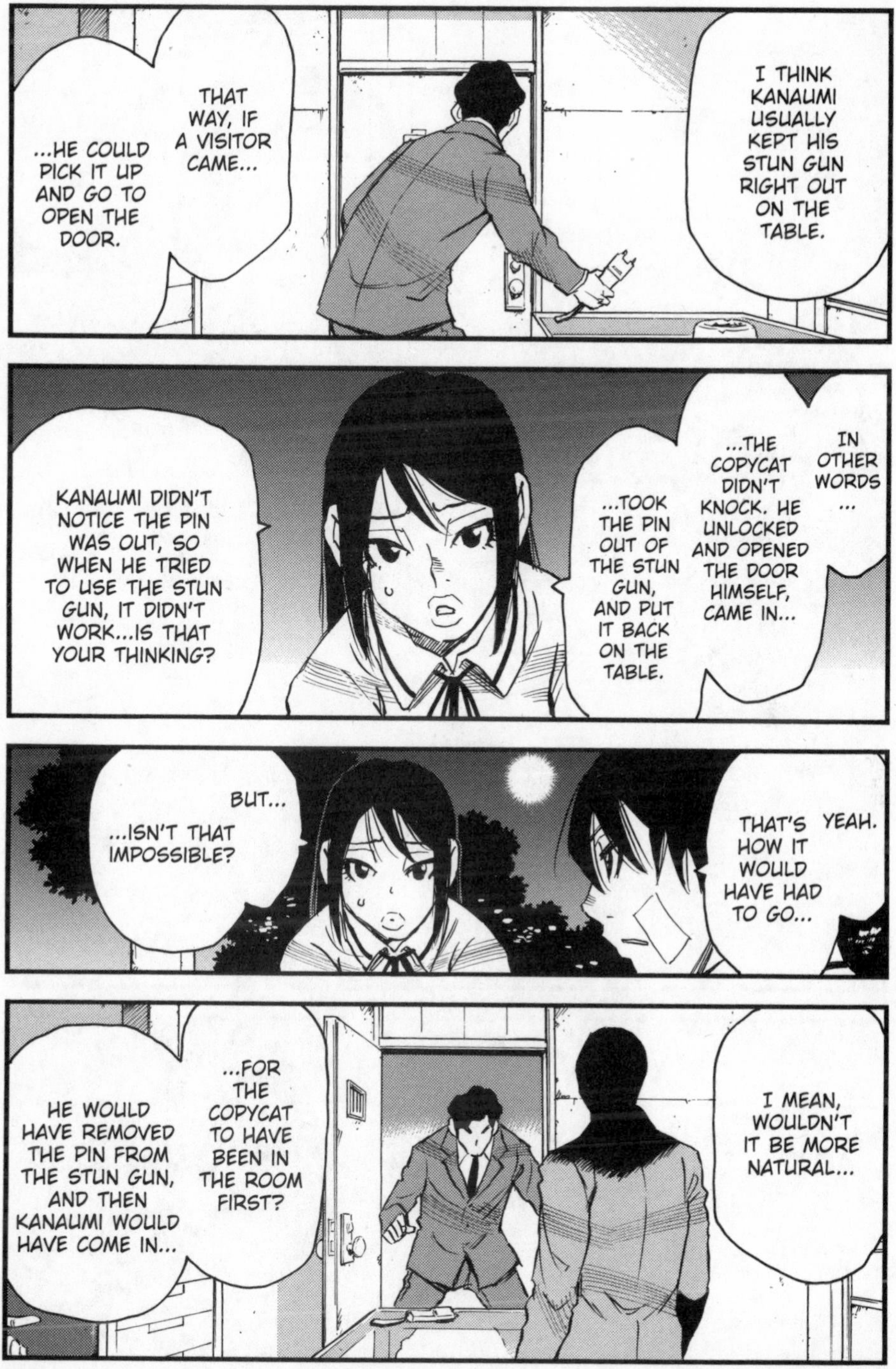
I THINK KANAUMI USUALLY KEPT HIS STUN GUN RIGHT OUT ON THE TABLE.
THAT WAY, IF A VISITOR CAME...
...HE COULD PICK IT UP AND GO TO OPEN THE DOOR.
IN OTHER WORDS...
...THE COPYCAT DIDN'T KNOCK. HE UNLOCKED AND OPENED THE DOOR HIMSELF, CAME IN...
...TOOK THE PIN OUT OF THE STUN GUN, AND PUT IT BACK ON THE TABLE.
KANAUMI DIDN'T NOTICE THE PIN WAS OUT, SO WHEN HE TRIED TO USE THE STUN GUN, IT DIDN'T WORK...IS THAT YOUR THINKING?
YEAH.
THAT'S HOW IT WOULD HAVE HAD TO GO...
BUT...
...ISN'T THAT IMPOSSIBLE?
I MEAN, WOULDN'T IT BE MORE NATURAL...
...FOR THE COPYCAT TO HAVE BEEN IN THE ROOM FIRST?
HE WOULD HAVE REMOVED THE PIN FROM THE STUN GUN, AND THEN KANAUMI WOULD HAVE COME IN...

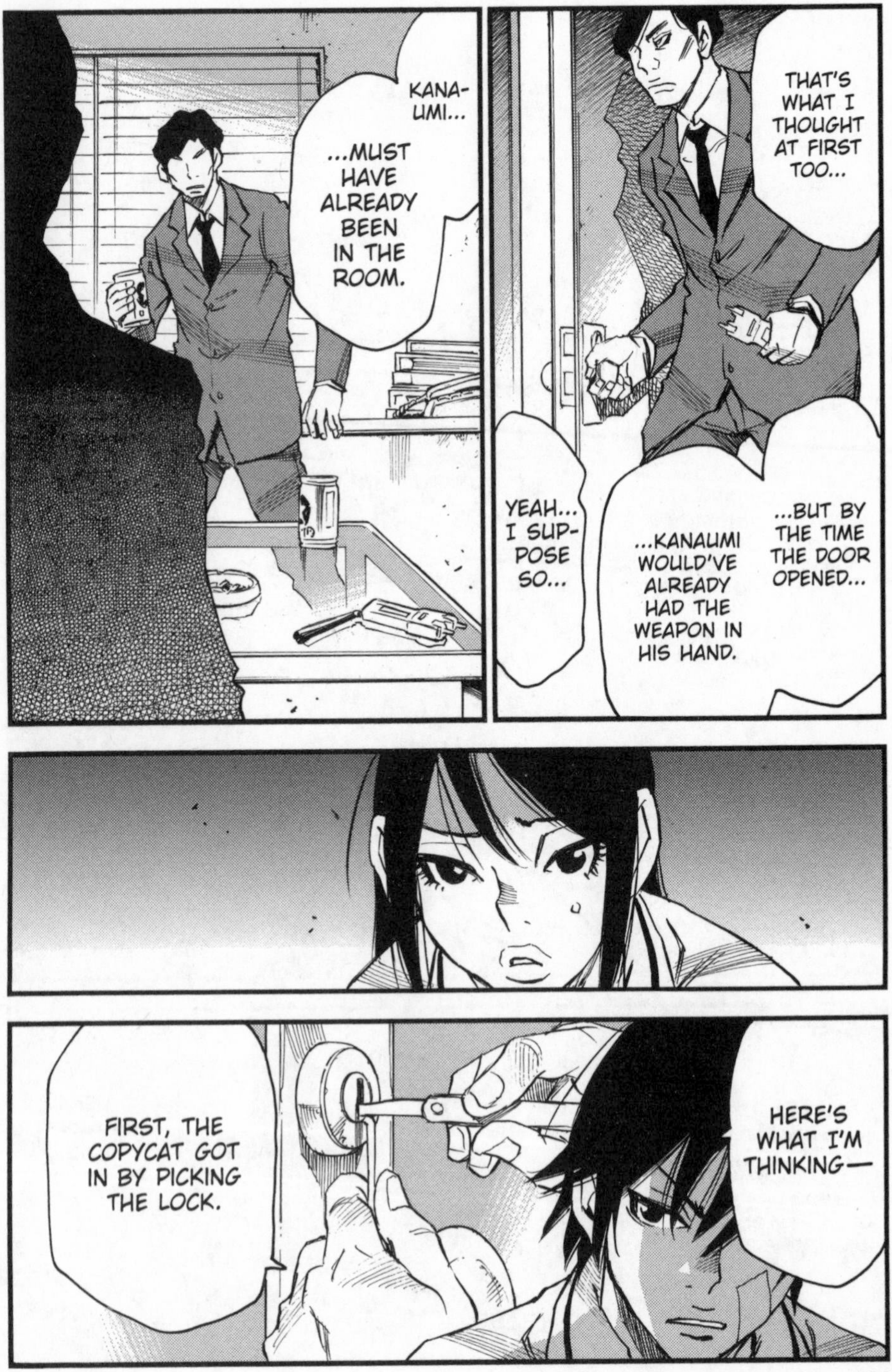
THAT'S WHAT I THOUGHT AT FIRST TOO...
...BUT BY THE TIME THE DOOR OPENED...
...KANAUMI WOULD'VE ALREADY HAD THE WEAPON IN HIS HAND.
YEAH... I SUP-POSE SO...
KANA-UMI...
...MUST HAVE ALREADY BEEN IN THE ROOM.
HERE'S WHAT I'M THINKING—
FIRST, THE COPYCAT GOT IN BY PICKING THE LOCK.

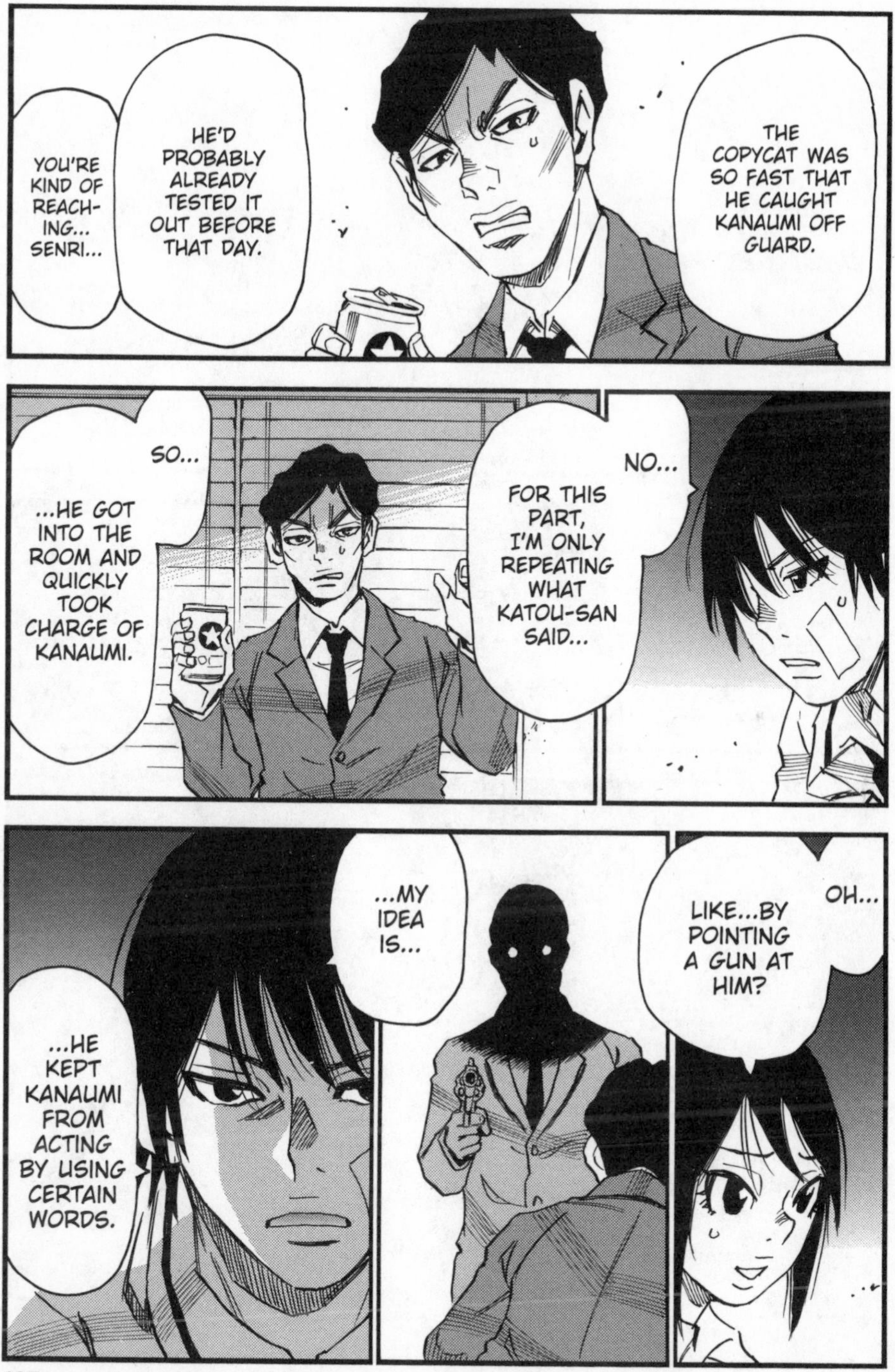
THE COPYCAT WAS SO FAST THAT HE CAUGHT KANAUMI OFF GUARD.
HE'D PROBABLY ALREADY TESTED IT OUT BEFORE THAT DAY.
YOU'RE KIND OF REACHING... SENRI...
NO...
FOR THIS PART, I'M ONLY REPEATING WHAT KATOU-SAN SAID...
SO...
...HE GOT INTO THE ROOM AND QUICKLY TOOK CHARGE OF KANAUMI.
OH...
LIKE...BY POINTING A GUN AT HIM?
...MY IDEA IS...
...HE KEPT KANAUMI FROM ACTING BY USING CERTAIN WORDS.

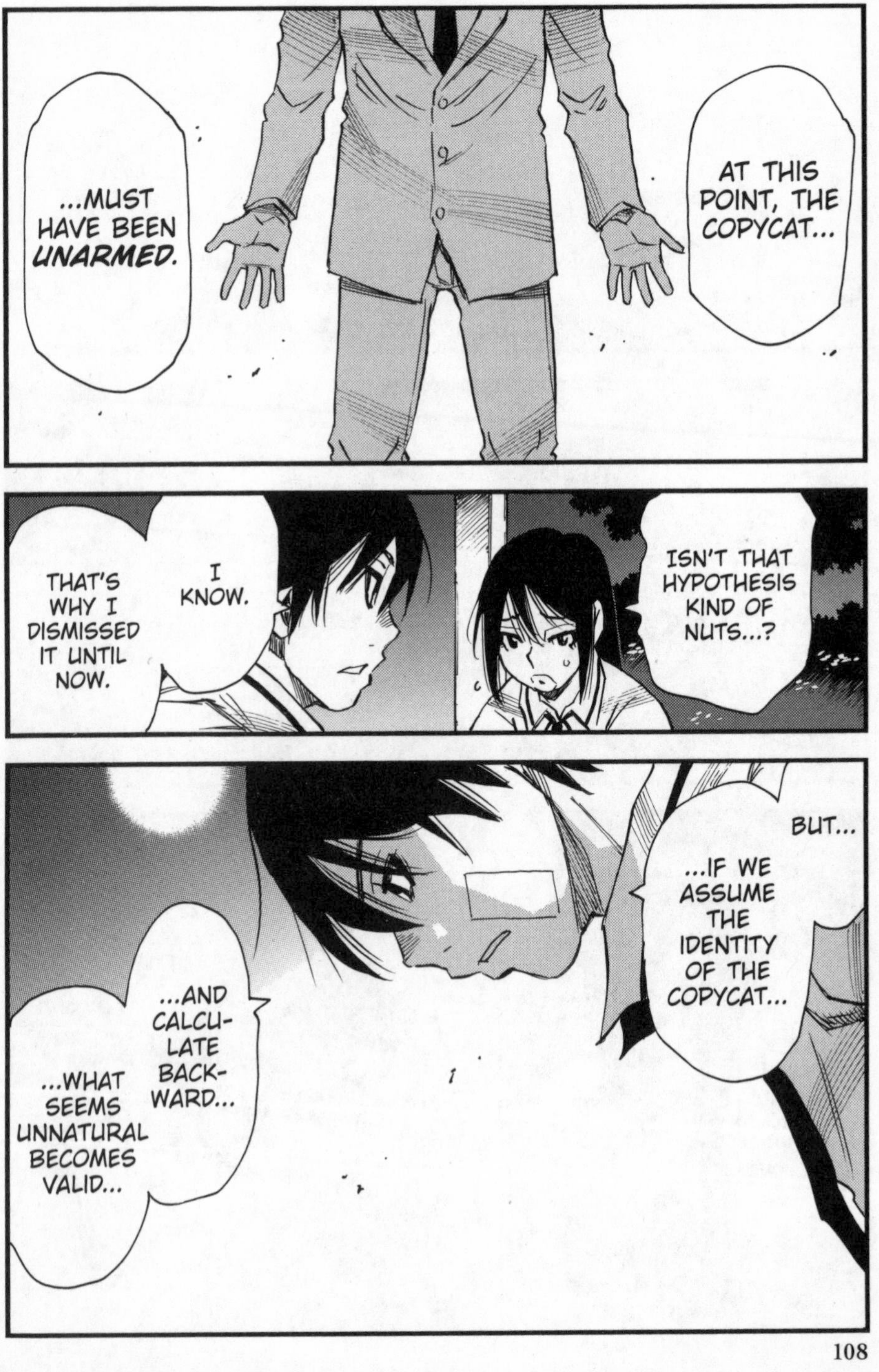
AT THIS POINT, THE COPYCAT...
...MUST HAVE BEEN *UNARMED.*
ISN'T THAT HYPOTHESIS KIND OF NUTS...?
I KNOW.
THAT'S WHY I DISMISSED IT UNTIL NOW.
BUT...
...IF WE ASSUME THE IDENTITY OF THE COPYCAT...
...AND CALCULATE BACKWARD...
...WHAT SEEMS UNNATURAL BECOMES VALID...

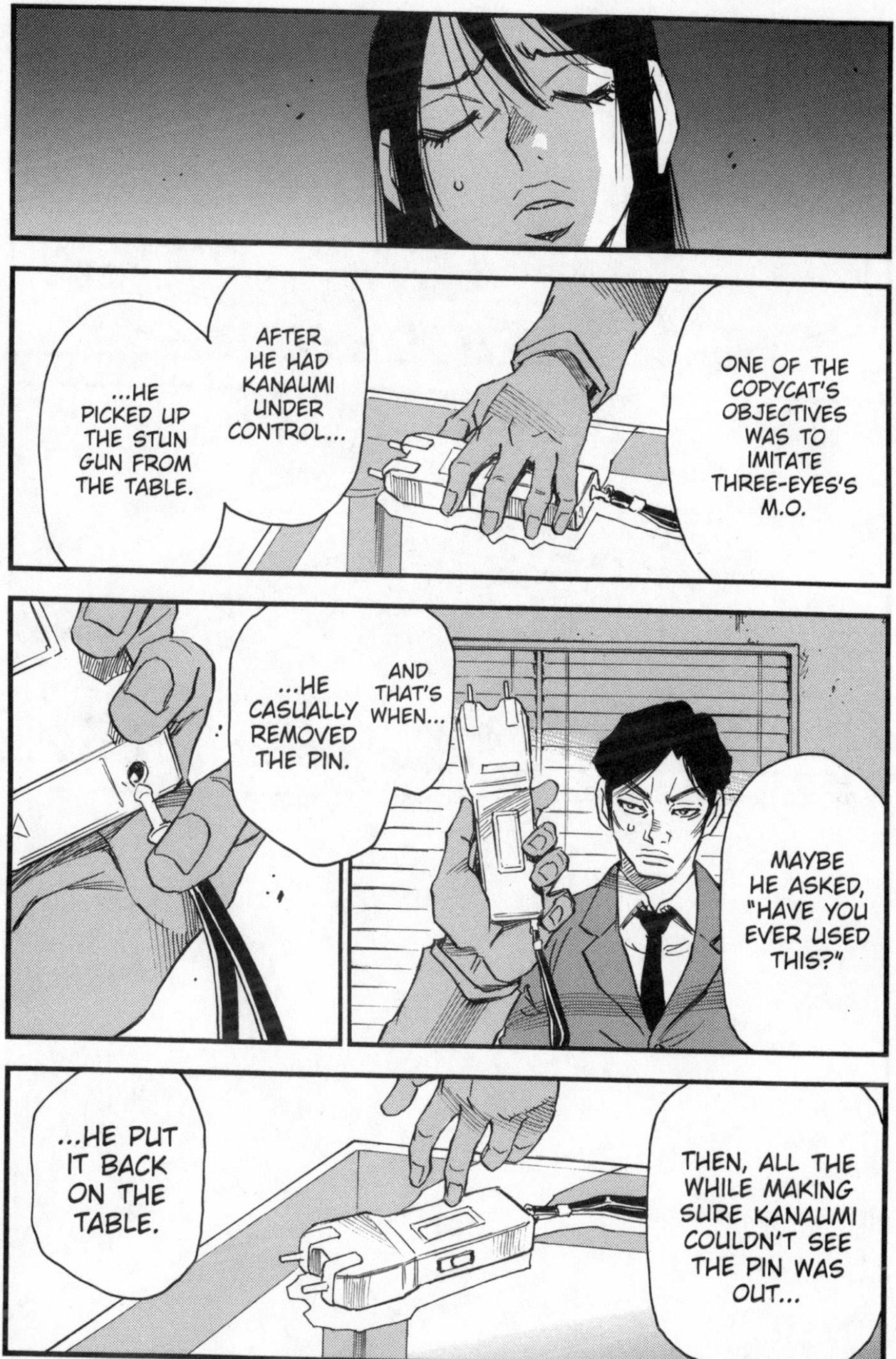
ONE OF THE COPYCAT'S OBJECTIVES WAS TO IMITATE THREE-EYES'S M.O.
AFTER HE HAD KANAUMI UNDER CONTROL...
...HE PICKED UP THE STUN GUN FROM THE TABLE.
MAYBE HE ASKED, "HAVE YOU EVER USED THIS?"
AND THAT'S WHEN...
...HE CASUALLY REMOVED THE PIN.
THEN, ALL THE WHILE MAKING SURE KANAUMI COULDN'T SEE THE PIN WAS OUT...
...HE PUT IT BACK ON THE TABLE.

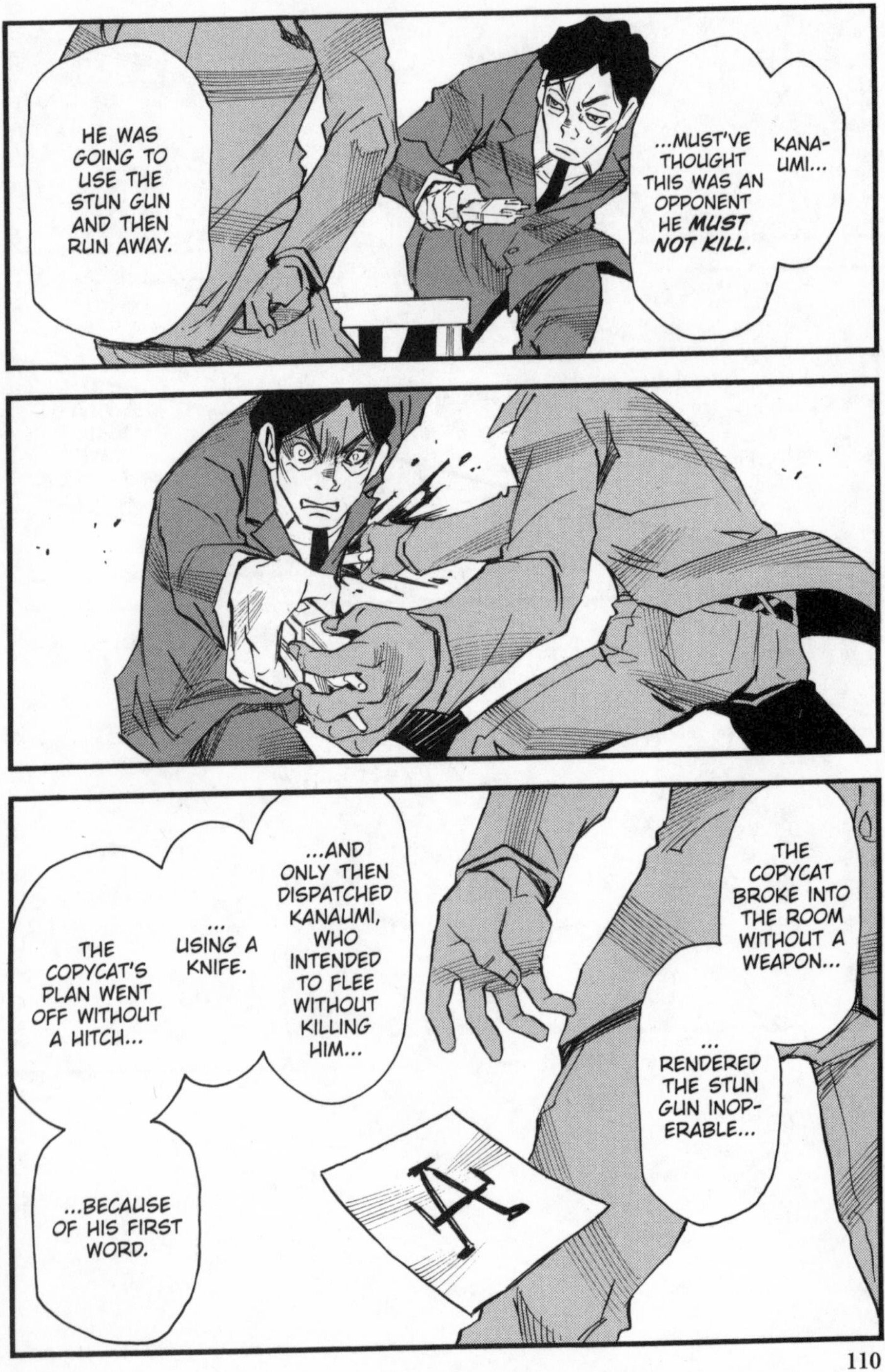
KANA-UMI...
...MUST'VE THOUGHT THIS WAS AN OPPONENT HE MUST NOT KILL.
HE WAS GOING TO USE THE STUN GUN AND THEN RUN AWAY.
THE COPYCAT BROKE INTO THE ROOM WITHOUT A WEAPON...
...RENDERED THE STUN GUN INOP-ERABLE...
...AND ONLY THEN DISPATCHED KANAUMI, WHO INTENDED TO FLEE WITHOUT KILLING HIM...
... USING A KNIFE.
THE COPYCAT'S PLAN WENT OFF WITHOUT A HITCH...
...BECAUSE OF HIS FIRST WORD.

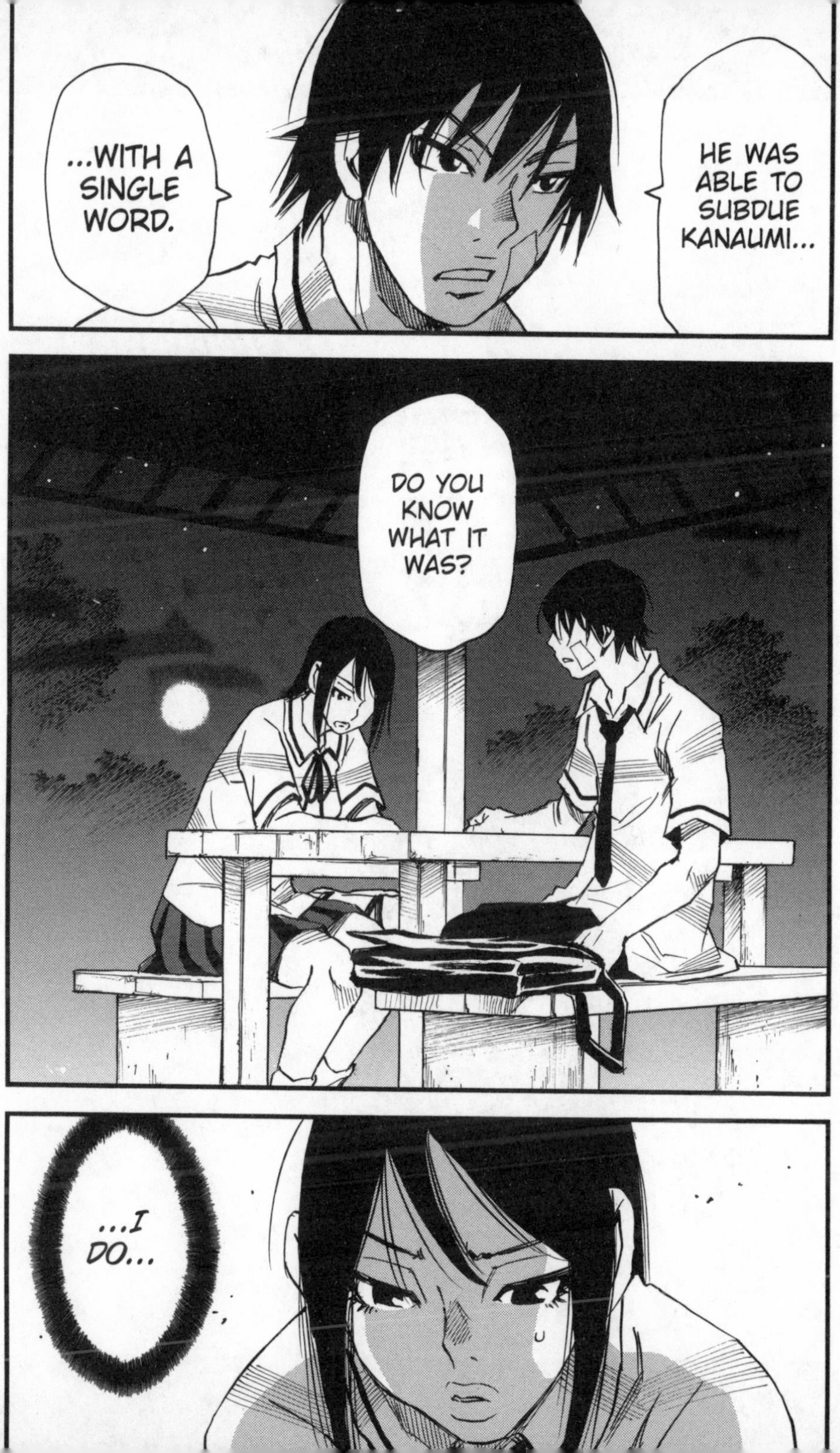
HE WAS ABLE TO SUBDUE KANAUMI...
...WITH A SINGLE WORD.
DO YOU KNOW WHAT IT WAS?
...I DO...

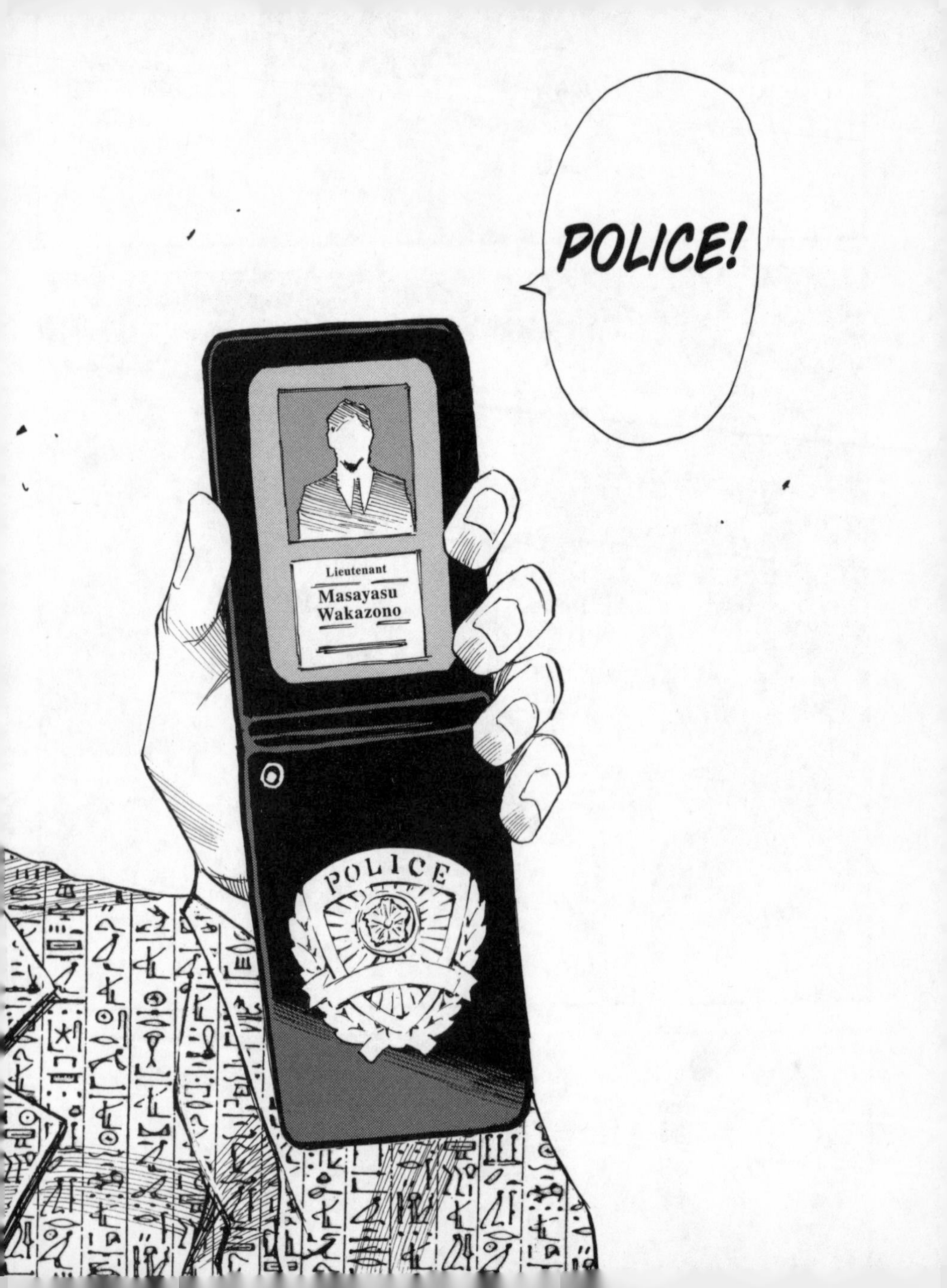
POLICE!
Lieutenant
Masayasu Wakazono
POLICE

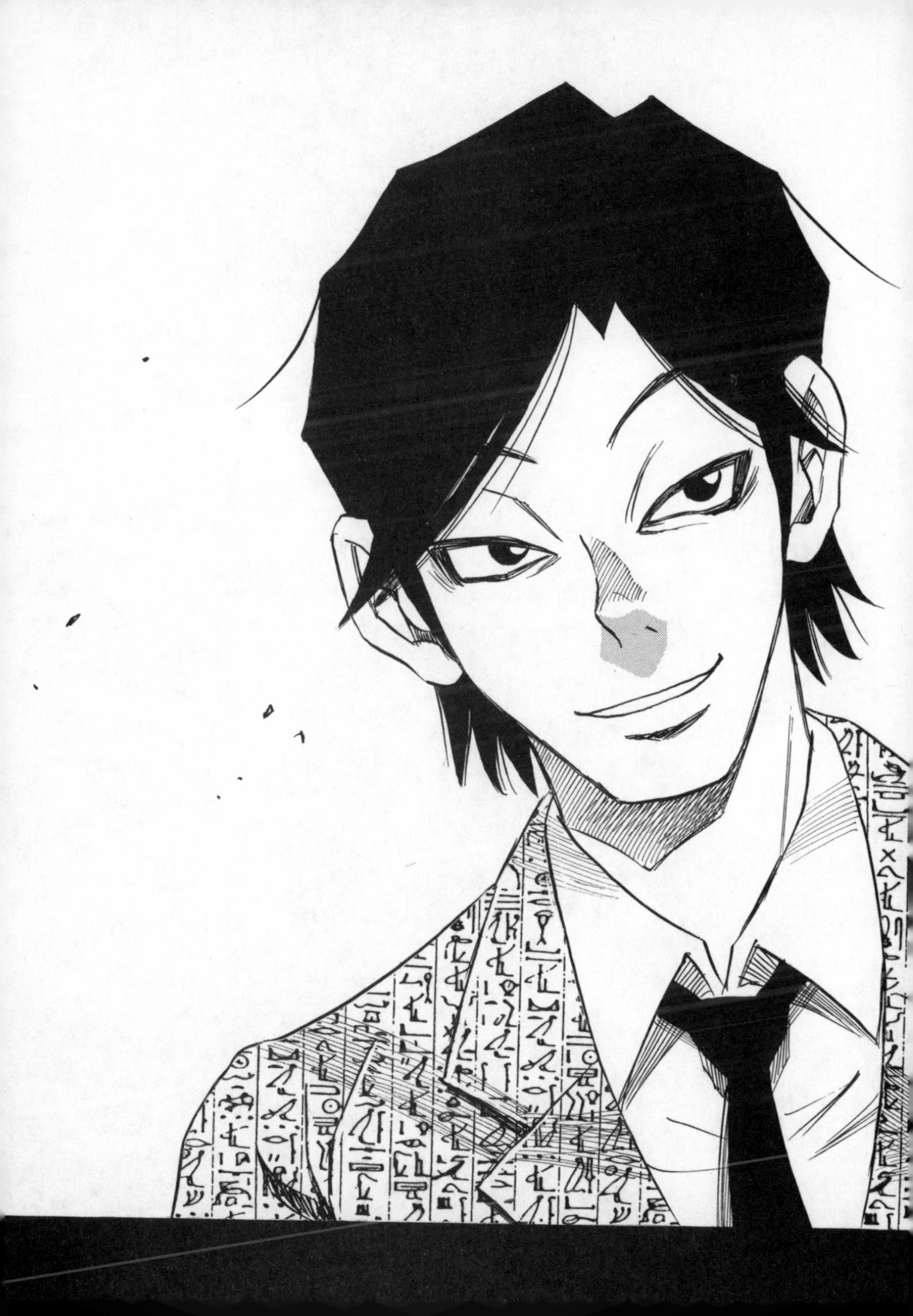

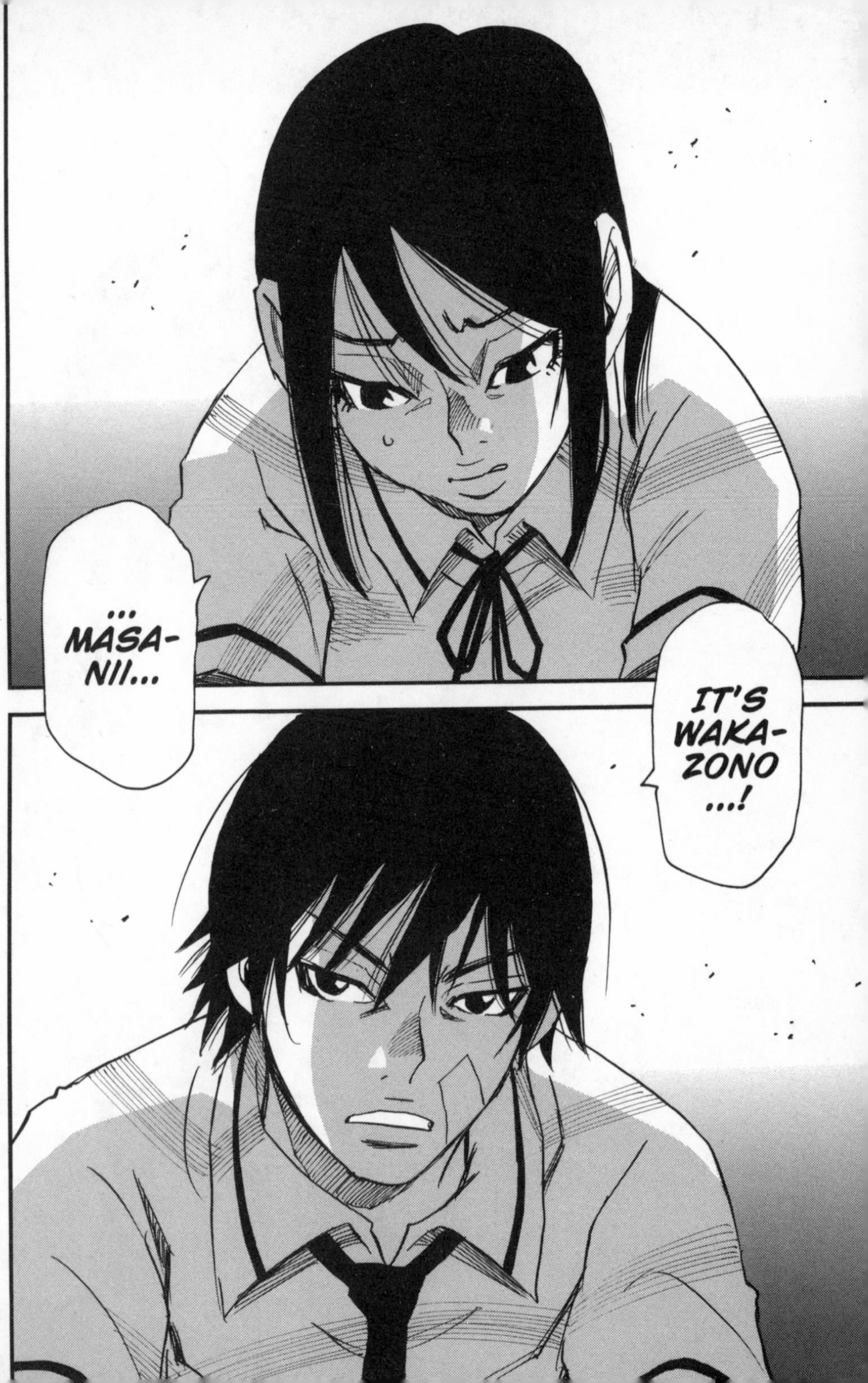
...MÄSA-NII...
IT'S WAKAZONO...!

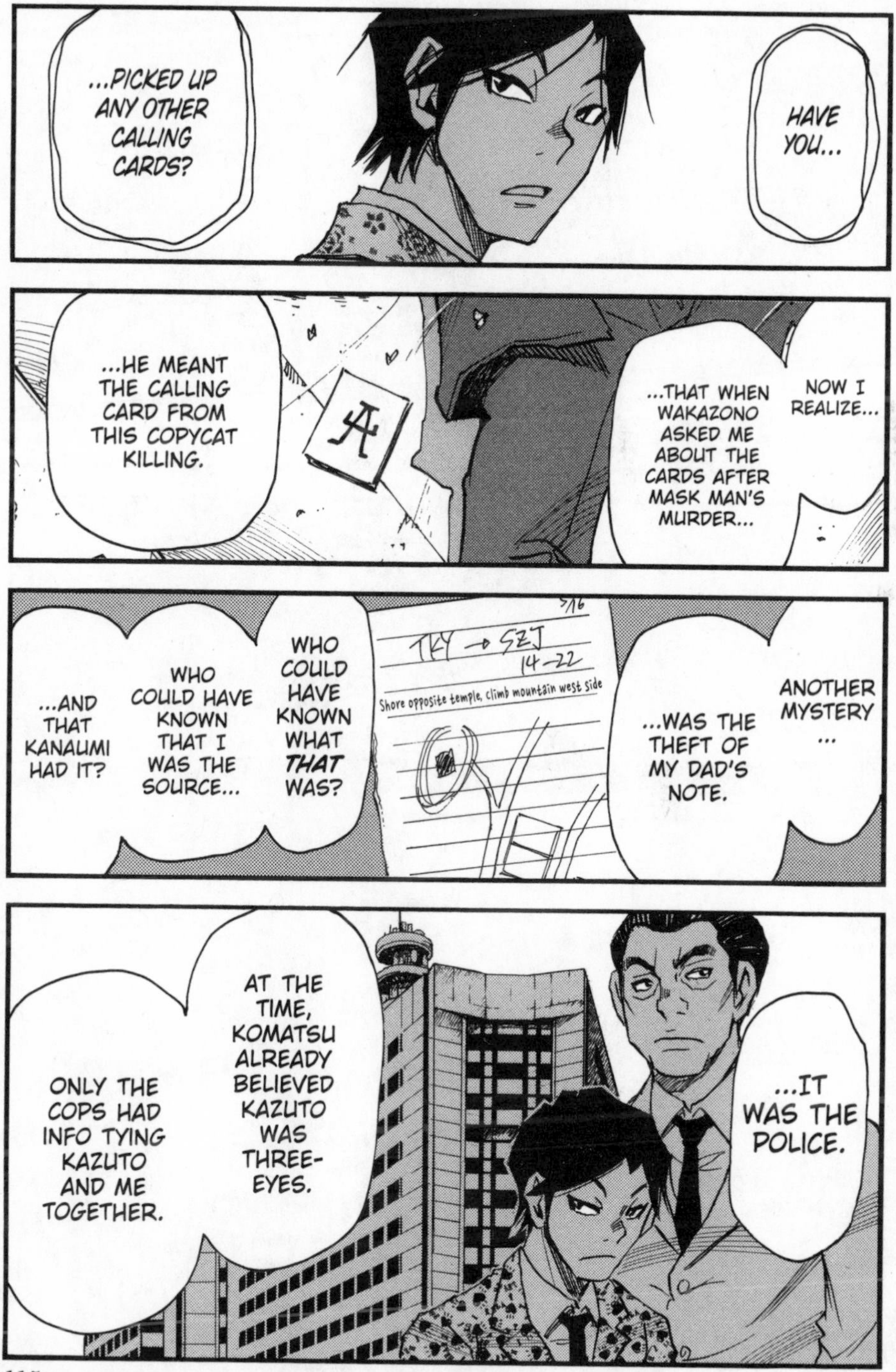
HAVE YOU...
...PICKED UP ANY OTHER CALLING CARDS?
NOW I REALIZE...
...THAT WHEN WAKAZONO ASKED ME ABOUT THE CARDS AFTER MASK MAN'S MURDER...
...HE MEANT THE CALLING CARD FROM THIS COPYCAT KILLING.
ANOTHER MYSTERY ...
...WAS THE THEFT OF MY DAD'S NOTE.
5/16
TKY → SZJ
14-22
Shore opposite temple, climb mountain west side
WHO COULD HAVE KNOWN WHAT *THAT* WAS?
WHO COULD HAVE KNOWN THAT I WAS THE SOURCE...
...AND THAT KANAUMI HAD IT?
...IT WAS THE POLICE.
AT THE TIME, KOMATSU ALREADY BELIEVED KAZUTO WAS THREE-EYES.
ONLY THE COPS HAD INFO TYING KAZUTO AND ME TOGETHER.

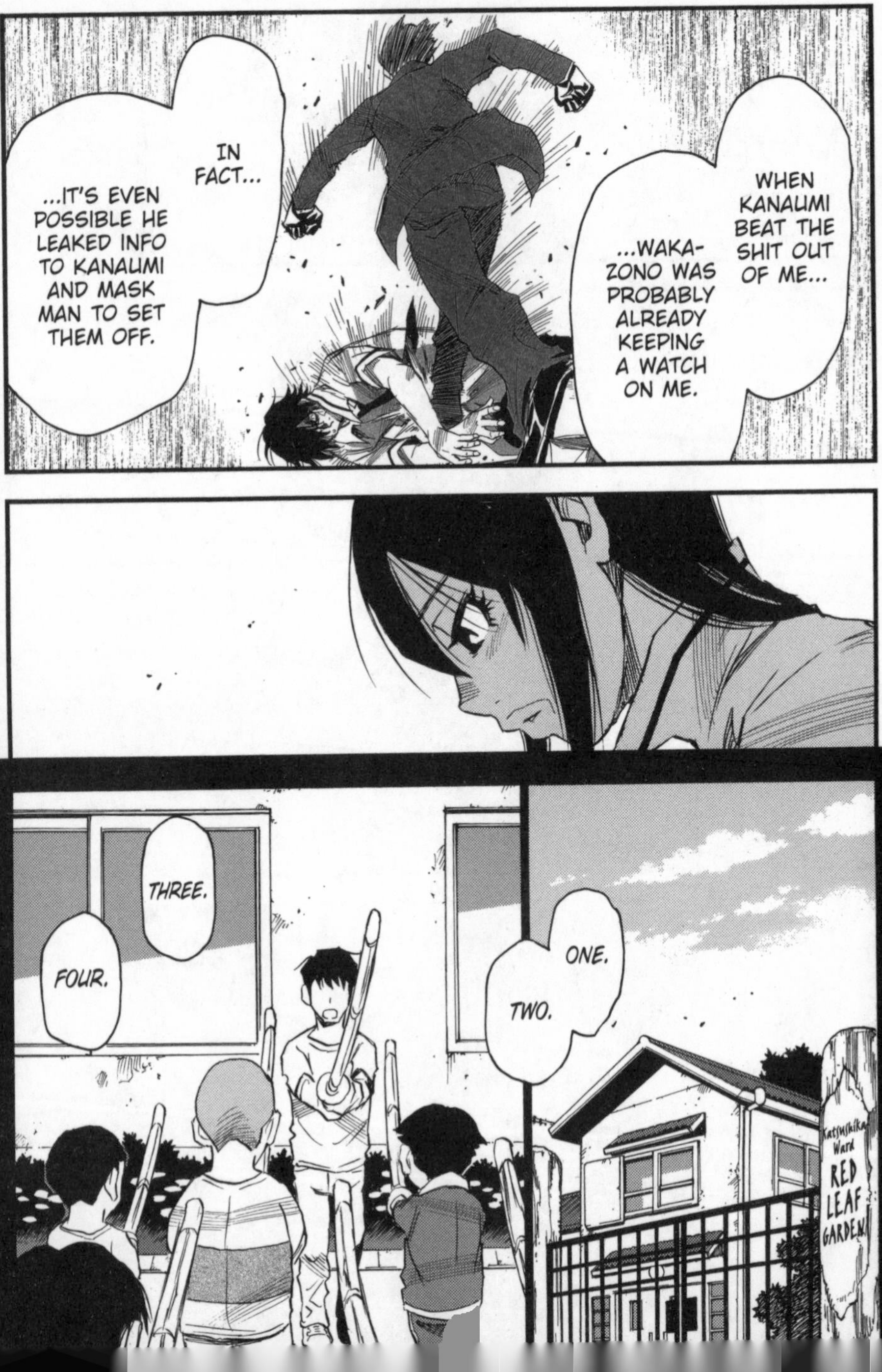
WHEN KANAUMI BEAT THE SHIT OUT OF ME...
...WAKA-ZONO WAS PROBABLY ALREADY KEEPING A WATCH ON ME.
IN FACT...
...IT'S EVEN POSSIBLE HE LEAKED INFO TO KANAUMI AND MASK MAN TO SET THEM OFF.
ONE.
TWO.
Katsushika Ward RED LEAF GARDEN
THREE.
FOUR.

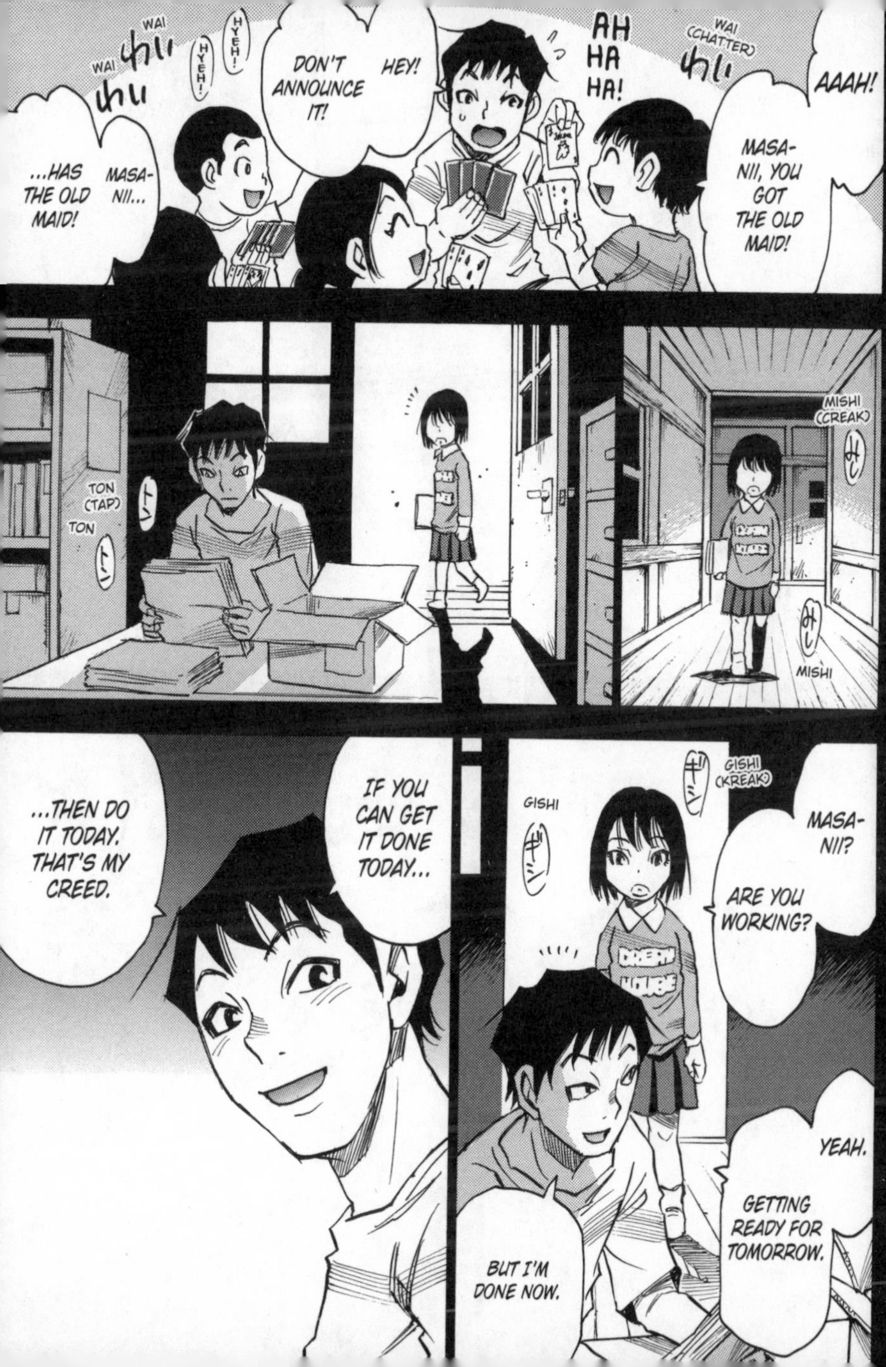
AAAH!
MASA-NII, YOU GOT THE OLD MAID!
WAI (CHATTER)
わい
AH HA HA!
HEY!
DON'T ANNOUNCE IT!
HYEH!
HYEH!
WAI
わい
WAI
わい
MASA-NII...
...HAS THE OLD MAID!
MISHI (CREAK)
みし
みし
MISHI
TON (TAP)
トン
TON
トン
GISHI (KREAK)
ギシ
GISHI
ギシ
MASA-NII?
ARE YOU WORKING?
YEAH.
GETTING READY FOR TOMORROW.
BUT I'M DONE NOW.
IF YOU CAN GET IT DONE TODAY...
...THEN DO IT TODAY. THAT'S MY CREED.

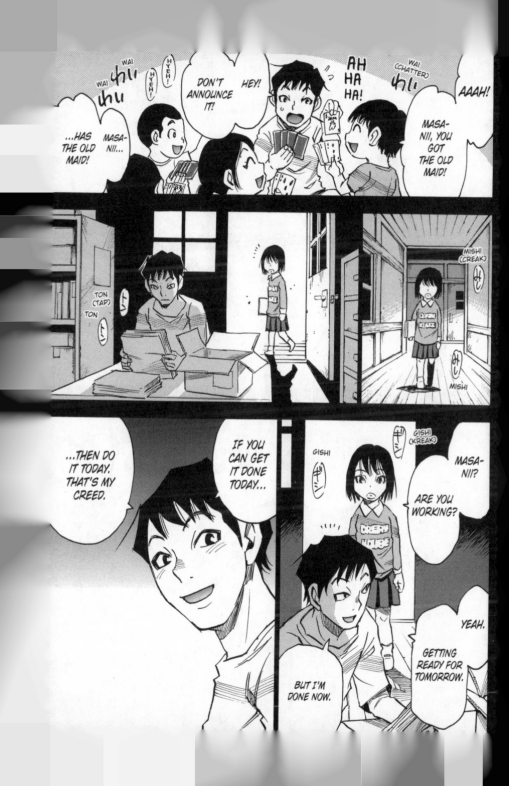

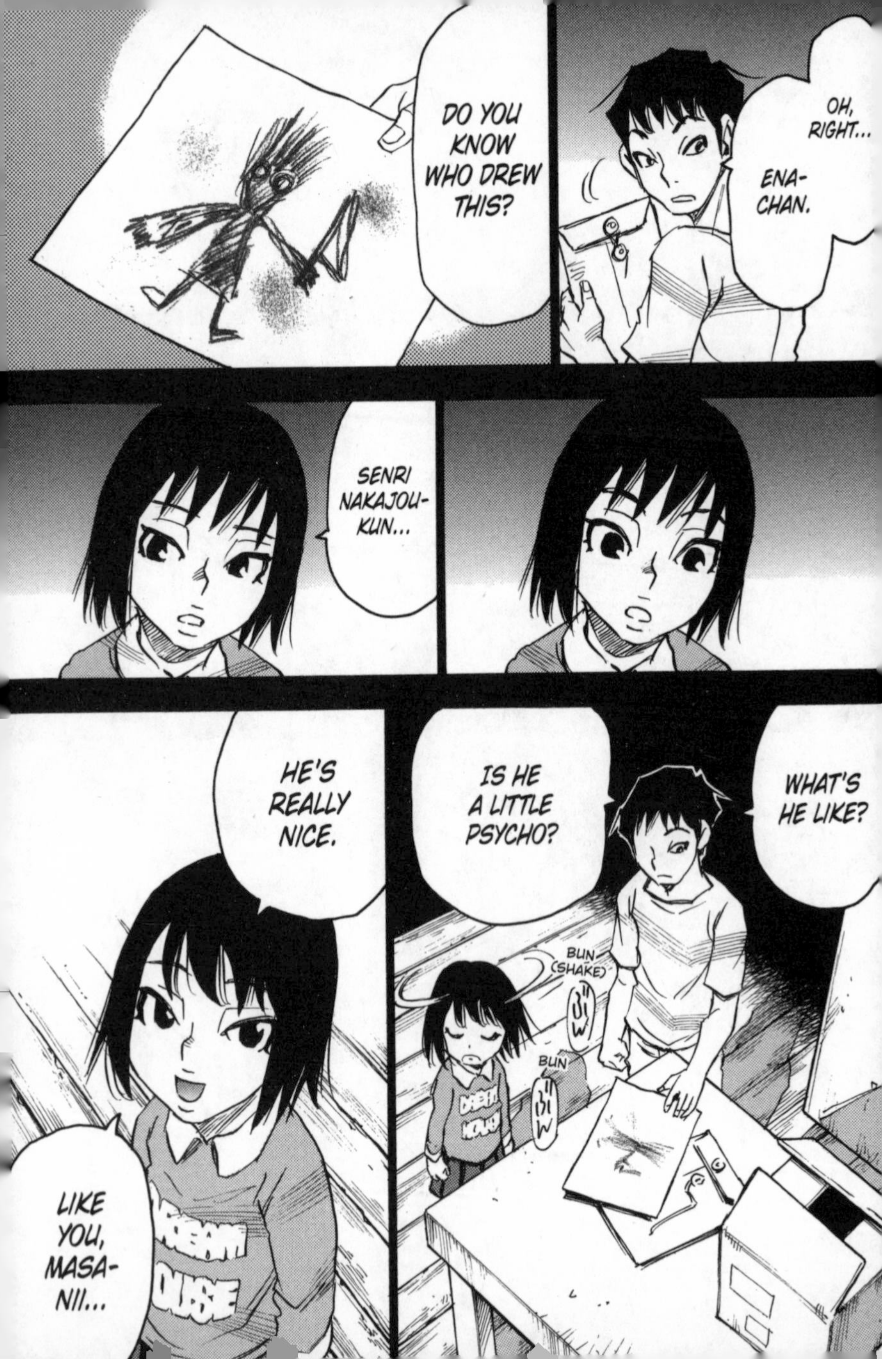
OH, RIGHT...
ENA-CHAN.
DO YOU KNOW WHO DREW THIS?
SENRI NAKAJOU-KUN...
WHAT'S HE LIKE?
IS HE A LITTLE PSYCHO?
BUN (SHAKE)
BUN
HE'S REALLY NICE.
LIKE YOU, MASA-NII...

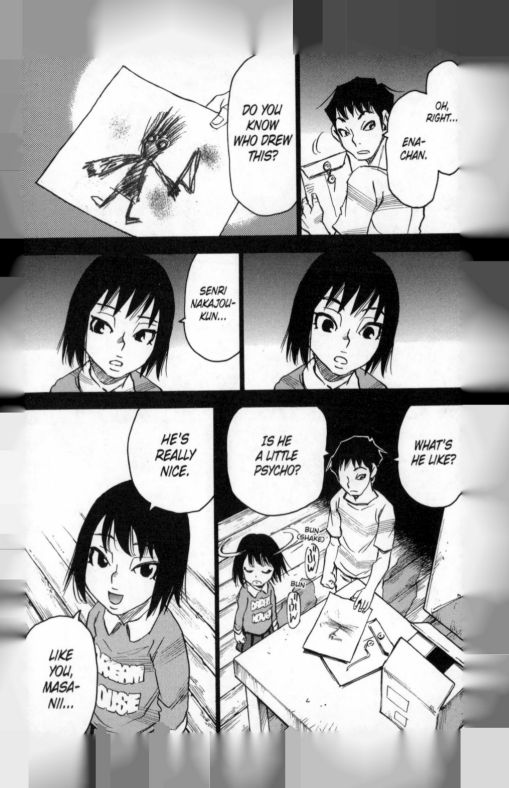

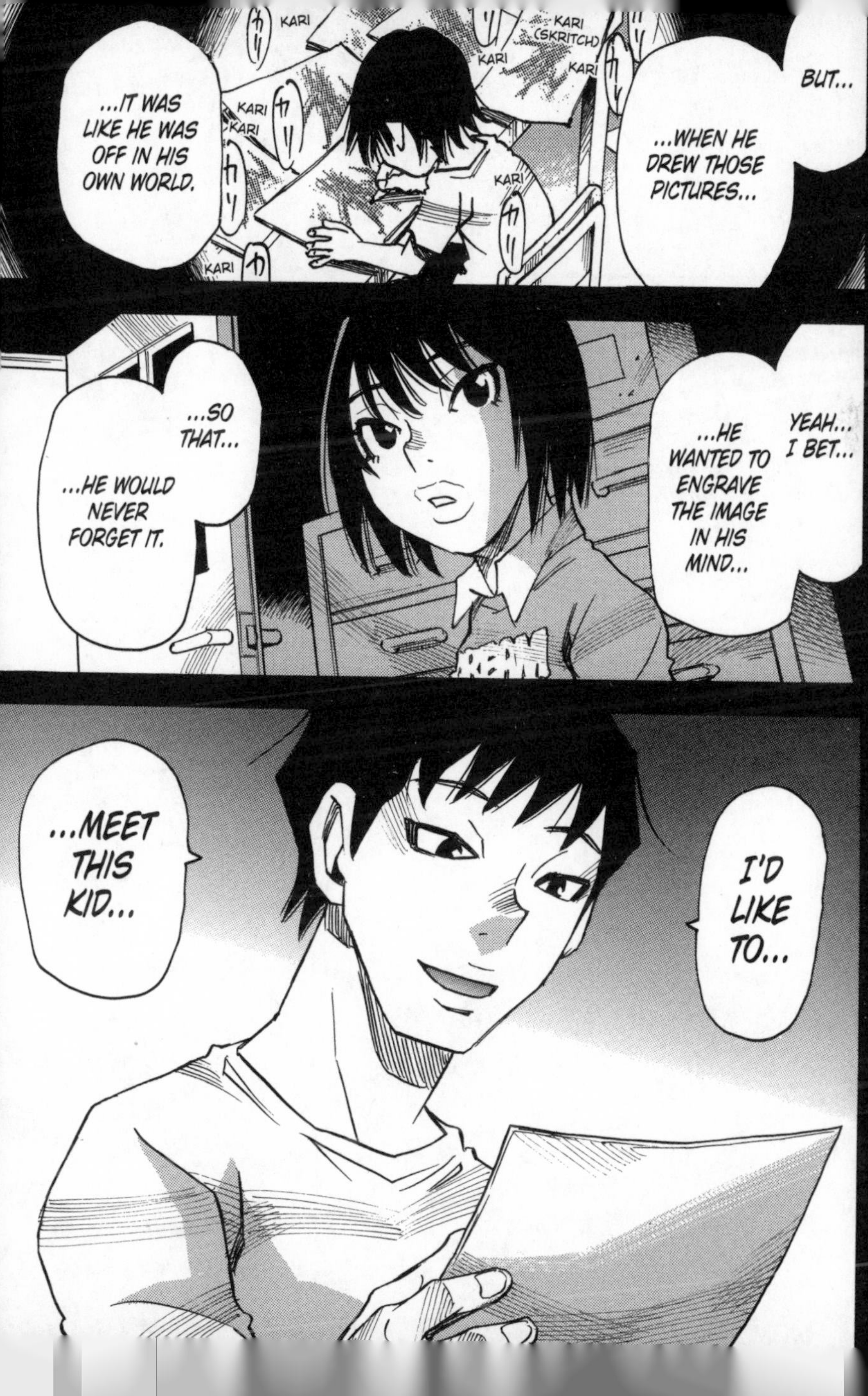
KARI (SKRITCH)
KARI
KARI
BUT...
...WHEN HE DREW THOSE PICTURES...
KARI
KARI
KARI
KARI
KARI
...IT WAS LIKE HE WAS OFF IN HIS OWN WORLD.
YEAH... I BET...
...HE WANTED TO ENGRAVE THE IMAGE IN HIS MIND...
...SO THAT...
...HE WOULD NEVER FORGET IT.
I'D LIKE TO...
...MEET THIS KID...

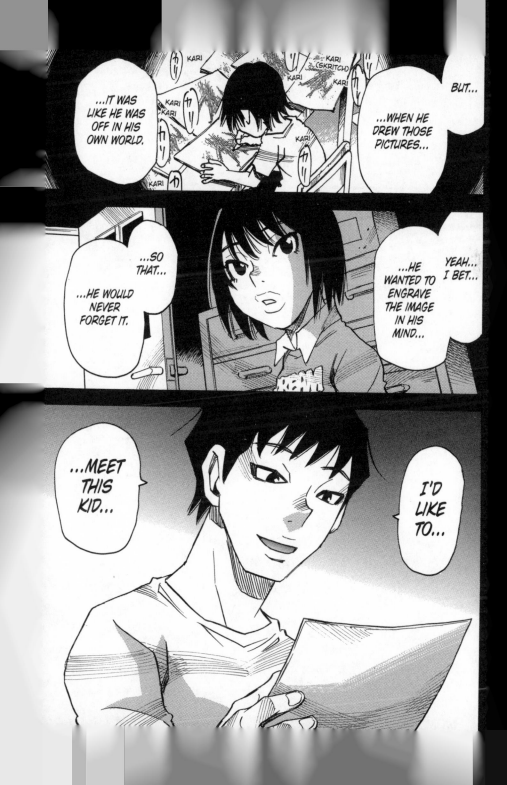

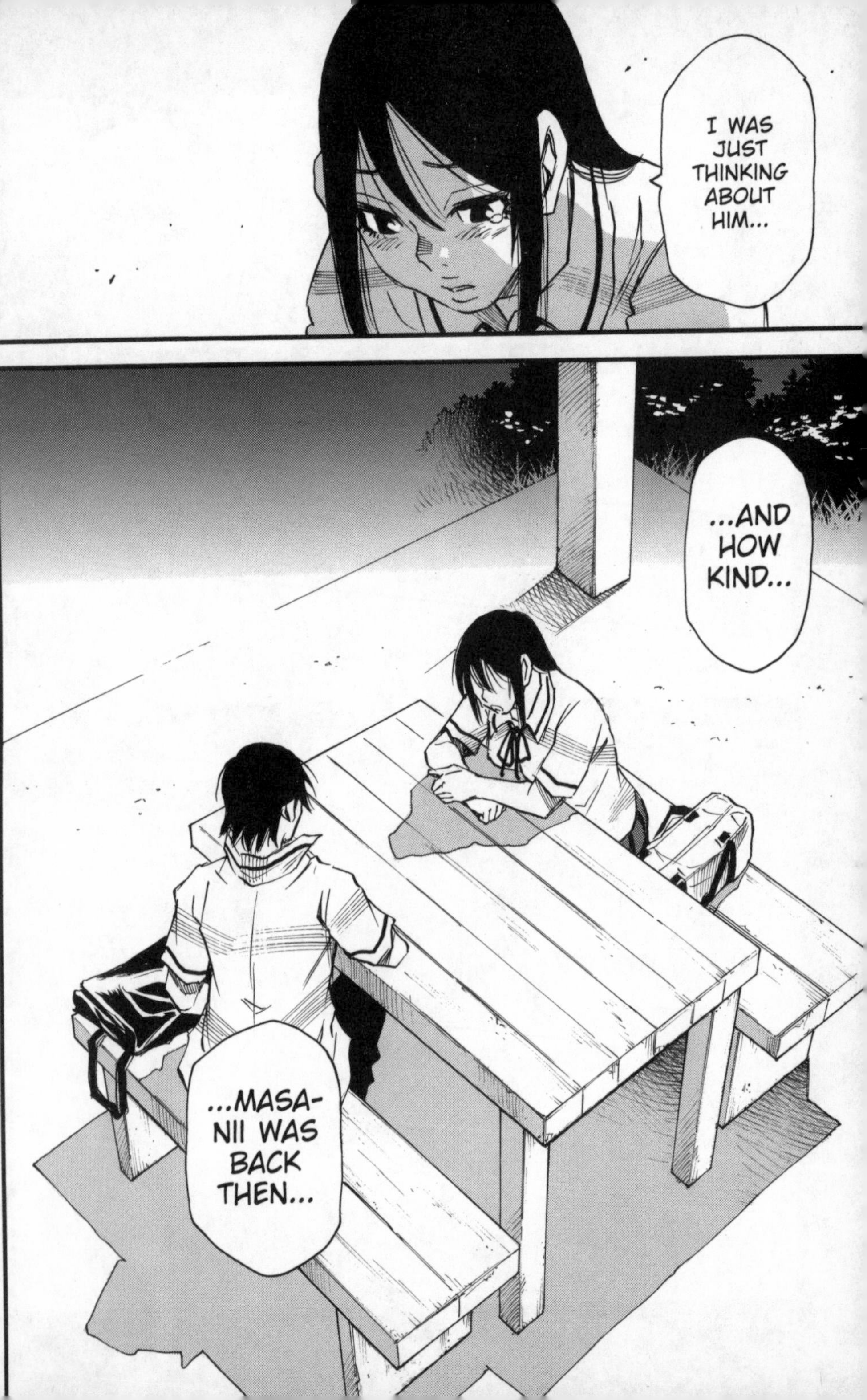
I WAS JUST THINKING ABOUT HIM...
...AND HOW KIND...
...MASA-NII WAS BACK THEN...

#40 END

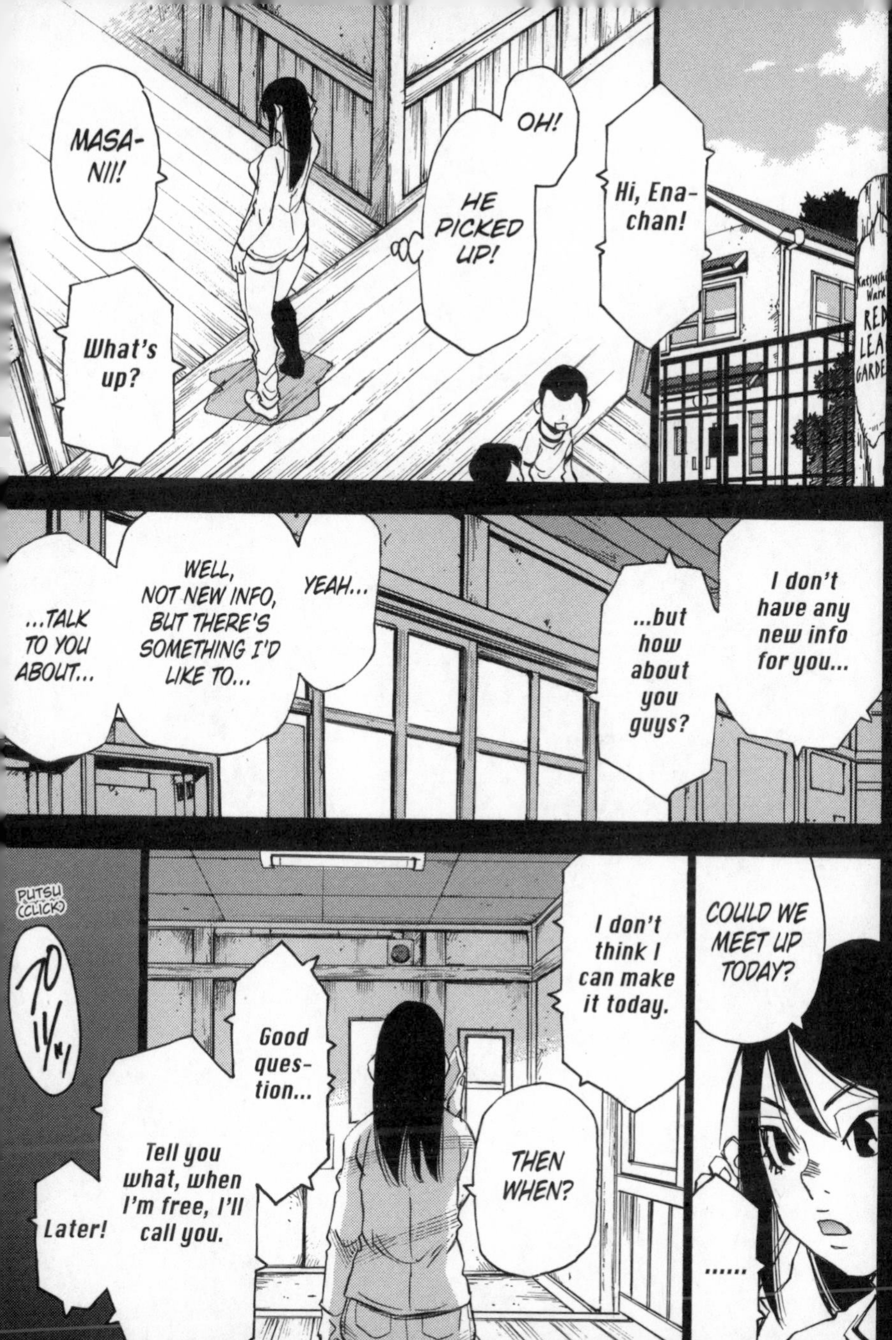
Hi, Ena-chan!
OH!
HE PICKED UP!
MASA-NII!
What's up?
I don't have any new info for you...
...but how about you guys?
YEAH...
WELL, NOT NEW INFO, BUT THERE'S SOMETHING I'D LIKE TO...
...TALK TO YOU ABOUT...
COULD WE MEET UP TODAY?
......
I don't think I can make it today.
THEN WHEN?
Good question...
Tell you what, when I'm free, I'll call you.
Later!
PUTSU (CLICK)

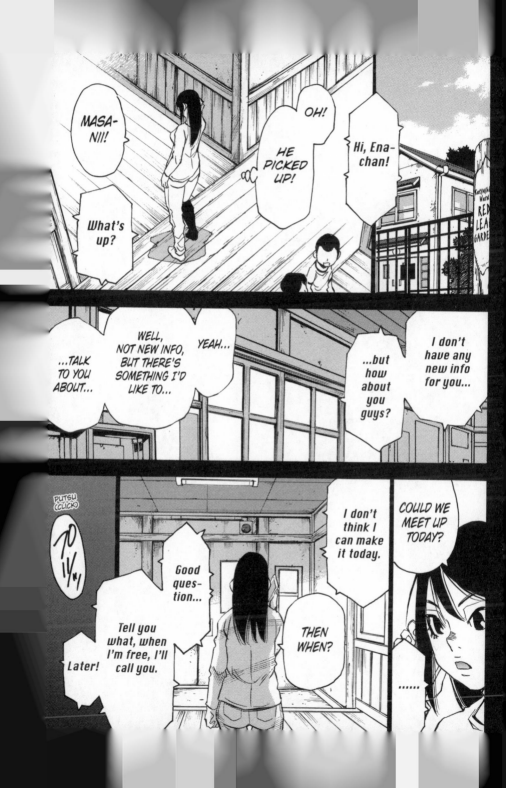

#41 Who Killed Whom

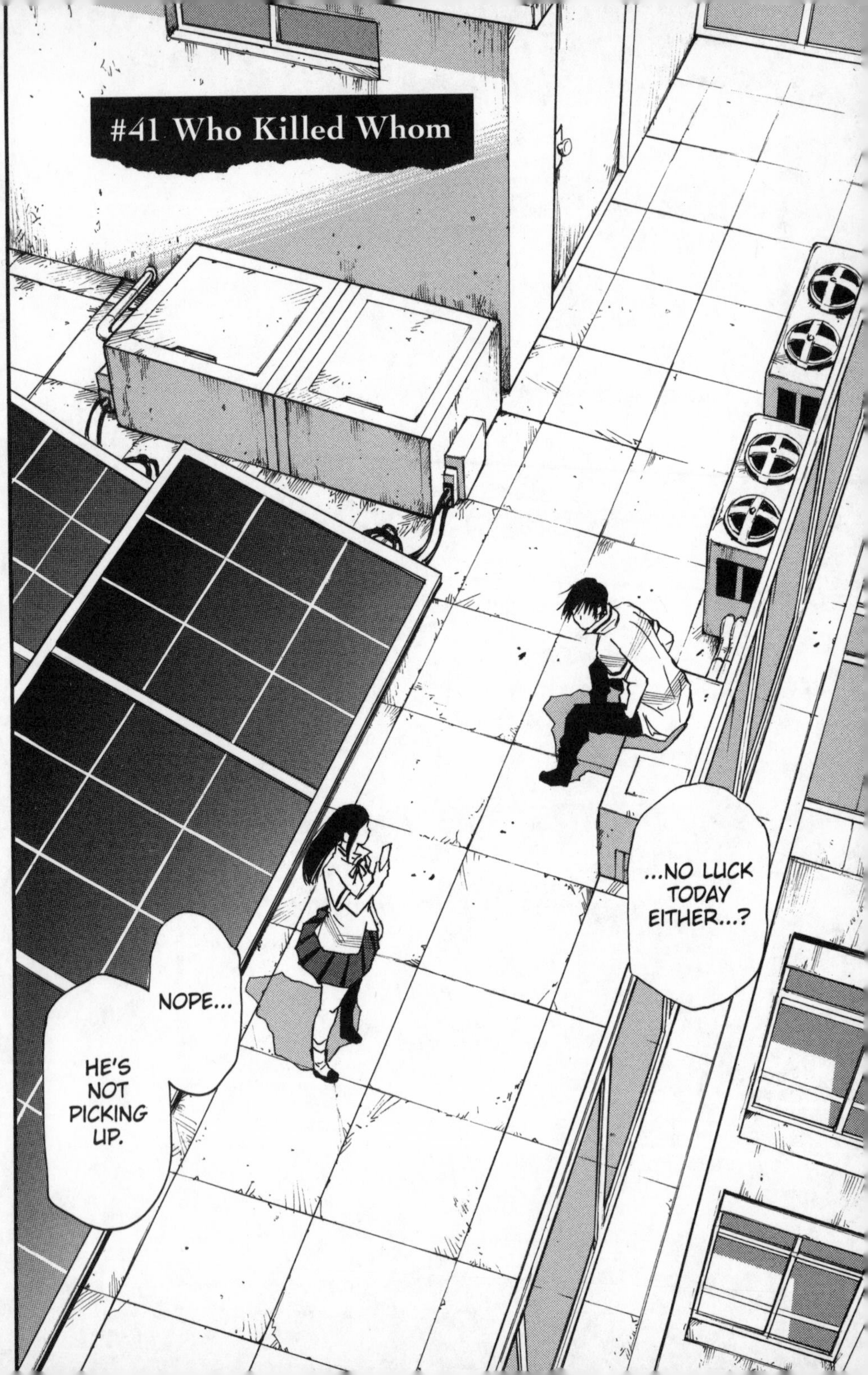
...NO LUCK TODAY EITHER...?
NOPE...
HE'S NOT PICKING UP.

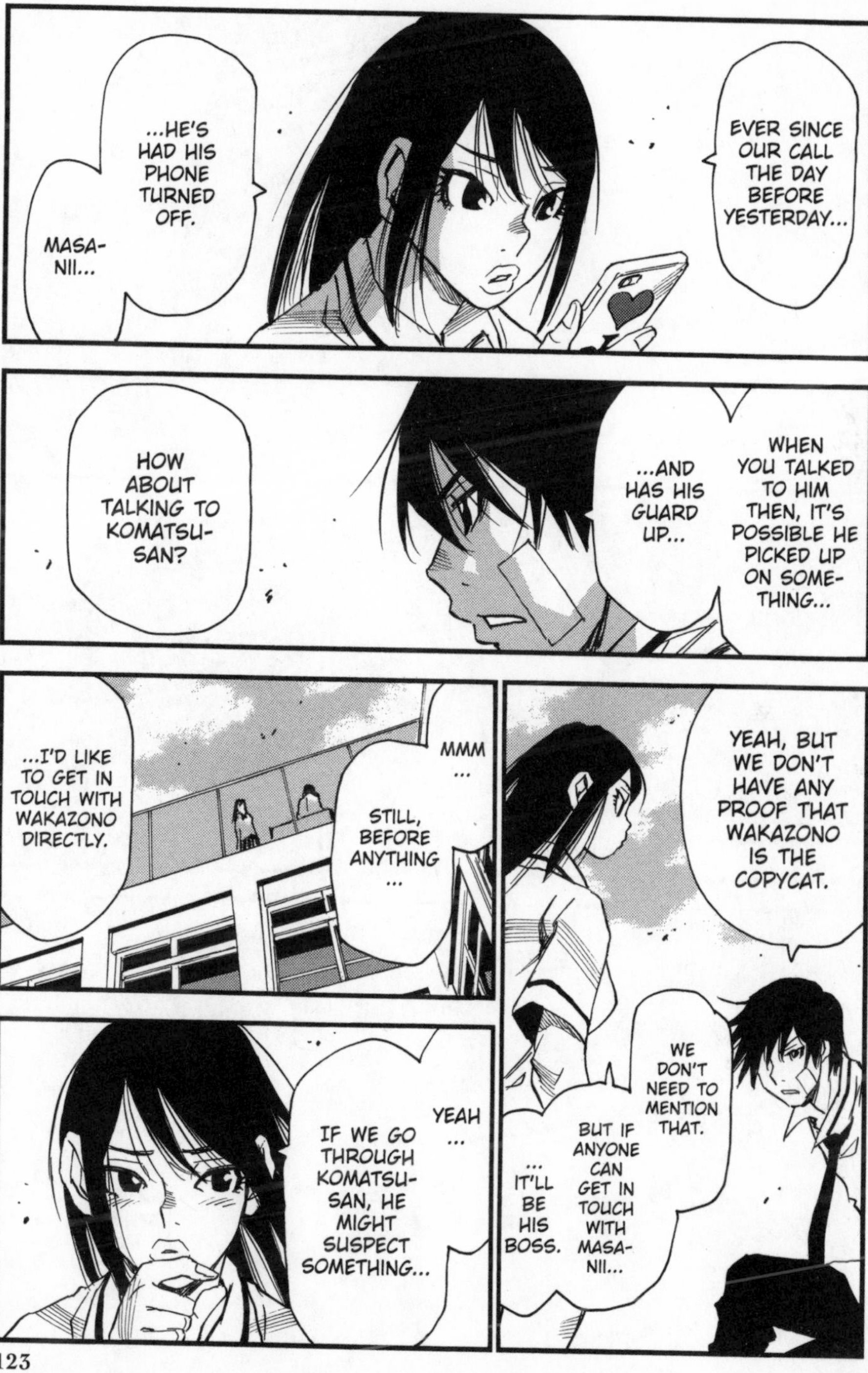
EVER SINCE OUR CALL THE DAY BEFORE YESTERDAY...
...HE'S HAD HIS PHONE TURNED OFF.
MASA-NII...
WHEN YOU TALKED TO HIM THEN, IT'S POSSIBLE HE PICKED UP ON SOME-THING...
...AND HAS HIS GUARD UP...
HOW ABOUT TALKING TO KOMATSU-SAN?
YEAH, BUT WE DON'T HAVE ANY PROOF THAT WAKAZONO IS THE COPYCAT.
WE DON'T NEED TO MENTION THAT.
BUT IF ANYONE CAN GET IN TOUCH WITH MASA-NII...
...IT'LL BE HIS BOSS.
MMM...
STILL, BEFORE ANYTHING...
...I'D LIKE TO GET IN TOUCH WITH WAKAZONO DIRECTLY.
YEAH...
IF WE GO THROUGH KOMATSU-SAN, HE MIGHT SUSPECT SOMETHING...

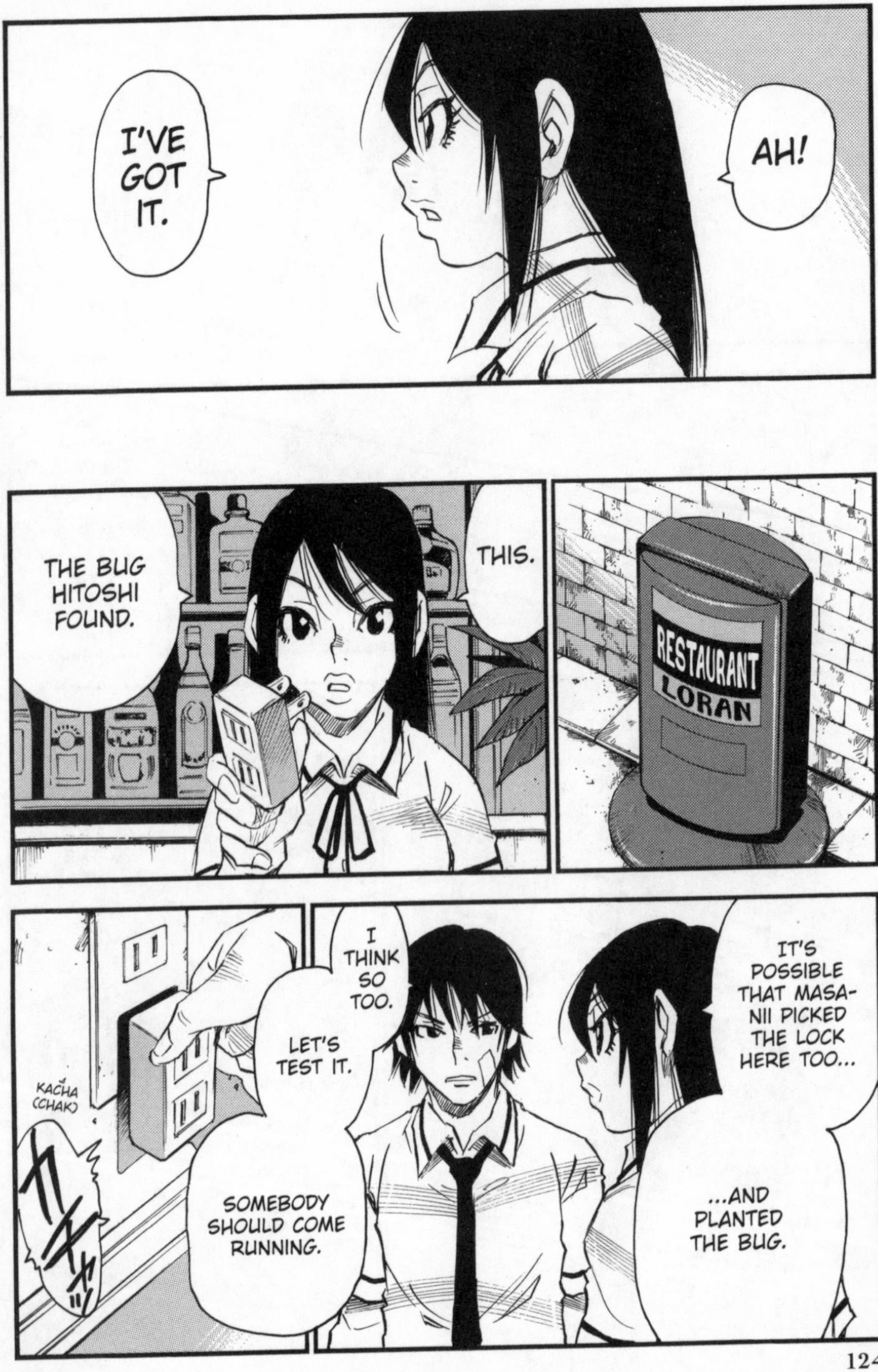
AH!
I'VE GOT IT.
RESTAURANT LORAN
THIS.
THE BUG HITOSHI FOUND.
IT'S POSSIBLE THAT MASA-NII PICKED THE LOCK HERE TOO...
...AND PLANTED THE BUG.
I THINK SO TOO.
LET'S TEST IT.
SOMEBODY SHOULD COME RUNNING.
KACHA (CHAK)

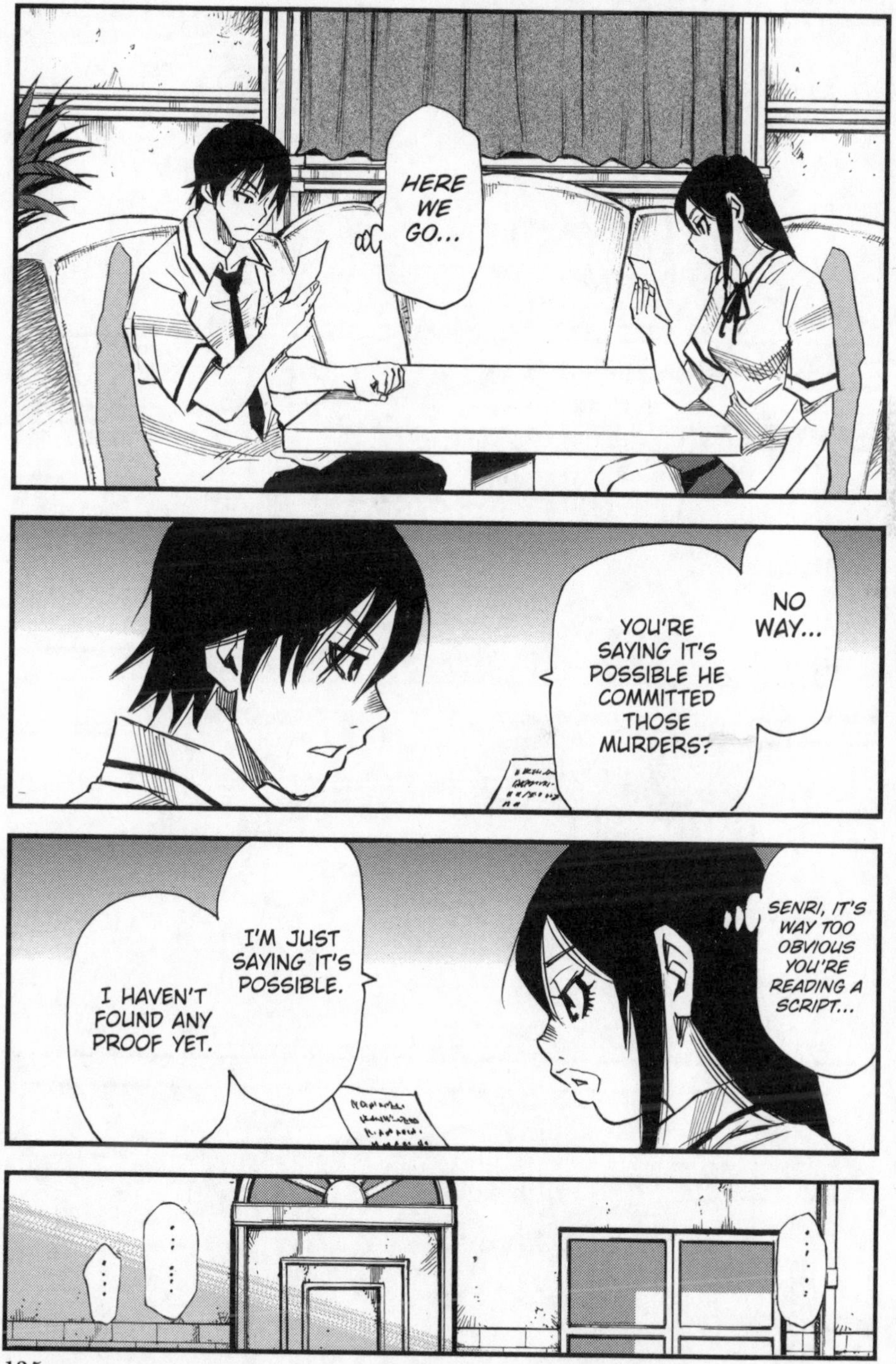
HERE WE GO...
NO WAY...
YOU'RE SAYING IT'S POSSIBLE HE COMMITTED THOSE MURDERS?
SENRI, IT'S WAY TOO OBVIOUS YOU'RE READING A SCRIPT...
I'M JUST SAYING IT'S POSSIBLE.
I HAVEN'T FOUND ANY PROOF YET.
....
... .
....

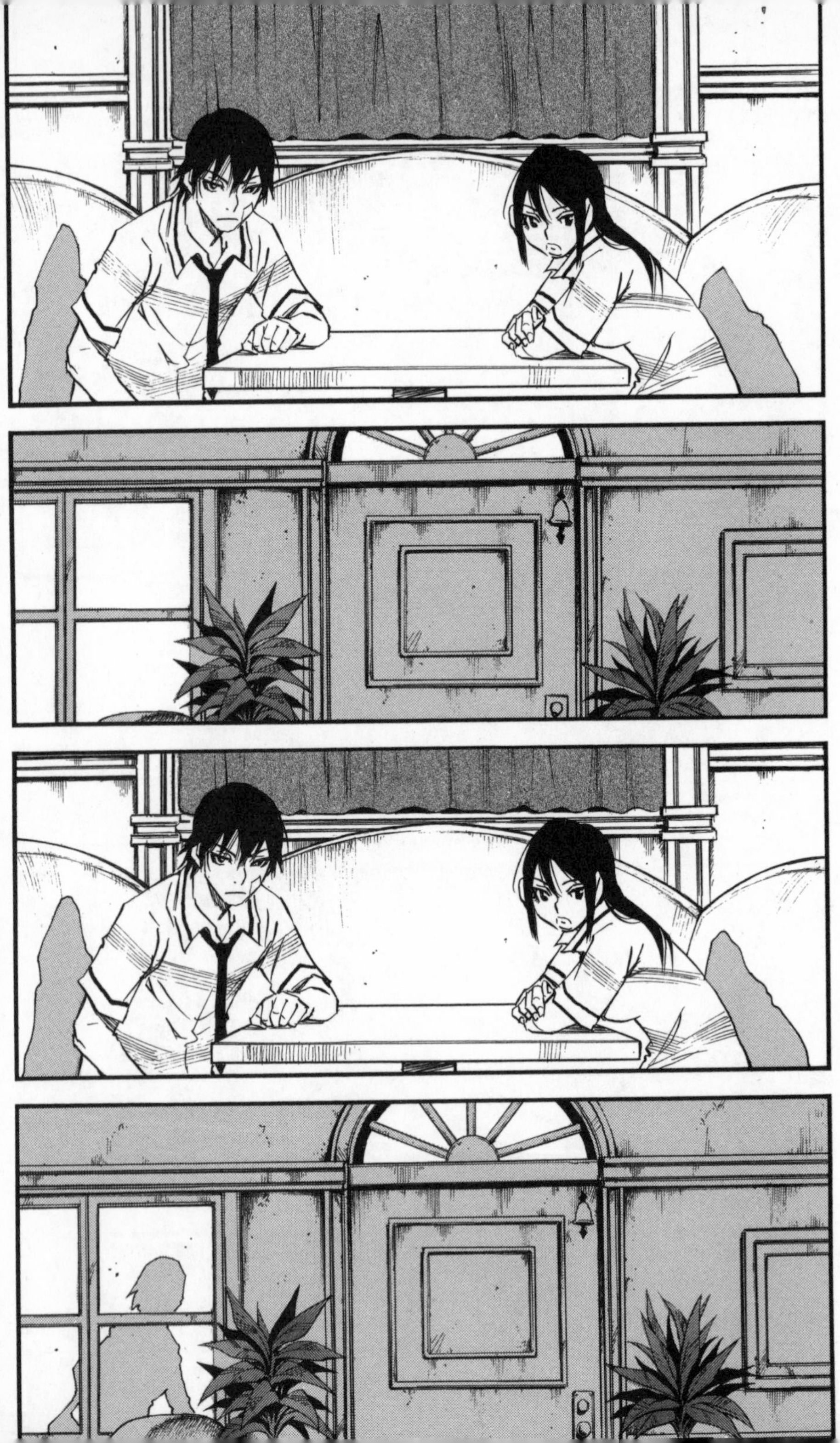

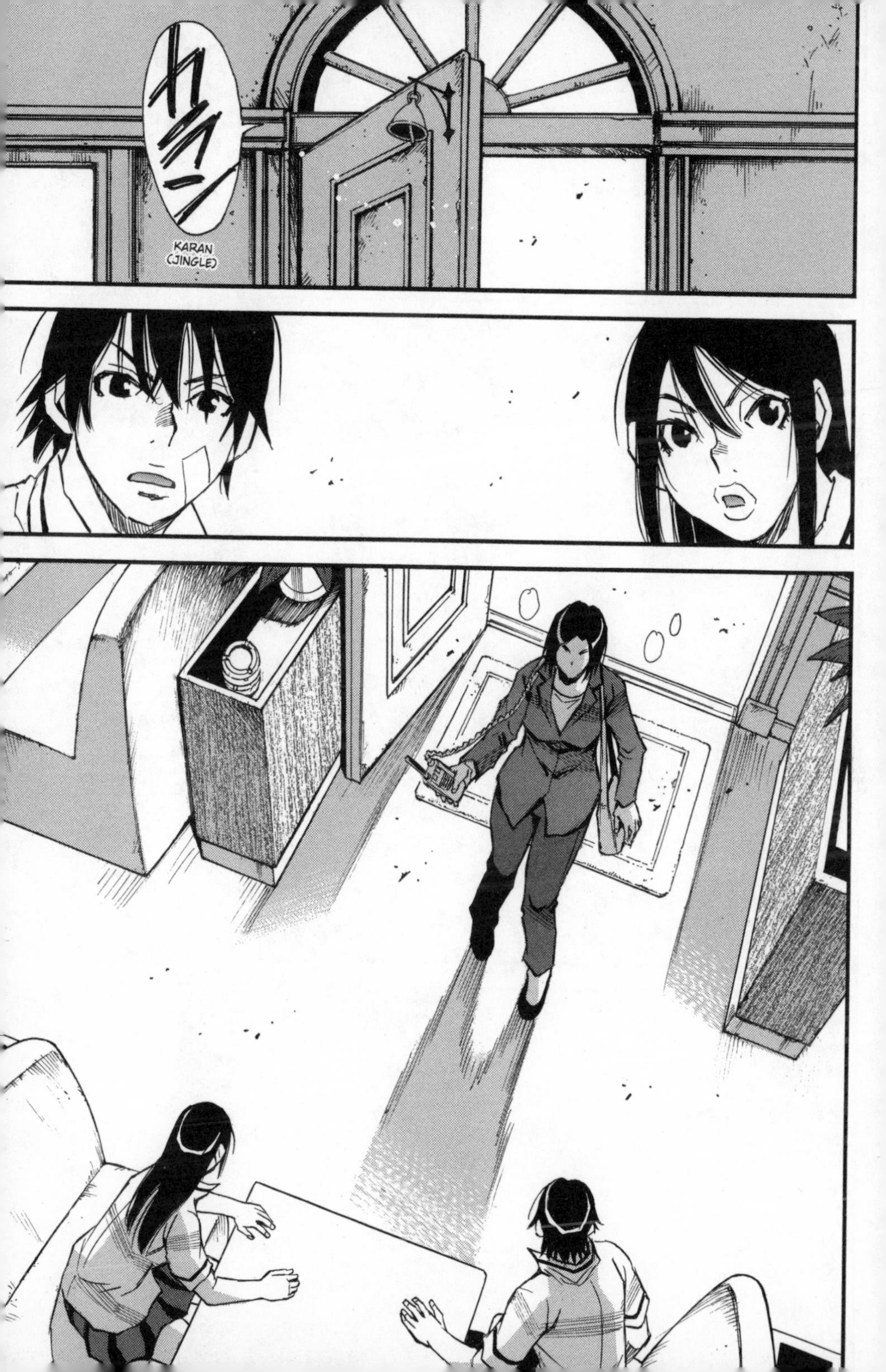
カラン
KARAN (JINGLE)

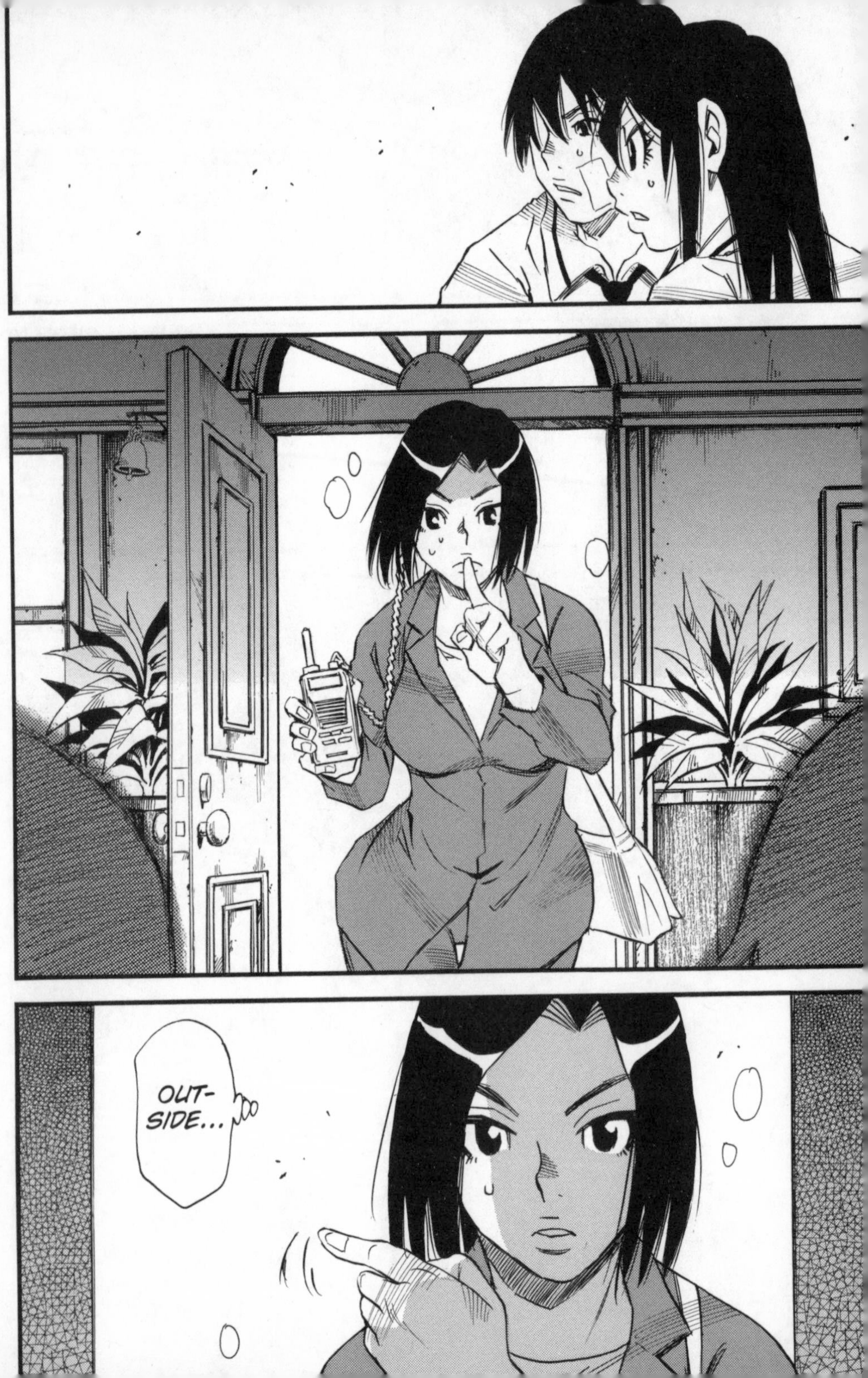
OUT-SIDE...

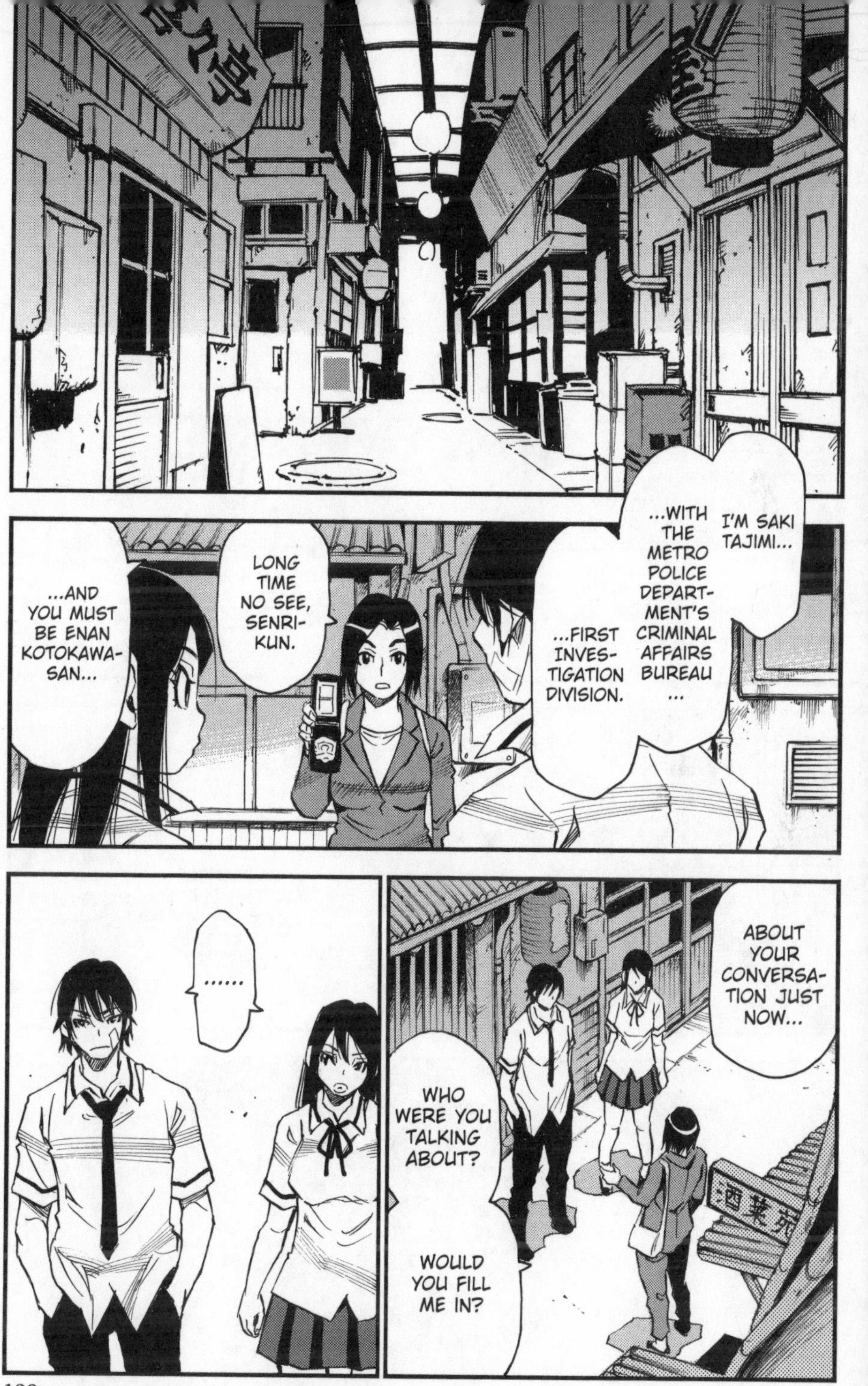
I'M SAKI TAJIMI...
...WITH THE METRO POLICE DEPARTMENT'S CRIMINAL AFFAIRS BUREAU...
...FIRST INVESTIGATION DIVISION.
LONG TIME NO SEE, SENRI-KUN.
...AND YOU MUST BE ENAN KOTOKAWA-SAN...
ABOUT YOUR CONVERSATION JUST NOW...
WHO WERE YOU TALKING ABOUT?
WOULD YOU FILL ME IN?
......

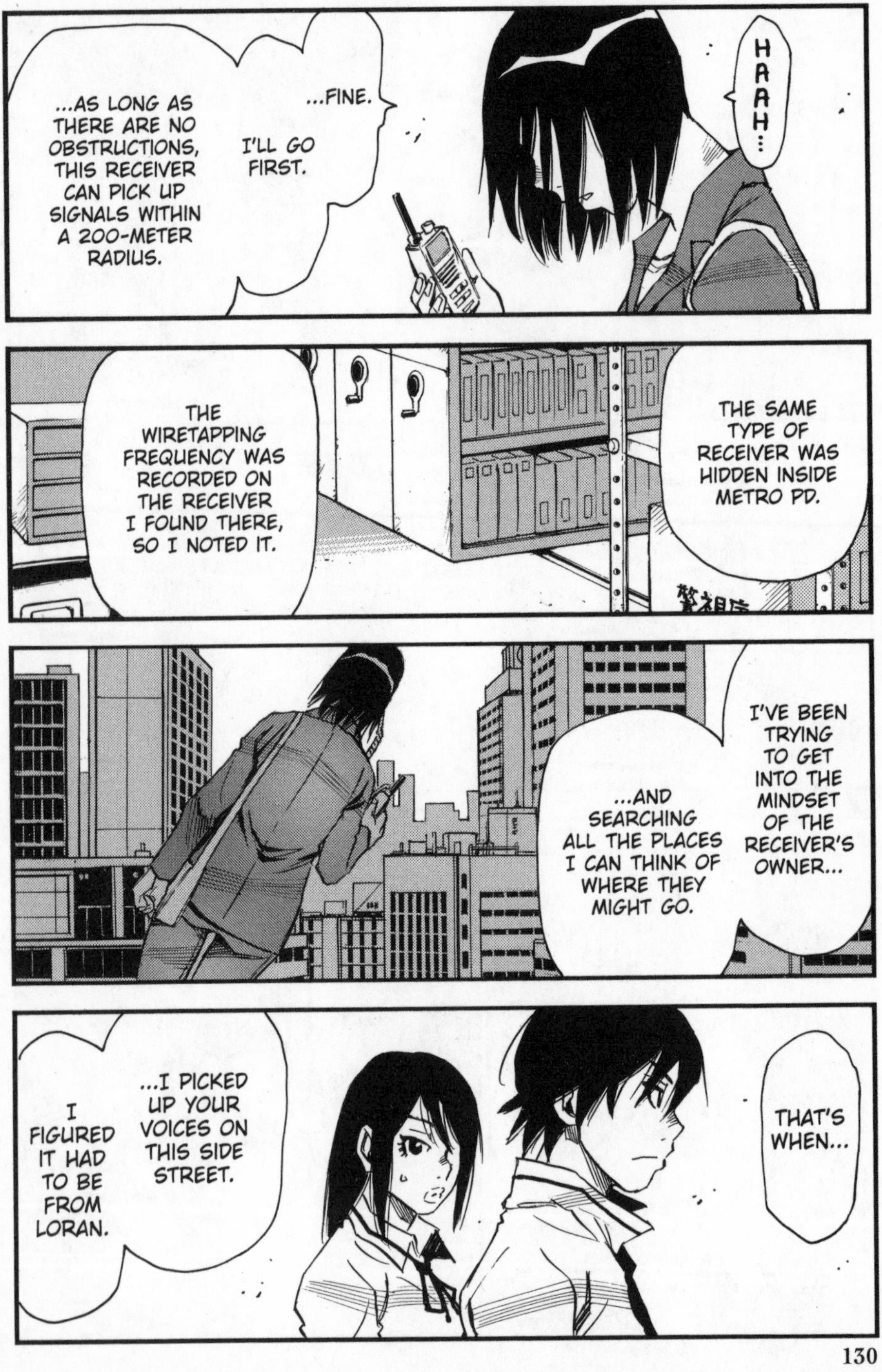
HAAH...
...FINE.
I'LL GO FIRST.
...AS LONG AS THERE ARE NO OBSTRUCTIONS, THIS RECEIVER CAN PICK UP SIGNALS WITHIN A 200-METER RADIUS.
THE SAME TYPE OF RECEIVER WAS HIDDEN INSIDE METRO PD.
THE WIRETAPPING FREQUENCY WAS RECORDED ON THE RECEIVER I FOUND THERE, SO I NOTED IT.
警視庁
I'VE BEEN TRYING TO GET INTO THE MINDSET OF THE RECEIVER'S OWNER...
...AND SEARCHING ALL THE PLACES I CAN THINK OF WHERE THEY MIGHT GO.
THAT'S WHEN...
...I PICKED UP YOUR VOICES ON THIS SIDE STREET.
I FIGURED IT HAD TO BE FROM LORAN.

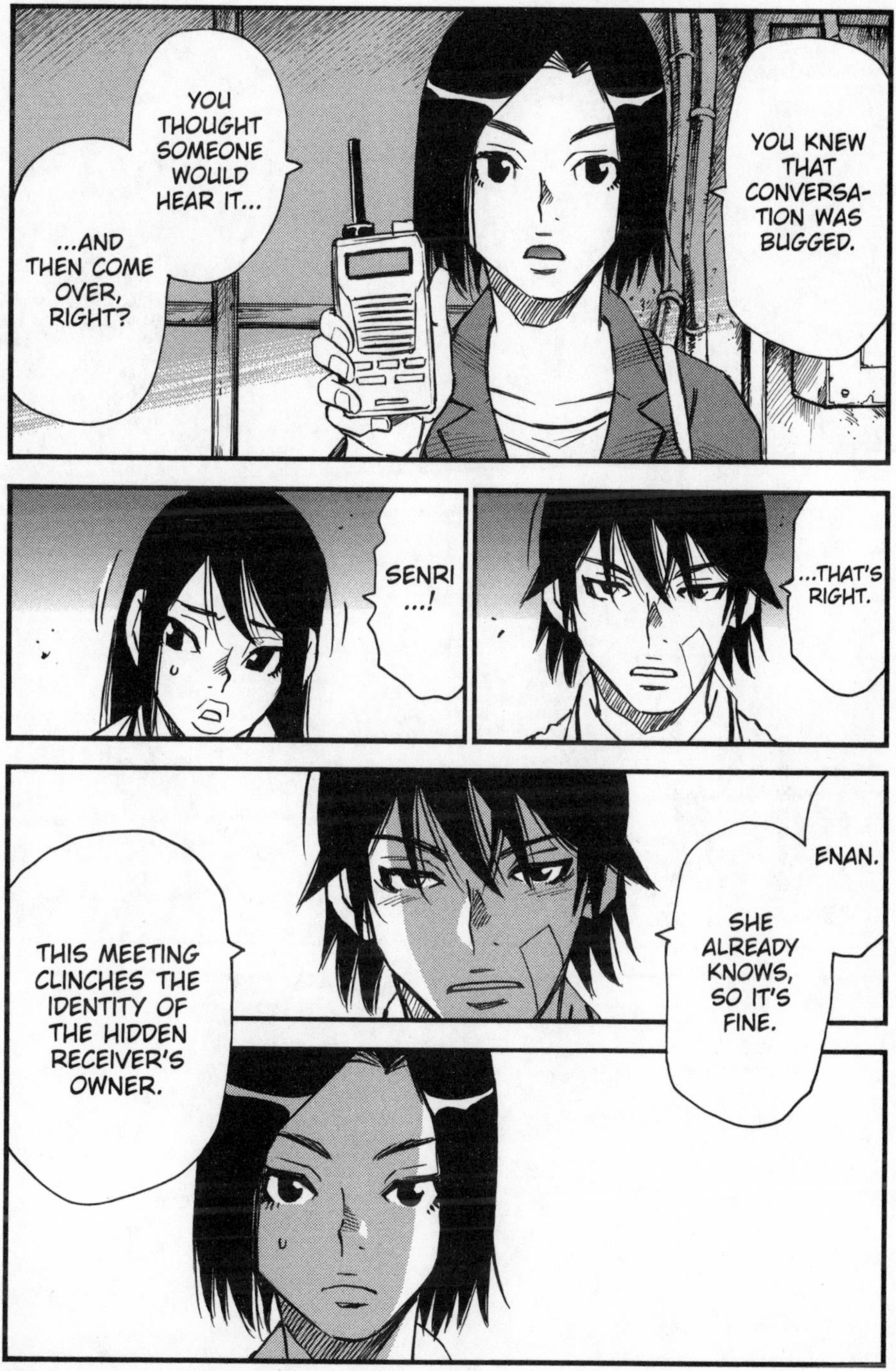
YOU KNEW THAT CONVERSATION WAS BUGGED.
YOU THOUGHT SOMEONE WOULD HEAR IT...
...AND THEN COME OVER, RIGHT?
...THAT'S RIGHT.
SENRI ...!
ENAN.
SHE ALREADY KNOWS, SO IT'S FINE.
THIS MEETING CLINCHES THE IDENTITY OF THE HIDDEN RECEIVER'S OWNER.

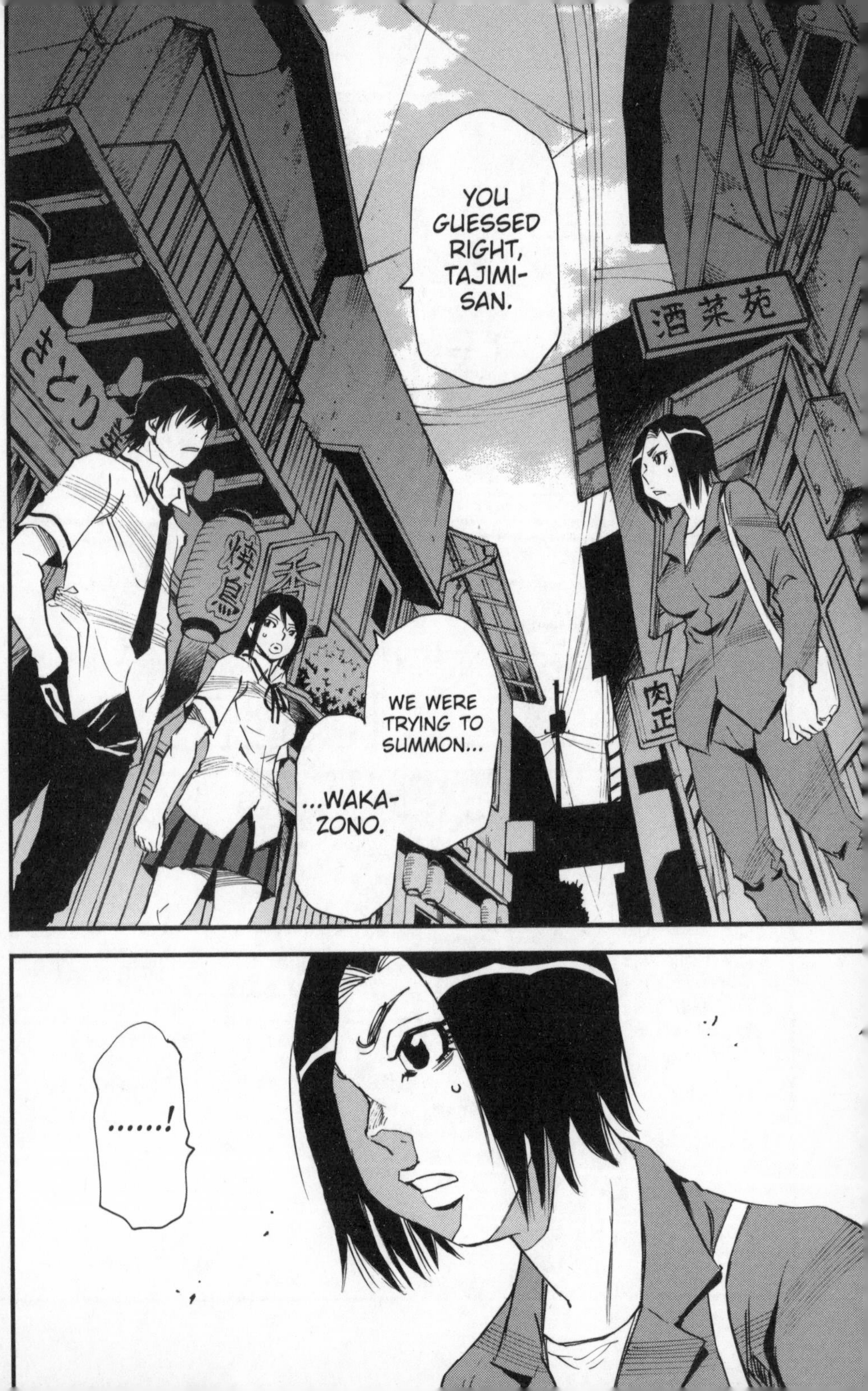
YOU GUESSED RIGHT, TAJIMI-SAN.
WE WERE TRYING TO SUMMON...
...WAKA-ZONO.
酒菜苑
焼鳥
肉正
......!

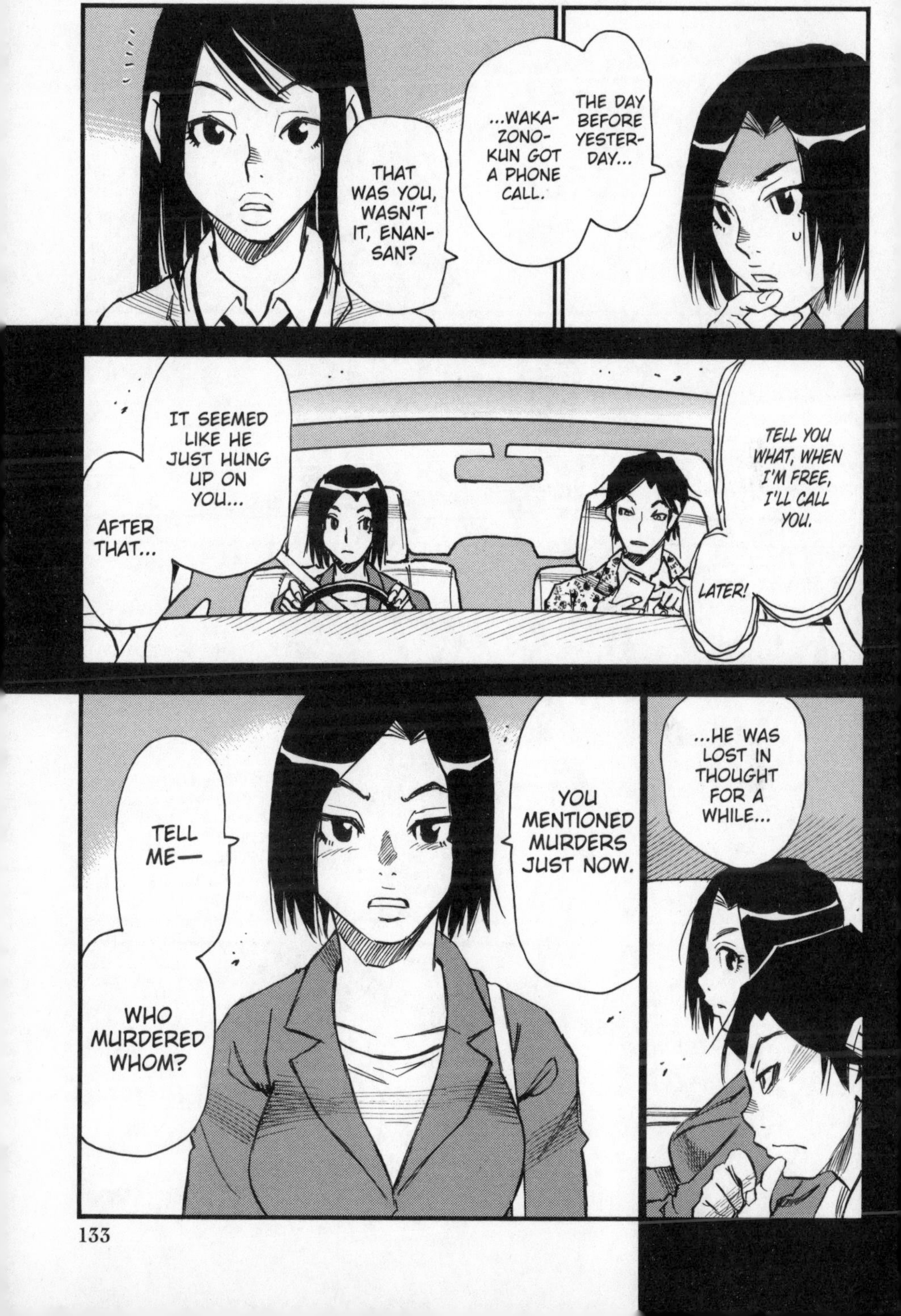
THE DAY BEFORE YESTER- DAY...
...WAKA- ZONO- KUN GOT A PHONE CALL.
THAT WAS YOU, WASN'T IT, ENAN- SAN?
TELL YOU WHAT, WHEN I'M FREE, I'LL CALL YOU.
LATER!
IT SEEMED LIKE HE JUST HUNG UP ON YOU...
AFTER THAT...
...HE WAS LOST IN THOUGHT FOR A WHILE...
YOU MENTIONED MURDERS JUST NOW.
TELL ME—
WHO MURDERED WHOM?

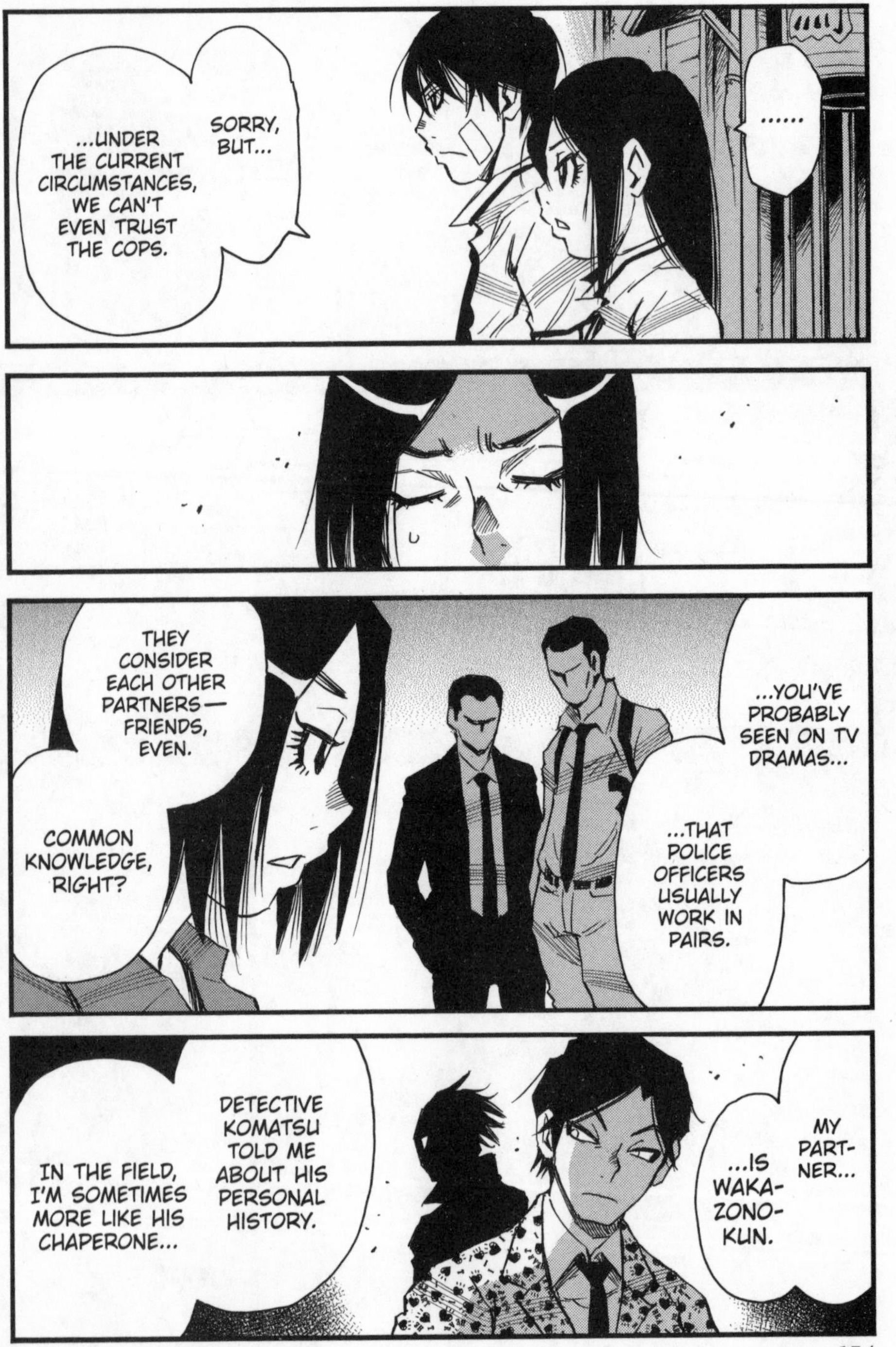
......
SORRY, BUT...
...UNDER THE CURRENT CIRCUMSTANCES, WE CAN'T EVEN TRUST THE COPS.
...YOU'VE PROBABLY SEEN ON TV DRAMAS...
...THAT POLICE OFFICERS USUALLY WORK IN PAIRS.
COMMON KNOWLEDGE, RIGHT?
THEY CONSIDER EACH OTHER PARTNERS—FRIENDS, EVEN.
MY PARTNER...
...IS WAKAZONO-KUN.
DETECTIVE KOMATSU TOLD ME ABOUT HIS PERSONAL HISTORY.
IN THE FIELD, I'M SOMETIMES MORE LIKE HIS CHAPERONE...

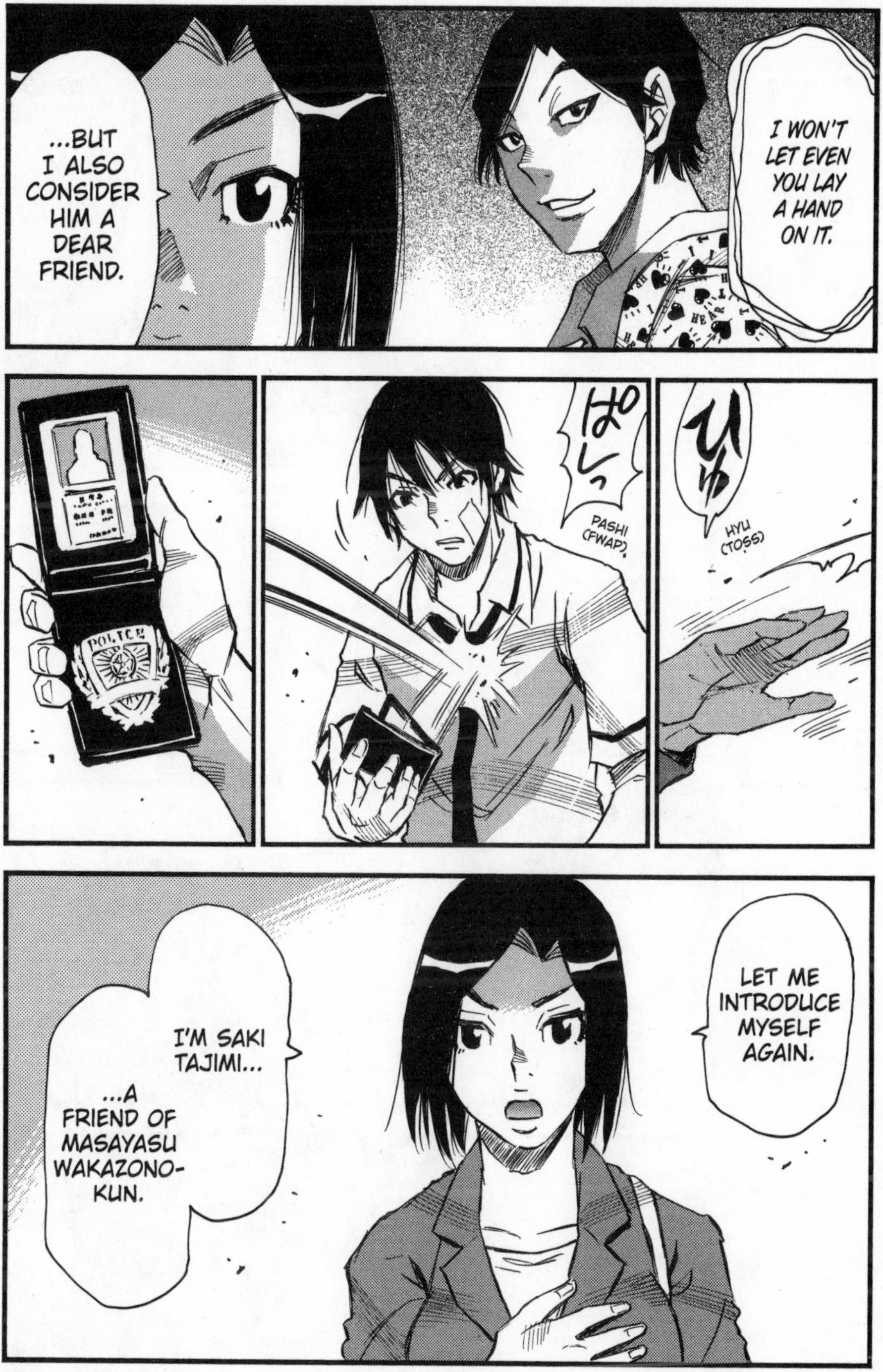
I WON'T LET EVEN YOU LAY A HAND ON IT.
...BUT I ALSO CONSIDER HIM A DEAR FRIEND.
ひゅ
HYU (TOSS)
ぱしっ
PASHI (FWAP)
POLICE
LET ME INTRODUCE MYSELF AGAIN.
I'M SAKI TAJIMI...
...A FRIEND OF MASAYASU WAKAZONO-KUN.

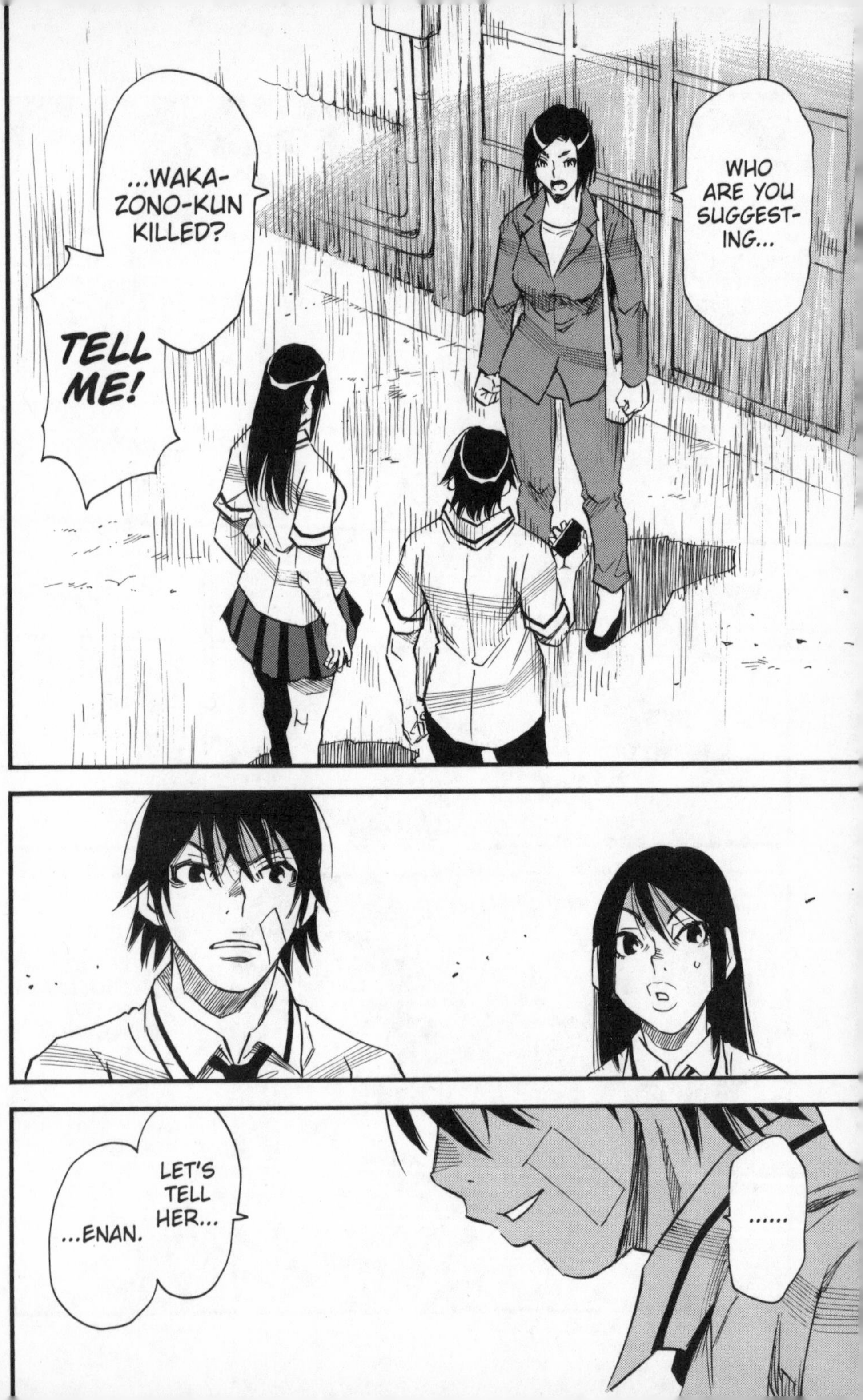
WHO ARE YOU SUGGEST-ING...
...WAKA-ZONO-KUN KILLED?
TELL ME!
......
LET'S TELL HER...
...ENAN.

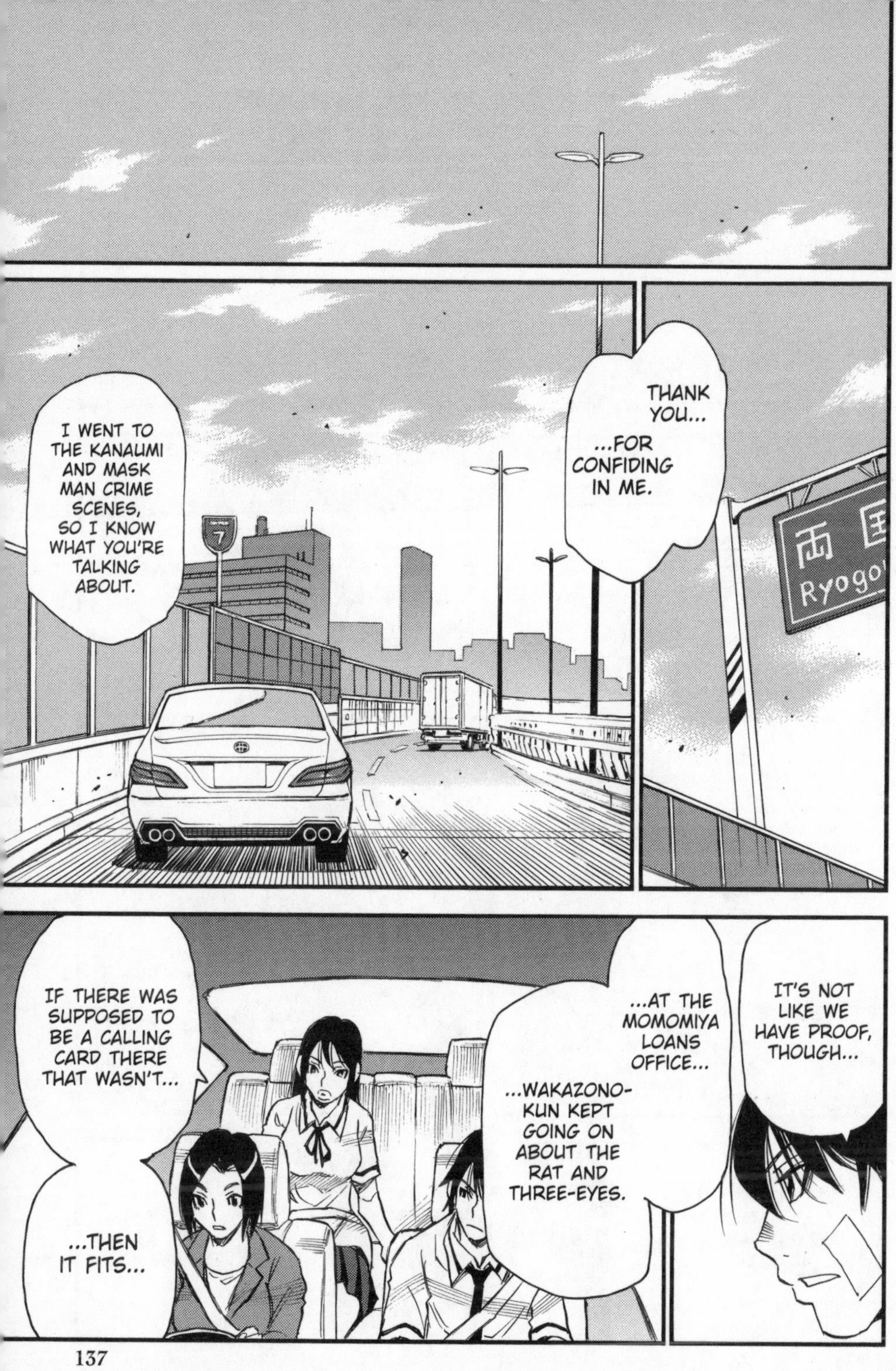
THANK YOU... ...FOR CONFIDING IN ME.
両国
Ryogo
I WENT TO THE KANAUMI AND MASK MAN CRIME SCENES, SO I KNOW WHAT YOU'RE TALKING ABOUT.
IT'S NOT LIKE WE HAVE PROOF, THOUGH...
...AT THE MOMOMIYA LOANS OFFICE...
...WAKAZONO-KUN KEPT GOING ON ABOUT THE RAT AND THREE-EYES.
IF THERE WAS SUPPOSED TO BE A CALLING CARD THERE THAT WASN'T...
...THEN IT FITS...

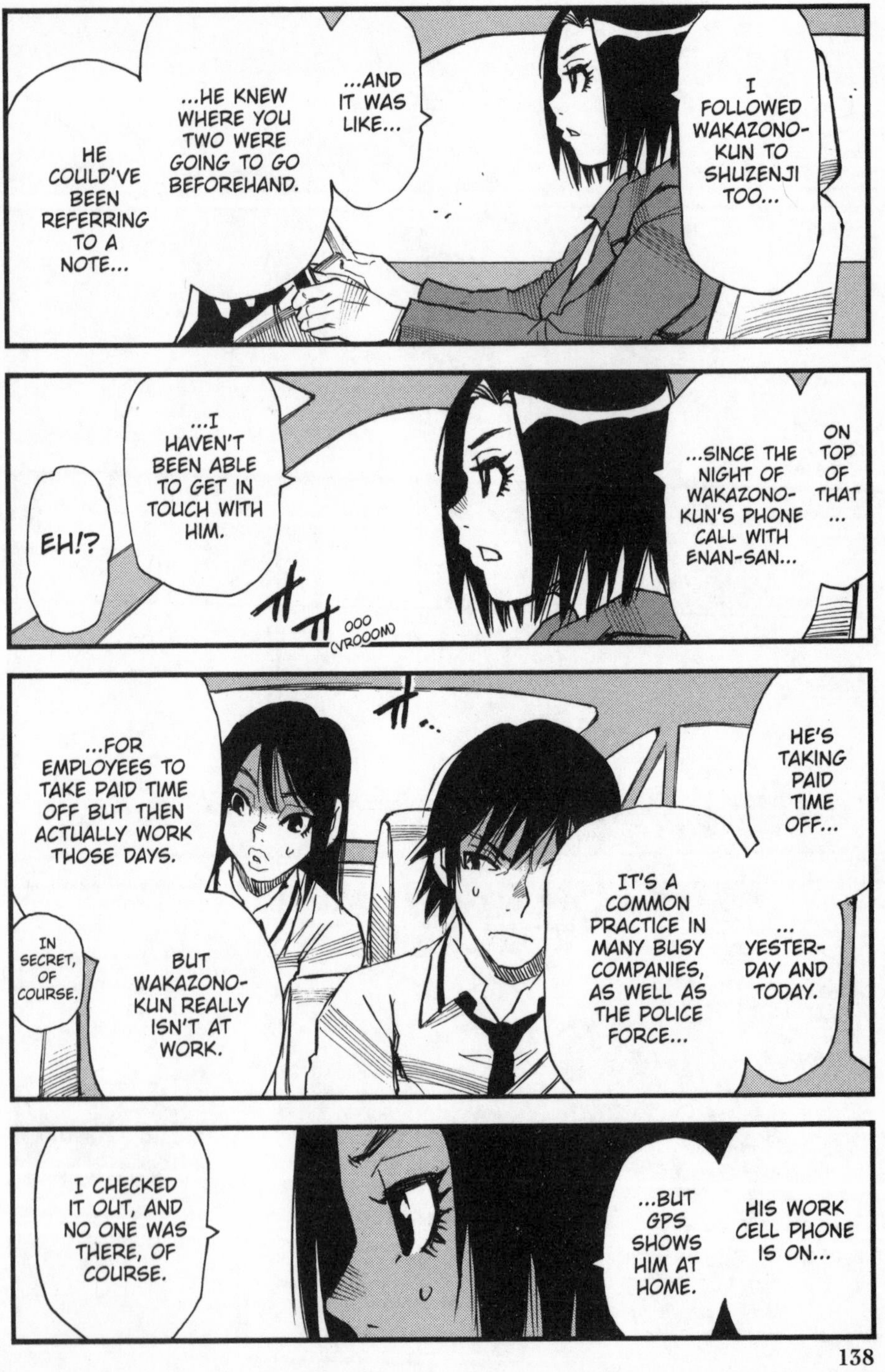
I FOLLOWED WAKAZONO-KUN TO SHUZENJI TOO...
...AND IT WAS LIKE...
...HE KNEW WHERE YOU TWO WERE GOING TO GO BEFOREHAND.
HE COULD'VE BEEN REFERRING TO A NOTE...
ON TOP OF THAT...
...SINCE THE NIGHT OF WAKAZONO-KUN'S PHONE CALL WITH ENAN-SAN...
...I HAVEN'T BEEN ABLE TO GET IN TOUCH WITH HIM.
EH!?
OOO (VROOOM)
HE'S TAKING PAID TIME OFF...
...YESTER-DAY AND TODAY.
IT'S A COMMON PRACTICE IN MANY BUSY COMPANIES, AS WELL AS THE POLICE FORCE...
...FOR EMPLOYEES TO TAKE PAID TIME OFF BUT THEN ACTUALLY WORK THOSE DAYS.
IN SECRET, OF COURSE.
BUT WAKAZONO-KUN REALLY ISN'T AT WORK.
HIS WORK CELL PHONE IS ON...
...BUT GPS SHOWS HIM AT HOME.
I CHECKED IT OUT, AND NO ONE WAS THERE, OF COURSE.

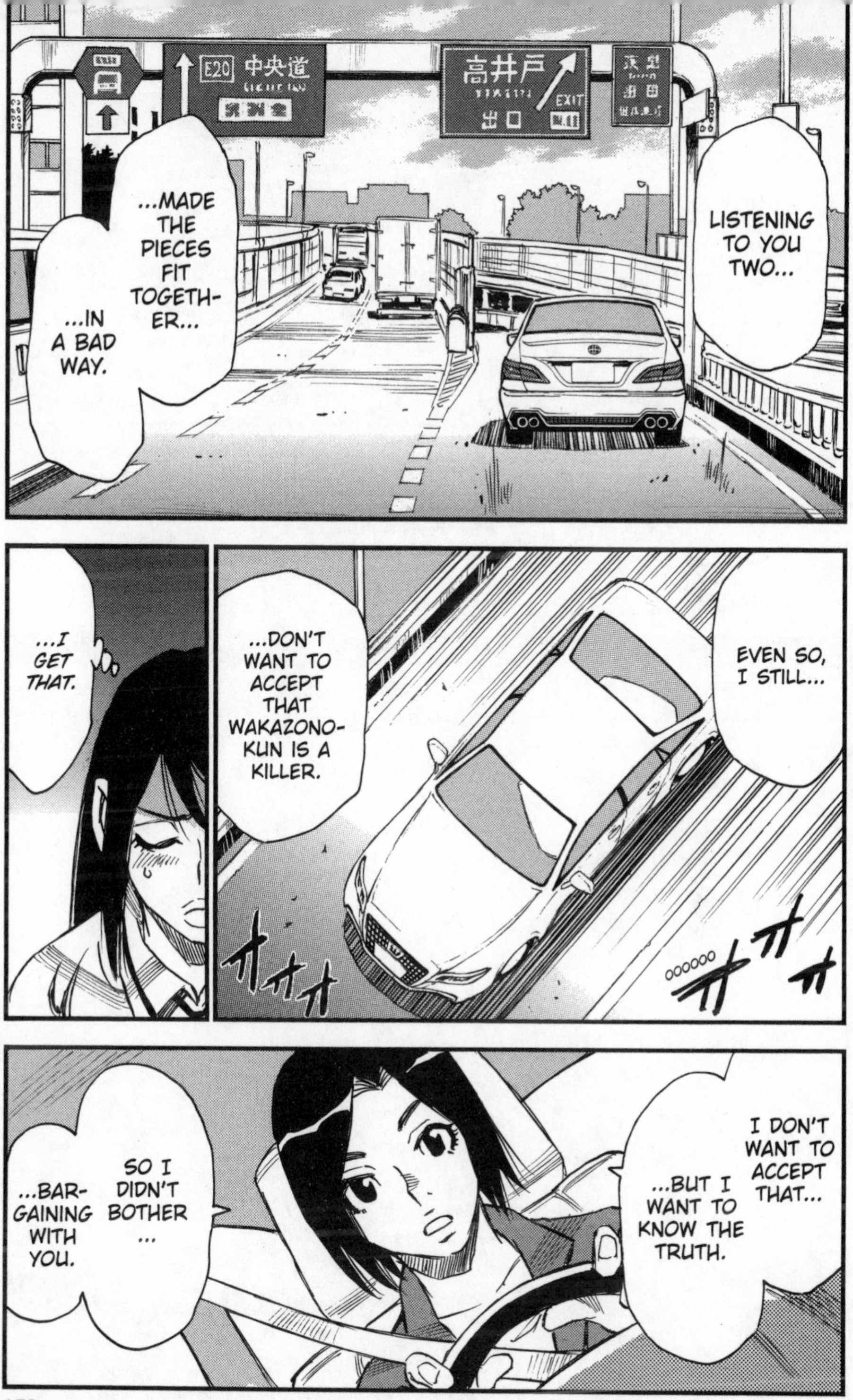
高井戸
EXIT
出口
E20
中央道
LISTENING TO YOU TWO...
...MADE THE PIECES FIT TOGETH-ER...
...IN A BAD WAY.
EVEN SO, I STILL...
...DON'T WANT TO ACCEPT THAT WAKAZONO-KUN IS A KILLER.
oooooo
...I GET THAT.
I DON'T WANT TO ACCEPT THAT...
...BUT I WANT TO KNOW THE TRUTH.
SO I DIDN'T BOTHER ...
...BAR-GAINING WITH YOU.

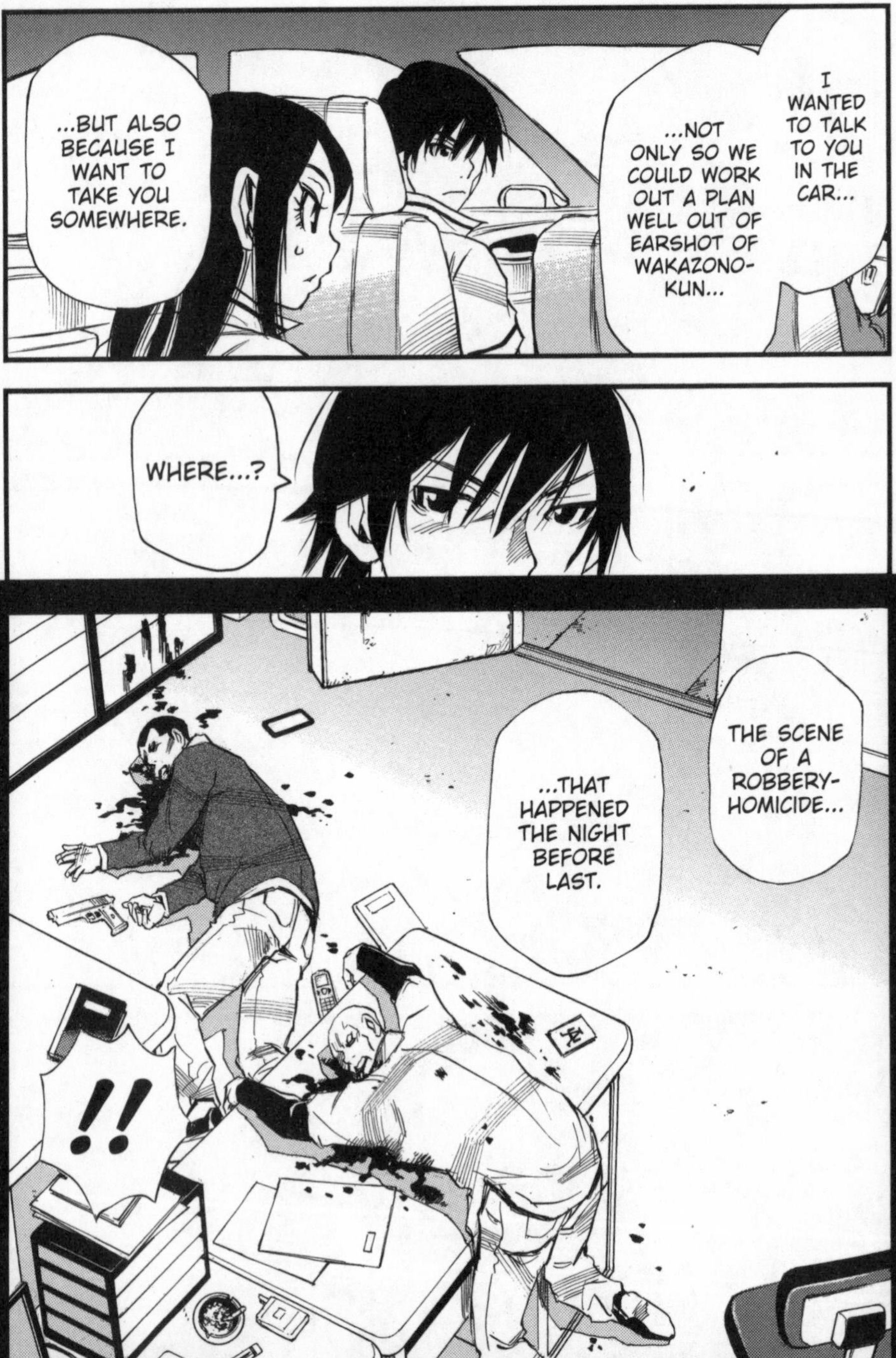
I WANTED TO TALK TO YOU IN THE CAR...
...NOT ONLY SO WE COULD WORK OUT A PLAN WELL OUT OF EARSHOT OF WAKAZONO-KUN...
...BUT ALSO BECAUSE I WANT TO TAKE YOU SOMEWHERE.
WHERE...?
THE SCENE OF A ROBBERY-HOMICIDE...
...THAT HAPPENED THE NIGHT BEFORE LAST.
!!

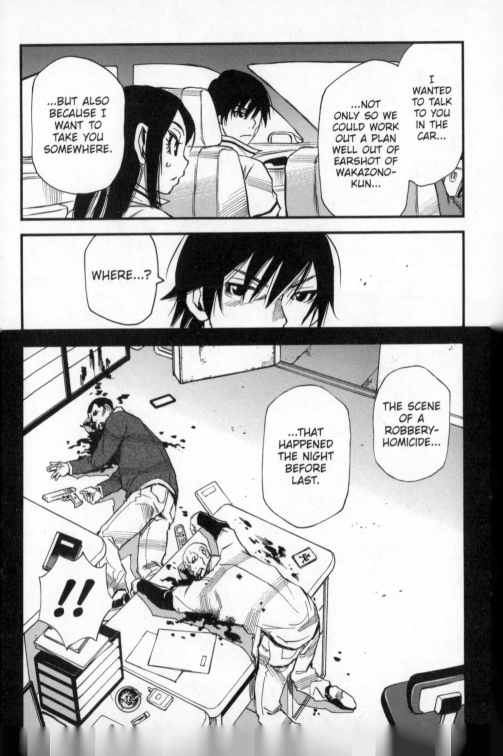

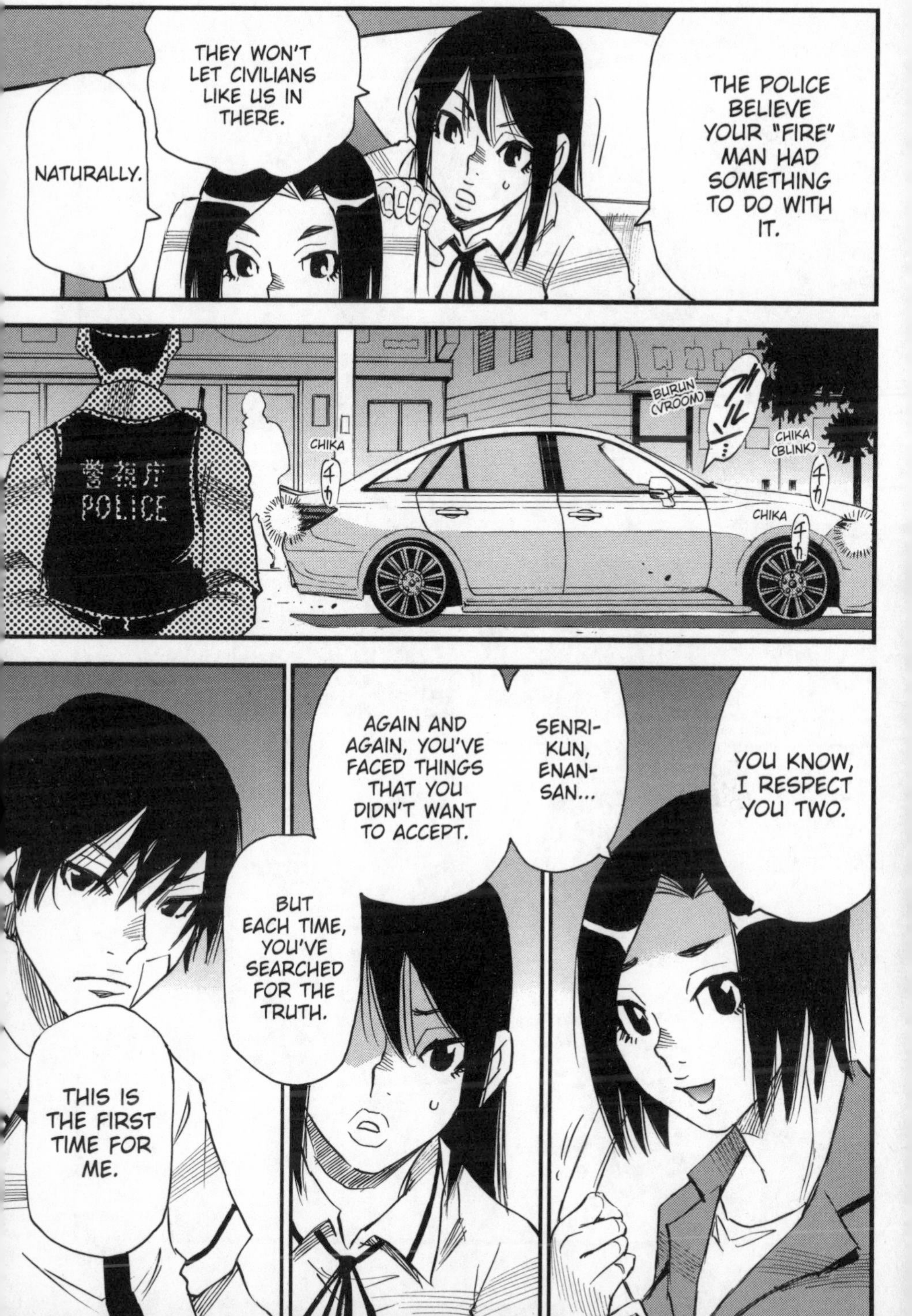
THE POLICE BELIEVE YOUR "FIRE" MAN HAD SOMETHING TO DO WITH IT.
THEY WON'T LET CIVILIANS LIKE US IN THERE.
NATURALLY.
CHIKA (BLINK)
チカ
CHIKA
チカ
ブルン…
BURUN (VROOM)
CHIKA
チカ
警視庁 POLICE
YOU KNOW, I RESPECT YOU TWO.
SENRI-KUN, ENAN-SAN...
AGAIN AND AGAIN, YOU'VE FACED THINGS THAT YOU DIDN'T WANT TO ACCEPT.
BUT EACH TIME, YOU'VE SEARCHED FOR THE TRUTH.
THIS IS THE FIRST TIME FOR ME.

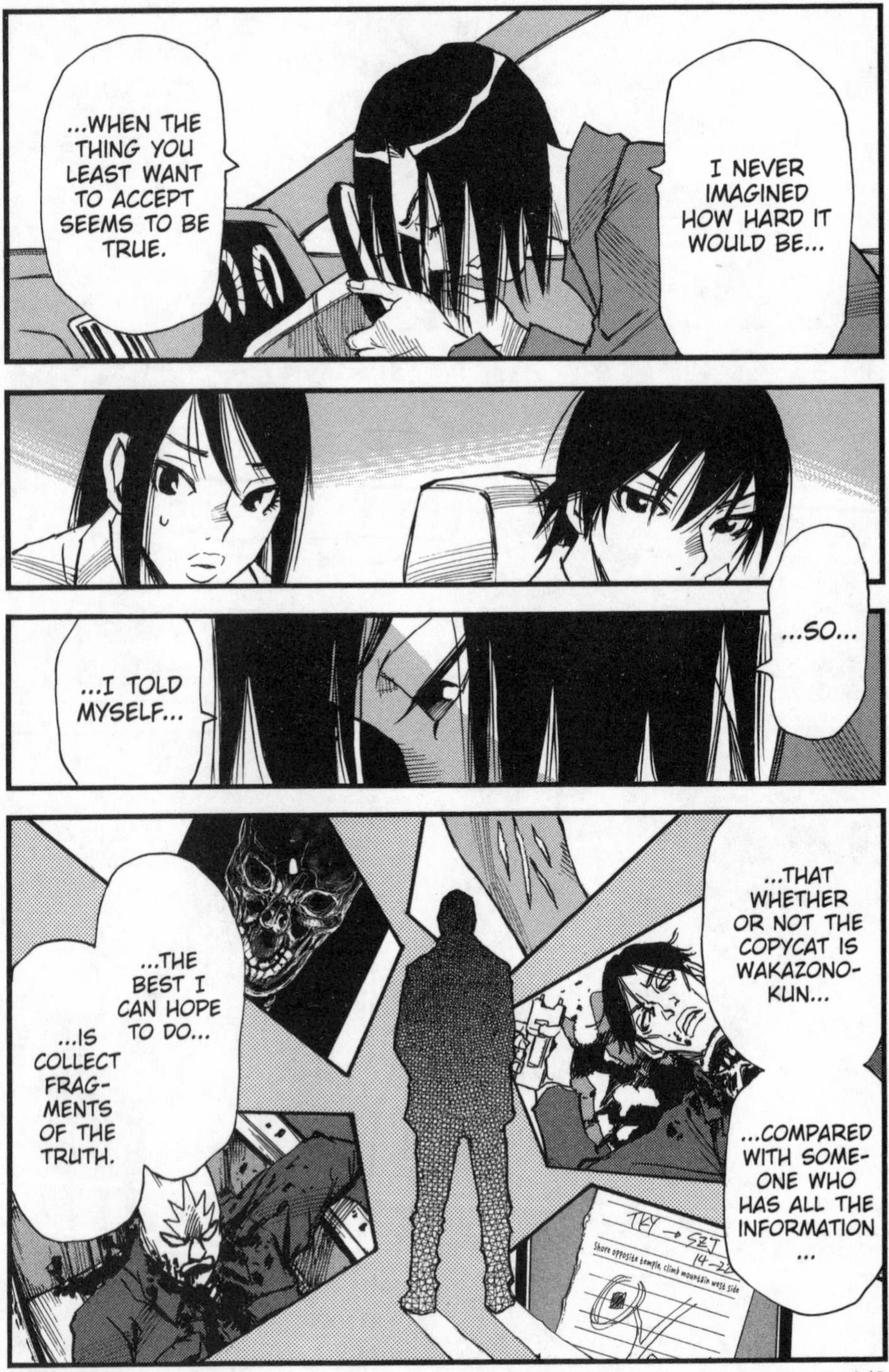
I NEVER IMAGINED HOW HARD IT WOULD BE...
...WHEN THE THING YOU LEAST WANT TO ACCEPT SEEMS TO BE TRUE.
...SO...
...I TOLD MYSELF...
...THAT WHETHER OR NOT THE COPYCAT IS WAKAZONO-KUN...
...COMPARED WITH SOME-ONE WHO HAS ALL THE INFORMATION ...
TKY → SZT
Shore opposite temple, climb mountain west side
...THE BEST I CAN HOPE TO DO...
...IS COLLECT FRAG-MENTS OF THE TRUTH.

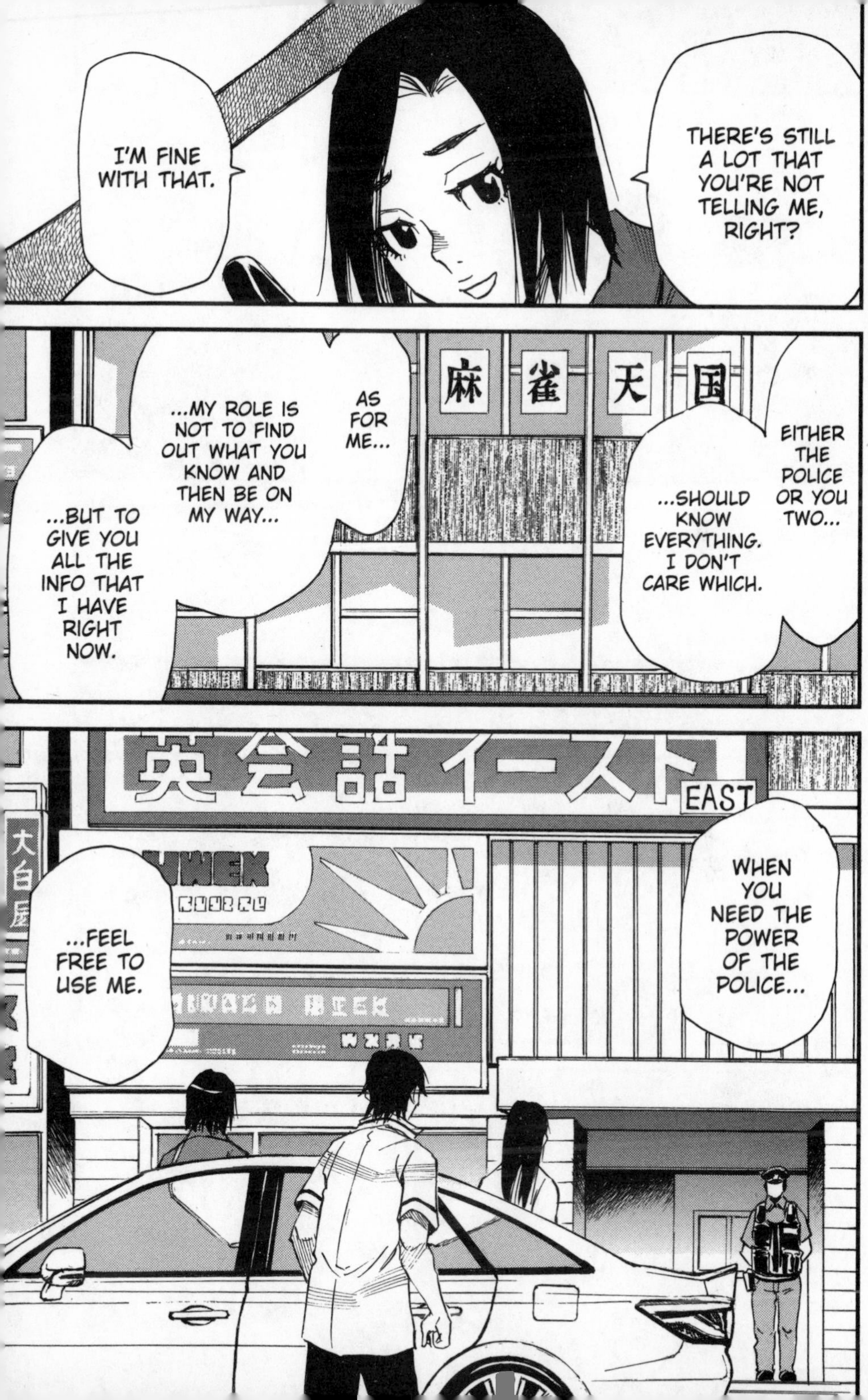

THERE'S STILL A LOT THAT YOU'RE NOT TELLING ME, RIGHT?
I'M FINE WITH THAT.
麻雀天国
EITHER THE POLICE OR YOU TWO...
...SHOULD KNOW EVERYTHING. I DON'T CARE WHICH.
AS FOR ME...
...MY ROLE IS NOT TO FIND OUT WHAT YOU KNOW AND THEN BE ON MY WAY...
...BUT TO GIVE YOU ALL THE INFO THAT I HAVE RIGHT NOW.
英会話イースト
EAST
WHEN YOU NEED THE POWER OF THE POLICE...
...FEEL FREE TO USE ME.

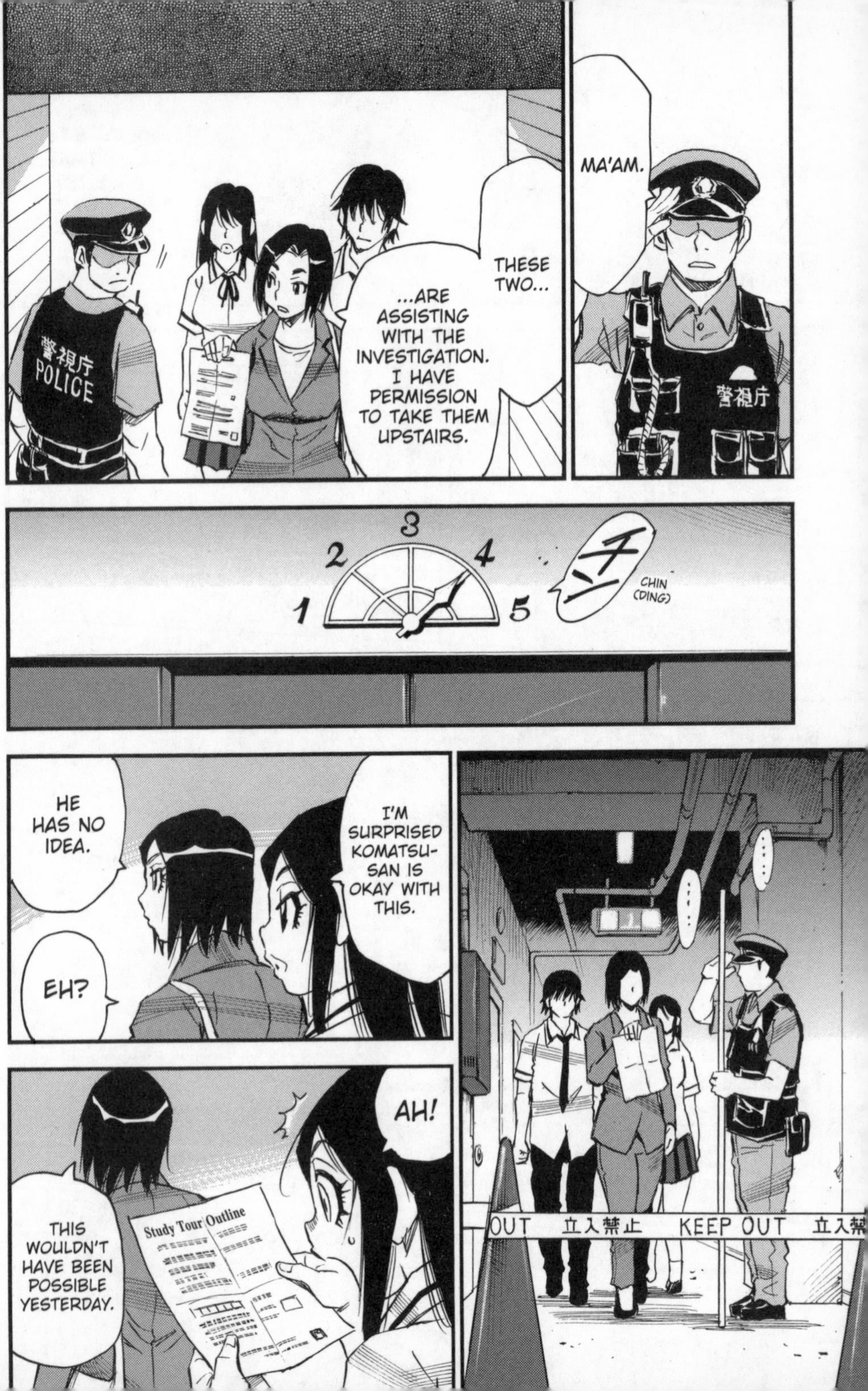
MA'AM.
警視庁
THESE TWO...
...ARE ASSISTING WITH THE INVESTIGATION. I HAVE PERMISSION TO TAKE THEM UPSTAIRS.
警視庁
POLICE
1 2 3 4 5
チン
CHIN (DING)
....
....
OUT 立入禁止 KEEP OUT 立入禁
I'M SURPRISED KOMATSU-SAN IS OKAY WITH THIS.
HE HAS NO IDEA.
EH?
AH!
THIS WOULDN'T HAVE BEEN POSSIBLE YESTERDAY.
Study Tour Outline

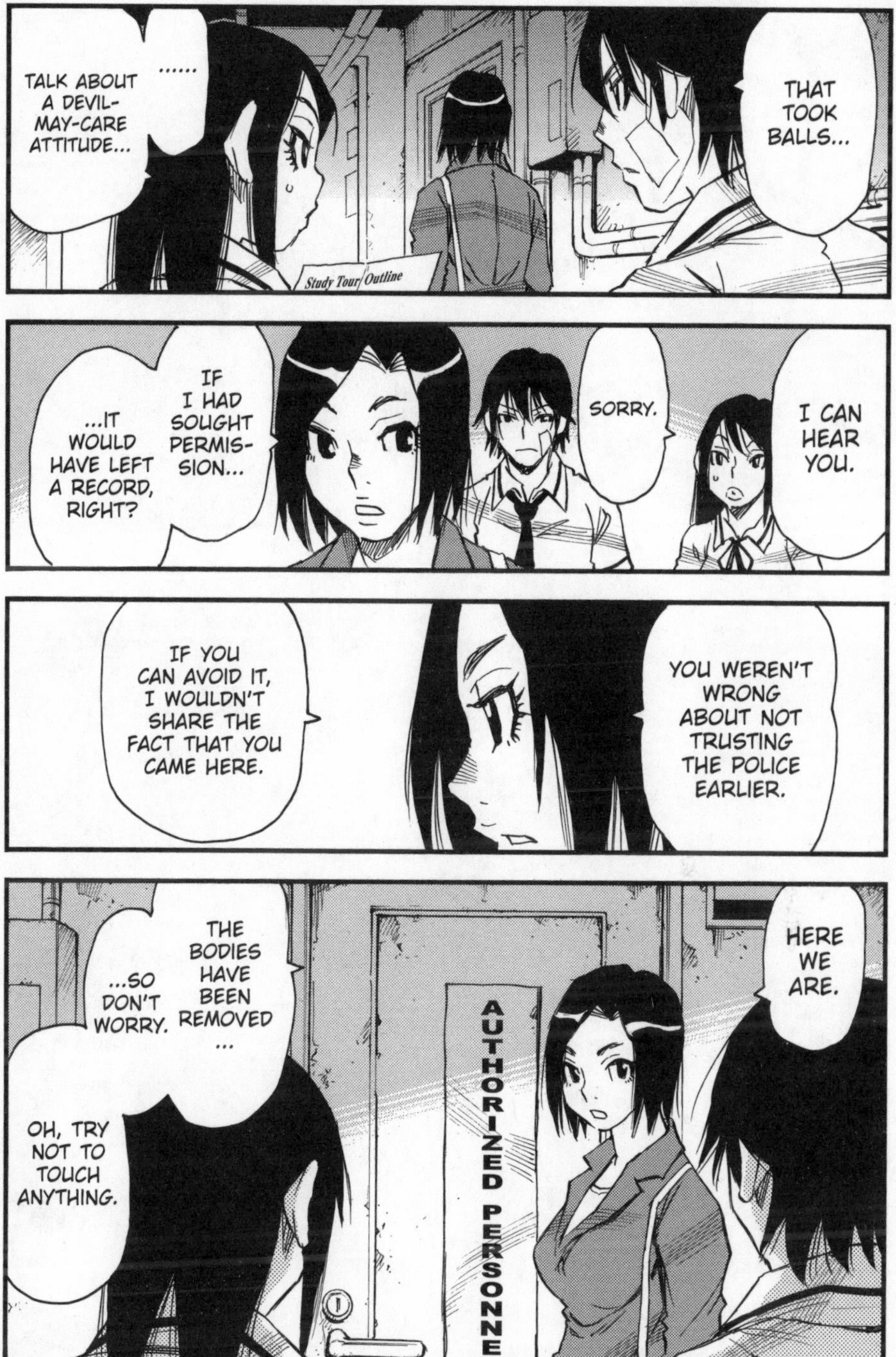
THAT TOOK BALLS...
......
TALK ABOUT A DEVIL-MAY-CARE ATTITUDE...
Study Tour Outline
I CAN HEAR YOU.
SORRY.
IF I HAD SOUGHT PERMISSION...
...IT WOULD HAVE LEFT A RECORD, RIGHT?
YOU WEREN'T WRONG ABOUT NOT TRUSTING THE POLICE EARLIER.
IF YOU CAN AVOID IT, I WOULDN'T SHARE THE FACT THAT YOU CAME HERE.
HERE WE ARE.
AUTHORIZED PERSONNE
THE BODIES HAVE BEEN REMOVED ...
...SO DON'T WORRY.
OH, TRY NOT TO TOUCH ANYTHING.

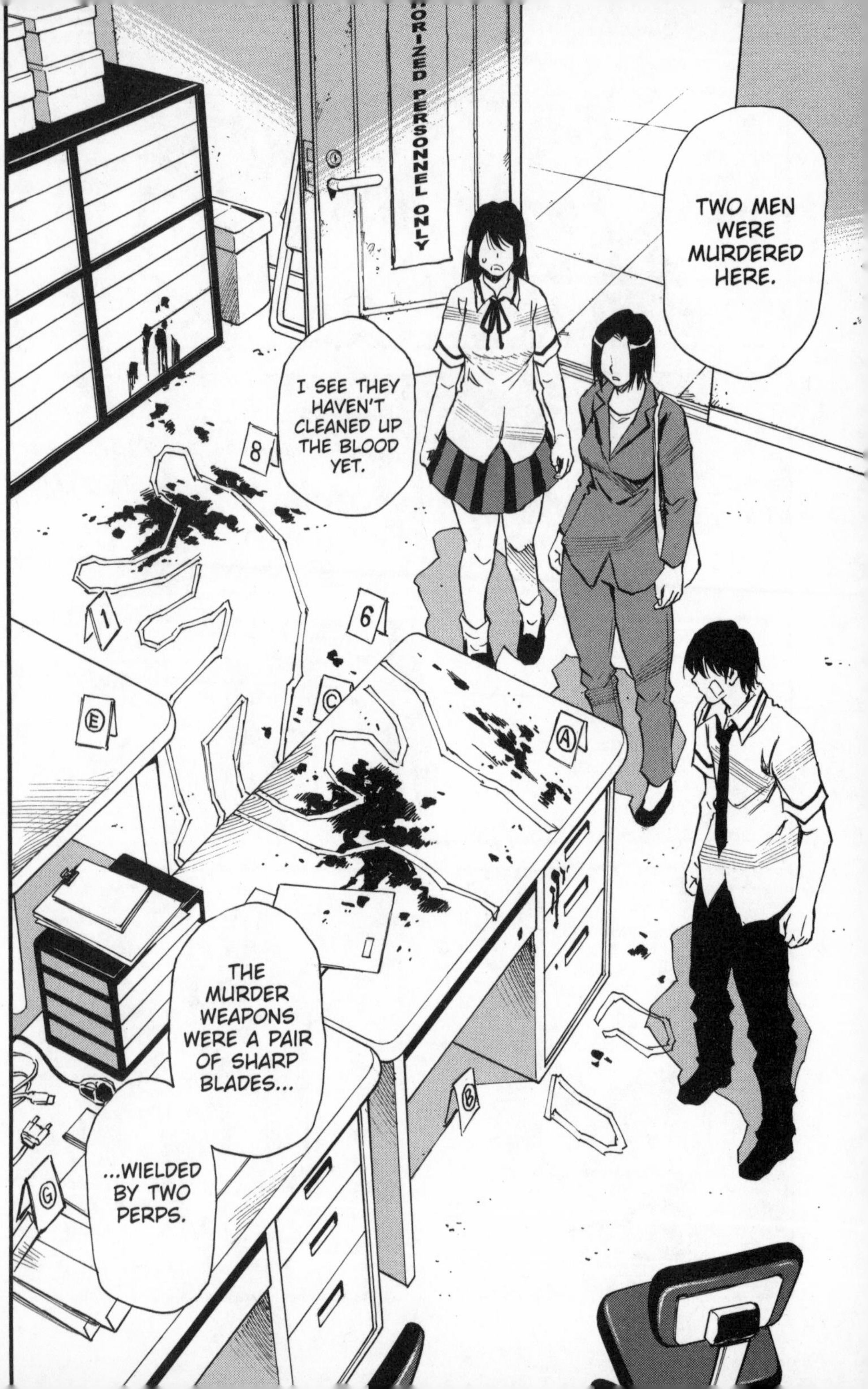
ORIZED PERSONNEL ONLY
TWO MEN WERE MURDERED HERE.
I SEE THEY HAVEN'T CLEANED UP THE BLOOD YET.
THE MURDER WEAPONS WERE A PAIR OF SHARP BLADES...
...WIELDED BY TWO PERPS.

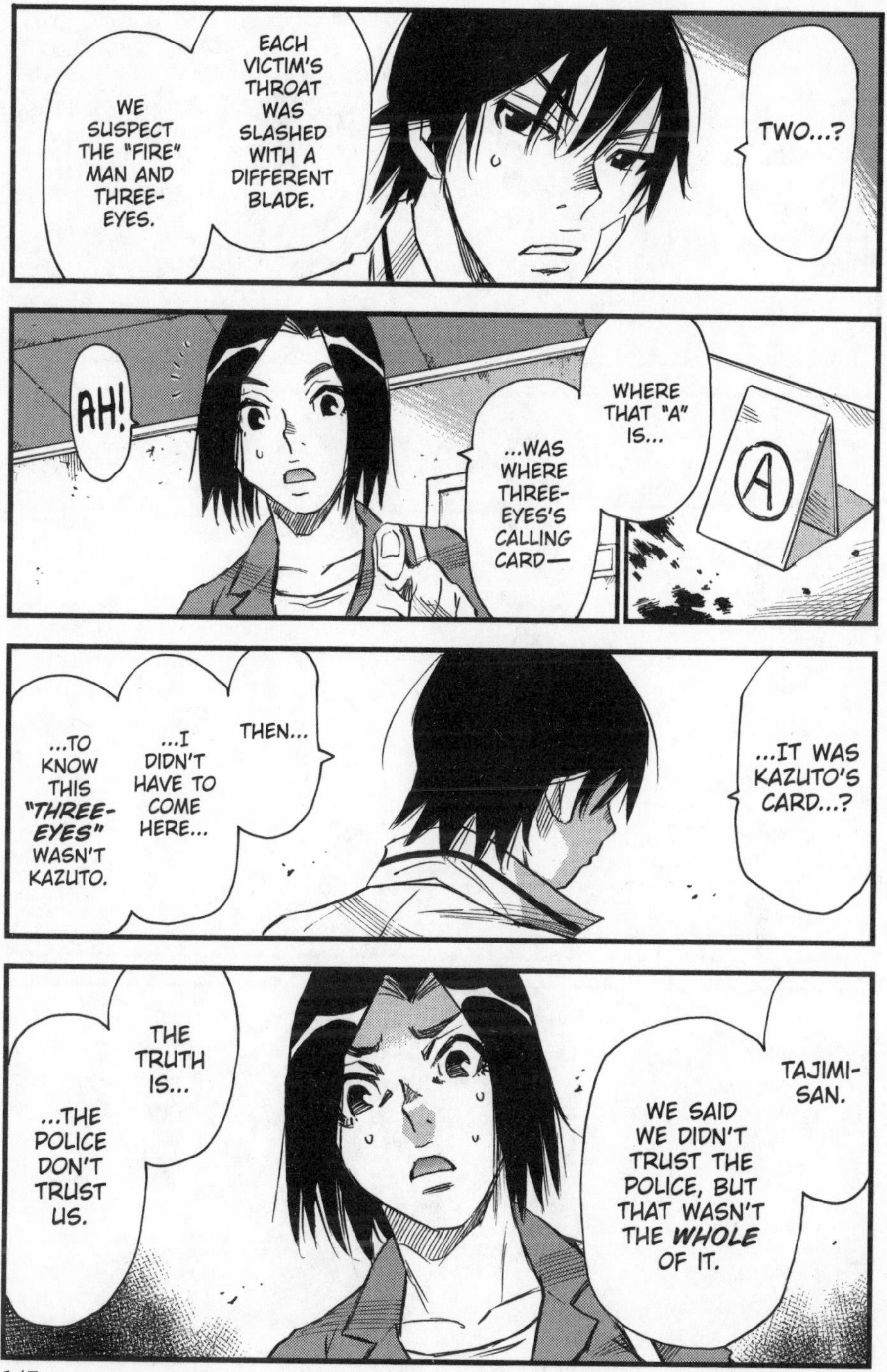
TWO...?
EACH VICTIM'S THROAT WAS SLASHED WITH A DIFFERENT BLADE.
WE SUSPECT THE "FIRE" MAN AND THREE-EYES.
A
WHERE THAT "A" IS...
...WAS WHERE THREE-EYES'S CALLING CARD—
AH!
...IT WAS KAZUTO'S CARD...?
THEN...
...I DIDN'T HAVE TO COME HERE...
...TO KNOW THIS *"THREE-EYES"* WASN'T KAZUTO.
TAJIMI-SAN.
WE SAID WE DIDN'T TRUST THE POLICE, BUT THAT WASN'T THE *WHOLE* OF IT.
THE TRUTH IS...
...THE POLICE DON'T TRUST US.

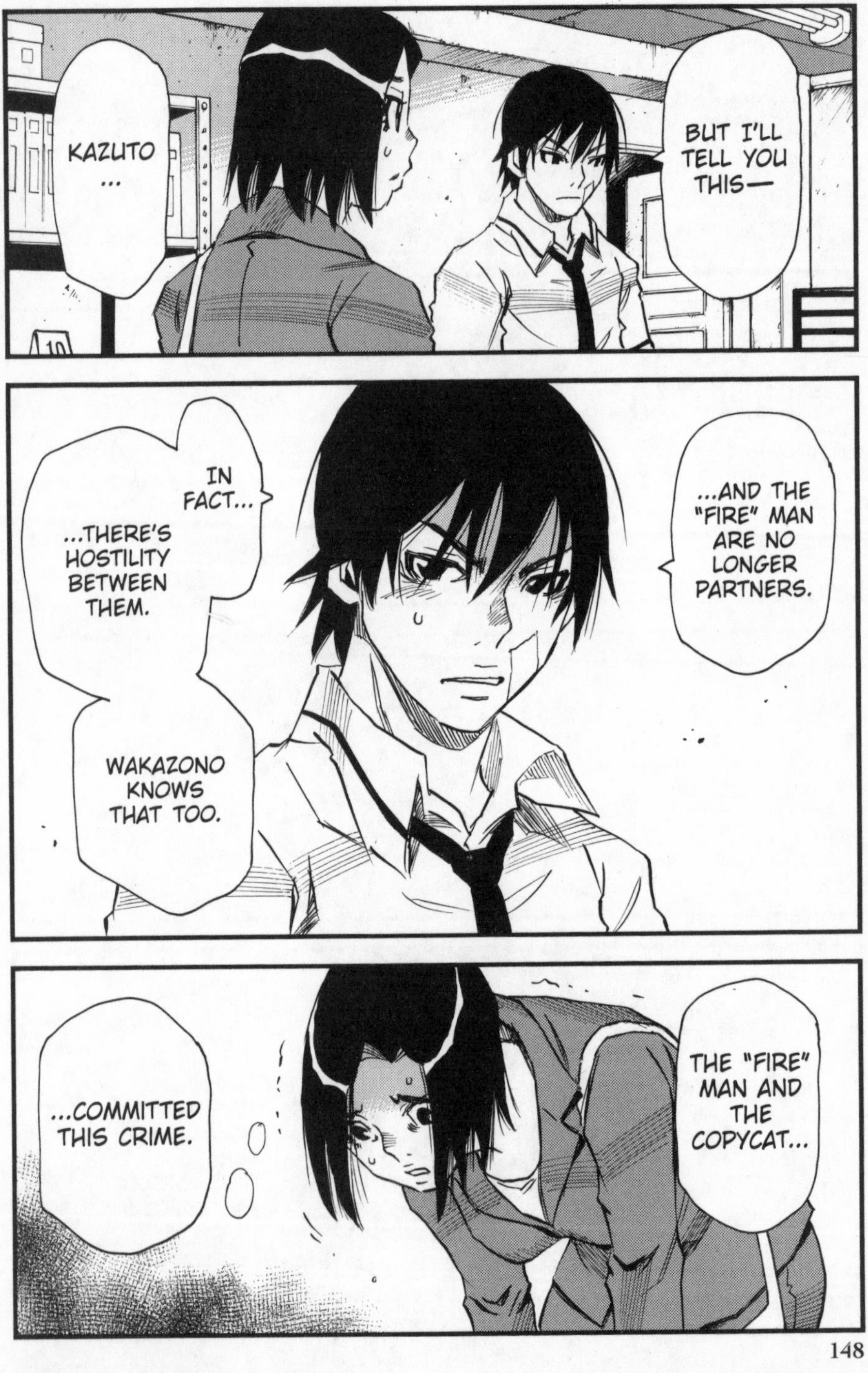
BUT I'LL TELL YOU THIS—
KAZUTO ...
...AND THE "FIRE" MAN ARE NO LONGER PARTNERS.
IN FACT...
...THERE'S HOSTILITY BETWEEN THEM.
WAKAZONO KNOWS THAT TOO.
THE "FIRE" MAN AND THE COPYCAT...
...COMMITTED THIS CRIME.

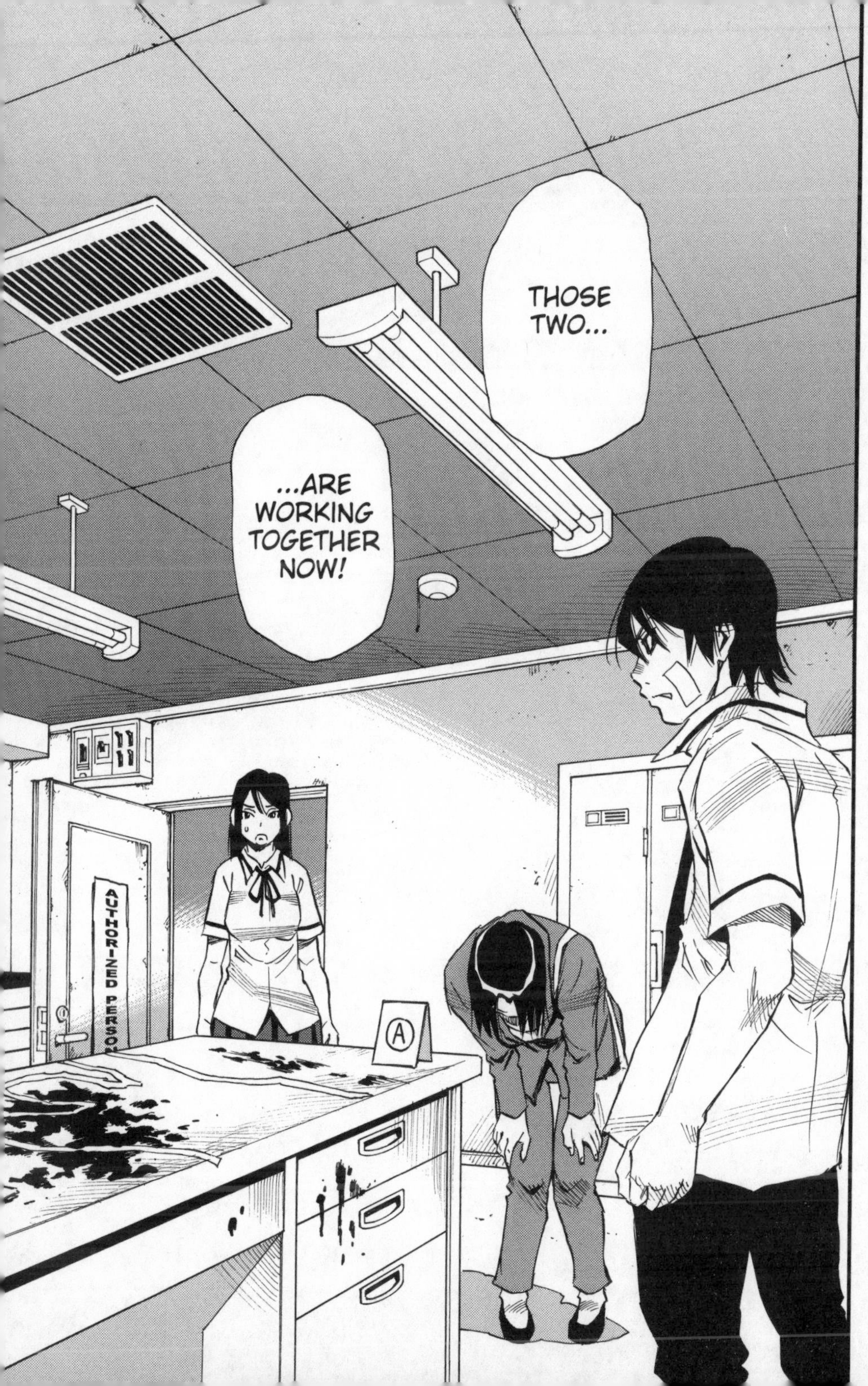
THOSE TWO...
...ARE WORKING TOGETHER NOW!
AUTHORIZED
A

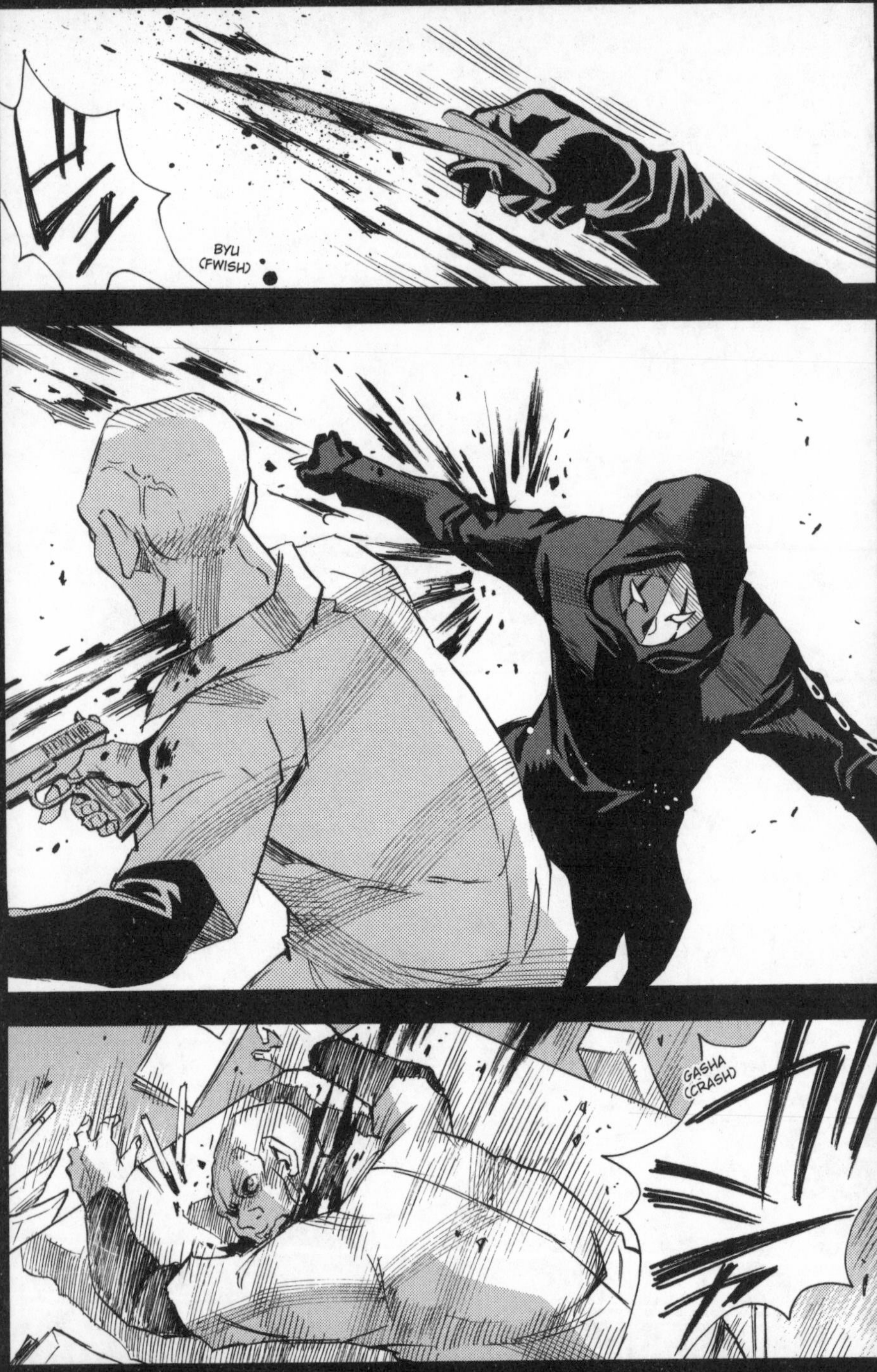
BYU
(FWISH)
GASHA
(CRASH)

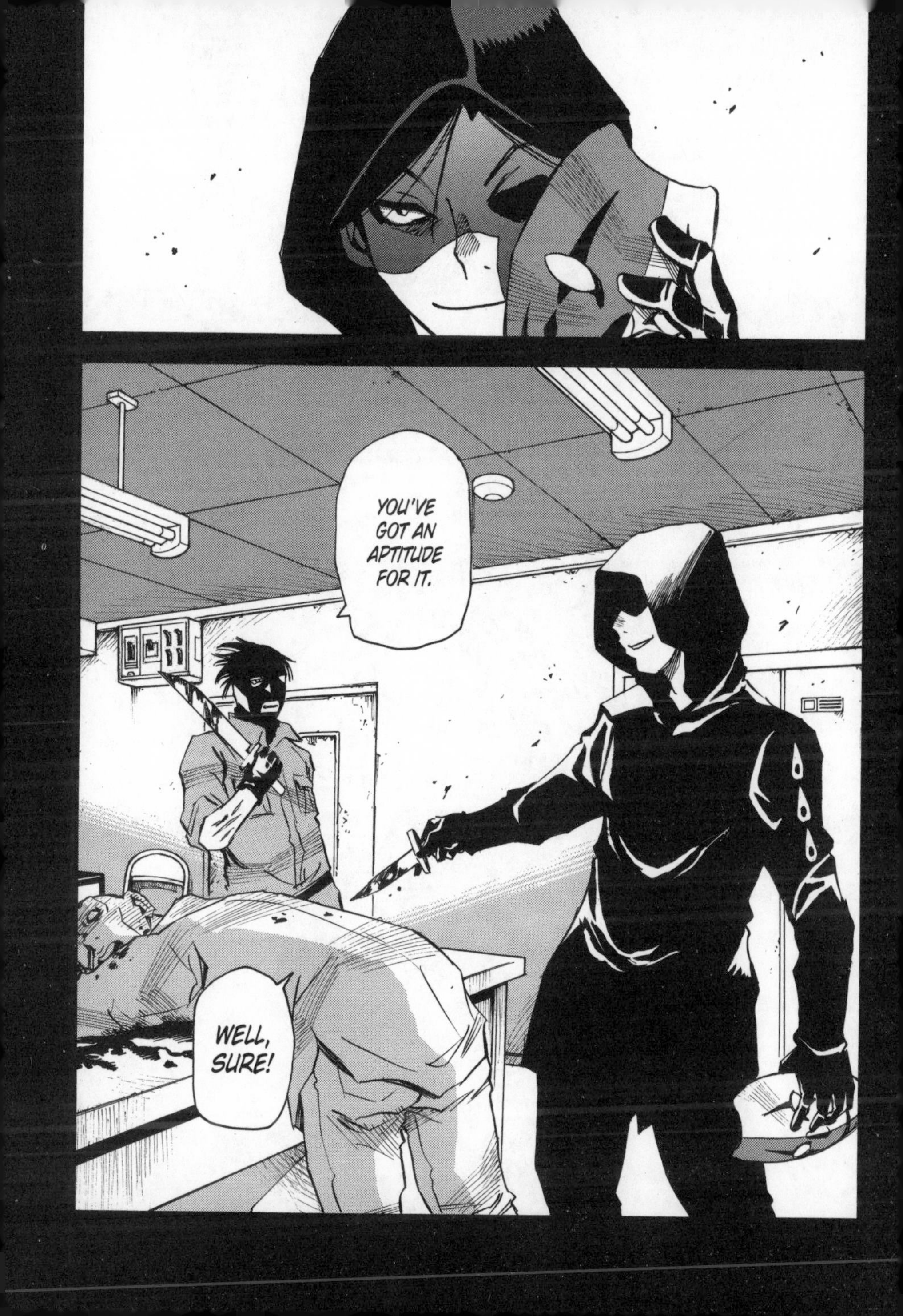
YOU'VE GOT AN APTITUDE FOR IT.
WELL, SURE!

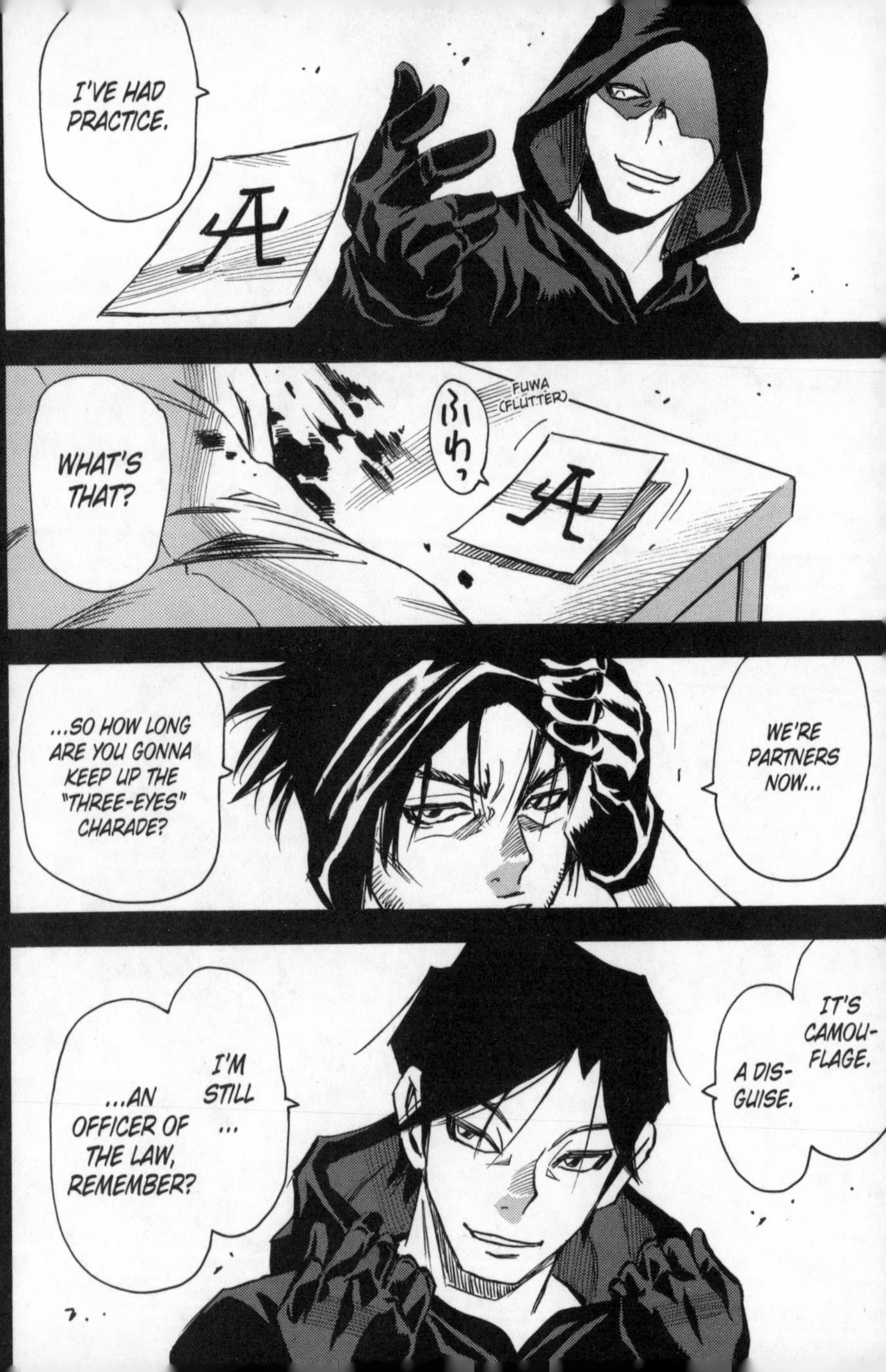
I'VE HAD PRACTICE.
ふわっ
FUWA (FLUTTER)
WHAT'S THAT?
WE'RE PARTNERS NOW...
...SO HOW LONG ARE YOU GONNA KEEP UP THE "THREE-EYES" CHARADE?
IT'S CAMOU-FLAGE.
A DIS-GUISE.
I'M STILL...
...AN OFFICER OF THE LAW, REMEMBER?

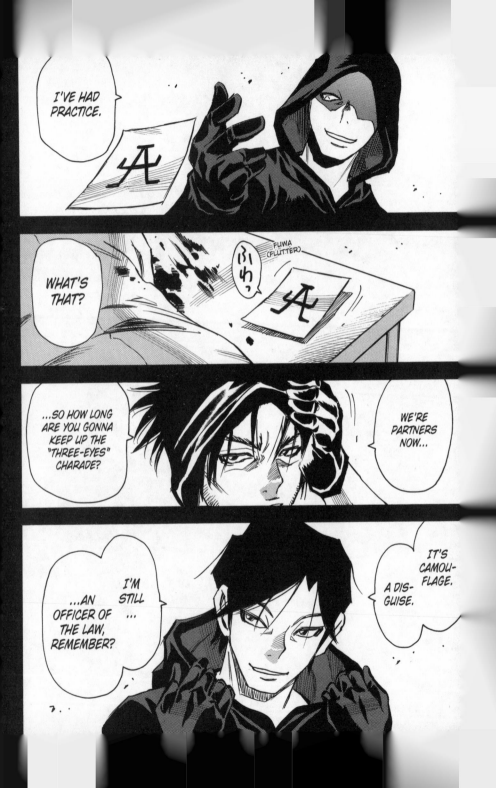

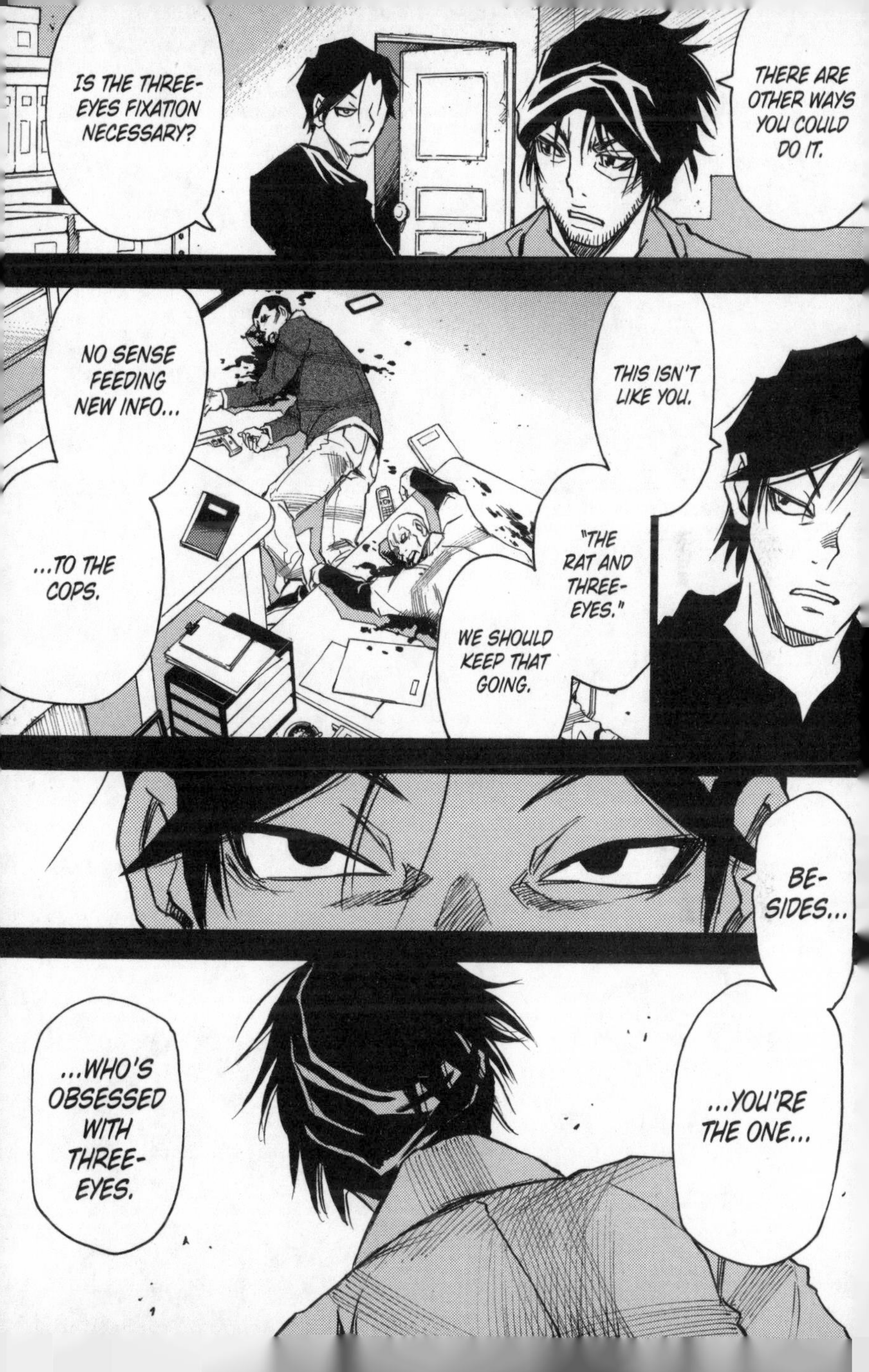
THERE ARE OTHER WAYS YOU COULD DO IT.
IS THE THREE-EYES FIXATION NECESSARY?
THIS ISN'T LIKE YOU.
"THE RAT AND THREE-EYES."
WE SHOULD KEEP THAT GOING.
NO SENSE FEEDING NEW INFO...
...TO THE COPS.
BE-SIDES...
...YOU'RE THE ONE...
...WHO'S OBSESSED WITH THREE-EYES.

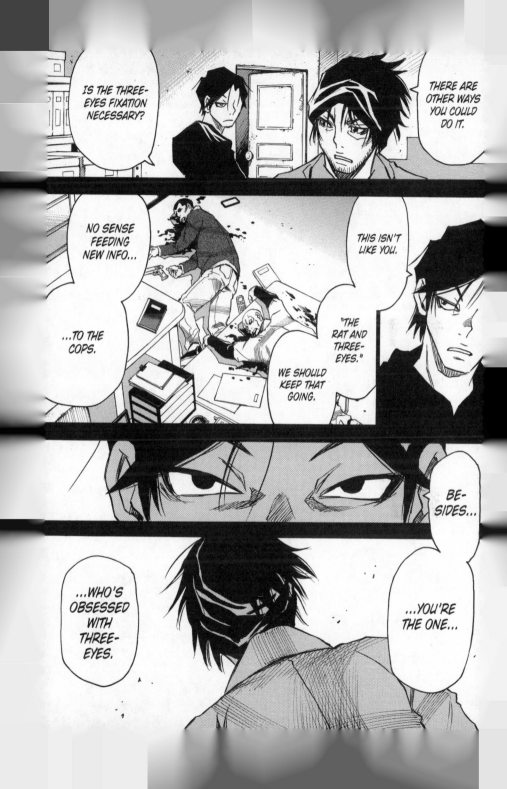

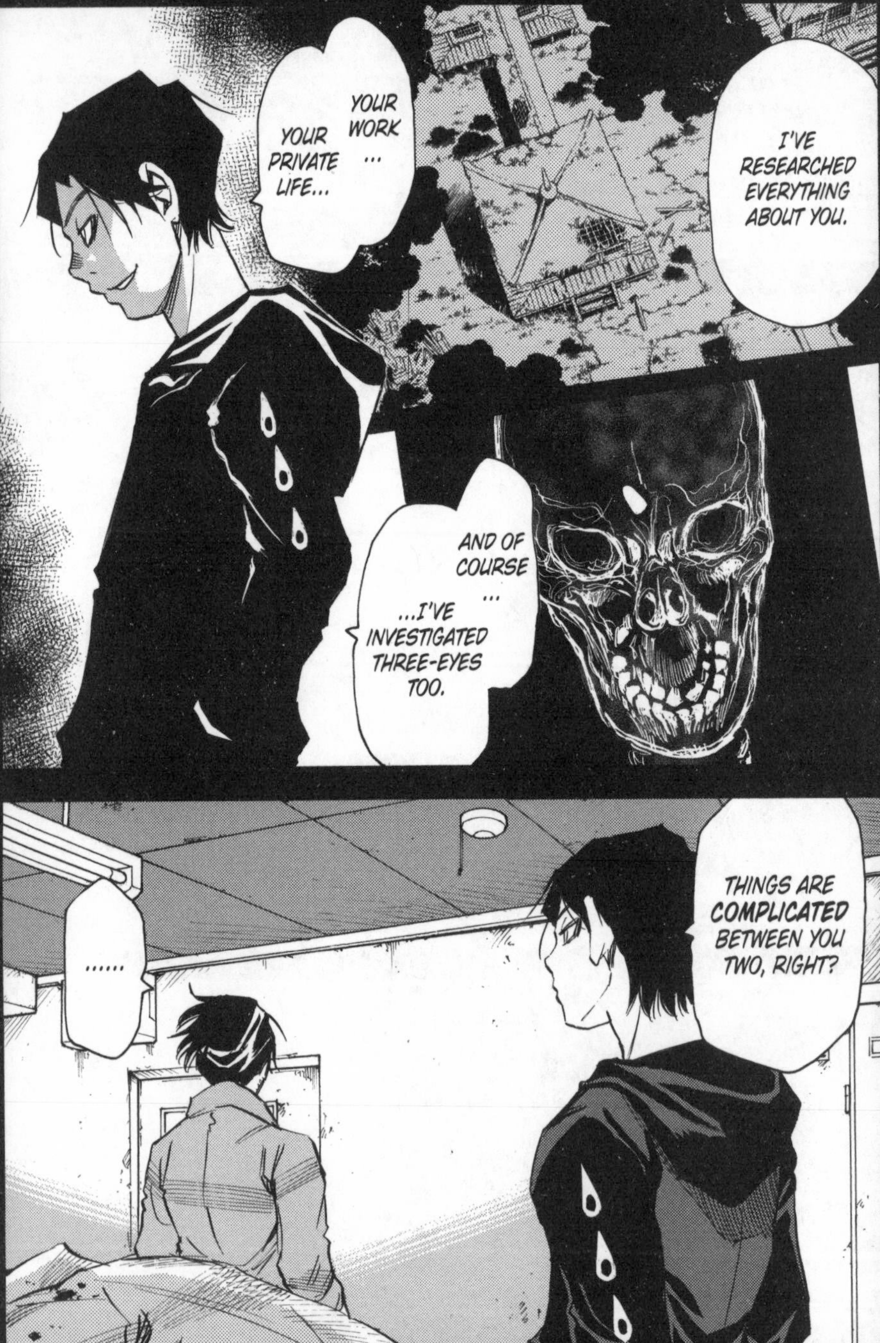
I'VE RESEARCHED EVERYTHING ABOUT YOU.
YOUR WORK ... YOUR PRIVATE LIFE...
AND OF COURSE ... ...I'VE INVESTIGATED THREE-EYES TOO.
THINGS ARE **COMPLICATED** BETWEEN YOU TWO, RIGHT?
......

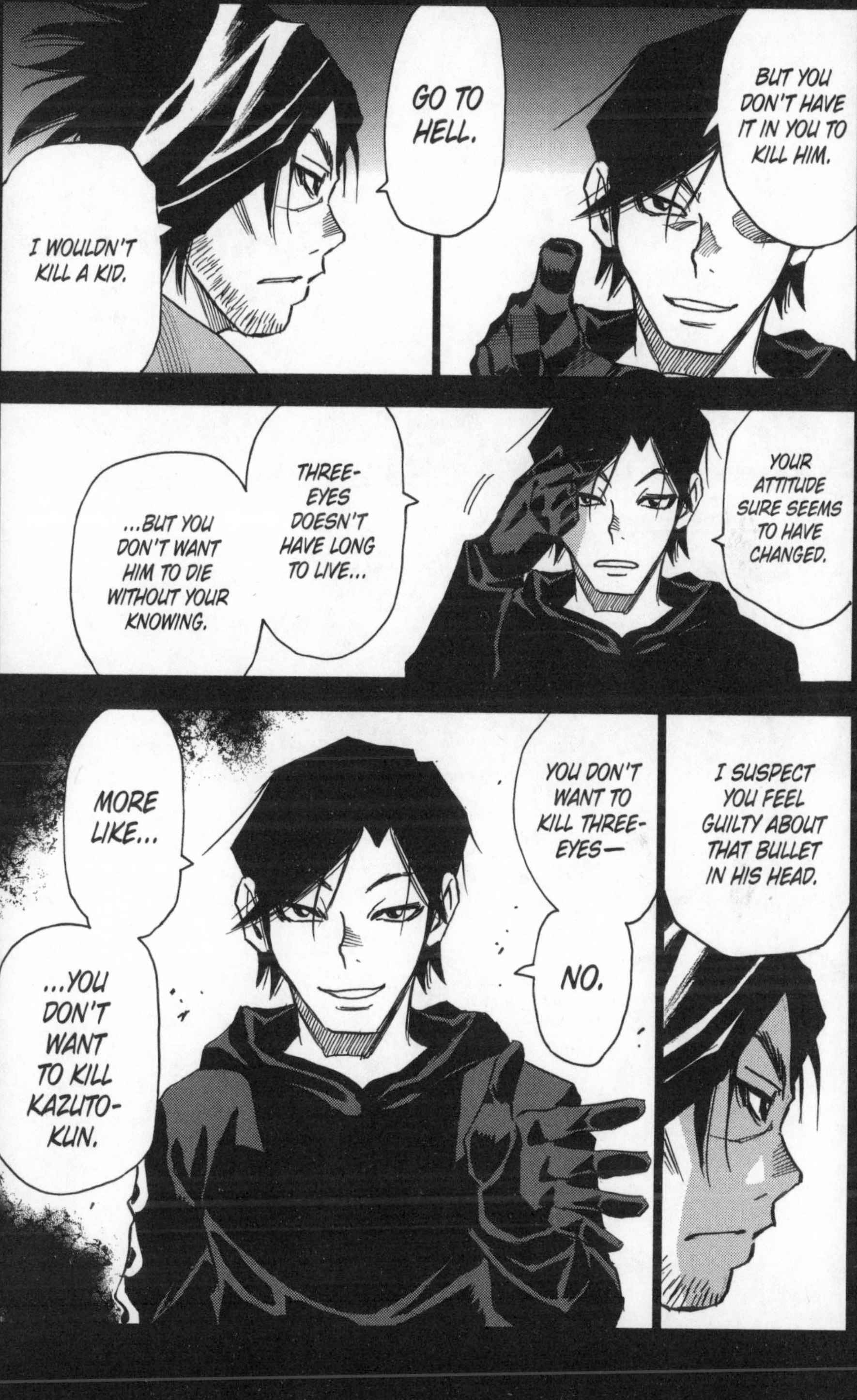
BUT YOU DON'T HAVE IT IN YOU TO KILL HIM.
GO TO HELL.
I WOULDN'T KILL A KID.
YOUR ATTITUDE SURE SEEMS TO HAVE CHANGED.
THREE-EYES DOESN'T HAVE LONG TO LIVE...
...BUT YOU DON'T WANT HIM TO DIE WITHOUT YOUR KNOWING.
I SUSPECT YOU FEEL GUILTY ABOUT THAT BULLET IN HIS HEAD.
YOU DON'T WANT TO KILL THREE-EYES—
NO.
MORE LIKE...
...YOU DON'T WANT TO KILL KAZUTO-KUN.

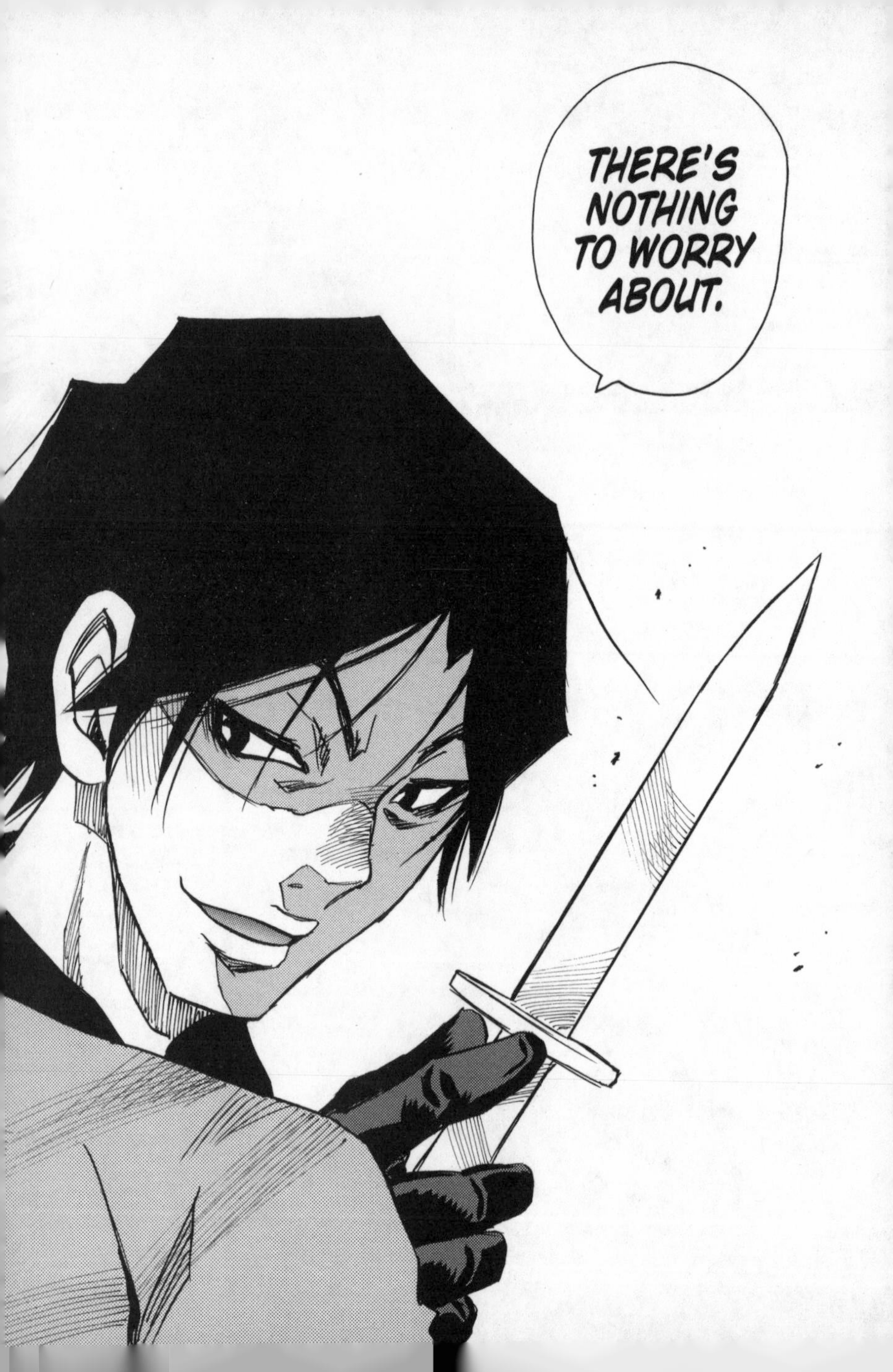
THERE'S NOTHING TO WORRY ABOUT.

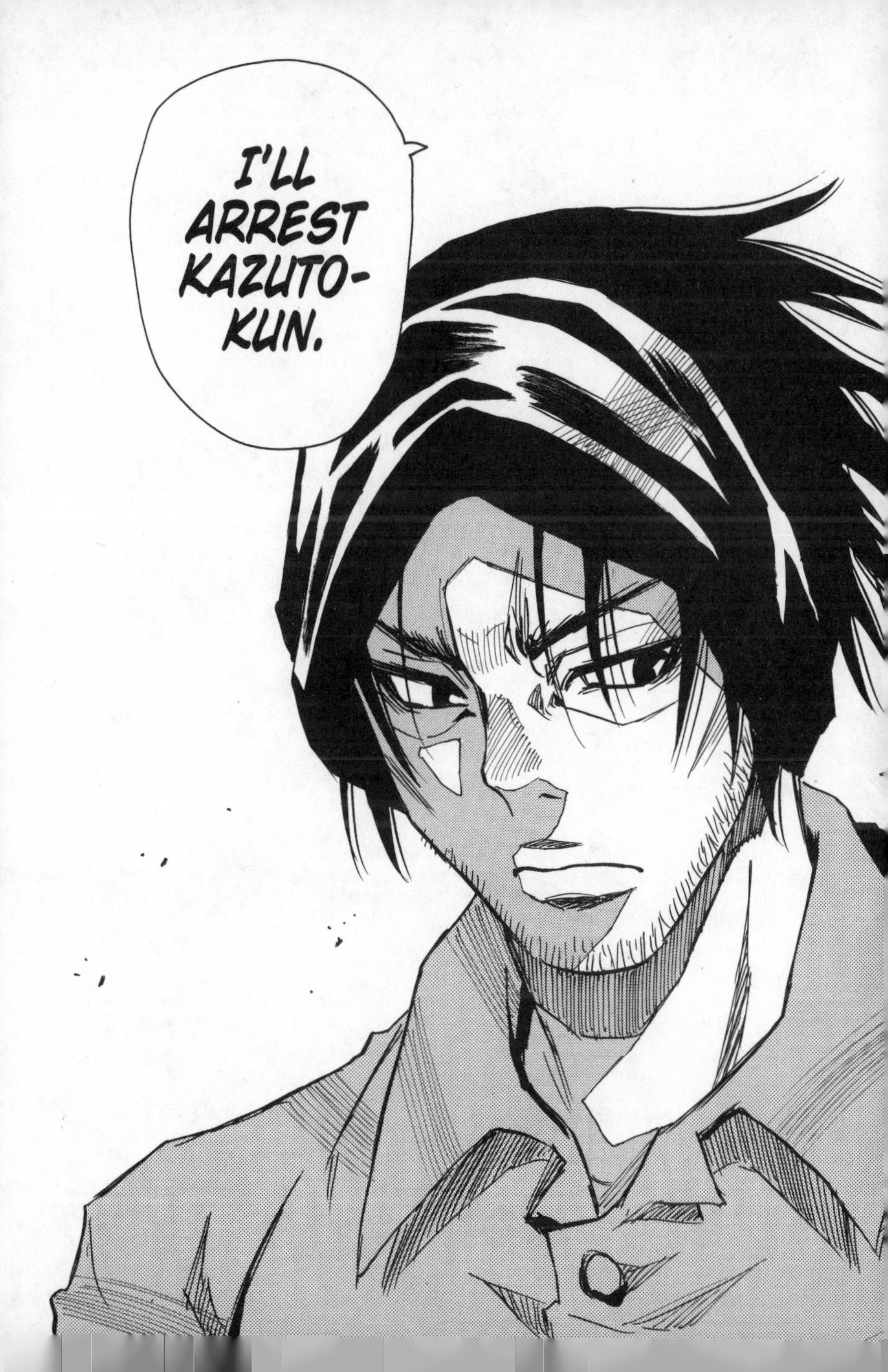
I'LL ARREST KAZUTO-KUN.

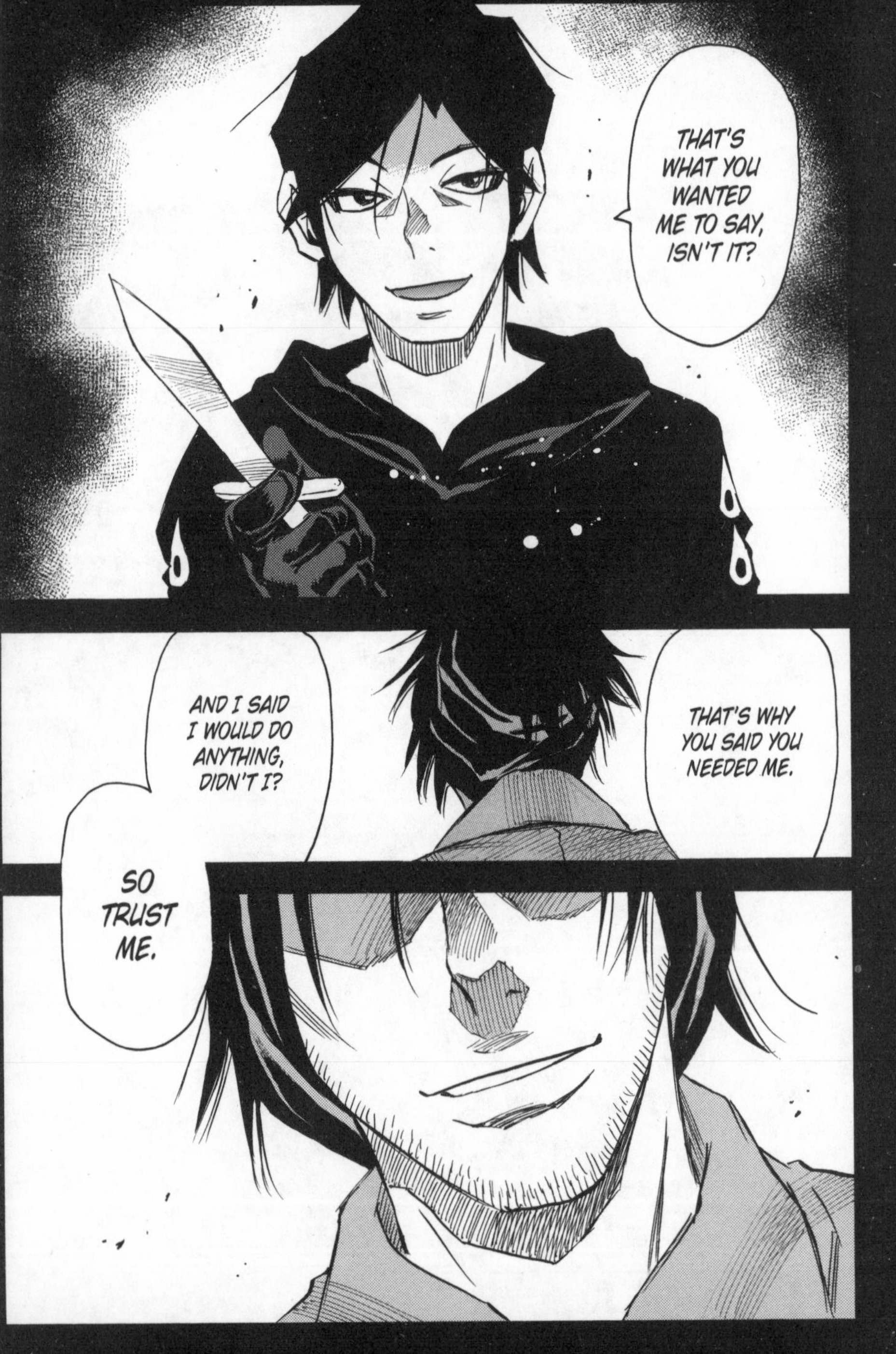
THAT'S WHAT YOU WANTED ME TO SAY, ISN'T IT?
THAT'S WHY YOU SAID YOU NEEDED ME.
AND I SAID I WOULD DO ANYTHING, DIDN'T I?
SO TRUST ME.

#41 END

THIS IS IT.

GI— (CREAK)

OKAY.

I'M GONNA OPEN IT.

GACHIN (CHIK)

GARA

GARA

GARA

GARA (RATTLE)

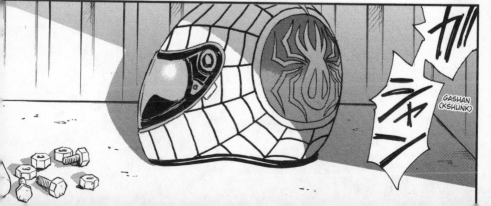

GASHAN (KSHUNK)

#42 For the Sake of That Kid

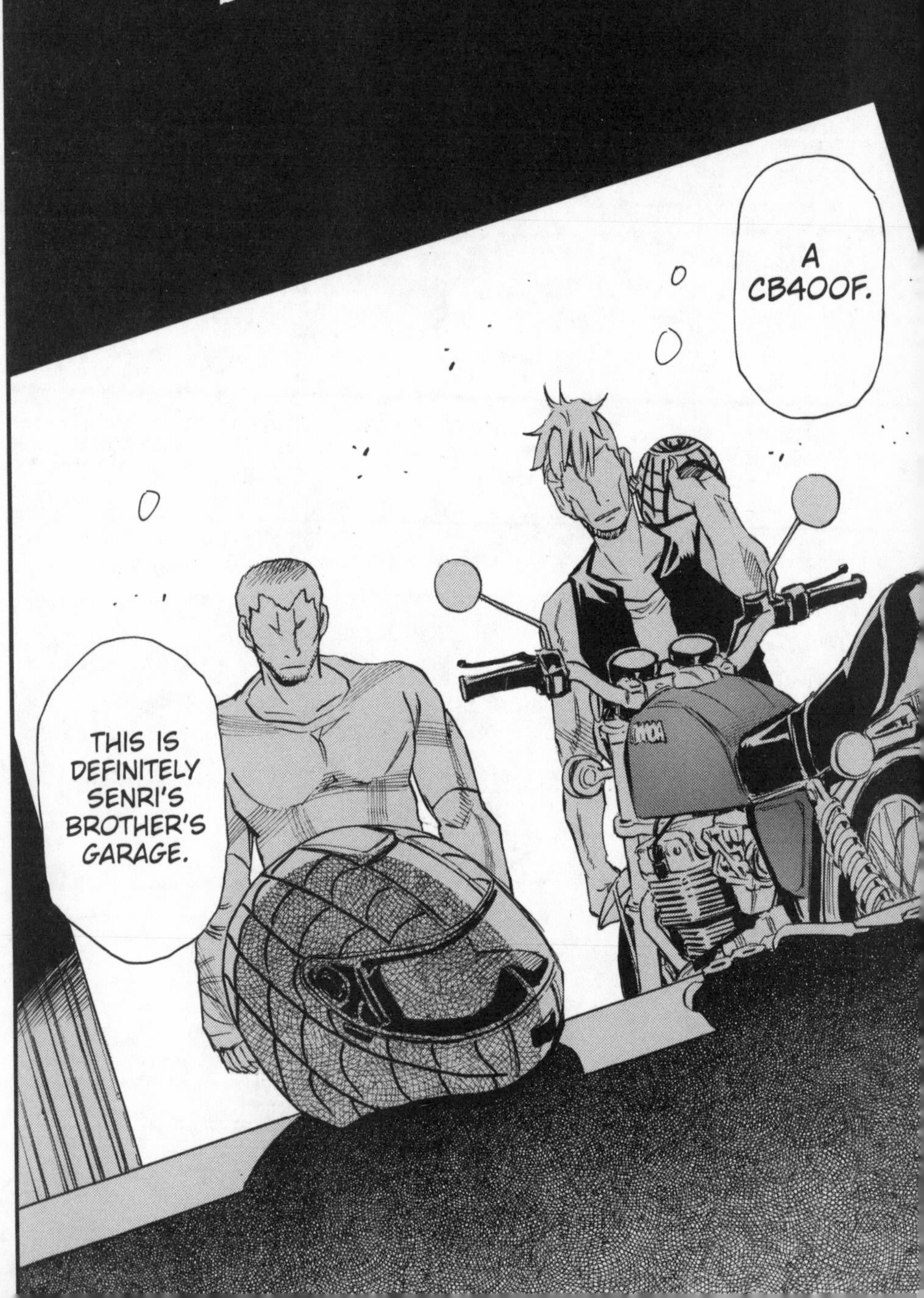
A CB400F.
THIS IS DEFINITELY SENRI'S BROTHER'S GARAGE.

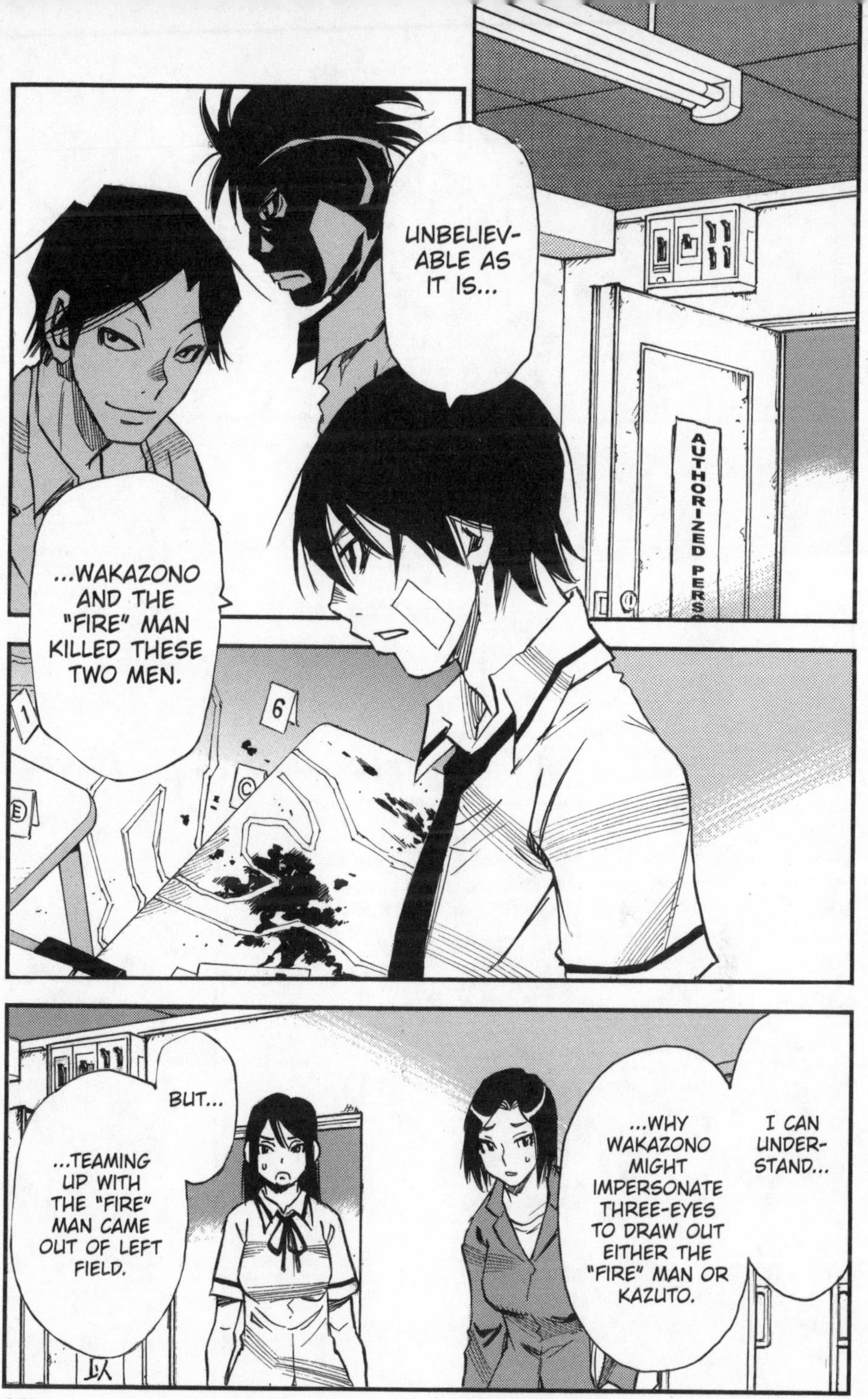
UNBELIEVABLE AS IT IS...
AUTHORIZED
...WAKAZONO AND THE "FIRE" MAN KILLED THESE TWO MEN.
I CAN UNDERSTAND...
...WHY WAKAZONO MIGHT IMPERSONATE THREE-EYES TO DRAW OUT EITHER THE "FIRE" MAN OR KAZUTO.
BUT...
...TEAMING UP WITH THE "FIRE" MAN CAME OUT OF LEFT FIELD.

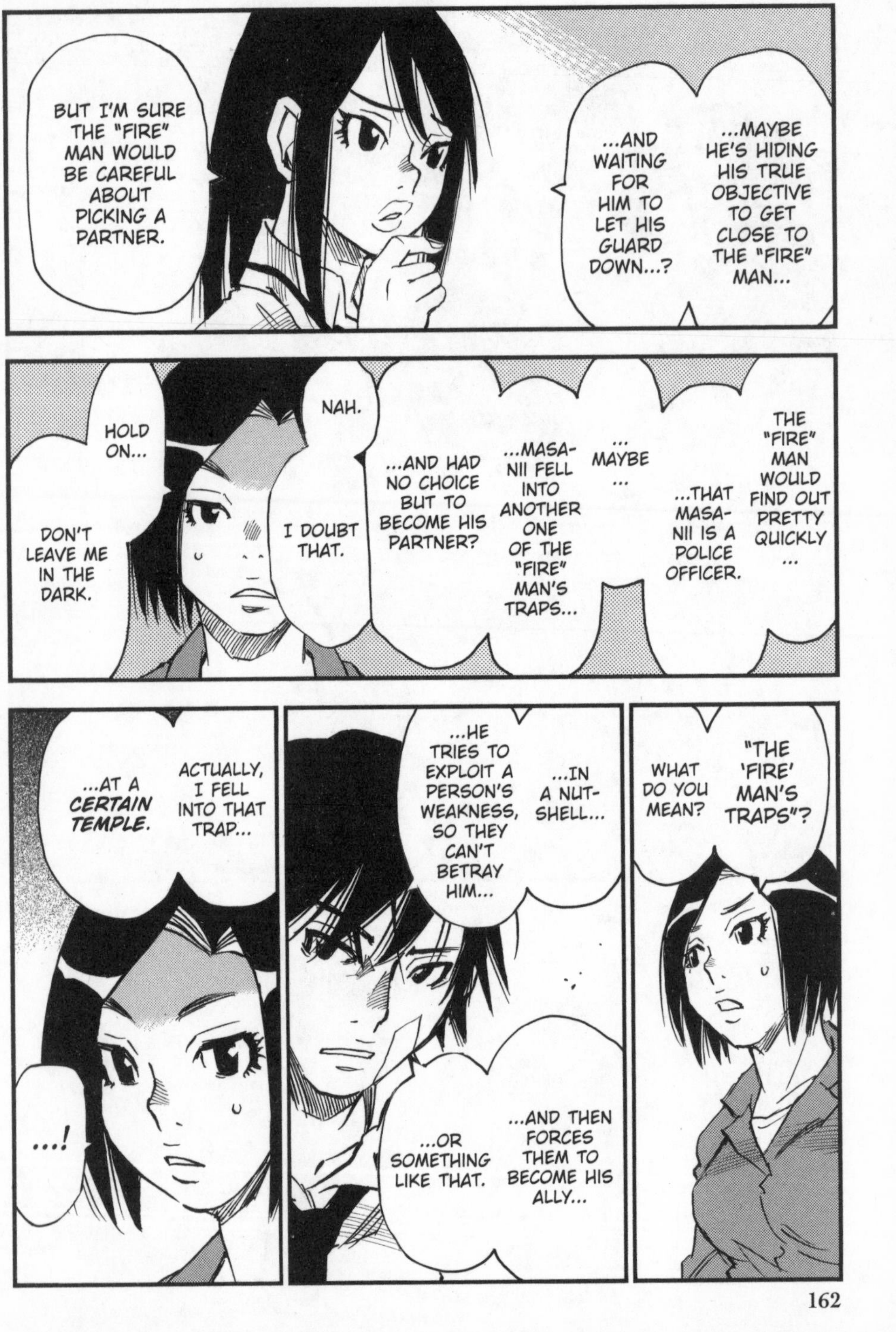
...MAYBE HE'S HIDING HIS TRUE OBJECTIVE TO GET CLOSE TO THE "FIRE" MAN...
...AND WAITING FOR HIM TO LET HIS GUARD DOWN...?
BUT I'M SURE THE "FIRE" MAN WOULD BE CAREFUL ABOUT PICKING A PARTNER.
THE "FIRE" MAN WOULD FIND OUT PRETTY QUICKLY ...
...THAT MASA-NII IS A POLICE OFFICER.
... MAYBE ...
...MASA-NII FELL INTO ANOTHER ONE OF THE "FIRE" MAN'S TRAPS...
...AND HAD NO CHOICE BUT TO BECOME HIS PARTNER?
NAH.
I DOUBT THAT.
HOLD ON...
DON'T LEAVE ME IN THE DARK.
"THE 'FIRE' MAN'S TRAPS"?
WHAT DO YOU MEAN?
...IN A NUT-SHELL...
...HE TRIES TO EXPLOIT A PERSON'S WEAKNESS, SO THEY CAN'T BETRAY HIM...
...AND THEN FORCES THEM TO BECOME HIS ALLY...
...OR SOMETHING LIKE THAT.
ACTUALLY, I FELL INTO THAT TRAP...
...AT A *CERTAIN TEMPLE*.
...!

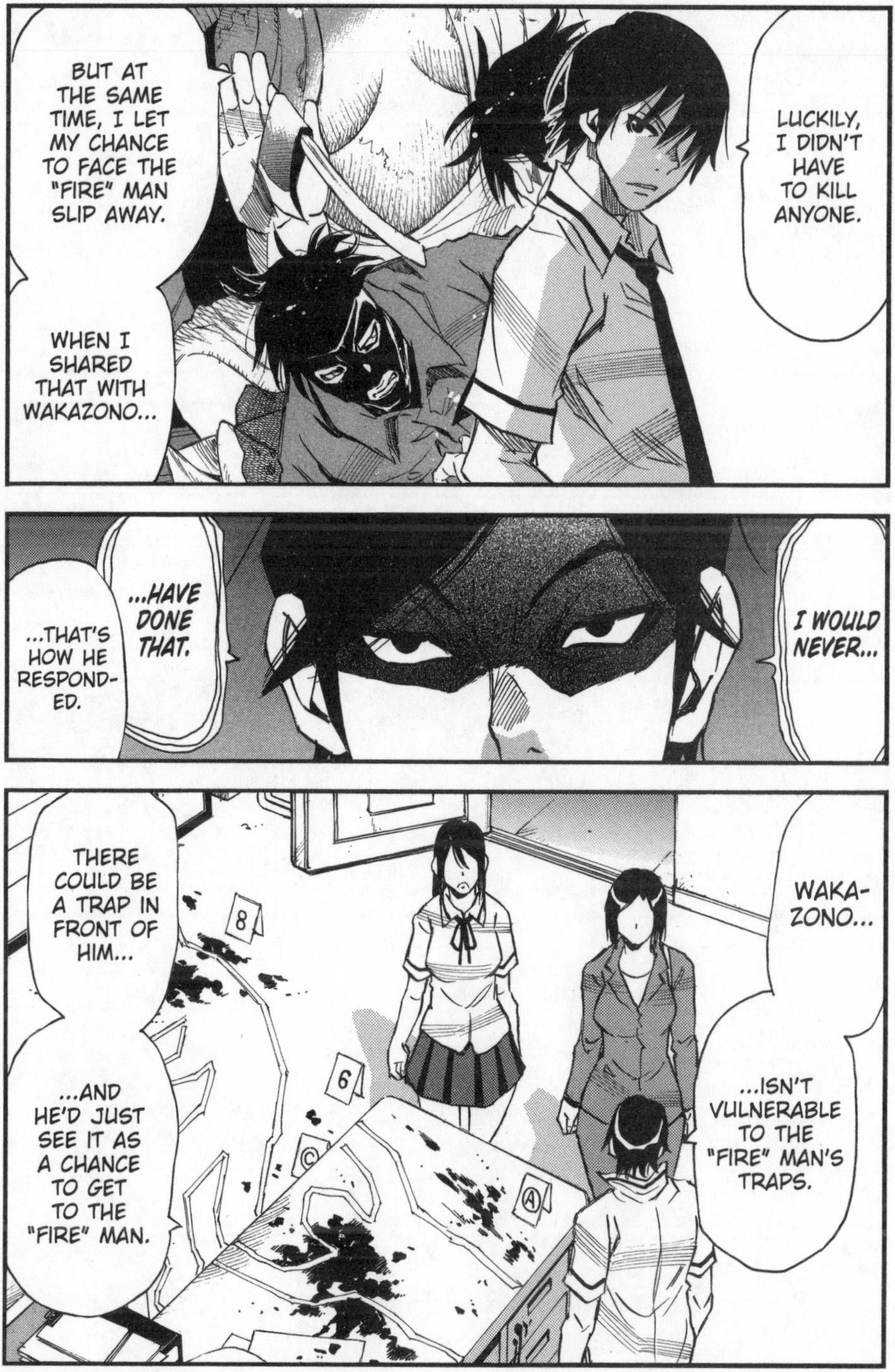
LUCKILY, I DIDN'T HAVE TO KILL ANYONE.
BUT AT THE SAME TIME, I LET MY CHANCE TO FACE THE "FIRE" MAN SLIP AWAY.
WHEN I SHARED THAT WITH WAKAZONO...
I WOULD NEVER...
...HAVE DONE THAT.
...THAT'S HOW HE RESPOND-ED.
WAKA-ZONO...
...ISN'T VULNERABLE TO THE "FIRE" MAN'S TRAPS.
THERE COULD BE A TRAP IN FRONT OF HIM...
...AND HE'D JUST SEE IT AS A CHANCE TO GET TO THE "FIRE" MAN.

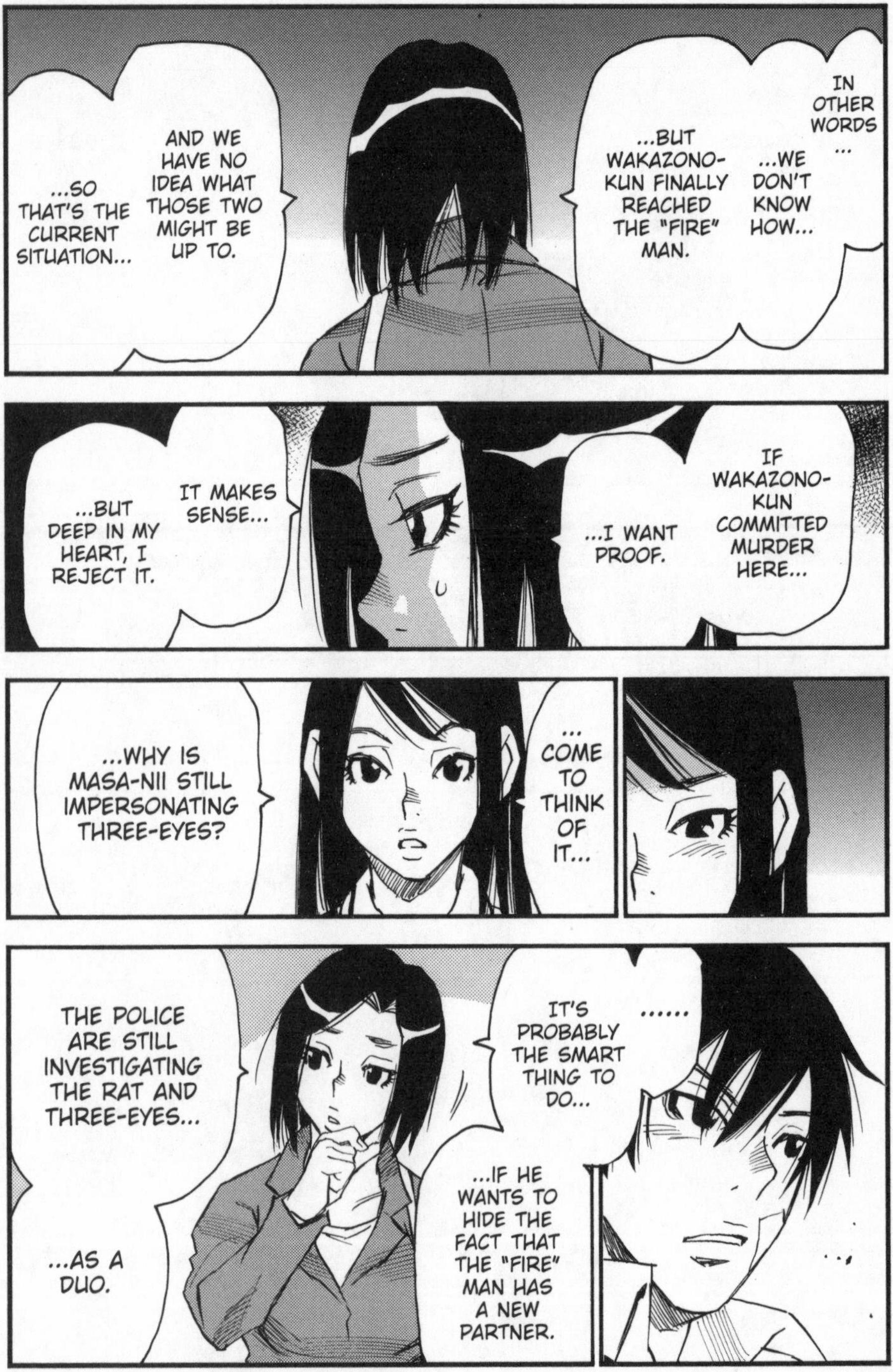
IN OTHER WORDS...
...WE DON'T KNOW HOW...
...BUT WAKAZONO-KUN FINALLY REACHED THE "FIRE" MAN.
AND WE HAVE NO IDEA WHAT THOSE TWO MIGHT BE UP TO.
...SO THAT'S THE CURRENT SITUATION...
IF WAKAZONO-KUN COMMITTED MURDER HERE...
...I WANT PROOF.
IT MAKES SENSE...
...BUT DEEP IN MY HEART, I REJECT IT.
...COME TO THINK OF IT...
...WHY IS MASA-NII STILL IMPERSONATING THREE-EYES?
......
IT'S PROBABLY THE SMART THING TO DO...
...IF HE WANTS TO HIDE THE FACT THAT THE "FIRE" MAN HAS A NEW PARTNER.
THE POLICE ARE STILL INVESTIGATING THE RAT AND THREE-EYES...
...AS A DUO.

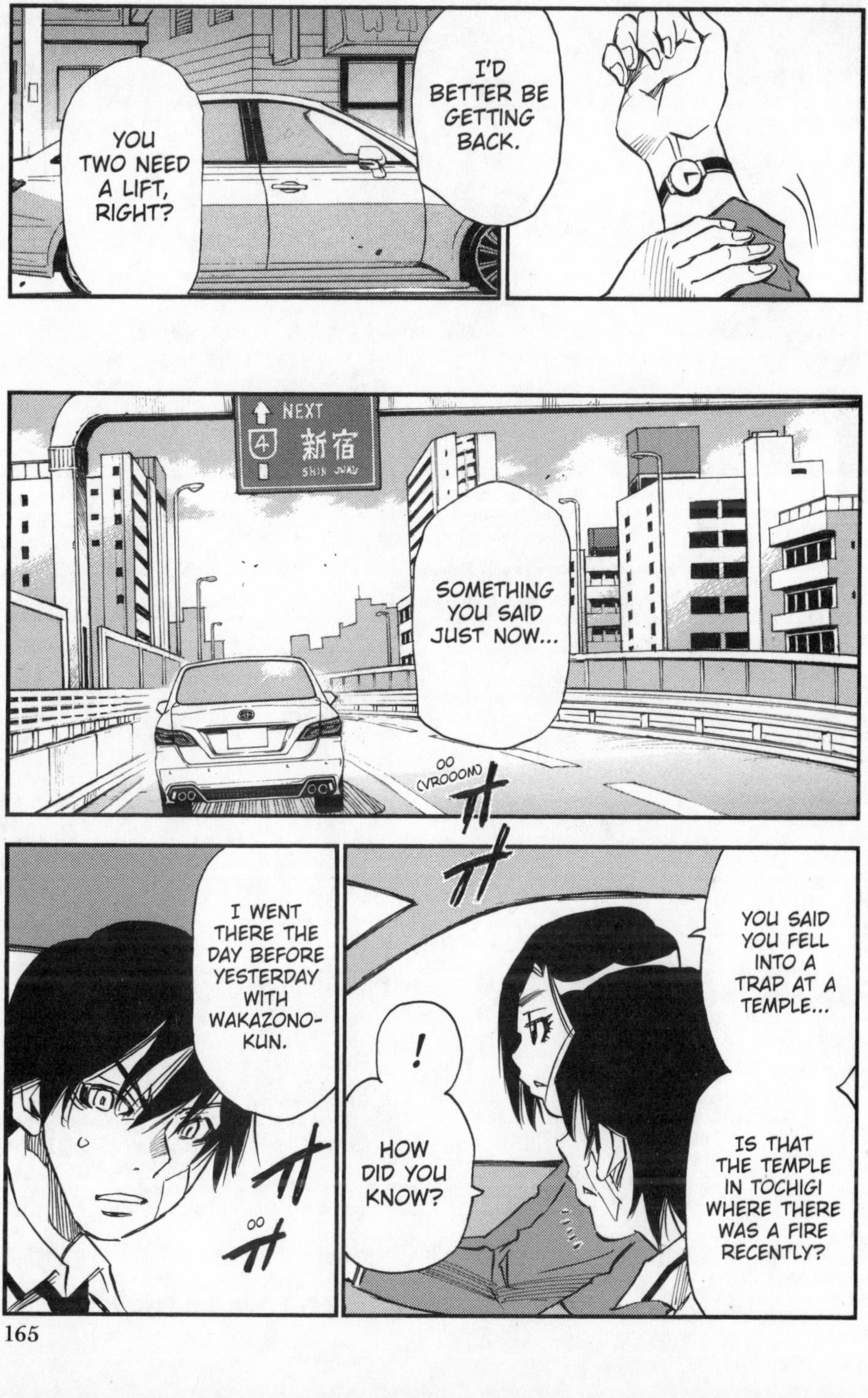
I'D BETTER BE GETTING BACK.
YOU TWO NEED A LIFT, RIGHT?
NEXT
4
新宿
SOMETHING YOU SAID JUST NOW...
OO (VROOOM)
YOU SAID YOU FELL INTO A TRAP AT A TEMPLE...
IS THAT THE TEMPLE IN TOCHIGI WHERE THERE WAS A FIRE RECENTLY?
!
HOW DID YOU KNOW?
I WENT THERE THE DAY BEFORE YESTERDAY WITH WAKAZONO-KUN.
OO

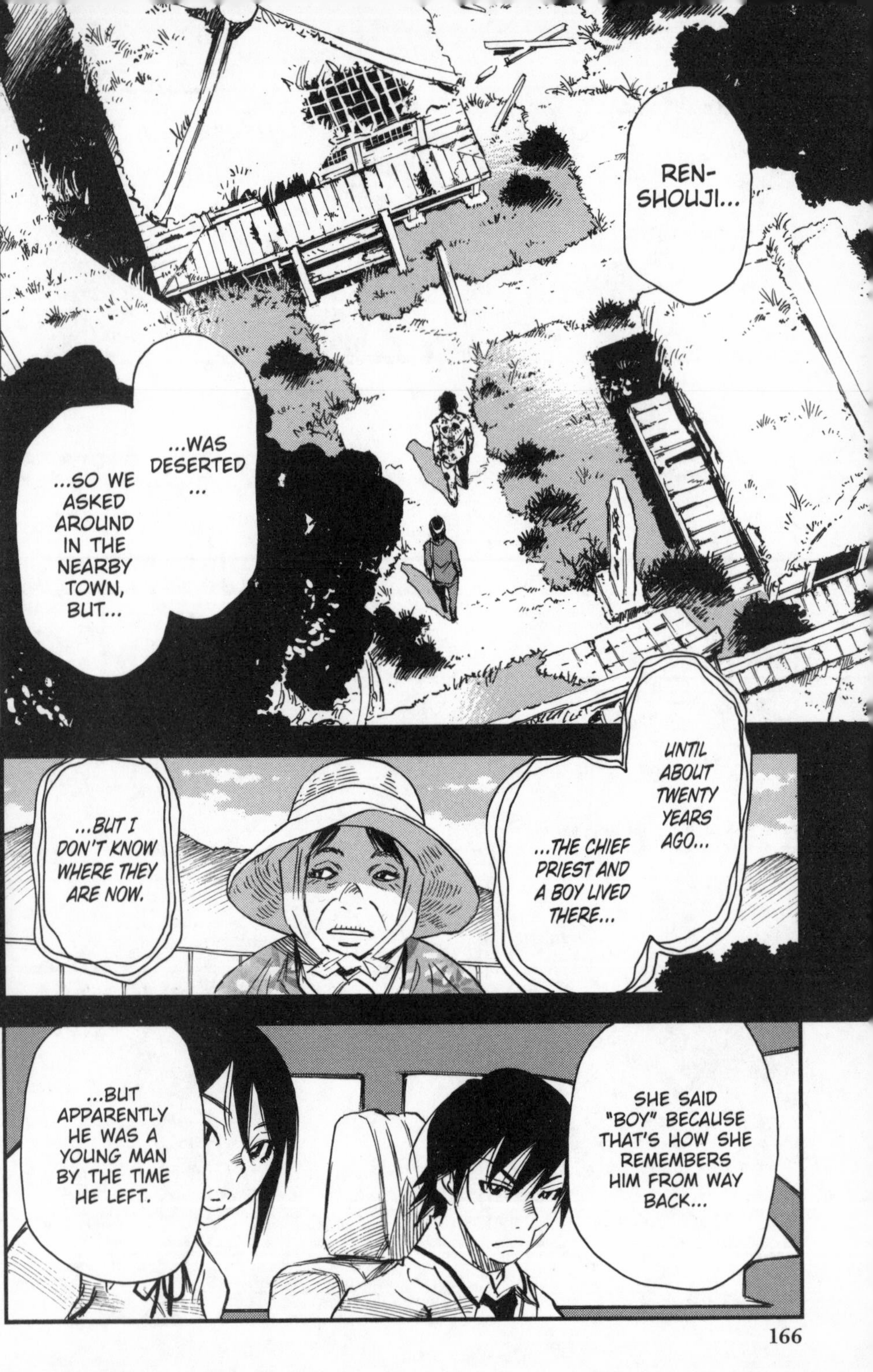
REN-SHOUJI...
...WAS DESERTED...
...SO WE ASKED AROUND IN THE NEARBY TOWN, BUT...
UNTIL ABOUT TWENTY YEARS AGO...
...THE CHIEF PRIEST AND A BOY LIVED THERE...
...BUT I DON'T KNOW WHERE THEY ARE NOW.
SHE SAID "BOY" BECAUSE THAT'S HOW SHE REMEMBERS HIM FROM WAY BACK...
...BUT APPARENTLY HE WAS A YOUNG MAN BY THE TIME HE LEFT.

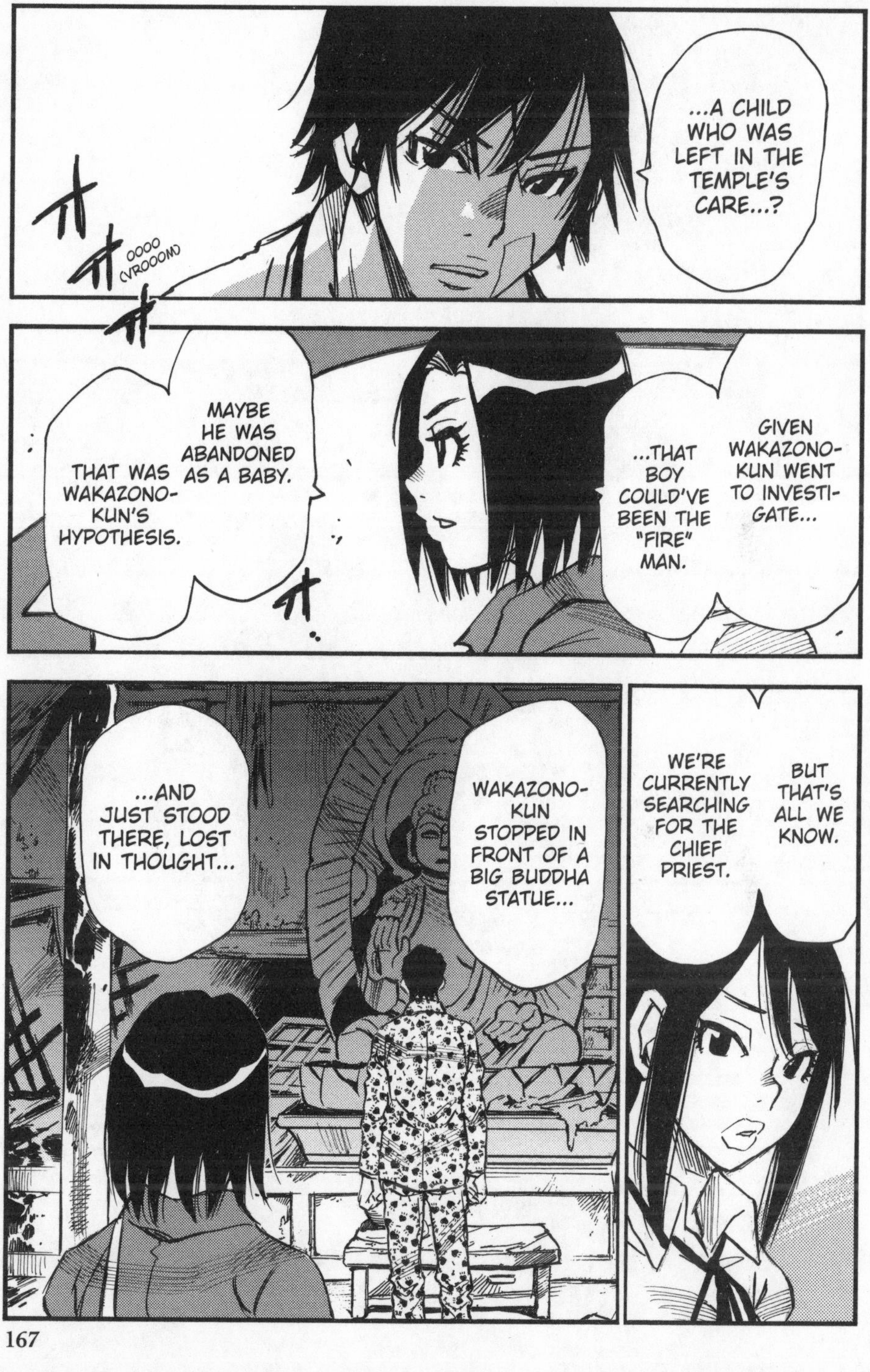
...A CHILD WHO WAS LEFT IN THE TEMPLE'S CARE...?
OOOO (VROOOM)
GIVEN WAKAZONO-KUN WENT TO INVESTI-GATE...
...THAT BOY COULD'VE BEEN THE "FIRE" MAN.
MAYBE HE WAS ABANDONED AS A BABY.
THAT WAS WAKAZONO-KUN'S HYPOTHESIS.
BUT THAT'S ALL WE KNOW.
WE'RE CURRENTLY SEARCHING FOR THE CHIEF PRIEST.
WAKAZONO-KUN STOPPED IN FRONT OF A BIG BUDDHA STATUE...
...AND JUST STOOD THERE, LOST IN THOUGHT...

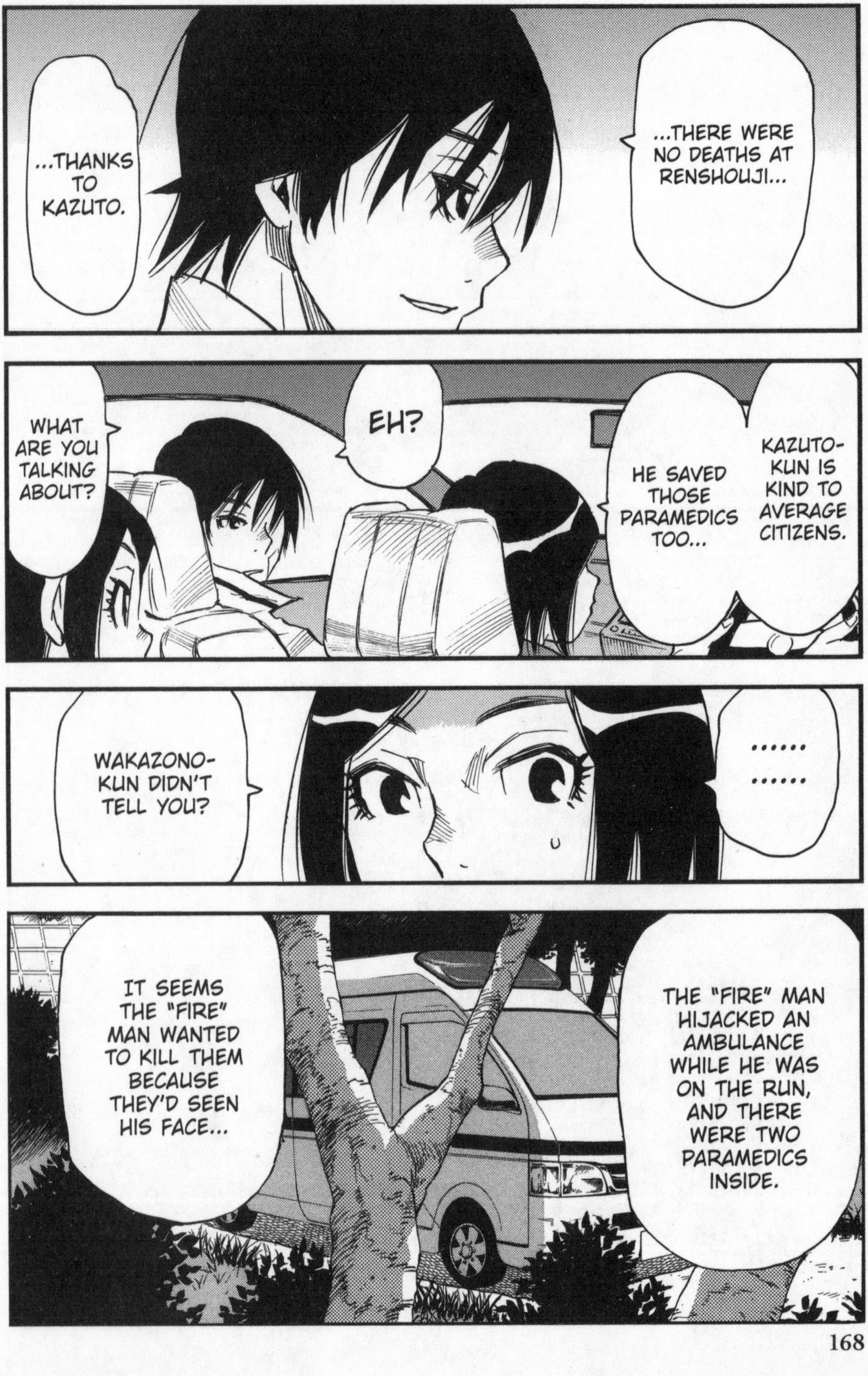
...THERE WERE NO DEATHS AT RENSHOUJI...
...THANKS TO KAZUTO.
KAZUTO-KUN IS KIND TO AVERAGE CITIZENS.
HE SAVED THOSE PARAMEDICS TOO...
EH?
WHAT ARE YOU TALKING ABOUT?
......
......
WAKAZONO-KUN DIDN'T TELL YOU?
THE "FIRE" MAN HIJACKED AN AMBULANCE WHILE HE WAS ON THE RUN, AND THERE WERE TWO PARAMEDICS INSIDE.
IT SEEMS THE "FIRE" MAN WANTED TO KILL THEM BECAUSE THEY'D SEEN HIS FACE...

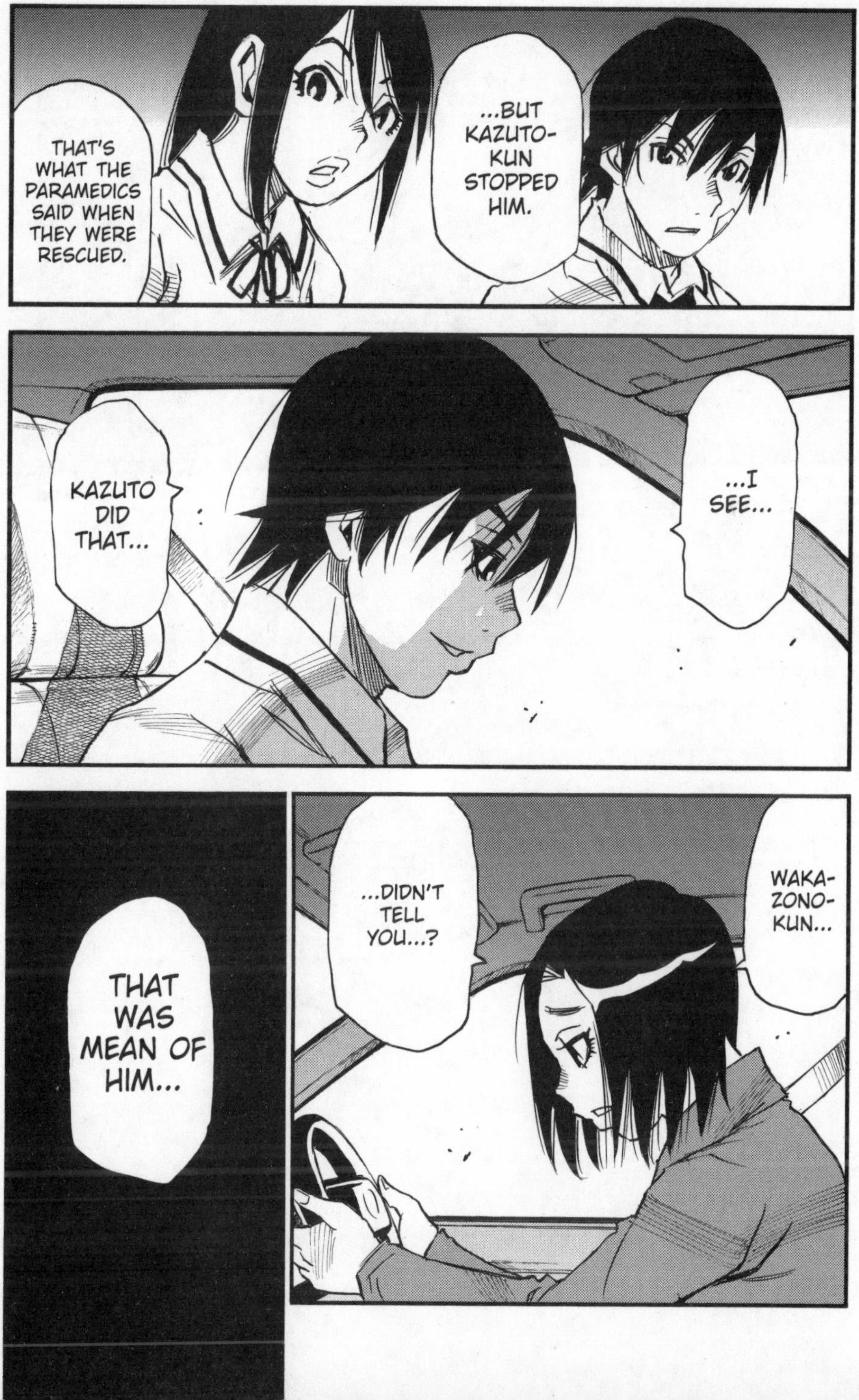
...BUT KAZUTO-KUN STOPPED HIM.
THAT'S WHAT THE PARAMEDICS SAID WHEN THEY WERE RESCUED.
...I SEE...
KAZUTO DID THAT...
WAKA-ZONO-KUN...
...DIDN'T TELL YOU...?
THAT WAS MEAN OF HIM...

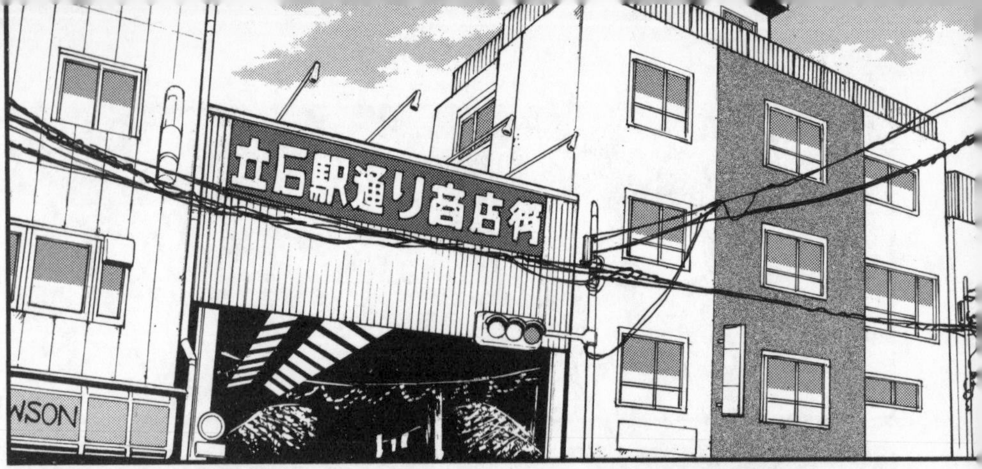
立石駅通り商店街

SIGN: TATEISHI STATION SHOPPING CENTER

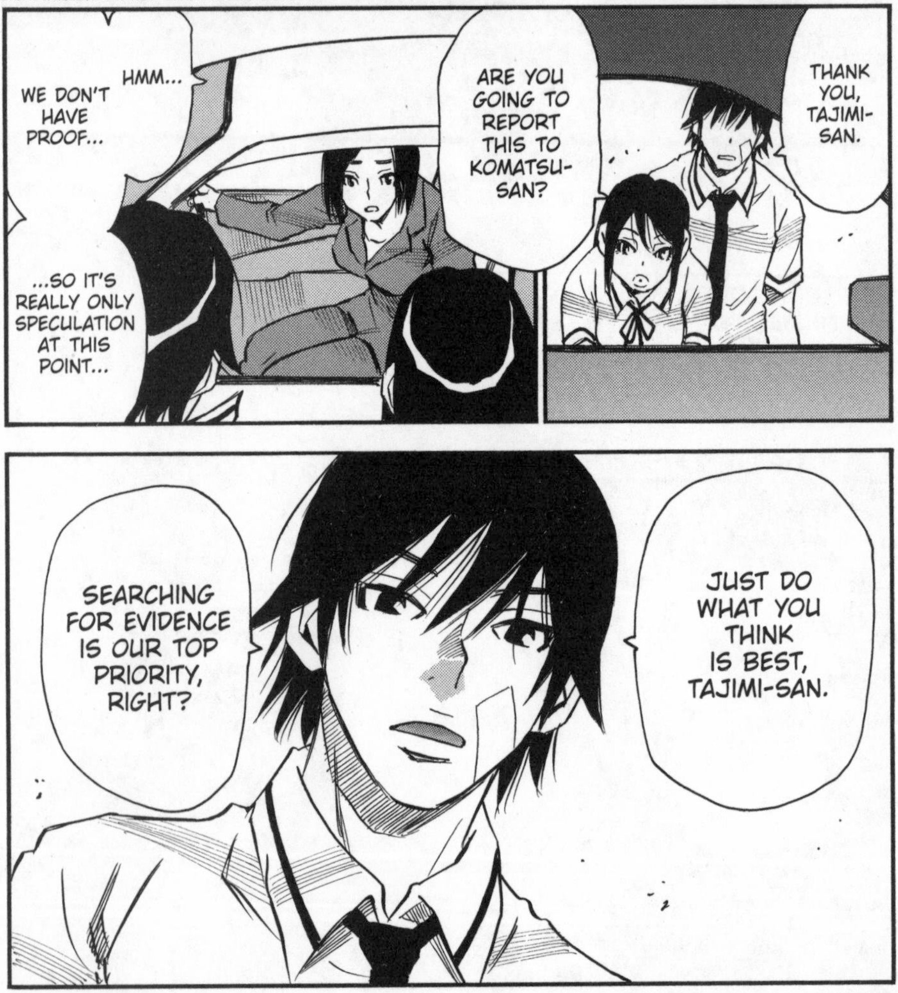
THANK YOU, TAJIMI-SAN.
ARE YOU GOING TO REPORT THIS TO KOMATSU-SAN?
HMM...
WE DON'T HAVE PROOF...
...SO IT'S REALLY ONLY SPECULATION AT THIS POINT...
JUST DO WHAT YOU THINK IS BEST, TAJIMI-SAN.
SEARCHING FOR EVIDENCE IS OUR TOP PRIORITY, RIGHT?

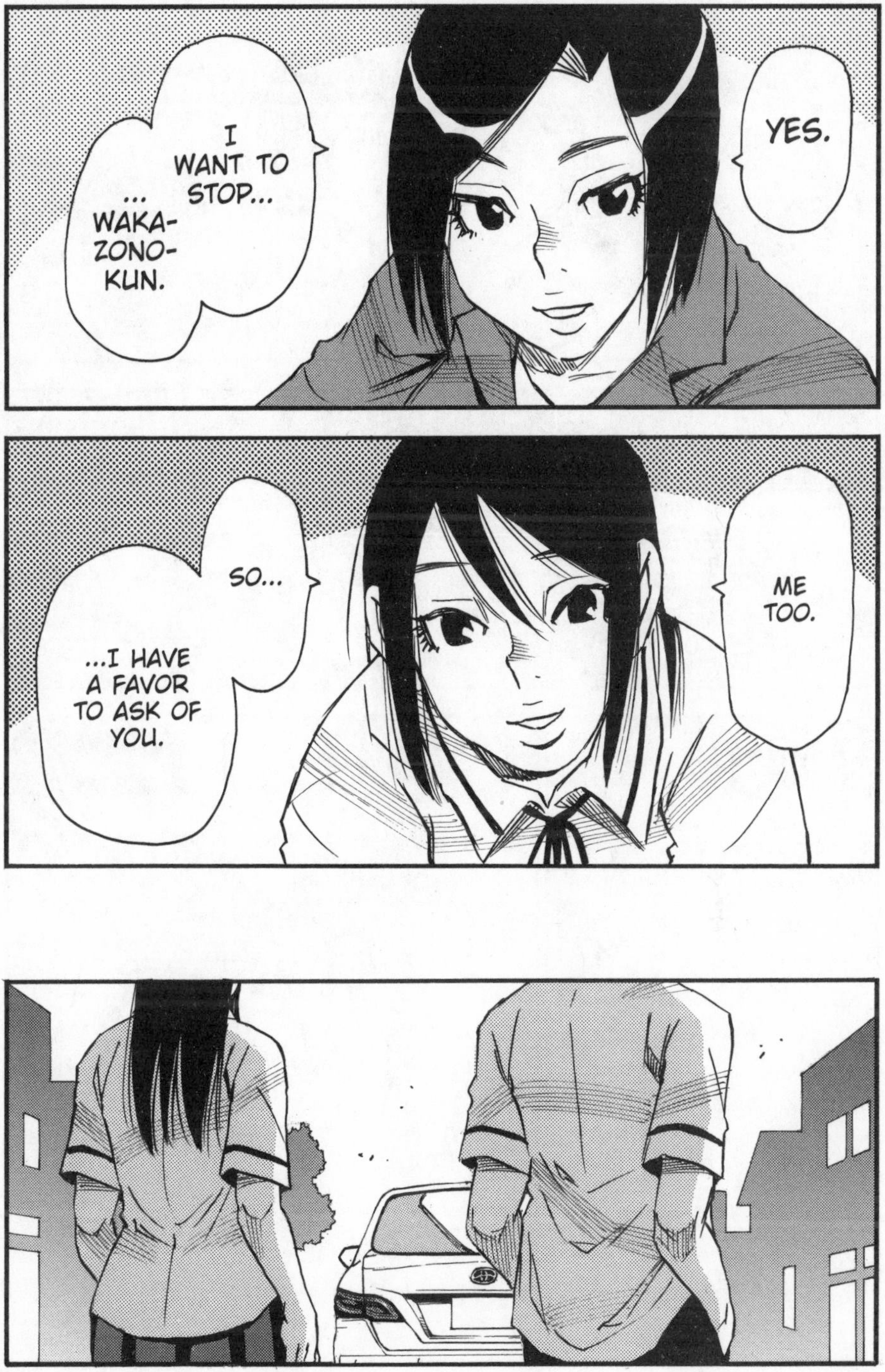
YES.
I WANT TO STOP...
...WAKA-ZONO-KUN.
ME TOO.
SO...
...I HAVE A FAVOR TO ASK OF YOU.

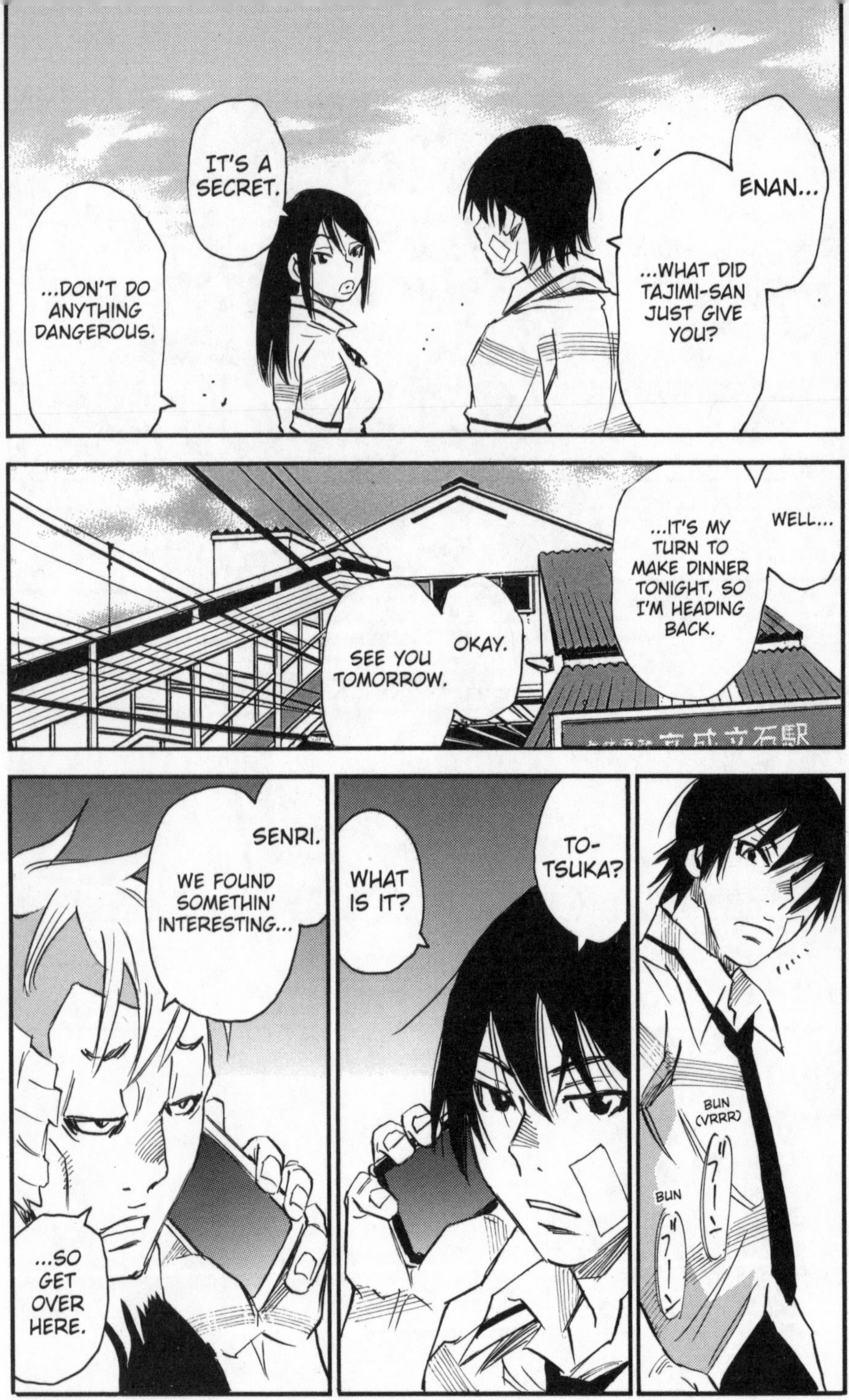
ENAN...
...WHAT DID TAJIMI-SAN JUST GIVE YOU?
IT'S A SECRET.
...DON'T DO ANYTHING DANGEROUS.
WELL...
...IT'S MY TURN TO MAKE DINNER TONIGHT, SO I'M HEADING BACK.
OKAY.
SEE YOU TOMORROW.
...
BUN (VRRR)
BUN
TO-TSUKA?
WHAT IS IT?
SENRI.
WE FOUND SOMETHIN' INTERESTING...
...SO GET OVER HERE.

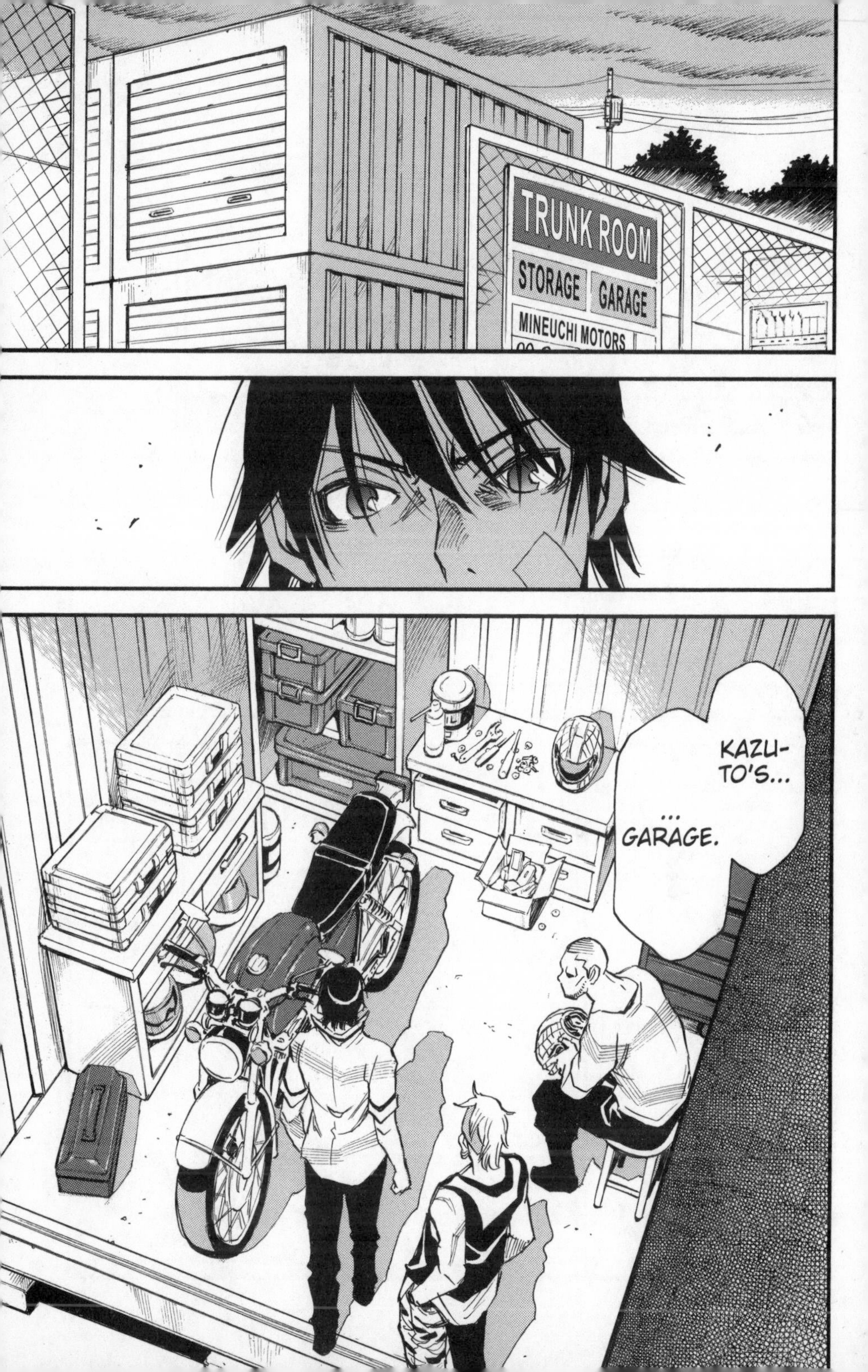
TRUNK ROOM
STORAGE
GARAGE
MINEUCHI MOTORS
KAZUTO'S... ...GARAGE.

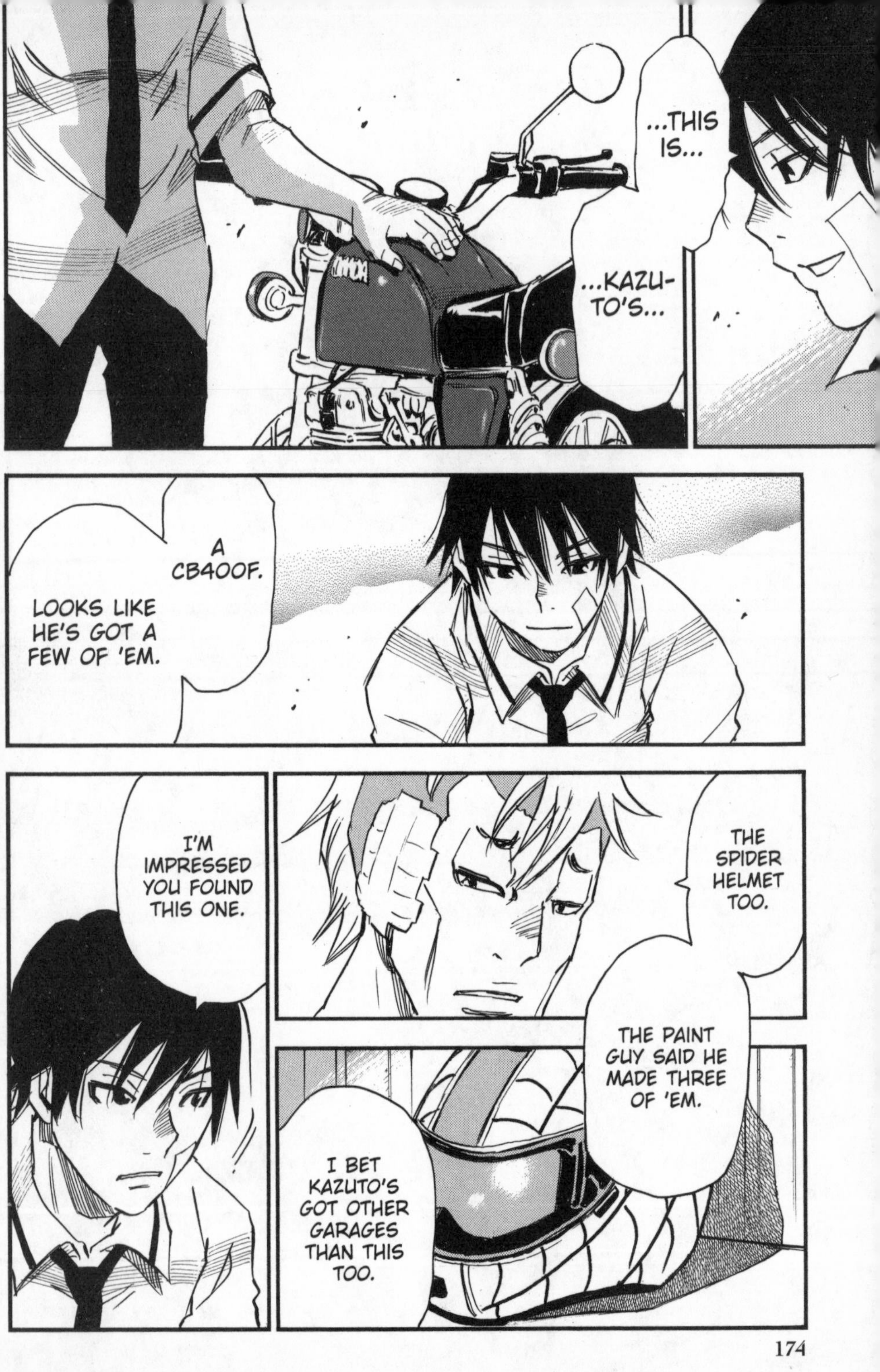
...THIS IS...
...KAZUTO'S...
A CB400F.
LOOKS LIKE HE'S GOT A FEW OF 'EM.
THE SPIDER HELMET TOO.
THE PAINT GUY SAID HE MADE THREE OF 'EM.
I BET KAZUTO'S GOT OTHER GARAGES THAN THIS TOO.
I'M IMPRESSED YOU FOUND THIS ONE.

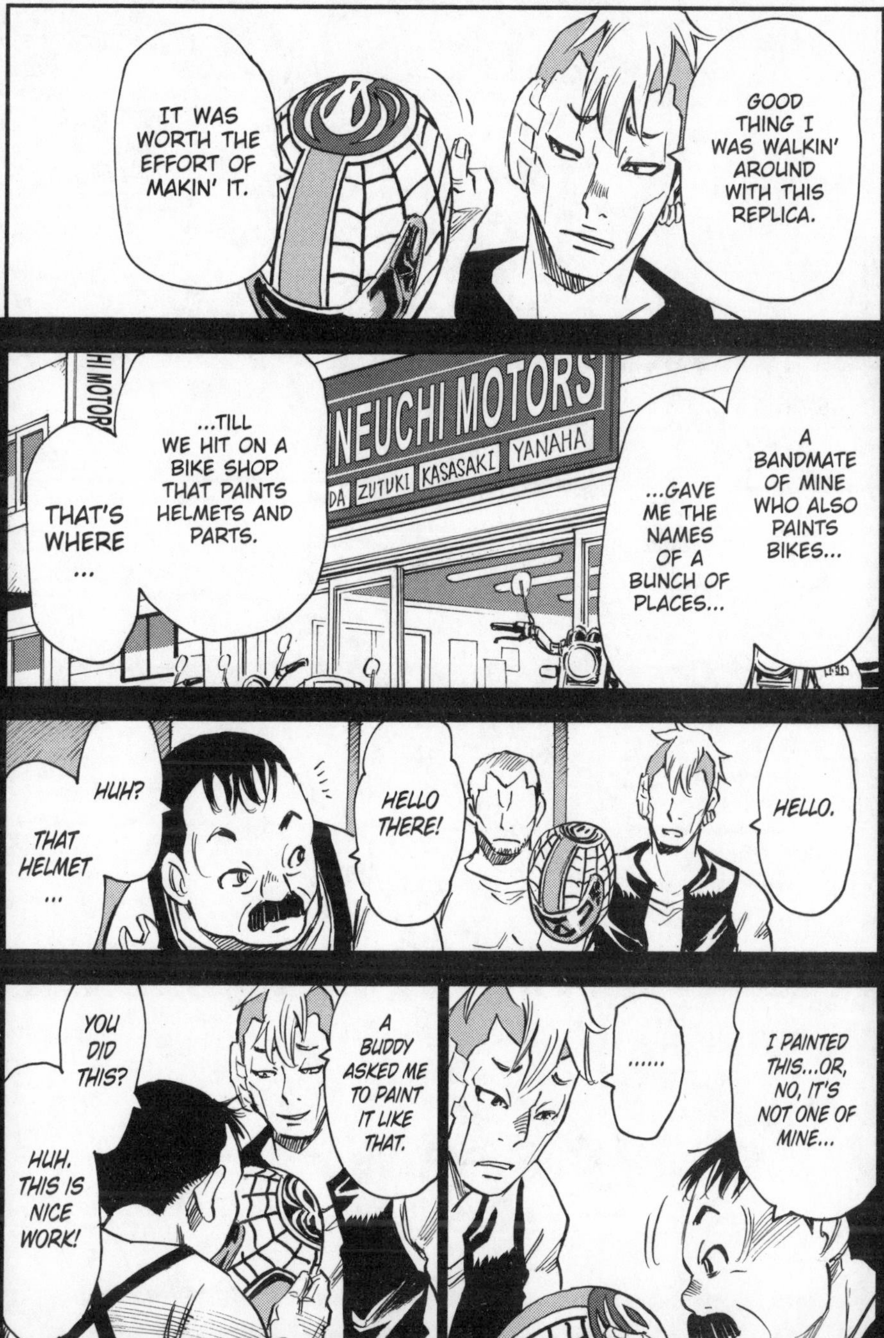
GOOD THING I WAS WALKIN' AROUND WITH THIS REPLICA.
IT WAS WORTH THE EFFORT OF MAKIN' IT.
INEUCHI MOTORS
YANAHA
KASASAKI
ZUTUKI
A BANDMATE OF MINE WHO ALSO PAINTS BIKES...
...GAVE ME THE NAMES OF A BUNCH OF PLACES...
...TILL WE HIT ON A BIKE SHOP THAT PAINTS HELMETS AND PARTS.
THAT'S WHERE ...
HELLO.
HELLO THERE!
HUH?
THAT HELMET ...
I PAINTED THIS...OR, NO, IT'S NOT ONE OF MINE...
......
A BUDDY ASKED ME TO PAINT IT LIKE THAT.
YOU DID THIS?
HUH. THIS IS NICE WORK!

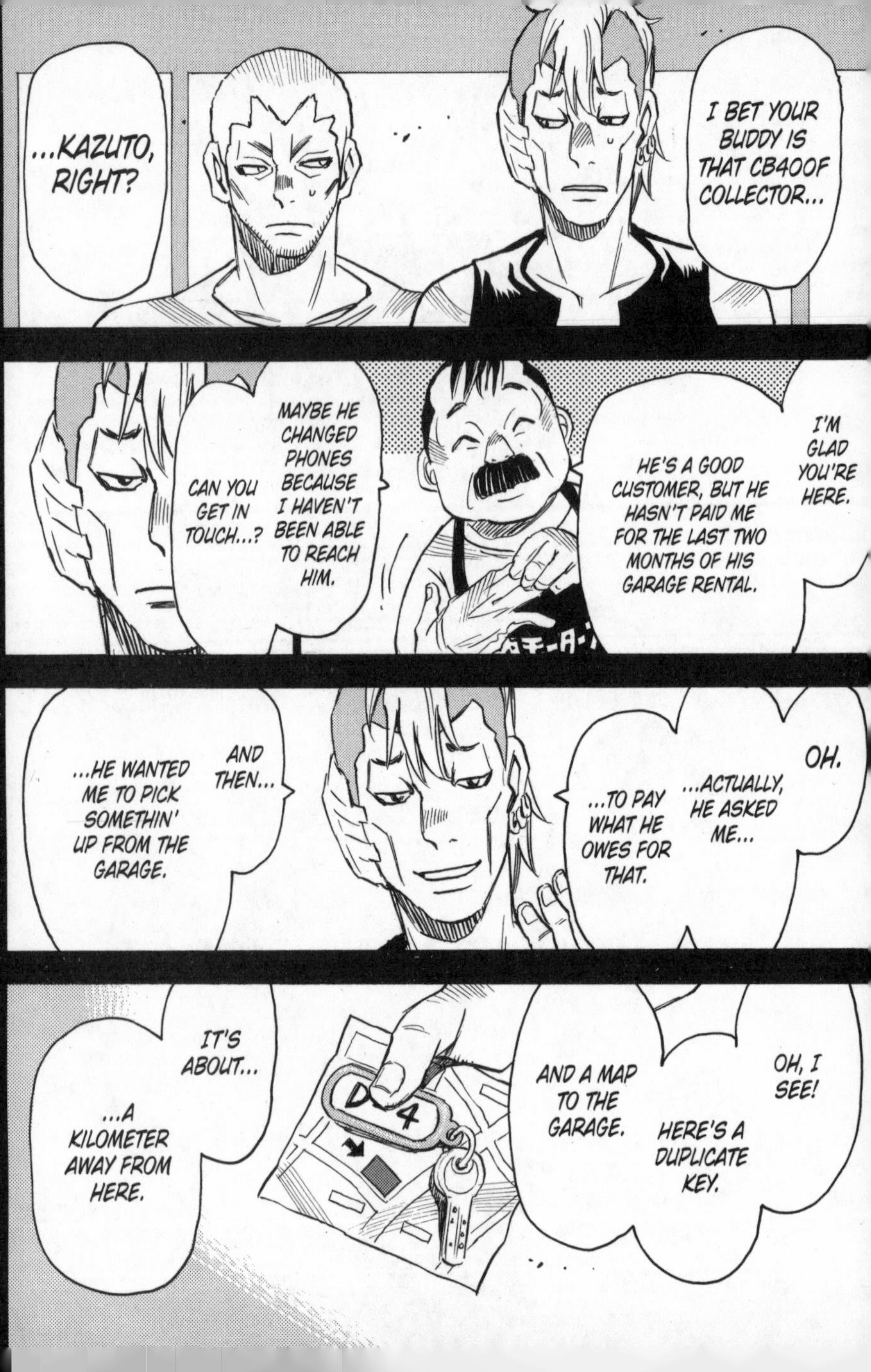
I BET YOUR BUDDY IS THAT CB400F COLLECTOR...
...KAZUTO, RIGHT?
I'M GLAD YOU'RE HERE.
HE'S A GOOD CUSTOMER, BUT HE HASN'T PAID ME FOR THE LAST TWO MONTHS OF HIS GARAGE RENTAL.
MAYBE HE CHANGED PHONES BECAUSE I HAVEN'T BEEN ABLE TO REACH HIM.
CAN YOU GET IN TOUCH...?
OH.
...ACTUALLY, HE ASKED ME...
...TO PAY WHAT HE OWES FOR THAT.
AND THEN...
...HE WANTED ME TO PICK SOMETHIN' UP FROM THE GARAGE.
OH, I SEE!
HERE'S A DUPLICATE KEY.
AND A MAP TO THE GARAGE.
IT'S ABOUT...
...A KILOMETER AWAY FROM HERE.

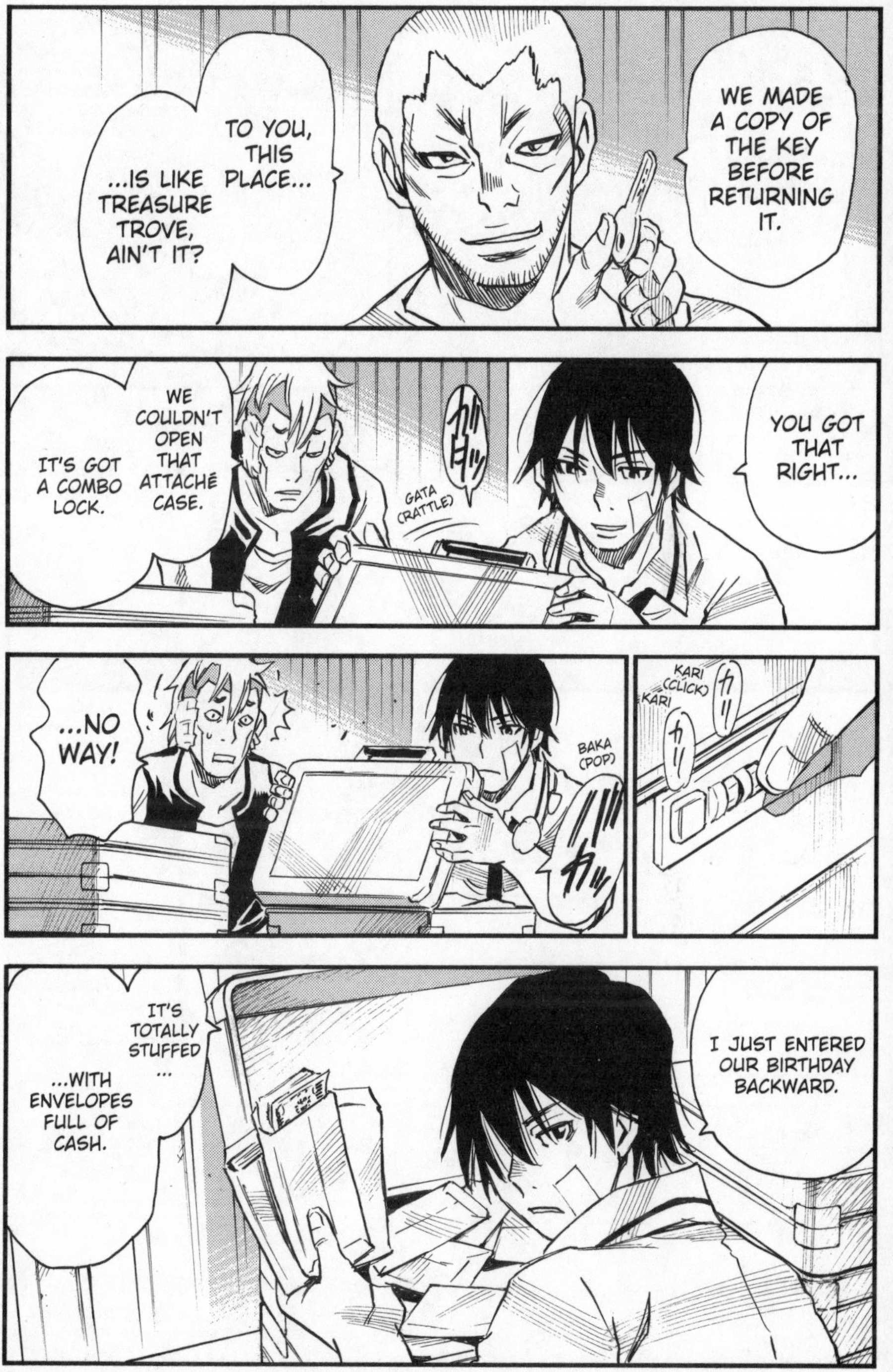

WE MADE A COPY OF THE KEY BEFORE RETURNING IT.
TO YOU, THIS PLACE...
...IS LIKE TREASURE TROVE, AIN'T IT?
YOU GOT THAT RIGHT...
GATA (RATTLE)
WE COULDN'T OPEN THAT ATTACHÉ CASE.
IT'S GOT A COMBO LOCK.
KARI (CLICK)
KARI
BAKA (POP)
...NO WAY!
I JUST ENTERED OUR BIRTHDAY BACKWARD.
IT'S TOTALLY STUFFED...
...WITH ENVELOPES FULL OF CASH.

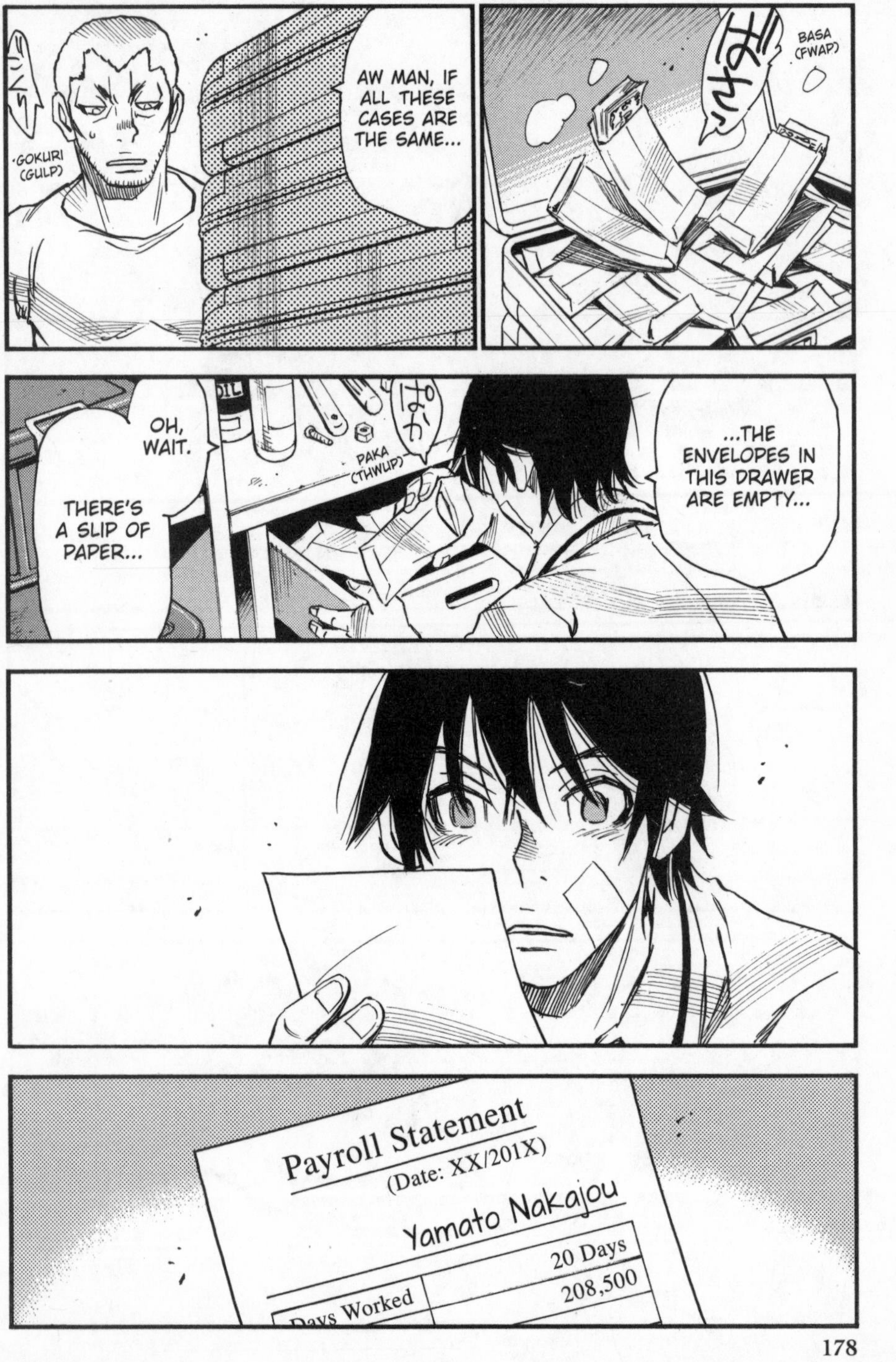
BASA (FWAP)
AW MAN, IF ALL THESE CASES ARE THE SAME...
GOKURI (GULP)
...THE ENVELOPES IN THIS DRAWER ARE EMPTY...
ぱか
PAKA (THWUP)
OH, WAIT.
THERE'S A SLIP OF PAPER...
Payroll Statement
(Date: XX/201X)
Yamato Nakajou
20 Days
208,500
Days Worked

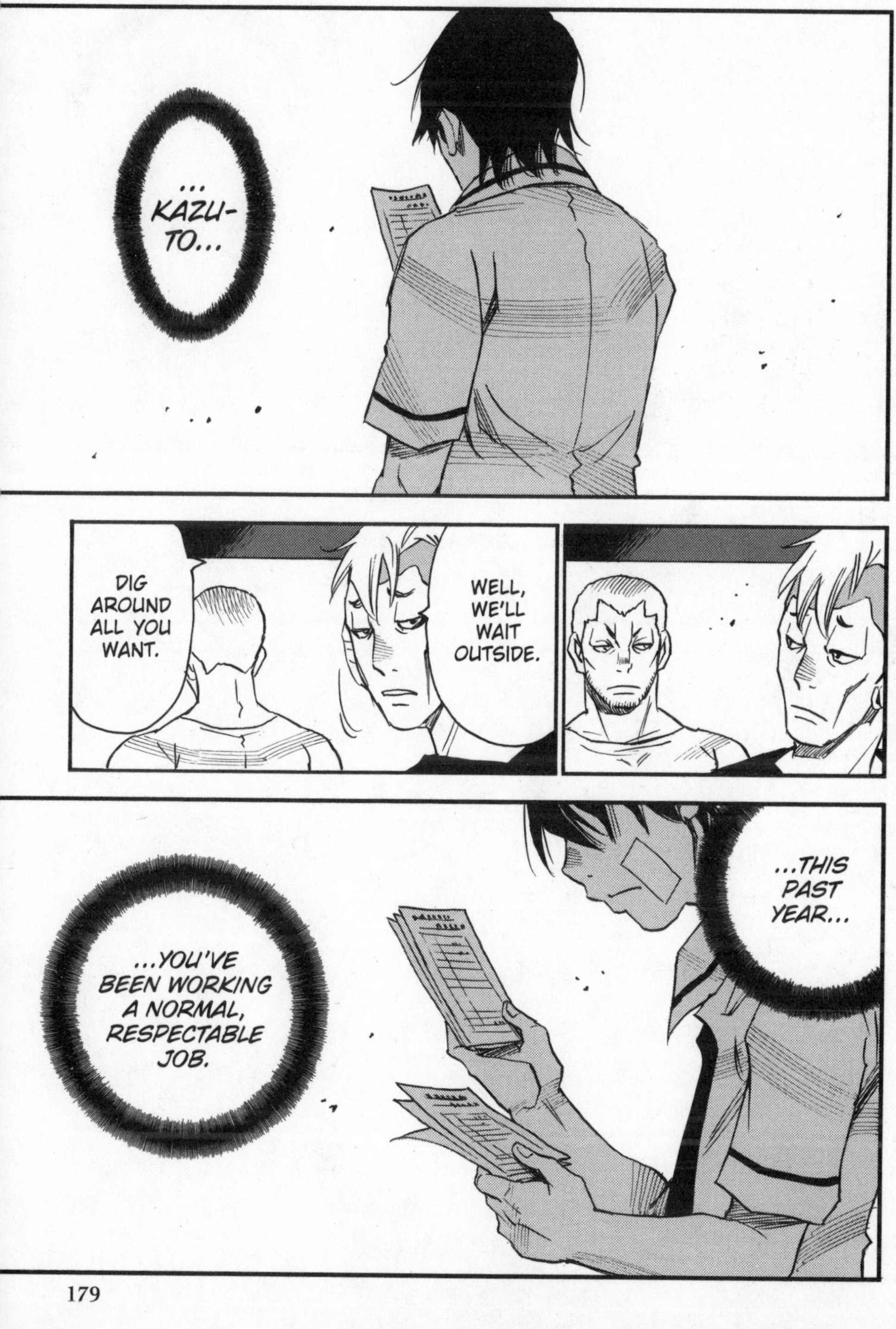
...KAZU-TO...
WELL, WE'LL WAIT OUTSIDE.
DIG AROUND ALL YOU WANT.
...THIS PAST YEAR...
...YOU'VE BEEN WORKING A NORMAL, RESPECTABLE JOB.

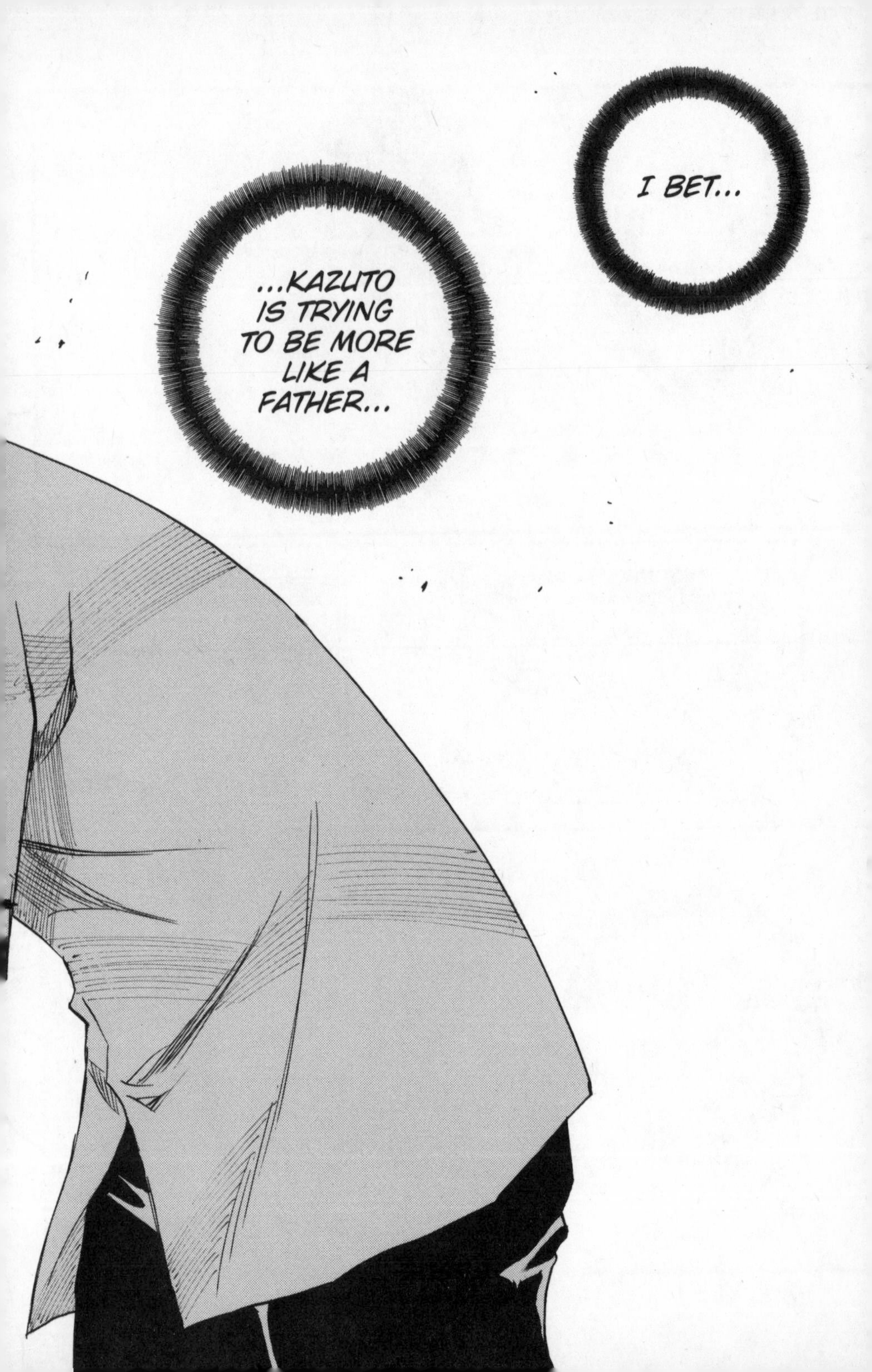
I BET...
...KAZUTO IS TRYING TO BE MORE LIKE A FATHER...

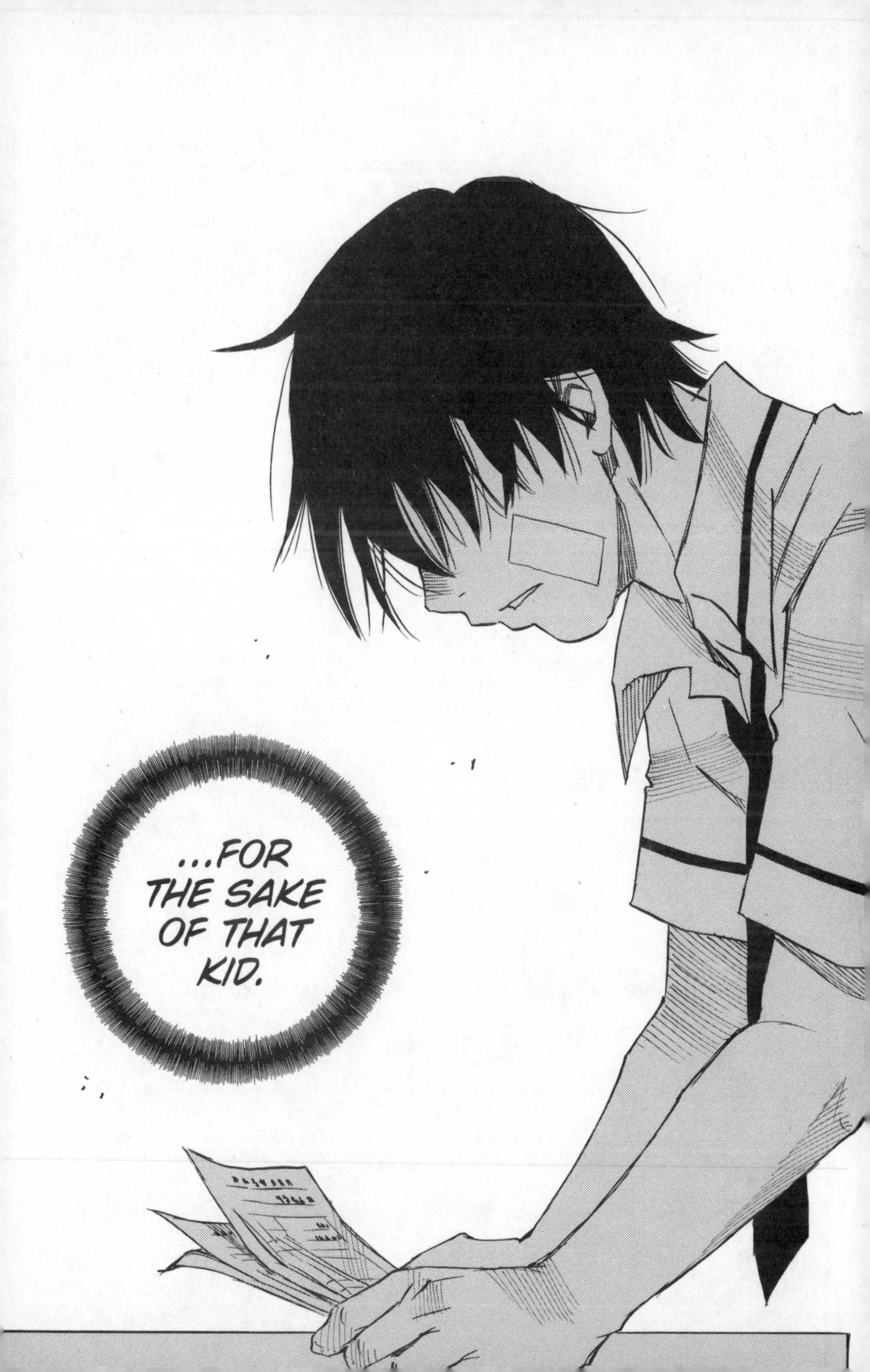
...FOR THE SAKE OF THAT KID.

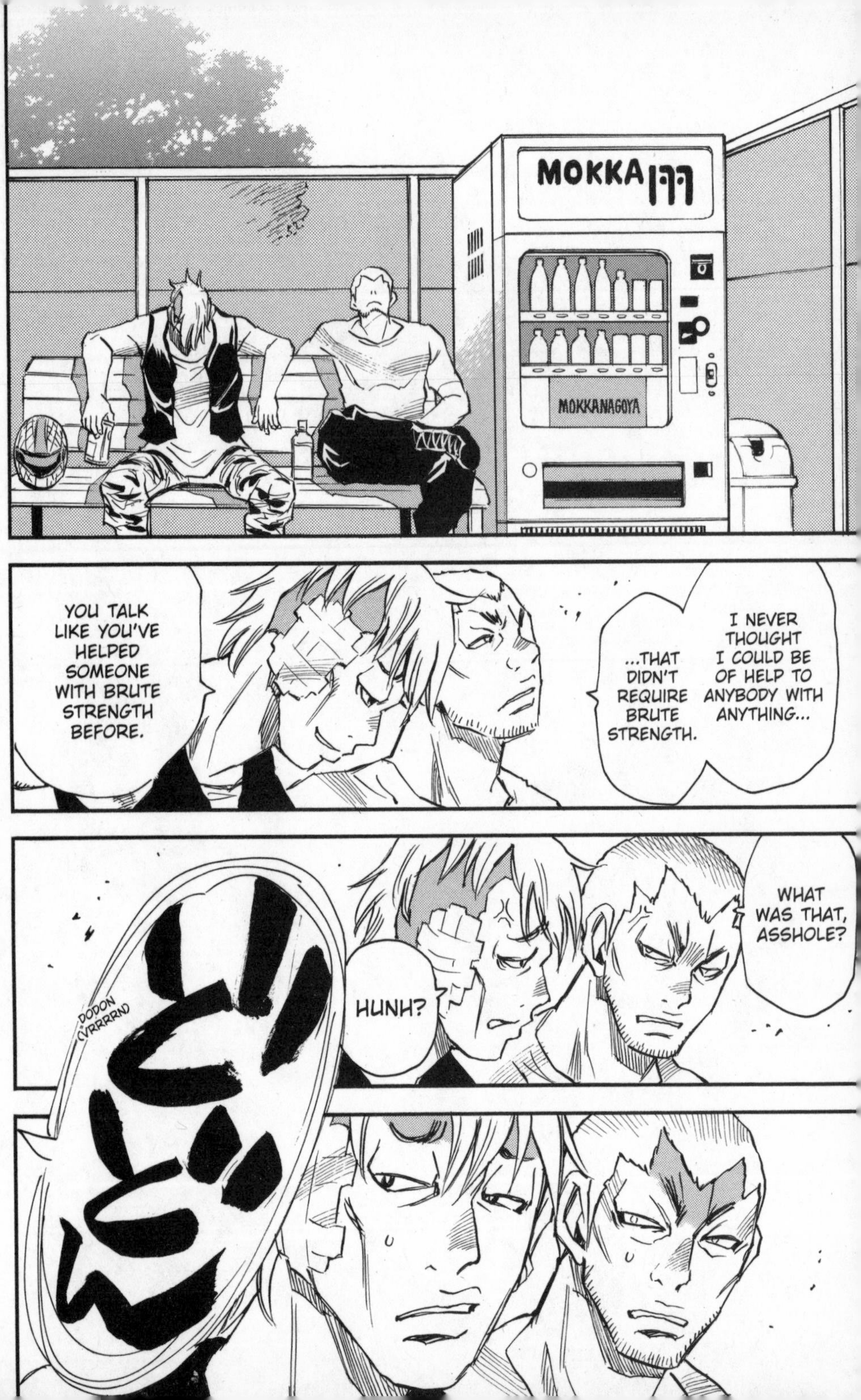
MOKKA
MOKKANAGOYA
I NEVER THOUGHT I COULD BE OF HELP TO ANYBODY WITH ANYTHING...
...THAT DIDN'T REQUIRE BRUTE STRENGTH.
YOU TALK LIKE YOU'VE HELPED SOMEONE WITH BRUTE STRENGTH BEFORE.
WHAT WAS THAT, ASSHOLE?
HUNH?
DODON (VRRRRN)

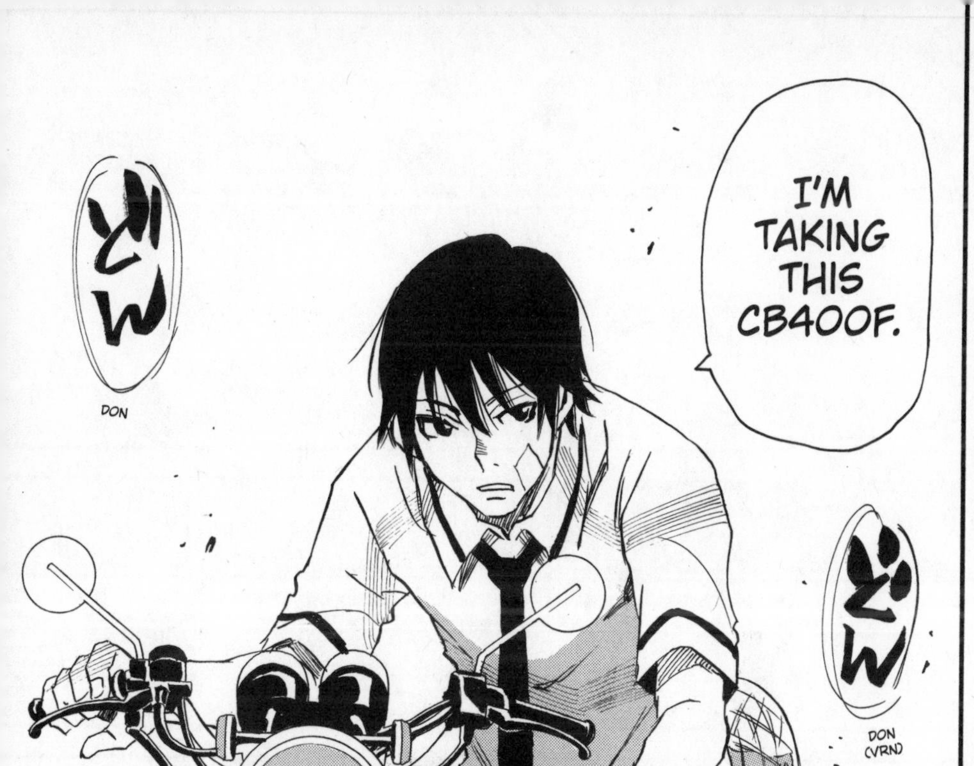
I'M TAKING THIS CB400F.
DON
DON (VRN)
DON
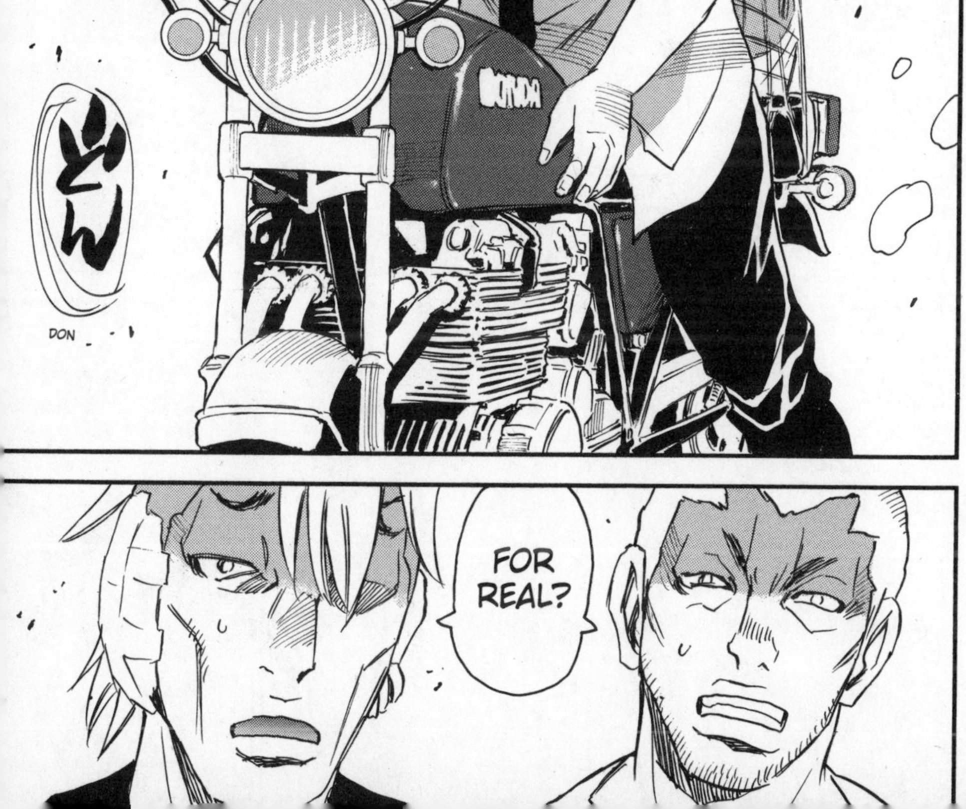
FOR REAL?

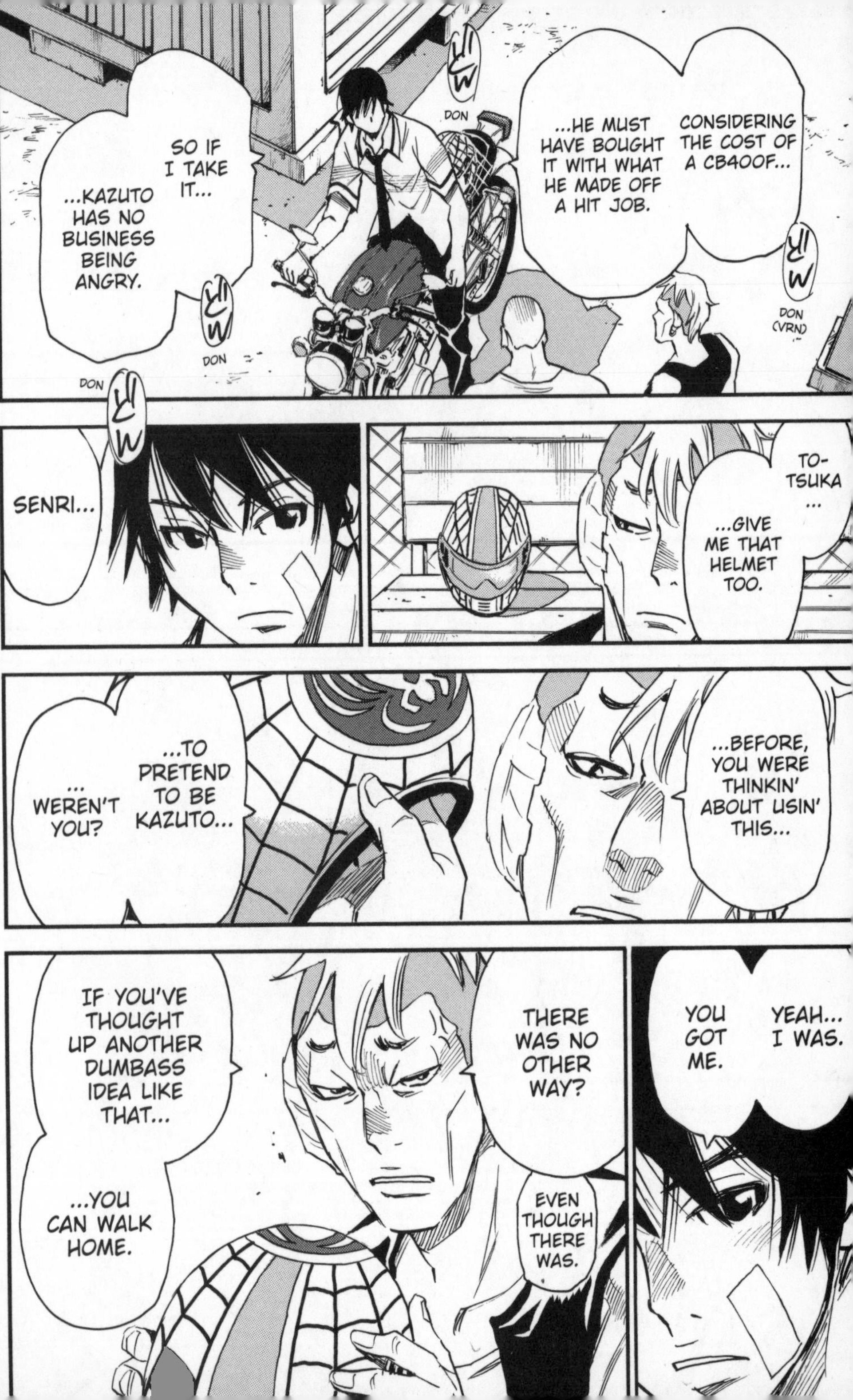
DON (VRN)
CONSIDERING THE COST OF A CB400F...
...HE MUST HAVE BOUGHT IT WITH WHAT HE MADE OFF A HIT JOB.
DON
SO IF I TAKE IT...
...KAZUTO HAS NO BUSINESS BEING ANGRY.
DON
DON
TO-TSUKA ...
...GIVE ME THAT HELMET TOO.
SENRI...
...BEFORE, YOU WERE THINKIN' ABOUT USIN' THIS...
...TO PRETEND TO BE KAZUTO...
... WEREN'T YOU?
YEAH... I WAS.
YOU GOT ME.
THERE WAS NO OTHER WAY?
EVEN THOUGH THERE WAS.
IF YOU'VE THOUGHT UP ANOTHER DUMBASS IDEA LIKE THAT...
...YOU CAN WALK HOME.

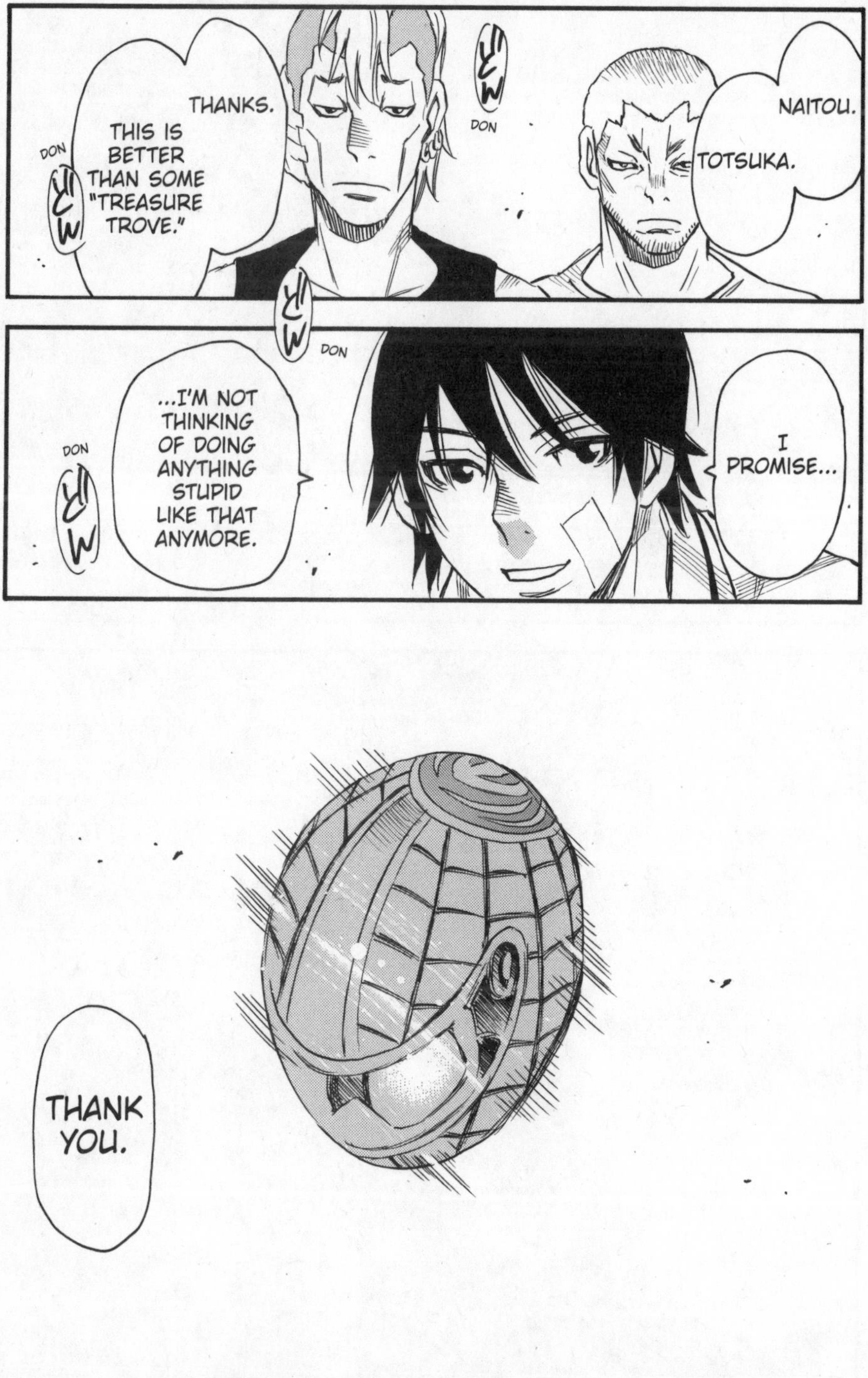
NAITOU. TOTSUKA.
DON
THANKS. THIS IS BETTER THAN SOME "TREASURE TROVE."
DON
DON
I PROMISE...
...I'M NOT THINKING OF DOING ANYTHING STUPID LIKE THAT ANYMORE.
DON
THANK YOU.

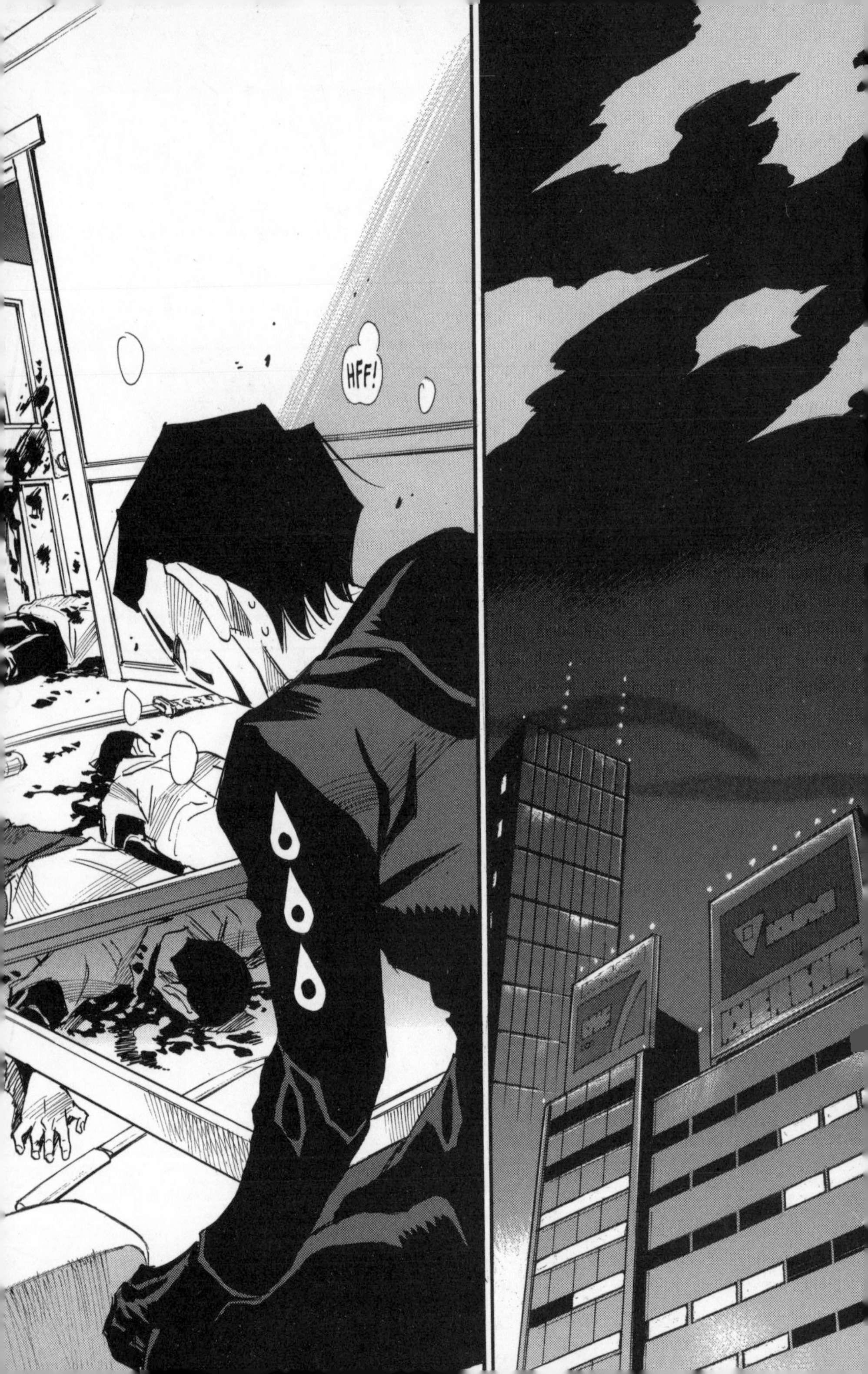
HFF!

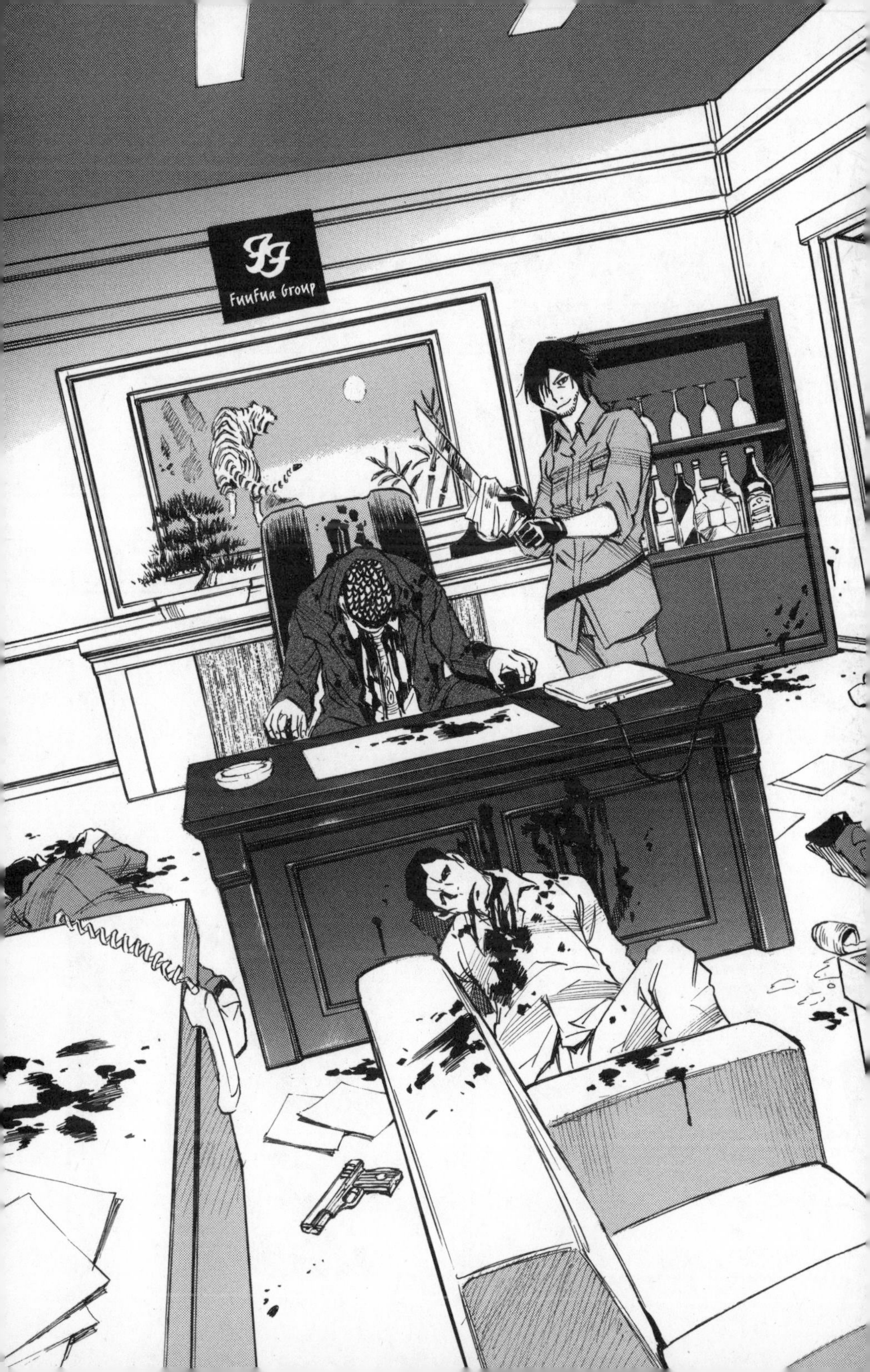
FuuFua Group

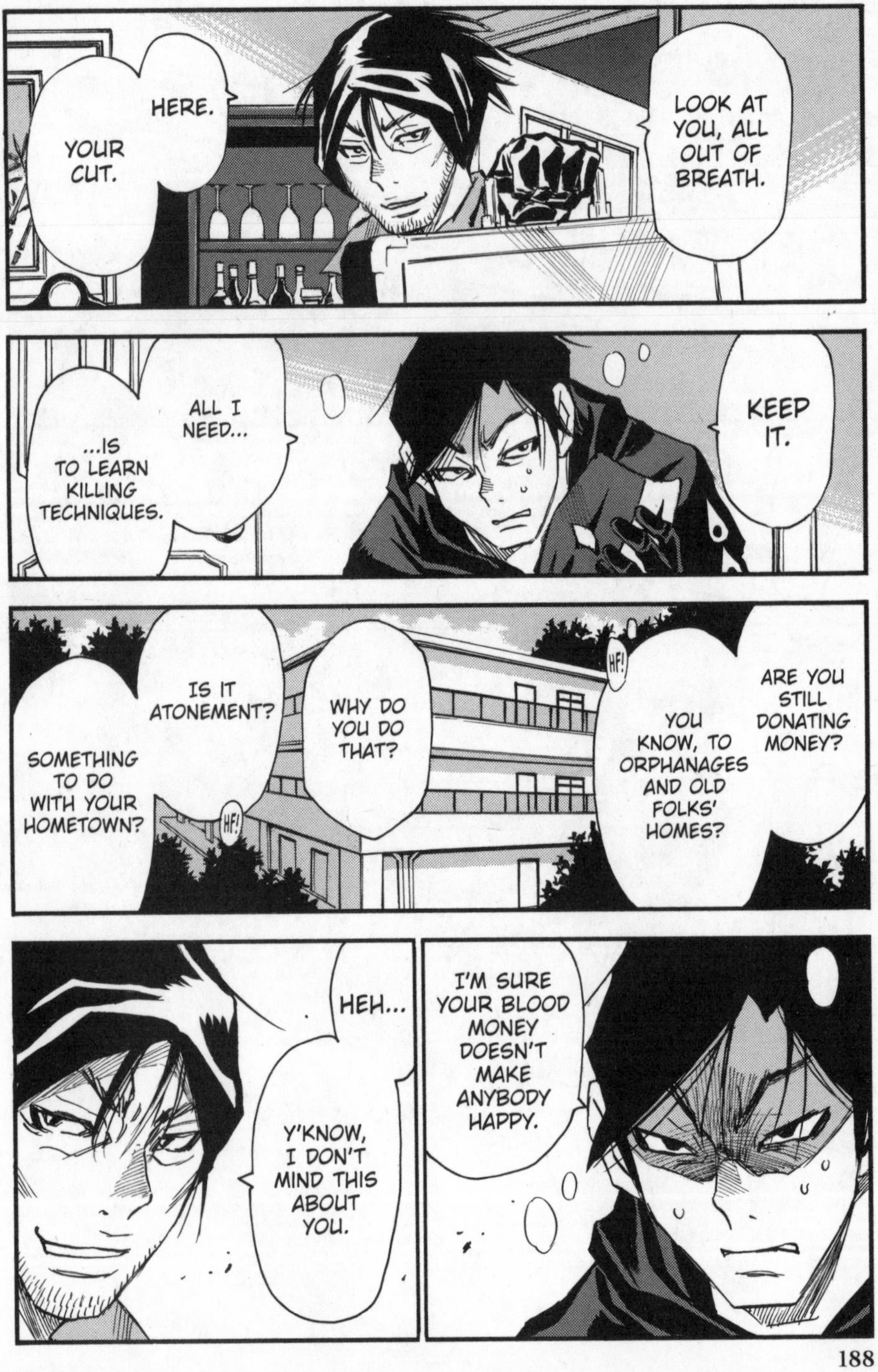
LOOK AT YOU, ALL OUT OF BREATH.
HERE.
YOUR CUT.
KEEP IT.
ALL I NEED...
...IS TO LEARN KILLING TECHNIQUES.
ARE YOU STILL DONATING MONEY?
YOU KNOW, TO ORPHANAGES AND OLD FOLKS' HOMES?
HF!
WHY DO YOU DO THAT?
IS IT ATONEMENT?
SOMETHING TO DO WITH YOUR HOMETOWN?
HF!
I'M SURE YOUR BLOOD MONEY DOESN'T MAKE ANYBODY HAPPY.
HEH...
Y'KNOW, I DON'T MIND THIS ABOUT YOU.

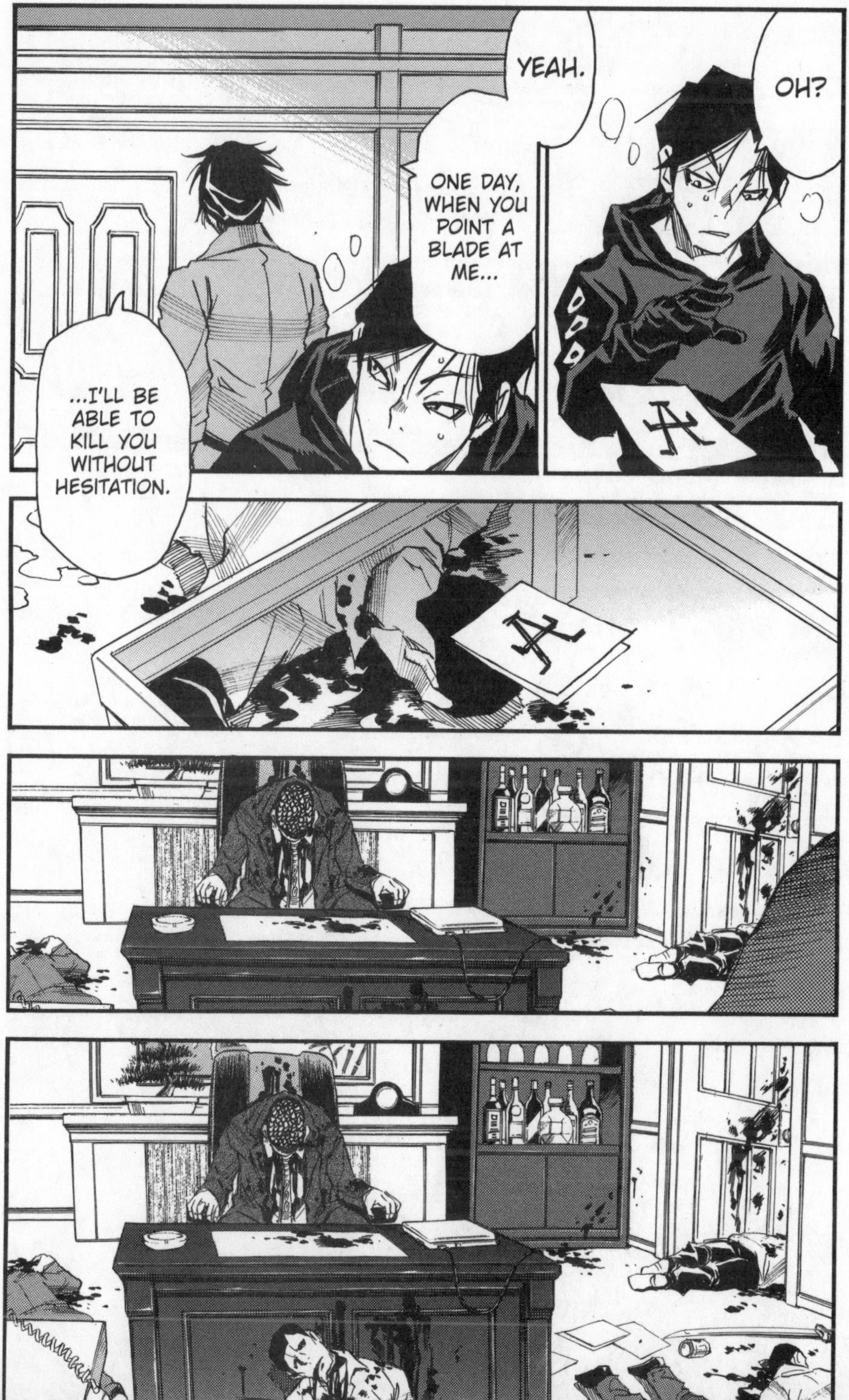
OH?
YEAH.
ONE DAY, WHEN YOU POINT A BLADE AT ME...
...I'LL BE ABLE TO KILL YOU WITHOUT HESITATION.

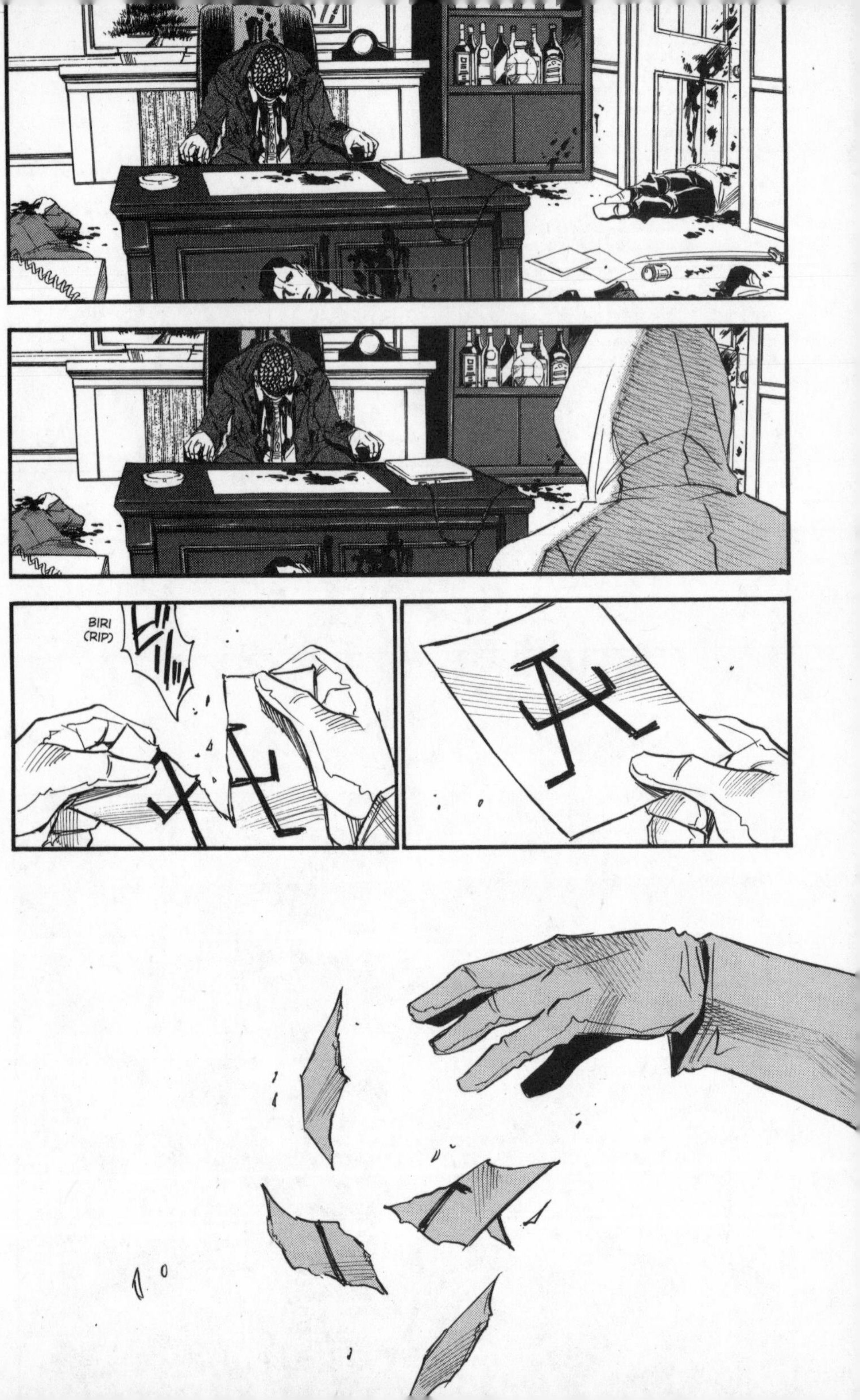
BIRI
(RIP)

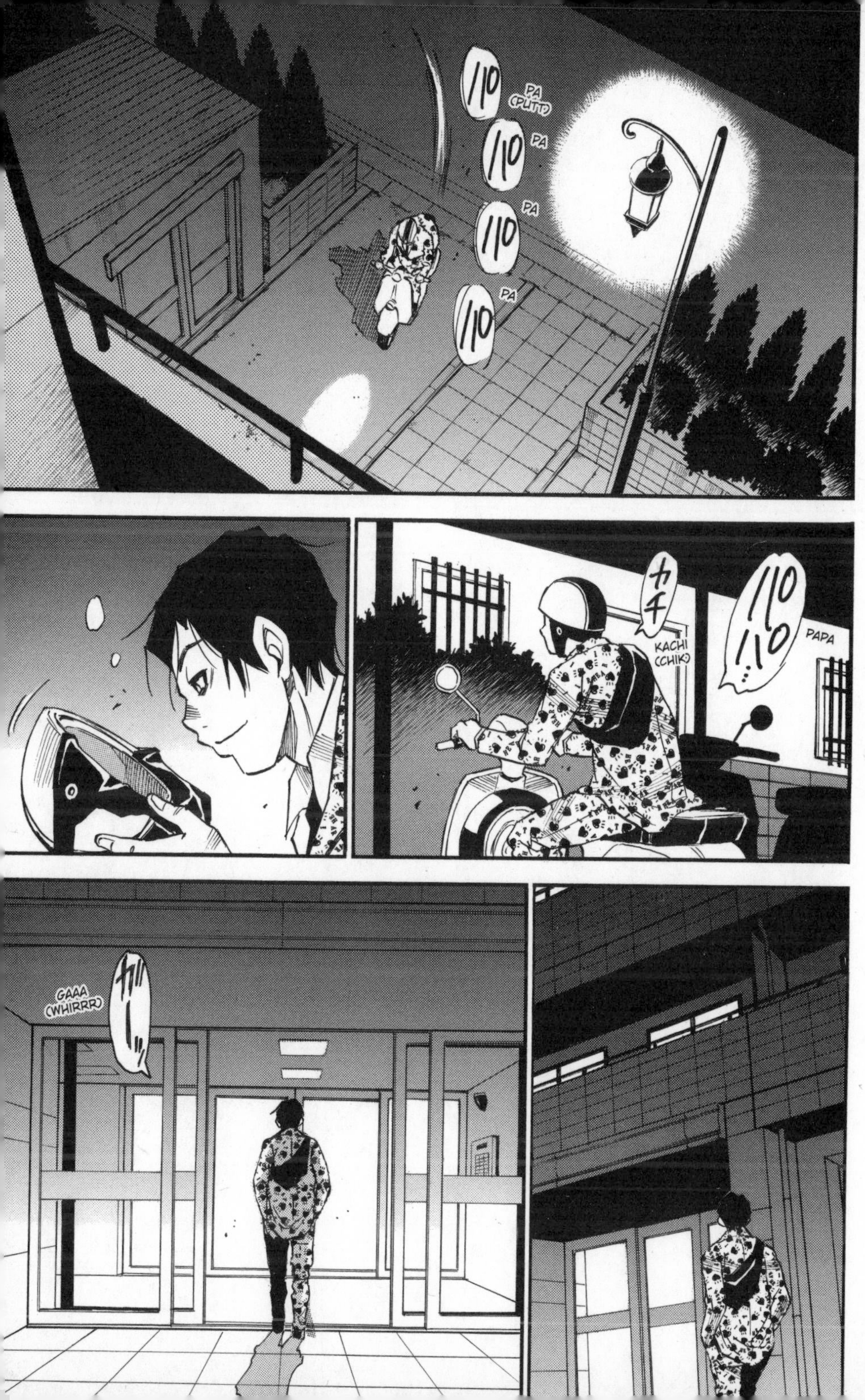
パ
PA (PUTT)
パ
PA
パ
PA
パ
PA
カチ
KACHI (CHIK)
パパ…
PAPA
ガー…
GAAA (WHIRRR)

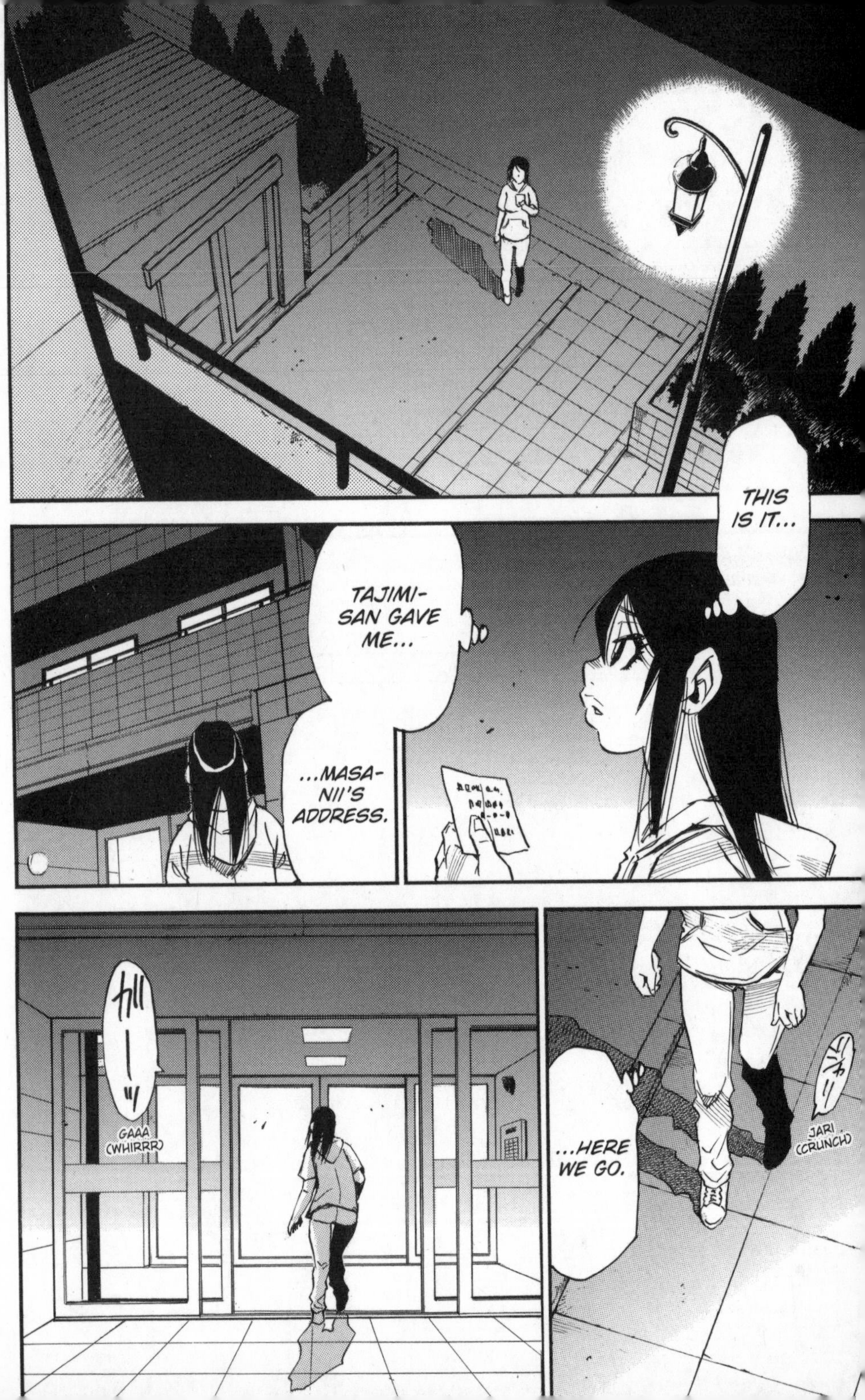
THIS IS IT...
TAJIMI-SAN GAVE ME...
...MASA-NII'S ADDRESS.
JARI (CRUNCH)
...HERE WE GO.
GAAA (WHIRRR)

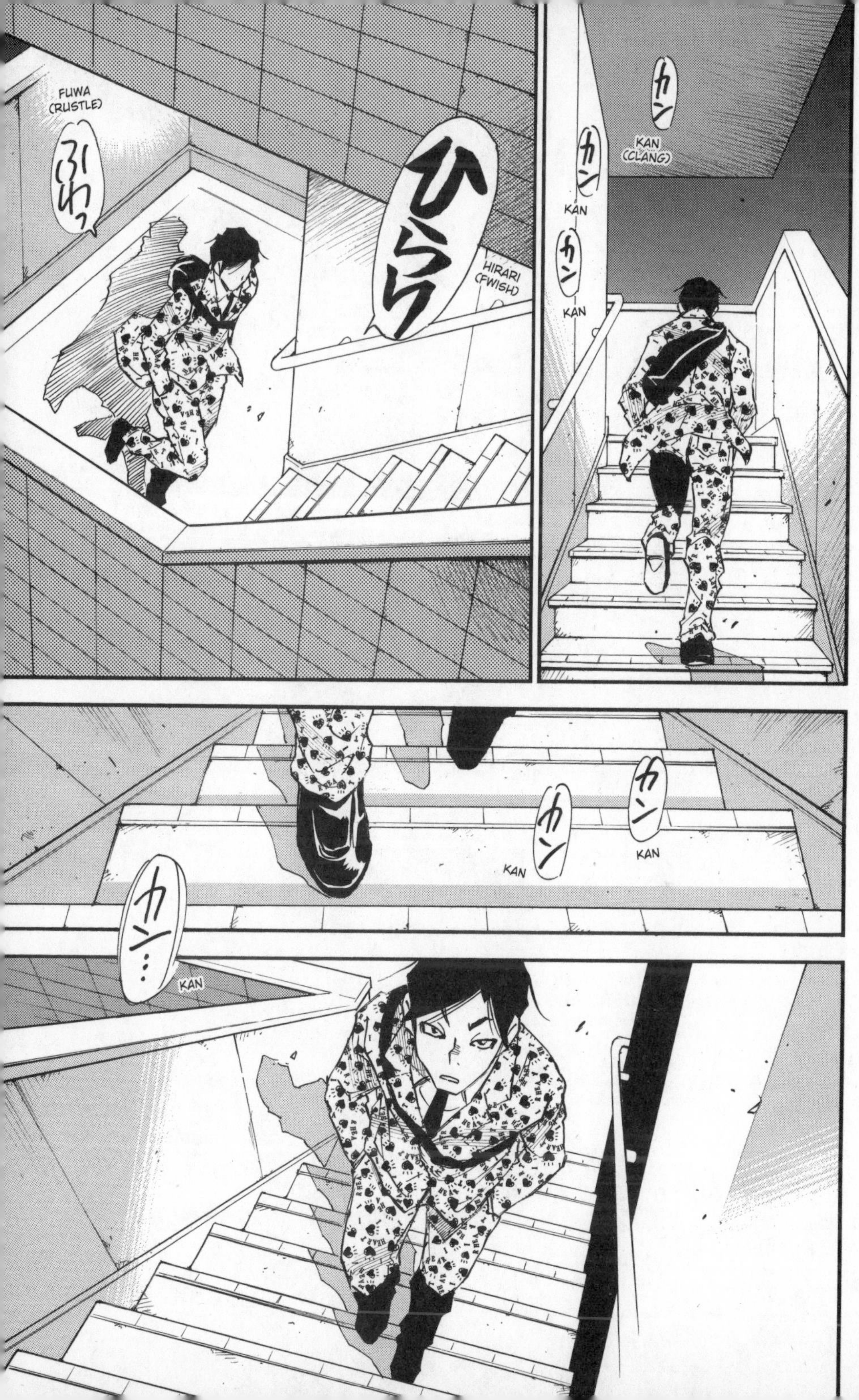
カン
KAN (CLANG)
カン
KAN
カン
KAN
ひらり
HIRARI (FWISH)
ふわっ
FUWA (RUSTLE)
カン
KAN
カン
KAN
カン…
KAN

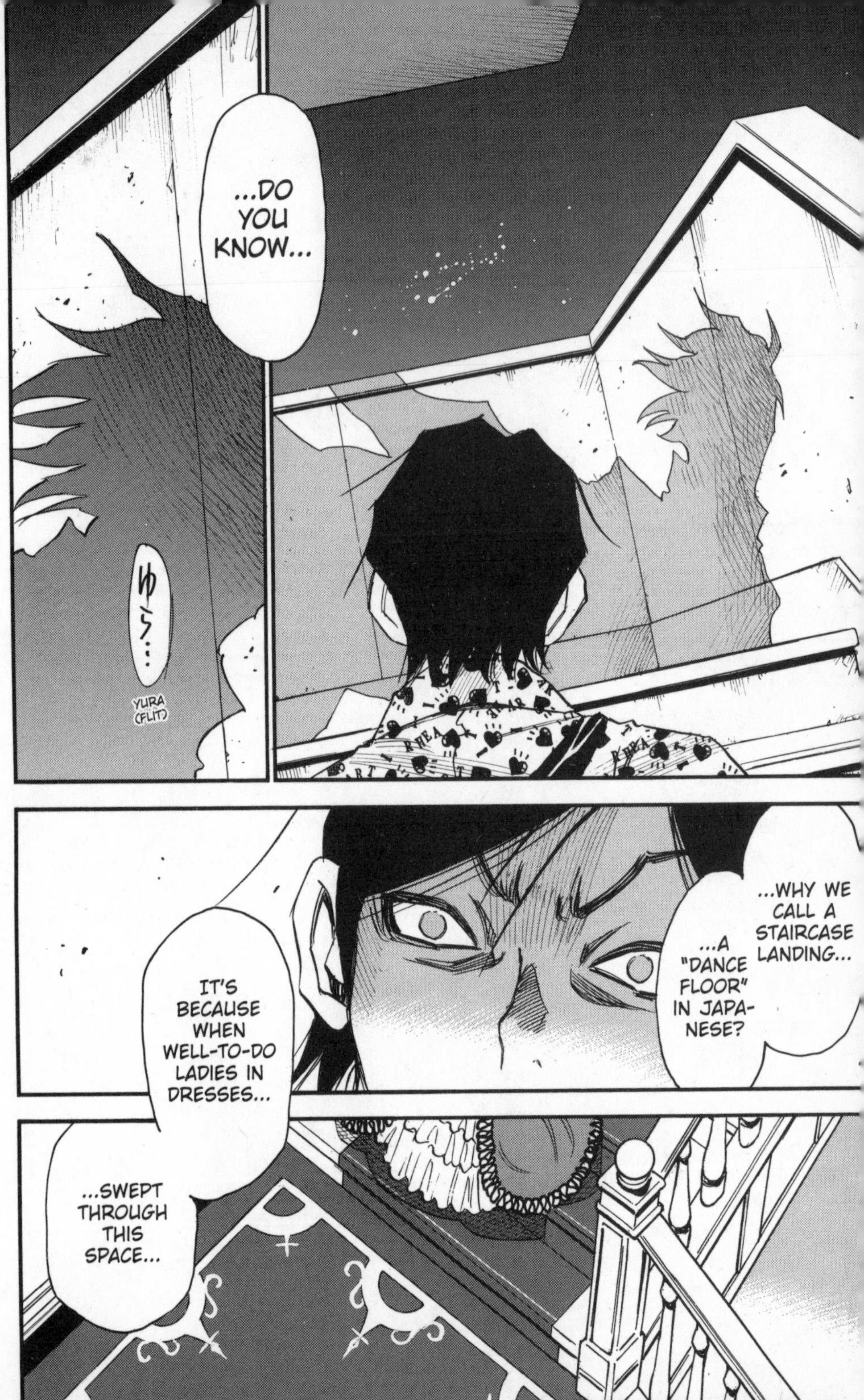
...DO YOU KNOW...
ゆら…
YURA (FLIT)
...WHY WE CALL A STAIRCASE LANDING...
...A "DANCE FLOOR" IN JAPANESE?
IT'S BECAUSE WHEN WELL-TO-DO LADIES IN DRESSES...
...SWEPT THROUGH THIS SPACE...

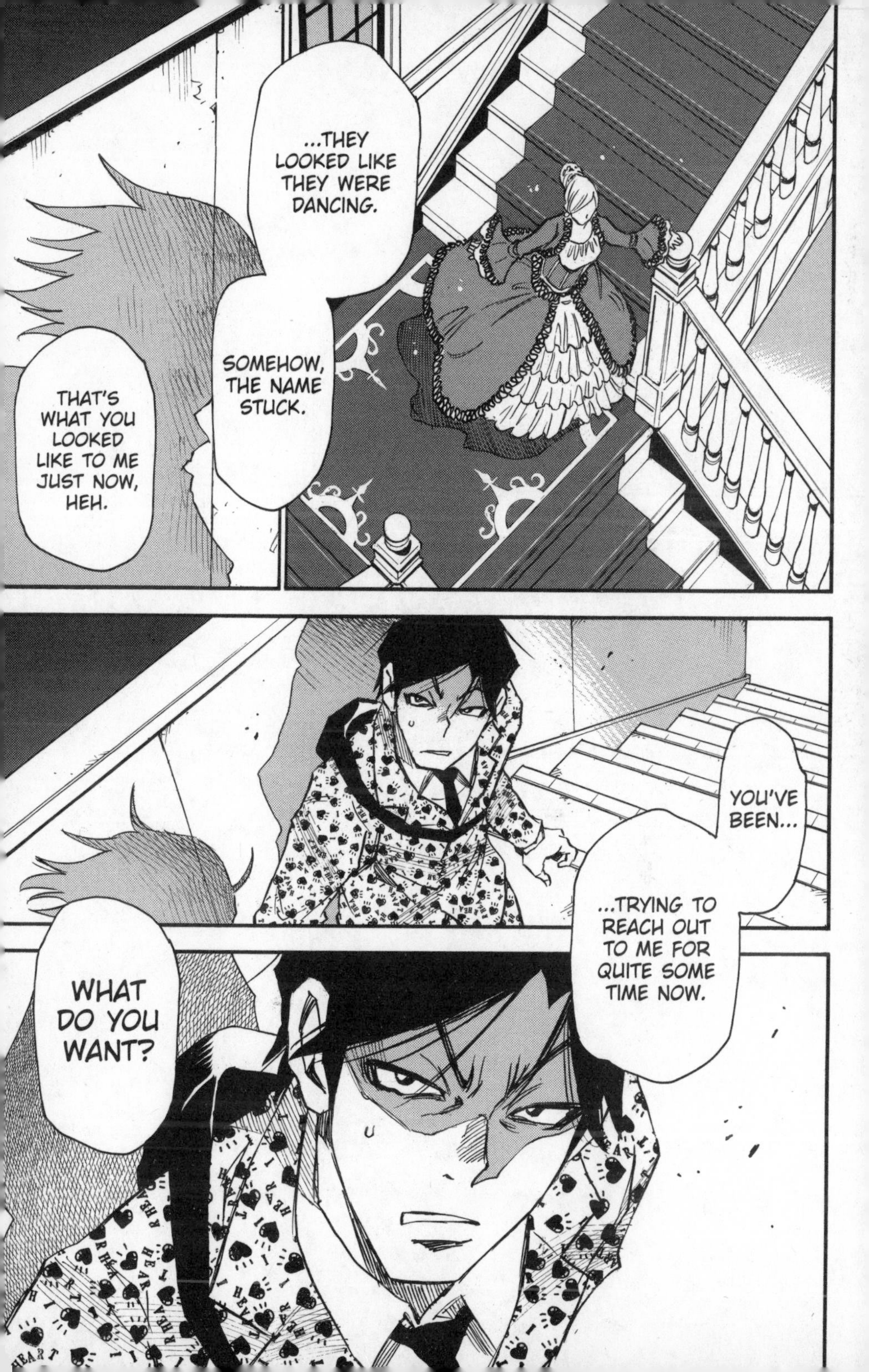
...THEY LOOKED LIKE THEY WERE DANCING.
SOMEHOW, THE NAME STUCK.
THAT'S WHAT YOU LOOKED LIKE TO ME JUST NOW, HEH.
YOU'VE BEEN...
...TRYING TO REACH OUT TO ME FOR QUITE SOME TIME NOW.
WHAT DO YOU WANT?

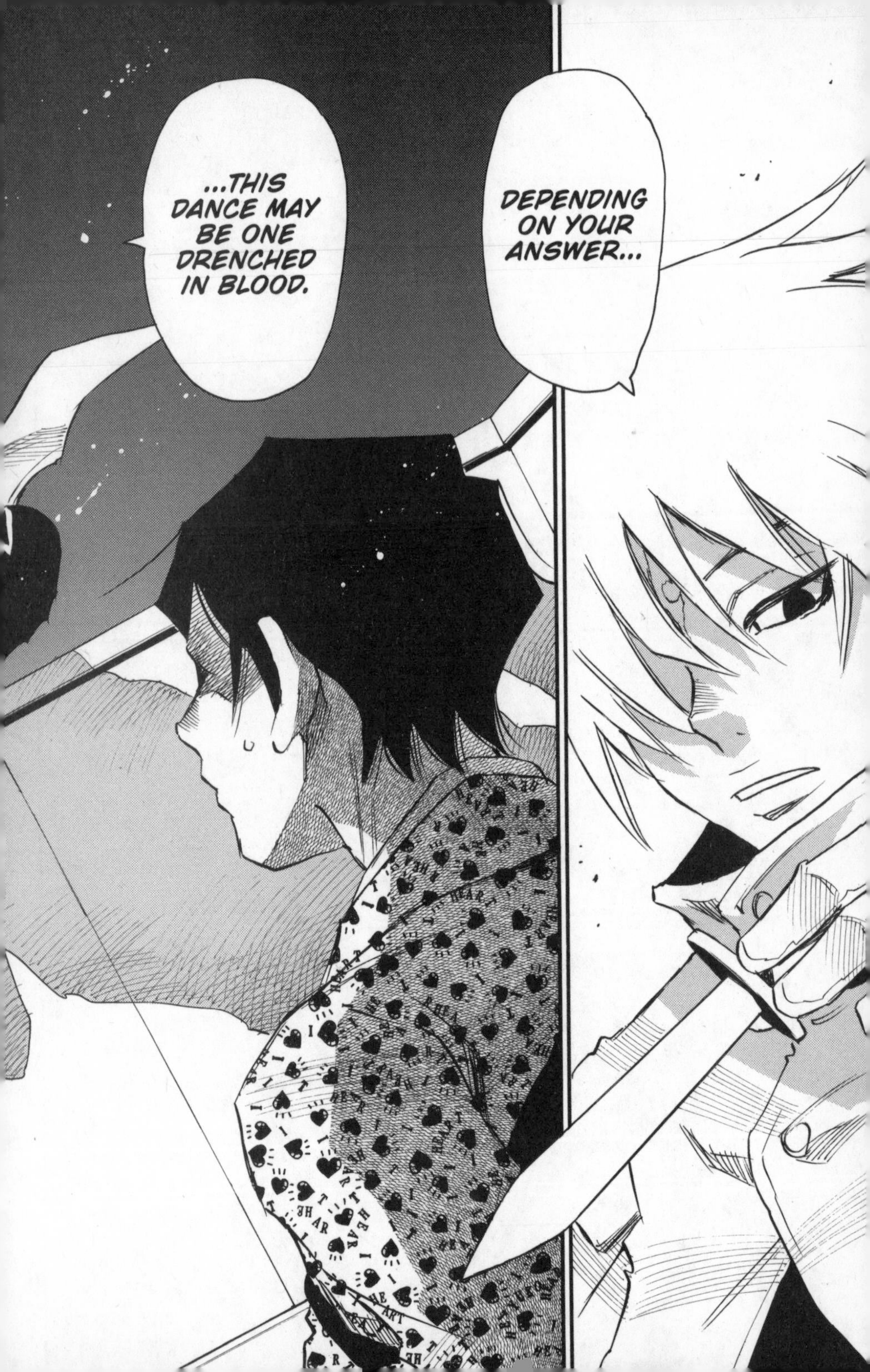
DEPENDING ON YOUR ANSWER...
...THIS DANCE MAY BE ONE DRENCHED IN BLOOD.

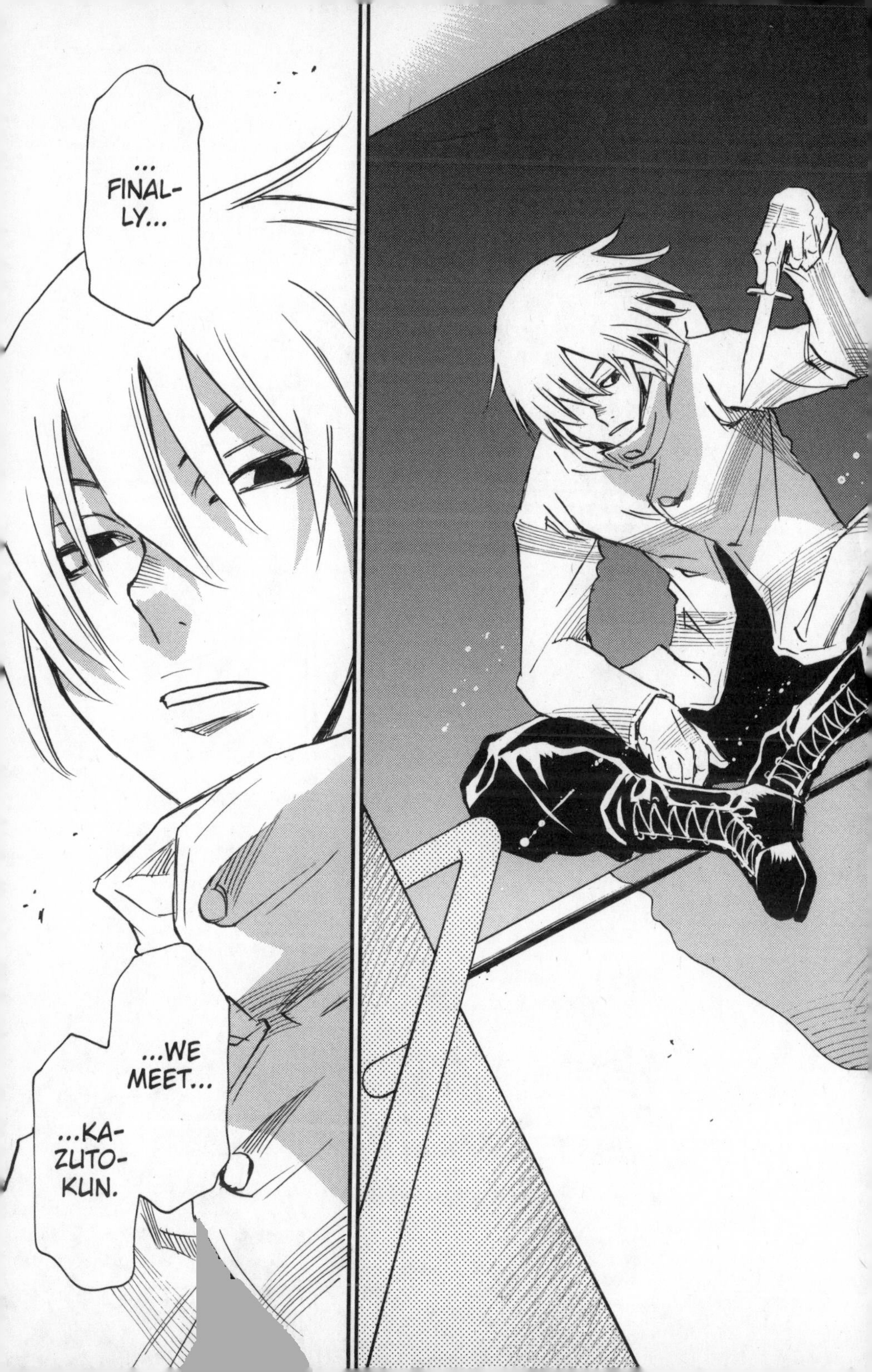
... FINAL-LY...
...WE MEET...
...KA-ZUTO-KUN.

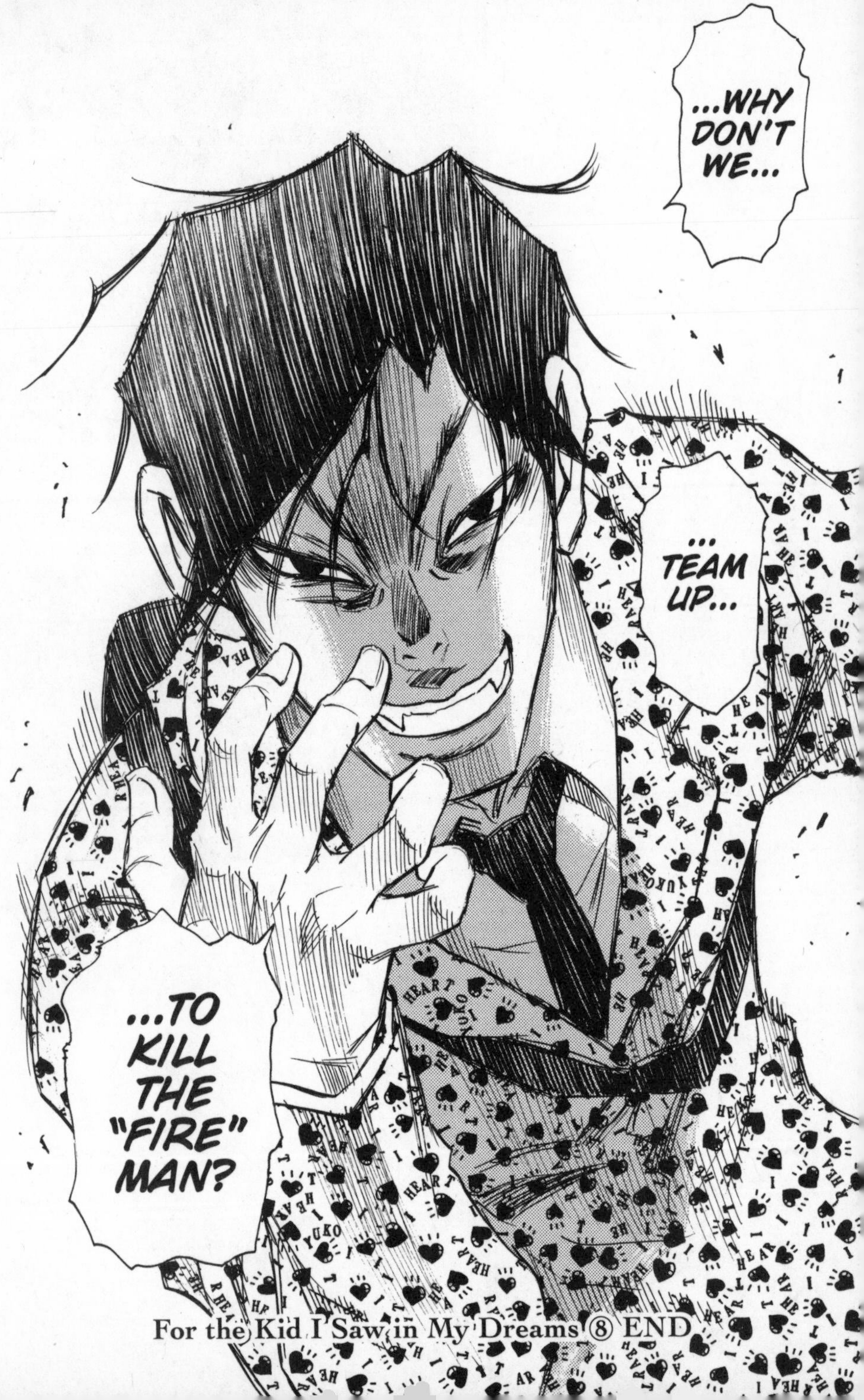
...WHY DON'T WE...
...TEAM UP...
...TO KILL THE "FIRE" MAN?
For the Kid I Saw in My Dreams ⑧ END

STAFF

Kei Sanbe

Yoichiro Tomita
Manami 18 Sai
Kouji Kikuta
Yasunobu

Keishi Kanesada

RESEARCH/PHOTOGRAPHY
ASSISTANCE
Houwa Toda

BOOK DESIGN
Yukio Hoshino
VOLARE inc.

EDITOR
Tsunenori Matsumiya

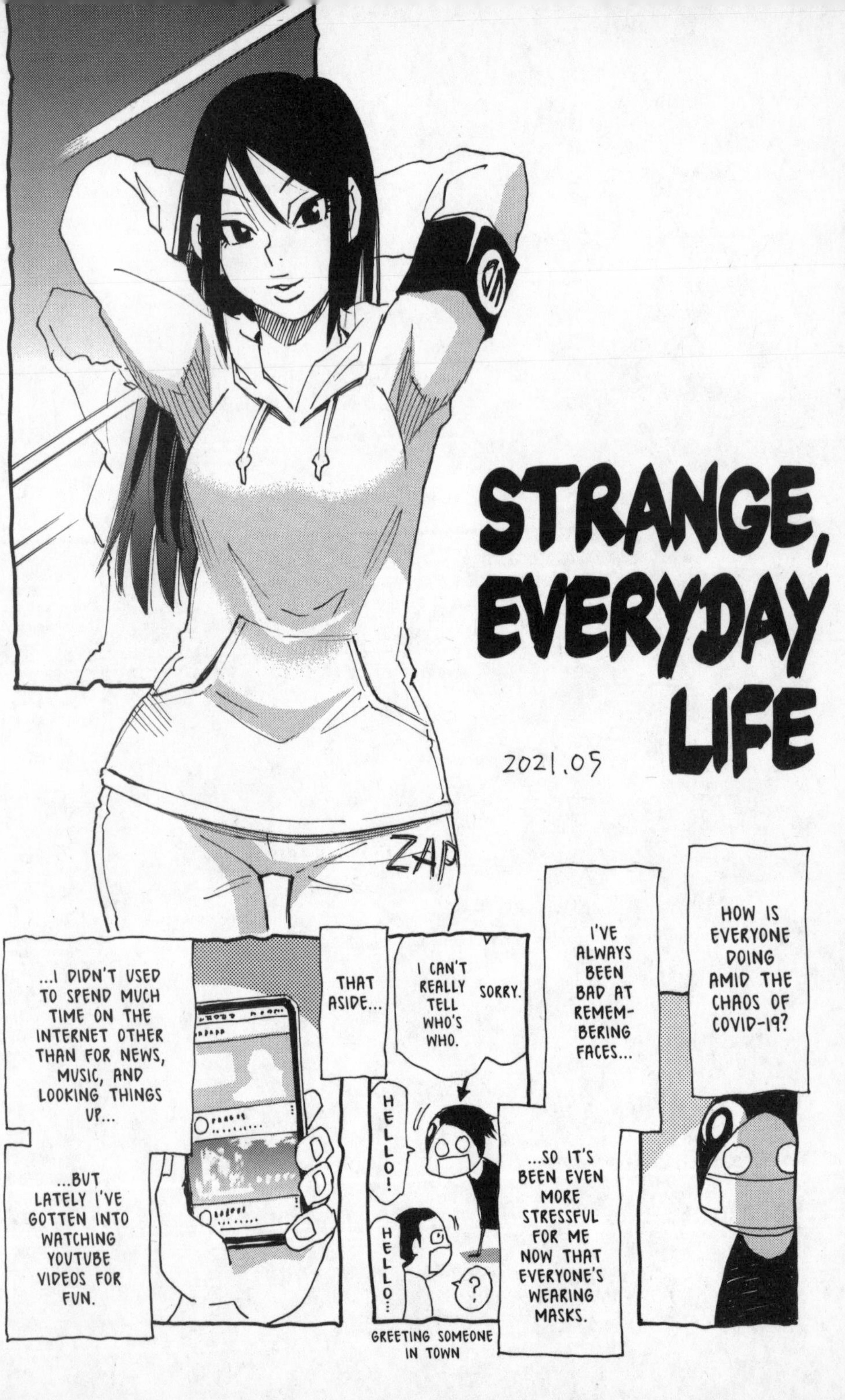
STRANGE, EVERYDAY LIFE
2021.05
ZAP
HOW IS EVERYONE DOING AMID THE CHAOS OF COVID-19?
I'VE ALWAYS BEEN BAD AT REMEMBERING FACES...
...SO IT'S BEEN EVEN MORE STRESSFUL FOR ME NOW THAT EVERYONE'S WEARING MASKS.
SORRY.
I CAN'T REALLY TELL WHO'S WHO.
HELLO!
HELLO...
?
GREETING SOMEONE IN TOWN
THAT ASIDE...
...I DIDN'T USED TO SPEND MUCH TIME ON THE INTERNET OTHER THAN FOR NEWS, MUSIC, AND LOOKING THINGS UP...
...BUT LATELY I'VE GOTTEN INTO WATCHING YOUTUBE VIDEOS FOR FUN.

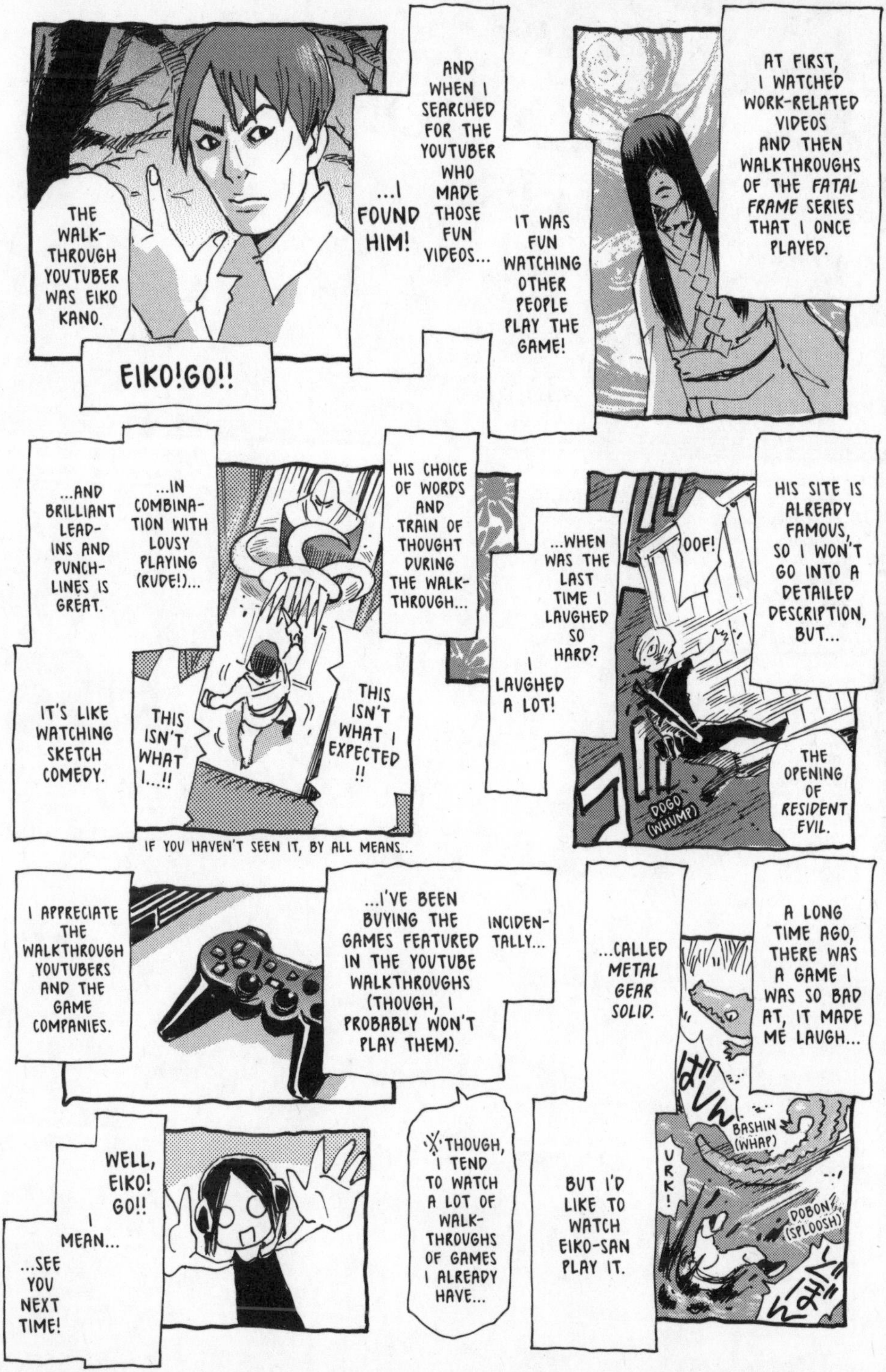
AT FIRST, I WATCHED WORK-RELATED VIDEOS AND THEN WALKTHROUGHS OF THE *FATAL FRAME* SERIES THAT I ONCE PLAYED.
IT WAS FUN WATCHING OTHER PEOPLE PLAY THE GAME!
AND WHEN I SEARCHED FOR THE YOUTUBER WHO MADE THOSE FUN VIDEOS...
...I FOUND HIM!
THE WALK-THROUGH YOUTUBER WAS EIKO KANO.
EIKO!GO!!
HIS SITE IS ALREADY FAMOUS, SO I WON'T GO INTO A DETAILED DESCRIPTION, BUT...
OOF!
THE OPENING OF *RESIDENT EVIL*.
DOGO (WHUMP)
...WHEN WAS THE LAST TIME I LAUGHED SO HARD?
I LAUGHED A LOT!
HIS CHOICE OF WORDS AND TRAIN OF THOUGHT DURING THE WALK-THROUGH...
...IN COMBINATION WITH LOUSY PLAYING (RUDE!)...
...AND BRILLIANT LEAD-INS AND PUNCH-LINES IS GREAT.
THIS ISN'T WHAT I EXPECTED!!
THIS ISN'T WHAT I...!!
IT'S LIKE WATCHING SKETCH COMEDY.
IF YOU HAVEN'T SEEN IT, BY ALL MEANS...
A LONG TIME AGO, THERE WAS A GAME I WAS SO BAD AT, IT MADE ME LAUGH...
...CALLED METAL GEAR SOLID.
BASHIN (WHAP)
URK!
DOBON (SPLOOSH)
BUT I'D LIKE TO WATCH EIKO-SAN PLAY IT.
※ THOUGH, I TEND TO WATCH A LOT OF WALK-THROUGHS OF GAMES I ALREADY HAVE...
INCIDEN-TALLY...
...I'VE BEEN BUYING THE GAMES FEATURED IN THE YOUTUBE WALKTHROUGHS (THOUGH, I PROBABLY WON'T PLAY THEM).
I APPRECIATE THE WALKTHROUGH YOUTUBERS AND THE GAME COMPANIES.
WELL, EIKO! GO!!
I MEAN...
...SEE YOU NEXT TIME!

TRANSLATION NOTES

Common Honorifics

no honorific: Indicates familiarity or closeness; if used without permission or reason, addressing someone in this manner would constitute an insult.

-san: The Japanese equivalent of Mr./Mrs./Miss. If a situation calls for politeness, this is the fail-safe honorific.

-sama: Conveys great respect; may also indicate the social status of the speaker is lower than that of the addressee.

-kun: Used most often when referring to boys, this indicates affection or familiarity. Occasionally used by older men among their peers, but it may also be used by anyone referring to a person of lower standing.

-chan: An affectionate honorific indicating familiarity used mostly in reference to girls; also used in reference to cute persons or animals of either gender.

(o)nii: A familiar way to refer to an older man of similar age.

-sensei: A respectful term for teachers, artists, or high-level professionals.

Currency Conversion

While conversion rates fluctuate daily, an easy estimate for Japanese Yen conversion is 100 JPY to 1 USD.

Page 42

Kendo: A Japanese martial art that utilizes bamboo swords. The word directly translates to "the way of the sword" in English.

For the Kid I Saw in My Dreams

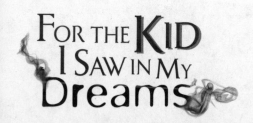

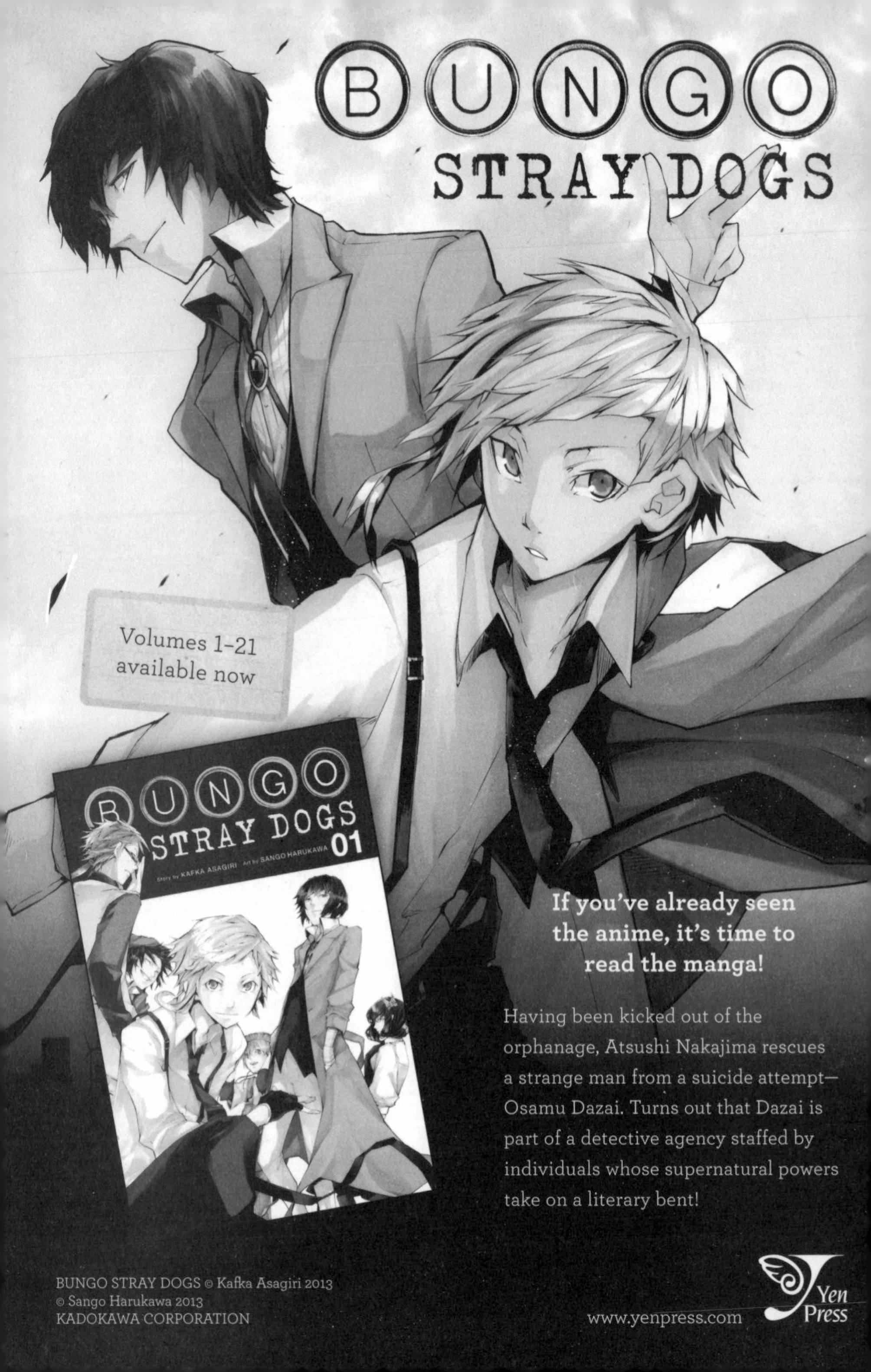
BUNGO
STRAY DOGS
Volumes 1–21
available now
BUNGO
STRAY DOGS
01
Story by KAFKA ASAGIRI Art by SANGO HARUKAWA
If you've already seen the anime, it's time to read the manga!
Having been kicked out of the orphanage, Atsushi Nakajima rescues a strange man from a suicide attempt—Osamu Dazai. Turns out that Dazai is part of a detective agency staffed by individuals whose supernatural powers take on a literary bent!
BUNGO STRAY DOGS © Kafka Asagiri 2013
© Sango Harukawa 2013
KADOKAWA CORPORATION
www.yenpress.com
Yen Press

THE Eminence IN Shadow

ONE BIG FAT LIE

AND A FEW TWISTED TRUTHS

Even in his past life, Cid's dream wasn't to become a protagonist or a final boss. He'd rather lie low as a minor character until it's prime time to reveal he's a mastermind...or at least, do the next best thing—pretend to be one! And now that he's been reborn into another world, he's ready to set the perfect conditions to live out his dreams to the fullest. Cid jokingly recruits members to his organization and makes up a whole backstory about an evil cult that they need to take down. Well, as luck would have it, these imaginary adversaries turn out to be the real deal—and everyone knows the truth but him!

 For more information
visit www.yenpress.com

IN STORES NOW!

KAGE NO JITSURYOKUSHA NI NARITAKUTE !
©Daisuke Aizawa 2018 Illustration: Touzai / KADOKAWA CORPORATION

The Detective Is Already Dead

The Detective Is Already Dead 1

nigozyu

Illustration by Umibouzu

When the story begins without its hero

Kimihiko Kimizuka has always been a magnet for trouble and intrigue. For as long as he can remember, he's been stumbling across murder scenes or receiving mysterious attache cases to transport. When he met Siesta, a brilliant detective fighting a secret war against an organization of pseudohumans, he couldn't resist the call to become her assistant and join her on an epic journey across the world.

...Until a year ago, that is. Now he's returned to a relatively normal and tepid life, knowing the adventure must be over. After all, the detective is already dead.

Volumes 1-2 available wherever books are sold!

YenPress.com

TANTEI HA MO, SHINDEIRU. Vol. 1
©nigozyu 2019
Illustration: Umibouzu
KADOKAWA CORPORATION

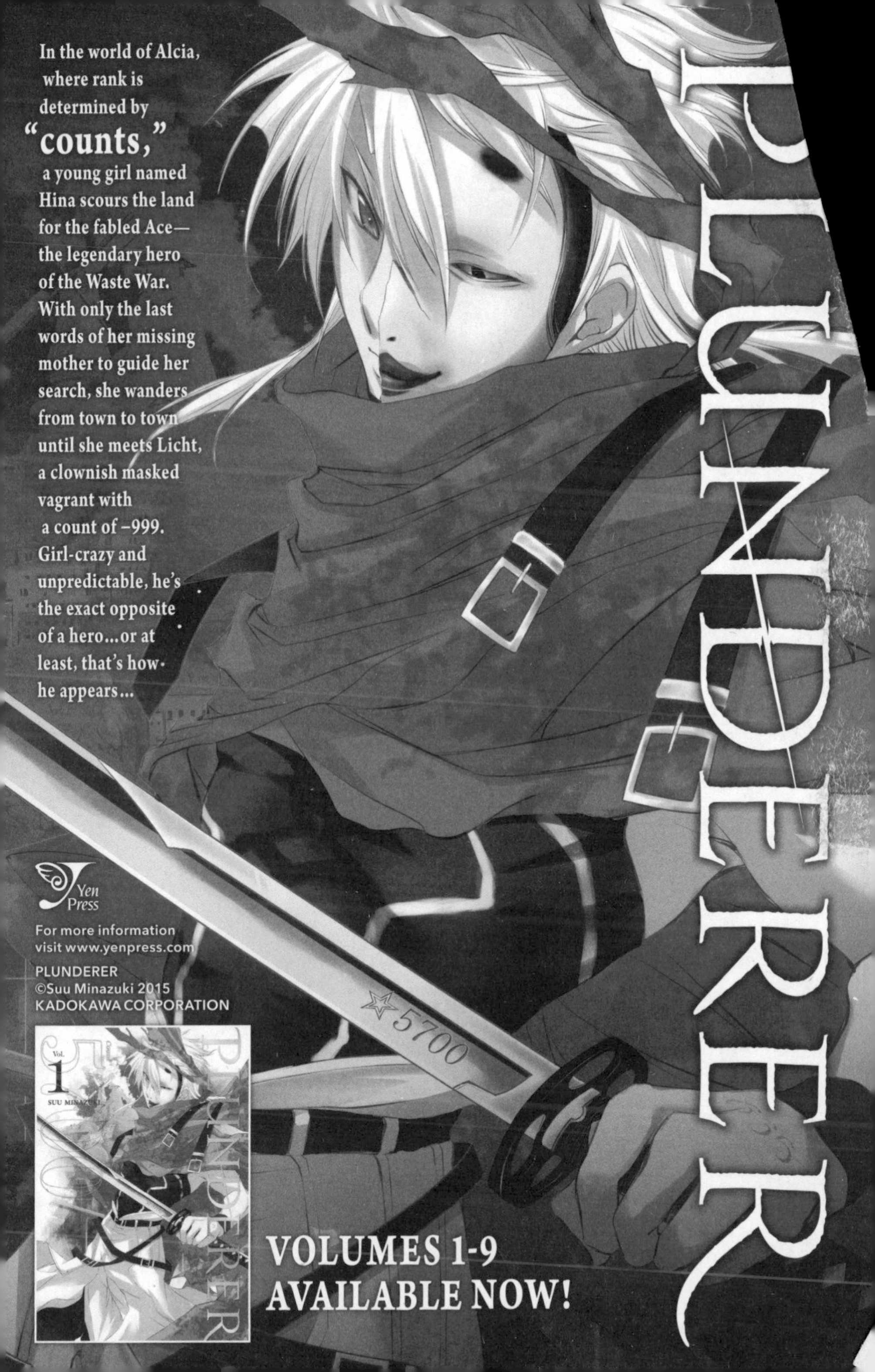

In the world of Alcia,
where rank is
determined by
"counts,"
a young girl named
Hina scours the land
for the fabled Ace—
the legendary hero
of the Waste War.
With only the last
words of her missing
mother to guide her
search, she wanders
from town to town
until she meets Licht,
a clownish masked
vagrant with
a count of −999.
Girl-crazy and
unpredictable, he's
the exact opposite
of a hero...or at
least, that's how
he appears...

For more information
visit www.yenpress.com

PLUNDERER
©Suu Minazuki 2015
KADOKAWA CORPORATION

PLUNDERER

VOLUMES 1-9
AVAILABLE NOW!

...KID I SAW IN MY Dreams 8

SANBE

TRANSLATION: SHELDON DRZKA ✦ LETTERING: ABIGAIL BLACKMAN

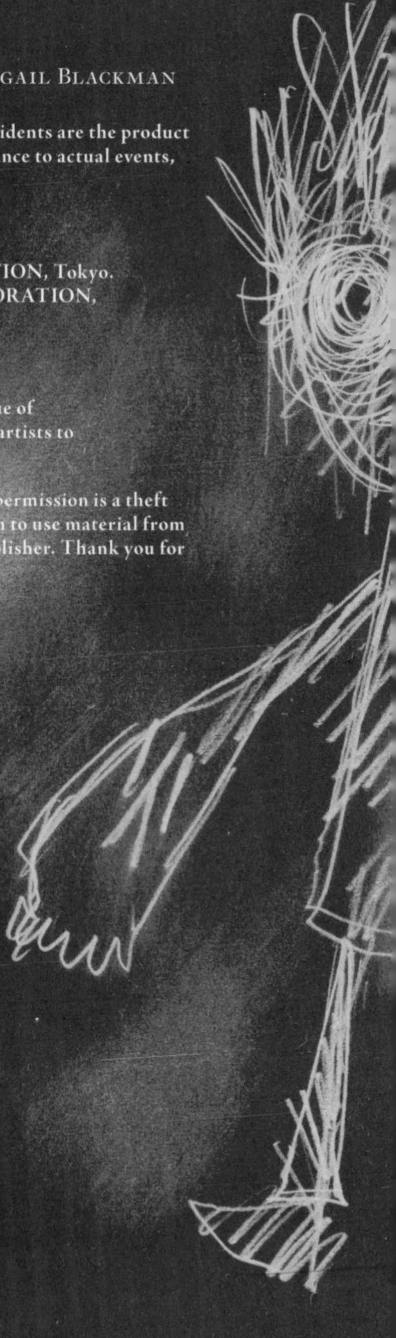

YUME DE MITA ANO KO NO TAME NI Volume 8
© Kei Sanbe 2021.
First published in Japan in 2021 by KADOKAWA CORPORATION, Tokyo.
English translation rights arranged with KADOKAWA CORPORATION,
Tokyo through TUTTLE-MORI AGENCY INC., Tokyo.

Yen Press
150 West 30th Street, 19th Floor
New York, NY 10001

Visit us at yenpress.com
facebook.com/yenpress
twitter.com/yenpress
yenpress.tumblr.com
instagram.com/yenpress

First Yen Press Edition: July 2022
Edited by Abigail Blackman &
Yen Press Editorial: Won Young Seo
Designed by Yen Press Design: Eddy Mingki, Wendy Chan

Yen Press is an imprint of Yen Press, LLC.
The Yen Press name and logo are trademarks of Yen Press, LLC.

The publisher is not responsible for websites (or their content)
that are not owned by the publisher.

Library of Congress Control Number: 2018958636

ISBNs: 978-1-9753-4491-7 (hardcover)
        978-1-9753-4492-4 (ebook)

10 9 8 7 6 5 4 3 2 1

WOR

Printed in the United States of America